Building the Knowledge Management Network

Best Practices, Tools, and Techniques for Putting Conversation to Work

Cliff Figallo

Nancy Rhine

Wiley Technology Publishing

Publisher: Robert Ipsen
Editor: Ben Ryan
Assistant Editor: Scott Amerman
Managing Editor: Pamela Hanley
New Media Editor: Brian Snapp
Text Design & Composition: Benchmark Productions, Inc.

Designations used by companies to distinguish their products are often claimed as trademarks. In all instances where Wiley Publishing, Inc., is aware of a claim, the product names appear in initial capital or all capital letters. Readers, however, should contact the appropriate companies for more complete information regarding trademarks and registration.

This book is printed on acid-free paper. ∞

Published by John Wiley & Sons, Inc.

Published simultaneously in Canada.

Limit of Liability/Disclaimer of Warranty: While the publisher and author have used their best efforts in preparing this book, they make no representations or warranties with respect to the accuracy of completeness of the contents of this book and specifically disclaim any implied warranties of merchantability or fitness for a particular purpose. No warranty may be created or extended by sales representatives or written sales materials. The advice and strategies contained herein may not be suitable for your situation. You should consult with a professional where appropriate. Neither the publisher nor author shall be liable for any loss of profit or any other commercial damages, including but not limited to special, incidental, consequential, or other damages.

For general information on our other products and services please contact our Customer Care Department within the United States at (800) 762-2974, outside the United States at (317) 572-3993 or fax (317) 572-4002.

Wiley also publishes its books in a variety of electronic formats. Some content that appears in print may not be available in electronic books.

Library of Congress Cataloging-in-Publication Data

ISBN 0-471-21549-X (paper : alk. paper)

Printed in the United States of America.

10 9 8 7 6 5 4 3 2 1

Contents

Acknowledgments

Knowledge networks depend for their success on the right social environment. We have worked within many such respectful, trusting, nurturing, and educational social environments, and those experiences have led us to write this book. We both spent many years learning together with hundreds of others in building a small, self-sufficient community in Tennessee. We applied what we learned in that challenging social experiment to the work we did in the early days of our first online communities at The WELL and Women.com. The members of those communities showed us the value of lowering the communications boundaries between management and customers. In those and in subsequent positions at AOL, Digital City, Salon.com, and PlanetRX, we observed the value of informal knowledge sharing through the Net. And so we thank the innumerable people we worked with and did our best to serve for being our teachers in collaboration in those virtual but still very personal environments.

We would not have traveled our respective paths toward community interaction were it not for the support and example of our families. And so we each acknowledge their parts in our development as leaders who look for the ways in which people agree rather than ways in which they disagree.

Nancy: I want to thank my mother and father, Bill and Dorothy Gerard, who have always exemplified the essential best practices of granting people the benefit of the doubt regardless of age, race, gender, or social standing. I have learned from them that 99 percent of the time people not only prove worthy of that trust, but even rise admirably to the occasion. Thanks also to my three daughters, Leah, Emmy, and Odessa, who are carrying this compassionate and intelligent legacy of their grandparents into the new millennium. It is, indeed, a fine way to live.

Cliff: Thanks to my parents, Bruno and Gwen, and to my kids who have kept my attention and care on people more than technology. Thanks to my coworkers through the years—whether building houses, installing village water systems, or managing online communities—for teaching me how to listen and work together for the common good.

We'd like to acknowledge all of those who provided the information and stories that have made this book happen. Special thanks go to Tom Brailsford of Hallmark for his generous insight into what may be the model of customer relationships for the future. And last, but not least, we express our appreciation for the support of our development editor at John Wiley & Sons, Scott Amerman, for gently leading us through the writing of this book.

Introduction

With this book in your hand, you're probably looking for ways to help your organization get smarter by making the most effective use of online conversations. In these pages we write about a basic human drive to share what we know. We reposition that age-old practice at the intersection of two social environments: the modernizing organization and the expanding electronic network.

Your company should know what this book reveals, because in this competitive and downsized economy, you are being forced to make the best use of your current human resource assets. You can't afford the high cost of replacing the knowledge of people you've trained and lost. You must find, harvest, and distribute current and relevant knowledge from a wide variety of trusted human sources in order to make decisions and innovations in today's hyperactive marketplace of things and ideas. Organizations today must change intelligently and constantly to survive. Ongoing, high-quality conversation is a key to making that kind of change possible.

Though online knowledge networks can involve sophisticated technology, this book is not, at its core, about technology; it's more about people and motivation. Though terms like application integration are important to understand in this context, you'll likely find terms like cultural evolution and self-governing systems to be more relevant to the successful adoption of useful online conversation as a productive process within your organization.

Even companies that value their knowledge networks can run into problems applying what they've learned to their business. There is a gap between *knowing* and *doing*. Putting conversation to work means bringing the right people with the requisite knowledge together and having their online interaction solve real and immediate problems. To reach that level of practical impact, there must be trust and commitment among the participants in addition to software and connectivity. For your organization, that means leading and fostering the kind of culture that motivates people to share what they know with their coworkers.

If there's a central theme to this book, it's *the importance of making the appropriate match between the culture and the technology for any given situation.* The cultural needs may pertain to your entire organization, specific teams within your organization, or the constituents who are served by your organization. In our approach, culture is in the driver's seat for selecting and configuring the technology, yet we also emphasize the inevitable influence of technology on the culture that uses it.

Twenty years ago, very few people had seen, much less used, a computer. Now there are hundreds of millions of daily computer users. Today, relatively few people use online conversation as an essential work tool, but we see a future where the skills and practices we describe in this book are common throughout organizations, and where workers are engaged in multiple discussions from their desktops or laptops. In that future, workers will use the Net to share the fresh ideas and experiences that will help guide their companies.

Why This Book Now?

During January and February 2002, the Pew Internet & American Life Project conducted a survey to gauge the involvement of people in *online communities.*[1] The survey found that 84 percent of Internet users have at one time or another contacted an online group. Referring to these 90 million Americans as Cyber Groupies, the study revealed that half of them claimed that the Internet had helped them connect with people who shared their interests, and that the average Cyber Groupie had contacted four different online groups.

Far from being a cold, lonely, and impersonal electronic medium, the Internet described by the Pew survey is an inhabited communication environment with a vibrant social life. People learn—through the simplicity of the Web interface and from one another—how to find, explore, and sustain social activity on the Net. Many Cyber Groupies engage with their online communities from the workplace. Some of them find their communities *within* the workplace. Yet these communities and the conversations that go on within them are invisible to most of the companies providing the intranets on which they live. More significantly, these communities are invisible to the leaders of those companies, who need to know more about what their workers know and are doing.

We've seen the end of the *first* big Internet boom. The dot-com meltdown signaled the end of only the first wave of commercial online innovation and experimentation. But much learning has taken place since the Internet became a commercial medium in 1993. Group communication through the Net is no longer the rare and esoteric practice that it was in the 1980s when we began managing online communities. Thousands of Web sites have since provided chat rooms and message boards. Email among groups of people has become another common meeting place. Instant messaging has become the means through which isolated keyboardists maintain a sense of immediate connection with their online buddies.

Meanwhile organizations—after years of adopting expensive technologies to keep meticulous track of operational numbers and statistics—have recognized that numeric information alone is not sufficient to guide them in today's fast-changing marketplace. Last year's sales figures don't tell them how to change production as new fads, technologies, and competitors suddenly crash into their markets. Millions of records of customer transactions don't inform them of their consumers' thinking after an event like the terrorist attacks on September 11 or a calamitous news story about their industry. Numbers about past performance have fooled many enterprises into thinking they knew what the future would bring.

The Net has speeded up both communication and change in attitudes, opinions, and habits. To anticipate and prepare for the future, organizations must learn more from their employees and from the people on whom they depend—customers, partners, and constituents. Today we need *dynamic* knowledge—current and constantly updated experience and thinking found only in the agile minds of living human beings and revealed most naturally and completely through human conversations.

This book addresses the modern organization at a point in time when many trial applications for the Net have been abandoned in favor of its powerful role as a communication medium—the purpose for which it was originally designed. We now have a significant percentage of consumers—both inside and outside of the organization—using the Net to connect and converse with others. Organizations are desperately seeking a competitive edge in a world defined by unexpected change, increasingly decentralized leadership and the instant interconnectivity of hundreds of millions. The consumer is far more informed than in the pre-Web days, and now expects to be able to communicate directly—and honestly—with the companies that make the products (s)he buys. We wrote this book now to teach organizations how to engage in the conversations that can make them integral parts of this new, expanding, and uncontrollable marketplace.

Who Should Read This Book

Chief executives make and approve strategy, and knowledge networking is a strategic tool. This book may be too instructional for executive reading matter, but its practical lessons should make its conceptual message more palatable to those who lead organizations.

It used to be said that executives would be the last ones to begin using email because they relied on secretaries to do all of their typing. They may have learned to type since then, but it's still true that the typical executive is the most distanced employee from the online interaction that takes place among the tiers of workers who long ago adopted email to help coordinate their projects and tasks. As remnants from the hierarchical model of organizations, those tiers form impenetrable firewalls between the executives and the creative conversations that hold the potential of transforming their organizations.

The Net is the great equalizer. It undermines hierarchies because networks don't recognize artificial separations between organizational layers. This has become common knowledge, but just as outdated legacy computer systems prevent many companies from progressing to the next level of technical integration, legacy organization charts keep many companies from realizing their networked potential. Executives should read this book to get a refresher on the philosophy of the network revolution, but also to get a better understanding of the different form of leadership that is necessary to keep their organizations in sync with that ongoing revolution. Leaders must understand the medium of online conversation to do a good job of leading people to use it well. We suspect that most company leaders still lack that understanding.

Managers, like executives, are leaders, but in being closer to the workers and their specific responsibilities, their role definitions are changing due to the self-organizing influence of the Net. Because managers direct the activities of working groups, they, too, need to understand the capabilities of the technology to support conversations so that they can begin to plan and lead their departments and teams within the emerging online meeting place. Managers should be regular participants in online forums for planning, innovation and knowledge sharing, and need to stay current with existing work-related online discussions among the people they supervise. Managers who truly understand the strengths and weaknesses of using online conversation as a working tool will get the most out of it.

It's more likely that workers and professionals have already begun to use the available online communications media to exchange mission critical information about their jobs or projects, but this book is for them, too. For although leadership from the top of the organization is a necessity for changing a culture to one that values creative conversation, the best conversations and best ideas are most likely to *bubble up* from the bottom of the organizational chart, where the actual work gets done and the company interfaces most directly with its customers. We hope this book inspires the spontaneous formation of online communities that can solve immediate problems and inspire the widespread use of online knowledge networks within receptive organizations.

Self-Organizing Systems:
What the Ants Know

We have spent a combined 30 years in the practice of online community—using the technology of networks to help people locate and engage with groups that bring them personal and professional support, useful ideas and trusted knowledge. With keyboards and words as their main tools for communication, members of these communities interact for mutual benefit; they get to know one another, learn from one another, and collaborate to achieve shared goals. They cannot be easily steered or controlled, for just as soon as you attempt to direct their activities, they are likely to cease their activity.

We've observed that as people become more familiar with one another, trust grows and the transfer of relevant knowledge between them becomes easier and more efficient. Learning begets more learning; people not only learn who knows what, they learn the most effective techniques for getting their fellow members to reveal and share what they know. We have found ourselves observing the organic formation and change that happens when people are given access to tools for building conversational relationships on the Net, and we've often described the experience as like watching ant farms.

In his new book, *Emergence*[2], Steven Johnson—a leading innovator in the use of the Web as a collaborative publishing medium—uses the behavior of ants to illustrate the principle of *self-organizing systems*. Johnson describes ant colonies as "having this miraculous ability to pull off complex engineering feats or resource management feats without an actual leadership dictating what any ants should be doing at any time."[3] Ants get all this done by following simple local rules through which, Johnson says in an interview, "the intelligence of the colony comes into being."

In our earliest experience with online community at the WELL, one of the groundbreaking experiments in group conversation among home-based personal computer users, we imposed only a few very simple rules, otherwise providing the members with access to the discussion tools to make with them what they would. Among other things, they built a knowledge-sharing community, broken down into hundreds of separate topic areas formed around personalities, expertise and relationships. We got to spend most of our time as system managers keeping the technology functioning, providing support for new members and paying the bills. The content and the database of conversations was created and owned by the members—the knowledge sources and the knowledge seekers who swapped roles constantly.

The traditional business world is gradually beginning to release control like we did, allowing the emergence of new culture, new social practices and new ways of organizing from the bottom up. Flattening the hierarchy and empowering the collaborative workplace is threatening to the traditional role of leadership and it presents a prospect of the future that is new and untried. Few executives, no matter how open-minded, want to follow the model of ant colonies in changing the cultures of their companies. But the Net represents the new collaborative environment, and in networks these ant-like organizing effects not only work well, they are natural social behaviors and thus are difficult to suppress.

The Net, looked at as a whole, is a demonstration of *emergent behaviors*. Most of the content on the Web has been created outside of any overall plan or leadership mandate. Most of the communities have been formed because there was an opportunity and need, rather than a directive from on high. Literally billions of Web pages have been produced based on the simple rules of HTML and Internet software.

To the modern organization, the most valuable thing about emergent behavior is its ability to quickly adapt to changing circumstances. A look back at the previous decade—or even the past year—should provide sufficient evidence that we live in times of ever-changing circumstances. The need to adapt constantly is upon every organization that hopes to survive. The goal going into the twenty-first century is not so much to be a dominant organization, but to be a *sustainable organization*.

Ants don't follow leaders, nor do they build and rely on projections for the future. They communicate intensively, react to situations, and adapt constantly as they build their colonies, gather and store their food and deal effectively with local disasters like rain and having large critters stomp on their front doors. For organizations to quickly adapt to sudden downturns in the market, terrorist attacks and war, oil embargoes and transportation disruptions, their people must develop the skills and habits to communicate fluently and effectively. Accomplishing that will take practice and cultural support as we describe in this book.

Knowledge and Management

The *Oxford English Dictionary* claims that the roots of the modern English word knowledge are in Old English terms meaning "confession" and "to play, give, move about." Knowledge would seem to come from inside and to be restless at the same time. This fits our experience with knowledge sharing, where people reveal what they hold in their minds within a social atmosphere that is informal, trusting, and generous.

As we managed online communities and taught clients how to implement them in business settings during the nineties, we repeatedly encountered references to the term knowledge management. Businesses first practiced this concept by keeping better records of their transactions and quantifiable operations so that less "knowledge" was lost to the organization. As we looked into the practice, we learned that what was originally called knowledge was more accurately redefined as information because it had lost its association with any human experience. We also found that many had begun to question anyone's ability to manage knowledge, it being the experiential content of the human mind. By the end of the year 2000, knowledge management had evolved into a quest for more effective access to *tacit knowledge*—the experiential human understanding that didn't lend itself to quantification or to management.

Organizations stand to lose tacit knowledge whenever an employee leaves the company or when an employee has no means or motivation to reveal what (s)he knows to others. We had seen years of voluntary and enthusiastic exchange of tacit knowledge in the online communities we managed, and recognized the importance and relevance of what we had learned about groups in conversation through the Net—that tacit knowledge is shared readily where there is trust and the recognition of mutual benefit in the exchange.

As millions of people have learned how to access and use the Web, they have realized its power as a communications channel between them and their families, associates, and fellow enthusiasts in a myriad of hobbies and interests. Such communications account for more of their time online than any other pursuit, including information searches and shopping. Interpersonal informal communication has proven to be the most compelling use—the "killer app"—of the Net.

In this book, we apply the best practices of online conversation to the needs for effective knowledge exchange, which forward-looking organizations now recognize as *their* most compelling application of electronic networking tools. In the following chapters we describe how the mechanistic and hierarchical models of business operation and organization are being transformed into more decentralized and as some describe it, "messy" models composed of independent links between individuals and their self-organizing groups. And as we lead you through these descriptions, we provide you with proven ideas, suggestions, and examples for transforming your team, your department, your organization into one that is smart, alert, and ready to deal with the challenges of these exciting and unpredictable times.

How This Book Is Organized

The drive to share what we know is as old as humankind itself, but using the Net to share knowledge for the good of organizations is a new concept. On a grassroots level it is happening now, and is just beginning to find support and understanding from the leaders of organizations. The first two chapters of Part 1 provide historical and organizational background that may help you recognize and deal with some of the most entrenched sources of resistance and hesitancy to change in your company. Chapter 3 describes how the building of knowledge networks should guide the formulation of appropriate business strategy for this tumultuous age.

Part 2 explores the two legs of online knowledge networking: culture and technology. Because technology is necessary to create the online environment, its influence cannot be separated from the resulting culture. Chapter 4 looks at the role of the information technology department (IT) in building and maintaining the technical platform for the knowledge network, and the ideal working relationship between the network and the technicians who are counted on to fix it, improve it and keep it available. We examine the needs of a knowledge sharing culture—for trust, leadership, and mutual rewards—and then describe the challenges you may face in bringing your established organizational culture online. The final chapter in this section matches specific goals, styles, and missions of knowledge networks with the online communications technologies that best fit them.

Part 3 provides true-life examples, best practices, and wise suggestions for implementing knowledge networks to fit different circumstances, now and in the near future. We begin by presenting a variety of solutions for initiating and supporting conversations within the organization—from the spontaneous gatherings of fellow specialists to the broad-based provision of company-wide online discussion systems. Then we move to the practice of conversing with external stakeholders—customers, consumers, partners, and constituents. The increasing sophistication of consumers is driving companies to catch up to them in online conversation skills in order to engage with them in mutually meaningful conversation. The relationship between empowered consumer and the attentive company is leading the evolution of the marketplace. We wrap up the book with educated musings on the future knowledge networks and online knowledge sharing, noting that the future is already here, but is being practiced by very few organizations.

The following paragraphs, moving from history toward the future, describe the contents of the chapters of this book.

Chapter 1: "Knowledge, History, and the Industrial Organization." Human history is filled with conversation and knowledge sharing. Though communication was much slower in the past than it is today, we got to where we are now in terms of technology, culture, economy, and government through the exchange and distribution of new ideas. This chapter establishes our heritage as natural collaborators where common goals are recognized. It also illustrates how the medium—whether oral tales, clay tablets, papyrus, or parchment sheets, or the wonder of the printed page—affects the spread of knowledge and its influence on society. Until the dawn of the industrial age, most people passed along their experiential working knowledge personally, to apprentices and coworkers. The transition to the assembly line reduced the number of workers whose skills could be defined as knowledge and introduced the idea of the worker as a cog in a machine. We are still dealing with this mechanistic model of the organization and its workers, which is why many companies have failed to recognize the importance of worker knowledge.

Chapter 2: "Using the Net to Share What People Know." This chapter looks at the evolution of modern management theories, spanning the transition from worker-as-cog to worker as holder of key knowledge. Moving from Industrial Age mentality to Information Age mentality, the accompanying transformation of management philosophy has been jolted by the widespread adoption of the Internet and the Web. Information management has become a necessity and, as the tools and connectivity have advanced, the concept of *knowledge networking* has been born. Although industrialization altered the definitions of "the worker" and of "the job," it could not extinguish the natural tendency to share with others what we know. With the rise of *mass markets*, sellers became distanced from the buyers, but the Net has reintroduced the ability for sellers and buyers to connect and converse. It has also provided more convenient means than was ever possible before for sharing knowledge among groups.

Chapter 3: "Strategy and Planning for the Knowledge Network." In formulating strategies for the foreseeable future, organizations must accept that change and surprise may be their most reliable guiding stars. Planning must therefore include the distinct possibility of sudden stops and abrupt changes in direction. Knowledge networks as adaptive social systems are not only appropriate elements in today's strategic planning, they are valuable contributors to such planning because they support the continuing exchanges of ideas, rumors, and circulating information that helps organizations prepare and brace themselves for changes that might otherwise blindside them. Incorporating knowledge networks into the company's strategic future requires leadership that understands how such networks function, for any top-down design of what is basically a bottom-up activity can render it dysfunctional. Likewise, in designing the platform for knowledge networking, the actual users are the best judges of utility and convenience. We revisit many of these points in the chapter about internal knowledge exchange.

Chapter 4, "The Role of IT in the Effective Knowledge Network." The IT manager and the IT department have important roles in supporting dynamic, self-guided knowledge networks though many people have "rolled their own" using basic email. That fact points out the need for simplicity in choosing and implementing technology. While it is tempting to think in terms of choosing or designing software that will do more work and thereby increase human productivity, there are important reasons for at least beginning with the simplest tools that will enable measurable improvement in knowledge exchange. One reason is cost. Another is in facilitating the building of a good working relationship between the IT department and the people looking to build the online knowledge network. Such collaboration is crucial if the knowledge network is going to be able to incrementally improve its working environment. The more people converse, the more prone they are to discover new ideas for making their conversations richer—whether those ideas demand the addition of new technical features or whole new technical platforms. The role of IT should be to aid in tool selection, initial installation, and maintenance and the integration of relevant information applications within the company that will support the cultivation of knowledge.

Chapter 5: "Fostering Knowledge-Sharing Culture." Conversational knowledge sharing can (and will) only take place in a supportive social atmosphere. Such a persistent environment is what we call a "culture." The knowledge network exists, first, within the organization's greater culture, yet it may grow out of a more local *subculture*—that of an area of expertise or a functional division within the organization. It will probably develop an even more unique subculture once it goes online. An online knowledge sharing culture requires certain conditions and nutrients just as an orchid can only grow within certain ranges of temperature, humidity, and soil conditions. Yet, unlike an orchid, an online knowledge network can adapt to changing conditions through its conversations and technology. So we describe method that can be used to provide ideal conditions for the germination and early growth of the knowledge network inside of your organization. These conditions include tolerance for diversity, incentives for sharing what people know and for learning the skills necessary to do that sharing, and leadership that makes it clear, in no uncertain terms, that the creative energy of employees is valued.

Chapter 6: "Taking Culture Online." The online world is different from the world of physical presence. People communicate differently and must compensate for what the virtual meeting place cannot provide in the way of contact and the subtleties of facial expression and tone of voice. Though we have technologies through which people can meet via video, this is very much the exception rather than the rule of online community activity. This chapter introduces the relationship between people and the interfaces that allow them to practice knowledge sharing in Cyberspace. Technical choices and design are important to the flow of information between people. They can block or inhibit that flow just as easily as they can make it possible ˙ even improve it. Unnecessary complexity is always to be avoided. Change for the sake of change is often counterproductive. Interfaces with which a culture is already comfortable should be leveraged. This chapter will be full of cautions and descriptions of technical pitfalls.

Chapter 7: "Choosing and Using Technology." The choice of technologies for supporting online conversation fall into several buckets: chat, instant messaging, message boards and broadband voice and video. The most important companion technologies involve content management and publishing. The frameworks for presenting these tools and content are intranets and the more specifically purposed portals. Our approach for recommending various combinations of these tools it to describe the groups and purposes for which they will be used. Small teams with a single project may be best served by simple email, while department-level collaboration may require the flexibility of a full-blown portal. Features that permit each participant to customize their use of an interface can be an attraction or a distraction, depending on the importance of the conversation and its longevity. There are many factors to consider in choosing technology, but initial simplicity, flexibility of design, and the ability to incrementally expand in power and features are the characteristics that describe every community's ideal knowledge sharing environment.

Chapter 8: "Initiating and Supporting Internal Conversation." This *how-to* chapter describes a process of analyzing what you've got in terms of knowledge needs, culture, and existing internal communities, and then clearly stating your goals. From that point, you can choose from the available options to design the most appropriate social and technical structure. We recommend practices based on our experience and those of other experts in the fields of knowledge networking and online community. Our recommendations will provide you with some shortcuts to effective internal conversation, but you may find the most value in our warnings against certain social or technical pitfalls that can doom the knowledge network before it can reach cruising speed. Some organizational prerequisites need to be in place if your company is to have a chance of learning from its own workers. And different techniques for sharing knowledge can be applied under different social or work-related circumstances, storytelling, and conversation facilitation being two of them. We describe three different models of knowledge networking communities: spontaneous, strategic, and transitory, each requiring different approaches to management and technical support.

Chapter 9: "Conversing with External Stakeholders." Perhaps the greatest difference between today's organization and that of a few years ago is the increased dependence on the external stakeholder that is the result of the Net. Because those stakeholders—consumers, customers, business partners, supporters, and investors—can now communicate so easily and repeatedly through email and the Web, they are more informed and willing to share what they know about your organization or your competition. The conversations about you are probably already happening, and your mission—should you decide to accept it—is to be a part of at least some of those conversations. The choice of meeting ground is not yours to make, though some pioneering companies have successfully invited consumers to join them on their home sites to help them understand the needs and preferences of customers. We describe the differences in expectations between business-to-customer (B2C) conversations and business-to-business (B2B) conversations, and how your organization can best initiate and motivate them. Organizations are looking for cost-effective ways to gain access to the vital tacit knowledge contained in the interests, experiences and opinions of their Web-connected stakeholders. Online conversation is an effective route to that knowledge.

Chapter 10, "The Path Ahead." Trends are at work and taking hold in large companies that can afford to experiment in new practices. Some of these involve conversational knowledge networks and some of what they discover and implement on a larger scale will be shared and adopted by smaller companies as reports of their success, best practices and value circulate. Some of the changes that will stimulate the formation of knowledge-sharing communities are technical, but most are cultural. Technologies that allow smoother integration of software applications will provide more powerful knowledge-sharing environments. The conversion of more CEOs to belief in the less-controlled, decentralized organization will open the doors to more creative participation by workers and consumers. Changes and enhancements to traditional accounting practices will assign value to collaboration and innovative conversation that is not there now. Whatever your organization does today to make its knowledge sharing more effective through the Net is only preparation for its reaching the status of a sustainable organization.

About the Web Site

As all books must be, this is a snapshot of what the field of conversational knowledge networking is like as of the beginning of the year 2002. This book is accompanied by a companion Web site, where additional information and ideas are being posted to update readers and interested Web surfers on this changing field. To access this information, go to www.wiley.com/compbooks/figallo.

Included on the site are templates for evaluating the support of knowledge sharing in an organization, a survey for identifying the right starting point for a knowledge networking initiative, a checklist for framing a strategy that includes knowledge networking, a short training course for community managers and facilitators, links to relevant software tools, and a discussion board where readers can interact with us and with one another.

PART

One

Cave Walls to CRTs: The Landscape of Knowledge Networking

The first three chapters of this book bring us up to date with the status of knowledge networking as we enter the 21st century. Chapter 1, "Knowledge, History, and the Industrial Organization," is meant to remind us that sharing what we know is an important part of our human heritage. Our current efforts to rediscover and reactivate these ancestral skills have been complicated in large part by the hierarchical management philosophies that grew out of industrialization and its emphasis on feeding the demands of mass markets. Chapter 2, "Using the Net to Share What People Know," takes us through the transition from Industrial Age mentality to Information Age mentality and the accompanying transformation of management philosophy that has come with the widespread adoption of the Internet and the Web. Information management has become a necessity, and as the tools and connectivity have advanced, the concept of knowledge networking has been born. Chapter 3, "Strategy and Planning for the Knowledge Network," considers the many challenges that organizations face in changing their cultures, perspectives, and habits to support the smooth and efficient flow of knowledge and competence among their workers using the new tools of the Net.

Knowledge, History, and the Industrial Organization

In this first chapter, we review how the human species has pursued and handed down knowledge through the ages as an integral function of society and how modern organizations applied—and ignored—this ancestral heritage as they faced the challenges of 20th-century management. Many of those challenges during the past 150 years were being confronted for the first time in the vast panorama of human history. Mass production, mass marketing, and the tremendous advances in transportation and communication combined to force the early leaders of industrialization to focus on improving production over improving collaboration. Because those leaders put their attention on mechanistic solutions to business problems, we now find our modern organizations encountering the same hurdles—though in far different forms—that our ancestors had to overcome in the distant past.

Our Ancestral Heritage

As the velocity of commerce and its associated information increased with the Industrial Age, organizations adopted command-and-control approaches to save and catalogue as much descriptive data as they could. Both communication among the holders of knowledge and the verbal sharing of information were deemphasized as business captains focused on worker specialization, even through most of the 20th century. Creating and meeting ever-growing demand were regarded as marketing, production, and distribution problems, not knowledge problems; hence, little was done to develop systems and cultures that honored knowledge as the great movers and shakers among our ancestors had done through many previous centuries.

Thus, we find ourselves in the present situation, where many organizations must relearn not only the subtle skills of person-to-person knowledge sharing but also the cultural norms and values necessary to make them effective. They must learn to do this within a greater understanding of the Net and of how social networking takes place within its virtual environment. Luckily, the social part has been learned by our species through our collective history, and the principles of knowledge networking have established some very deep roots.

Illuminating a Dark Space

Thirty-five thousand years ago, at the base of a cliff in what is now southeastern France, members of a nomadic hunting tribe crawled through a dark, wet, and narrow passage into a cavern. Holding crude torches before them, they groped deeper into the damp gloom, past the evidence of bears that had made the cave their home. They built a small fire to light the space, and after mixing clays and water for their medium, they painted depictions of the creatures they often encountered stalking the hills and river bottoms around them. Leopards, lions, bison, rhinoceroses, and bears were not the animals they hunted, but the animals that threatened them.

These artists, in a chamber both frightening and barely accessible, were recording what they knew, for what reasons we 21st-century humans can't be sure. But as humans, we attribute some purpose to their deeds: to appease their gods, to appeal to the spirits of their predators, or maybe to initiate their young men as hunters.

Clearly, those artists—possibly our direct ancestors—were intentionally passing along experiential knowledge of value to their tribe and their apprentices at the dawn of human civilization. We can imagine the conversations that took place around these pictures, in the cave itself, and around the tribal campfire. In the process of creating their message pictures, they were unwittingly leaving evidence for us, the future descendants they could never have envisioned.

Knowledge sharing has become a natural part of our social behavior. Our ability to communicate defines our humanity, and our tendency is to tell each other what we know, especially when what we know is of interest to the other. Humans are also toolmakers and tool users. This book is about using the tools of the Internet to practice what we've always known how to do, but in the context of the organization rather than the family or tribe.

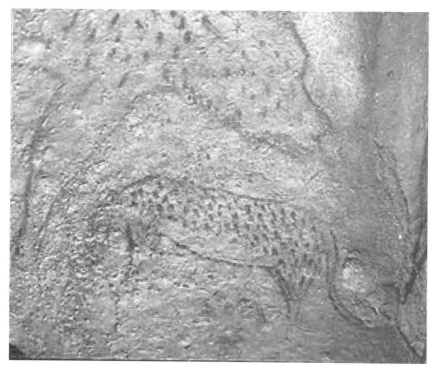

Figure 1.1   Lions and leopards and bears! Oh my! Recording wildlife sightings for the tribe in 33,000 B.C.

Panel of the Panther Chauvet-Pont-d'Arc. Photo courtesy of French Ministry of Culture and Communication, Régional Direction for Cultural Affairs—Rhône-Alpes region—Regional department of archeology

The Net as Today's Cave Wall

This is not a history book, but it uses examples from history to remind you, its readers, that knowledge sharing has defined our civilization. Communicating abstract ideas to one another has distinguished our species from all other animals. We've been innovating, testing, and practicing knowledge transfer for a long, long time, and much of what we'll describe in these pages is more natural to us than many organizations apparently realize.

In the context of present-day networked organizations, most managers are challenged in adapting natural conversational behaviors, which people have been refining at least since Paleolithic times, to communications media that, in the timeline of human history, appeared only moments ago. Certainly some adaptation is required, but resistance has become entrenched within the business climate that developed during more than a century of industrial expansion and technical advances. Fortunately, some of those technical advances are now able to foster a return to the "old ways" that proved themselves for all but the last little smidgen of human progress.

The Internet is today's cave wall where tens of millions of artists have now recorded their observations, experiences, learnings, and—perhaps less nobly— their sales pitches. The organization is still adjusting to its newfound ability to provide open access to the Net's information, entertainment, communication, and ideas within the work environment. Many organizations are still reluctant to provide that access because the excesses and abuses of the adolescent Internet have been so well publicized for business leaders to see.

Fear of the Unknown

No company wants its employees to spend their time at work surfing pornographic Web sites or wasting hours rambling in chat rooms. Yet, on the other side of the coin, examples that clearly demonstrate the benefits of allowing the workforce to collaborate socially through the Net and to use the Internet for valid research are often regarded as too anecdotal, too expensive, or too threatening to internal order, accountability, and efficiency.

The exchange of organizational knowledge through personal interaction on the Net has not yet been widely embraced because decision makers claim to lack proof that it is cost-effective. We will provide evidence that it is, but the following examples from history suggest that organizational leaders must be patient in adapting to this new global medium. After all, our ancestors learned cooperatively—through the glacially slow invention of progressively stronger media—for thousands of years. Now that media are developing so much faster than before, it shouldn't surprise us that change is outpacing our ability to keep up and make the best use of the latest and greatest technologies. This struggle to keep up applies on both the individual and organizational levels.

Adapting to Accelerating Change

The pace of cultural change through history has, for the most part, been slow and incremental. But judging by the 1990s, we are now expected to adjust almost yearly to tremendous advances in our ability to communicate around the planet. Can organizations change their cultures to keep up with the torrid pace of technology and information?

Compared to any new medium before it, the Net has been adopted by the overall population (at least in the developed world) at a lightning pace, maybe too fast for most organizations to adapt their cultures to its peculiarities. Our recommendations in this book will focus on careful, step-by-step approaches to learning to use the Net as a meeting place for knowledge exchange. Most organizations must learn to crawl before they try to walk, or they're likely to tumble and assume, prematurely, that they're just not *meant* to walk.

GRADUAL SCHOOL AND SUDDEN SCHOOL

In Buddhism, there was once a split between those who believed that enlightenment required study, meditation, and patience and those who believed that enlightenment could be ignited through a flash of realization. These were referred to, respectively, as the "gradual school" and the "sudden school." Zen Buddhism is known for the insight-jolting stories and questions called koans. You're probably familiar with the classic riddle: What is the sound of one hand clapping? Deep focus on such answerless riddles could instantly open new doors in the mind, but not every Buddhist monk was ready to have those doors opened.

Adoption of Net culture can be reached by either the long, careful, systematic path or by a sudden decision to revolutionize the company and its ways. The full conversion to networked culture will take time, training, and patience by most organizations. For the exceptional others, it will be intuited instantly, bringing a sudden and dramatic change in outlook and practice.

We believe that all organizations are meant to walk and that they will benefit by learning to share knowledge through networked conversation. But we also believe that one can be too careful, too fearful of what might happen by taking the plunge. The Net's rewards often come through the unplanned magic of serendipity, as many advances in human knowledge seem to have done. The change in our ability to communicate as groups has happened, and it's not likely to be reversed. We should, therefore, make the best use possible of the technical advances we have created for ourselves and our world.

What's New and What's Not?

Many of today's most successful organizations and businesses have become humongous, hurried, and complex compared to any that we include in our brief summary of human history. It used to take a despot to manage large human forces and projects, but the old *command-and-control* hierarchical model is yielding, slowly but steadily, to the *networked* organization in direct response to the competitive (and collaborative) influence of today's new media. Managing in a networked environment is one of the skills we will describe in this book.

Given the size of organizations today and the tremendous reach of the Net, history hints persuasively that there may be an optimum size for communities that can effectively share knowledge and then have disproportionate influence. Within huge organizations, these naturally scaled collaborative groups need to be identified and leveraged. Groups small enough for all members to essentially know one another are less likely to be held back by inhibitions brought by the presence of strangers. The examples and guides we provide in this book will therefore be based on *effectively scaled* knowledge communities.

Though our focus is on conversational knowledge sharing using the new media of technical networks, we emphasize in this chapter that the purely social aspects of this practice are not new. Modern organizations don't have to reinvent knowledge networks; they've been under iterative development for countless generations. The current challenge is to adapt knowledge networks to the needs of the modern organization and to the new environment of Cyberspace.

HISTORY'S RELEVANT LESSONS

Knowledge transfer is a natural human behavior
Fully adapting group communication to any new medium takes time
Today's organizations are bigger and more complex than ever
Networked management structure is a new concept
Communities for effective knowledge exchange have size limits

---

Show and Tell in the Knowledge Space

When the paintings described earlier were discovered in Chauvet Cave near Avignon, France in 1994, they were hailed as some of the greatest early evidence of communication by visual images and of the cerebral capacity for associative thinking. As Robert Hughes explained, reporting on the discovery in *Time* magazine, "Art, at its root, is association—the power to make one thing stand for and symbolize another, to create the agreements by which some marks on a surface denote, say, an animal, not just to the mark-maker but to others."[1] Making these symbols recognizable to others illustrates one crucial principle of knowledge networking: the use of a *commonly understood language*.

The choice of a cave as a location for displaying their art certainly had some reasoning behind it. Of course, we can't know for certain if caves were chosen to protect the paintings from the weather or to demonstrate the bravery of the warriors who had to enter the lair of the ferocious cave bear to paint and see them. Maybe the difficult entry and the inhospitably dark environment lent enough danger and mystery to the location to enhance its ritualistic purpose. Whatever the reason, knowledge was recorded, stored, and passed along in a dedicated *space*, another key element of good knowledge networking. The cave itself lent special importance to what the community learned from its contents.

Surely these paintings were created and preserved for some *purpose* beyond the quality of their art. Though we can recognize most of the animal forms, we can't understand the *context* of their creation. We may be the distant descendants of the cave painters, but the best we can do is guess that these paintings had meaning and solved problems for the clan. They could have created them to keep clan members safe, to keep them fed, or simply to allay their fears. In the lingo of modern knowledge management, the art in Chauvet Cave would be described as *local knowledge*—understood and appreciated by its immediate community but of no clear relevance to the rest of us. The cave paintings are thus like many of the facts and figures that corporations take care to preserve: of limited practical use to people who discover them once the originators are gone.

CAVE PAINTINGS AND PRINCIPLES OF THE KNOWLEDGE NETWORK

1. **Common lexicon:** The tribal community recognizes the animals and symbols on the cave wall
2. **The knowledge space:** The cave itself and its limited access make it a special place for sharing knowledge
3. **Recordkeeping and access:** Pictures are drawn to record what the artists knew for others
4. **Context and purpose:** The tribe understands the meaning and importance of the animal figures on the cave wall
5. **Knowledge communities:** The tribe itself shares and benefits from the special meaning and purpose of the paintings

---

Stories, Rituals, Trust, and Culture

Trust is the cornerstone of knowledge-sharing cultures. The one certain show-stopper to revealing our knowledge to others is mistrust—the perception that The Other is our competitor or enemy and might use what we tell them against us.

Historically, we have opened up to others when they were recognized as part of our family or tribe. When The Other is unfamiliar, stories about them and their background become the common foundations for building trust from the ground up. Rituals renew and celebrate trust within a culture, and rituals are often where new or old knowledge is exchanged and affirmed. Cave painting appears to have been a ritual, and tribes probably performed other rituals around the magical depictions that shamans painted and acted out in their presence.

Powerful stories such as creation myths, heroic legends, and battle sagas have been passed along verbally as part of tribal ritual (as with the !Kung tribe of the Kalahari; see Figure 1.2) for countless generations. More than mere accounts of events and personalities, these stories carry and transmit the accumulated history and wisdom of their ancestral societies, imparting the thinly veiled instructions for living in what was (even millennia before the Internal Revenue Service) a very complex world.

Oral tradition was the primary vehicle for spreading lore, learning, and myth through society for tens of thousands of years, preceding the proliferation and public interpretation of cave drawings and pictograms. In the marketplaces and bazaars of early civilization, people traded more than goods and services. As in

Figure 1.2 Grandfather makes a big impression as experience, lore, and legend are passed on to a new tribal generation.

!Kung family of the Kalahari, Courtesy of AOL Time-Warner, Inc.

many ethnic marketplaces still active today, they also exchanged news, tales, gossip, and helpful tips on where to find the best raw materials, which vendors were reliable, and who overpriced goods or sold shoddy products.

A recent business bestseller, *The Cluetrain Manifesto*,[2] is based on the idea that "markets are conversations." If you visit a living marketplace—your local farmers' market as opposed to a modern supermarket—you'll see the truth in that idea. People take the time to ask the tomato farmer about growing techniques and microclimate. The local home baker learns from buyers about possible distribution outlets. The market is as much a social interaction as a commercial one. Ancient peoples in a market much like the one shown in Figure 1.3 must have shared wondrous accounts of things seen over the horizon and of new techniques and tools that would help them accomplish life's arduous tasks.

The marketplace conversation was (and still is) ritualistic, not so much like a religious ceremony but like a repeated behavior that defined cultural relationships and the flow of information and opinion. It was a ritual of *cross-pollination* between the various cultures that met regularly at the crossroads or port towns that naturally became centers of commerce.

People working within groups and organizations participate in similar rituals today, of course. However, there is wide variation in the extent to which leadership sanctions, allows, or encourages the creation and oral sharing of lore, myth, tales, or anything that is not accountable as "official business." The Internet has become the virtual crossroads where different cultures intersect and interact. Within the organization, these cultural crossroads also exist, but by restricting social exchange and marketplace conversation, management policy may stunt the growth and vitality of its organizational culture.

Ancient Media and Content

Our ancestors began writing some 5,000 years ago, recording events and transactions that made it possible for people of succeeding eras, including our own, to access some of what was known, understood, and believed about life and

Figure 1.3   Ye olde marketplace was as much a place to learn as it was a place to buy, sell, and barter.

Chronicles of Ulrich de Richental: Open Market, Courtesy of CORBIS, Inc.

cosmology thousands of years in the past. Thus, we know about the flooding in Mesopotamia and the handing over of The Laws to Hammurabi by the Sumerian deity. Judeo-Christian-Islamic culture became most familiar with these stories through their Old Testament versions of Noah's Ark and Moses receiving the Ten Commandments.

The communications media of ancient times evolved slowly. First employing fragile clay tablets and sturdy stone walls to hold their writings and drawings, recordkeepers eventually began using animal hide parchment, which was the writing surface of the Dead Sea Scrolls. The Egyptians used the stalks of papyrus reeds, pounded together, to form the earliest version of paper—a medium that was to serve the ancient Greeks well in spreading their heroic poems and revolutionary philosophical theories.

KEY ADVANCES IN ANCIENT KNOWLEDGE TRANSFER

1. Pictograms on walls recorded achievements and events
2. Clay tablets lent portability to written records
3. Papyrus allowed more to be written, faster
4. The Phoenician alphabet used a limited set of symbols for more flexible communication
5. The Library at Alexandria accumulated written knowledge and encouraged debate and conversation
6. Socrates, Plato, and Aristotle modeled the knowledge classroom and the practice of formal argument

---

The scribes of Sumeria and ancient Egypt left behind records like the one shown in Figure 1.4 revealing certain aspects of events, accounting, and commerce in their times. But evidently, they did little to distribute how-to knowledge among their contemporaries. (Most organizations began their use of computer networks following similar priorities.) It was a long time before efforts were made to deliberately save and make available recorded knowledge on media other than temple walls, sculptures, and clay tablets—media that were both lasting and portable.

Advanced knowledge—beyond what was required for day-to-day subsistence agriculture and home life—was concentrated in the halls of royalty, the counting rooms of merchants, and in the minds of priests and scribes who handed it down, through direct teaching and demonstration, to their apprentices. The rudimentary written languages of those early civilizations were limited in their ability to do more than recount events and record transactions. One could only tell limited stories through the use of different arrangements of wedge-shaped impressions and pictures of people, animals, and implements.

The Phoenicians developed the first standard alphabet around 1100 B.C. However, it wasn't until the Greeks invented symbols for vowels in the middle of the eighth century B.C. that humankind had a tool to express *general knowledge* in addition to the recording of *specific knowledge* about commerce and events. This was a tremendous breakthrough because it became possible to express meaning using a total of only 26 symbols.

As Charles Van Doren writes in *A History of Knowledge*,[3] "Perhaps the human race is unable to think and know generally if individuals cannot write down their thoughts so that others can clearly understand them." This ability made it much easier for local knowledge to be made useful beyond the originating communities. Alphabetical writing and paper extended early knowledge networks beyond the closed and privileged confines of the royal court.

Figure 1.4 Pressing a stylus into soft clay in various configurations served the earliest bookkeepers for recording transactions.
Courtesy of Gianni Dagli Orti/Corbis.

The First Knowledge Center

The Egyptian empire began around 3000 B.C., but because its Nile-based agricultural civilization was so stable and protected by the surrounding desert, its culture was conservative and reluctant to change and advance its knowledge. Its leaders enjoyed the safety of their kingdom's isolation, and it was not until Egypt began interacting with the more intellectually aggressive Greeks that one of its leaders was inspired to take an action that opened its ancient and imperturbable civilization to the influences of other advanced peoples.

At the beginning of the third century B.C., Egypt's king, Ptolemy I Soter, built the original Library of Alexandria. His purpose was to house a copy of every known book, which was to serve as a center for knowledge exchange and debate among scholars and scientists from all over the known world. Dialogue in the knowledge space of Alexandria led to many significant advances in philosophy and the sciences.

It was there that the scholar Eratosthenes devised the first accurate measurement of the circumference of Earth. Euclid completed his *Elements* there, detailing the study of geometry. Kallimachos of Kyrene, Alexandria's most famous librarian, created the first subject catalogue for 120,000 scrolls of the library's holdings, dividing all knowledge into eight major categories: oratory, history, laws, philosophy, medicine, lyric poetry, tragedy, and miscellany. His citations described something of each author's life, his works, and the number of lines in each work. Though it was by no means comprehensive, the library was the first attempt at a grand index to knowledge and a precursor to the Dewey decimal system and today's online databases of books and information.

Conversation as a Basis for New Learning

The oldest recorded stories are honored as classics in our literature, and to this day, we look to many of them for guiding principles in our personal, religious, political, and cultural lives. Universal truths demonstrated through accounts of early human social interaction seem just as valid today, even after so many centuries of progress and change. Homer's *Iliad* and *Odyssey*, Greek mythology and drama, and biblical histories and the Psalms all describe human situations and express emotions to which we modern people can relate. These stories began as oral accounts and were eventually translated and transcribed into written form. But even after the standardization of writing, oral communication continued to play an important part in developing new directions for knowledge.

The philosophers Socrates, Plato, and Aristotle recognized the importance of creating and enabling *social context*—leading discourse in which new and controversial ideas would flourish. Socrates encouraged his students to question the conventional thinking of the times, an approach that led to his being forced to drink poisonous hemlock. Plato emphasized the value of nurturing spirited dialogue in pursuit of an elusive truth and created a place to support that dialogue: the School of Athens, pictured in Figure 1.5. Aristotle, a student of Plato, took his quest in a different direction, creating a school that he called the Lyceum where he focused on the empirical (observable) nature of knowledge, leading eventually to the development of the scientific method.

Plutarch, who lived centuries later, helped to revive these heroes of ancient Greek thought in his biographical writings, and he hosted conversations at his home near the Temple of Apollo. The roots of modern teaching institutions and universities were thus set in Western society. Only through questioning the known, these philosophical pioneers taught, could people arrive at the truth.

Figure 1.5 Plato's School of Athens, a philosophical think tank where the teacher surrounded himself with a "society of learner-companions."
Courtesy of Archivo Iconografico, S.A./Corbis.

Leaders of Intellectual Ferment

What we know of Western history tells us that a very few individuals—such as Plato and Aristotle in Classical Greek times and Petrarch and Boccaccio in the pre-Renaissance period—led the introduction of new knowledge and new ways of thinking to their respective cultures.

Francesco Petrarch almost single-handedly revived classical learning after the Dark Ages. Many consider Giovanni Boccaccio, a contemporary of Petrarch, to have been the first "Renaissance man," studying the arts, science, and philosophy and reconciling them in his writings. Together, these two stimulated interest in old Greek and Roman literature and science and thus awakened the long-dormant pursuit of new knowledge in Europe.

Western and Eastern cultures alike have always relied on both mythical and real-life heroes to lead them in new directions and to model new values and practices. After centuries of withdrawal into theocratic and feudal governance, Western culture needed these maverick champions, though neither gained universal recognition or acceptance during his own time, to snap it out of its inward-focused complacency.

Even as the bubonic plague wiped out much of the European population, the new ideas adapted from ancient ones by Petrarch and Boccaccio found an avid audience and a small but eager network of supporters. Thus, two curious, brilliant, and ambitious individuals sparked a revival of critical thinking that would soon blossom into the Renaissance.

The First Mass Medium

Just as they served Petrarch and Boccaccio, handwritten accounts of knowledge seekers' works had fueled intellectual exploration for centuries, but access to such documents remained difficult, even for the privileged classes. Illiteracy was endemic in spite of the realizations and discoveries of classical philosophers.

The Dark Ages marked a long period in Western civilization when even the expansive thinking of the Greeks was forgotten. The isolated pockets of literacy in monasteries and courts of royalty lacked the means and motivation to disseminate what had been discovered and revealed centuries in the past. An exclusive priesthood still controlled the book medium. But a technical invention coupled improbably with a terrible disease brought a revolutionary solution to the problem of limited access to recorded knowledge.

Gutenberg and the Serendipity of the Black Death

In *A History of Knowledge*, Van Doren describes how one of the most horrific scourges ever to afflict humankind helped create the conditions that launched one of the greatest surges in understanding and intellect ever to elevate human-ity. Three situations converged to turn the first use of a clever invention into one of the great events in human history.

In 1347, the bubonic plague was brought to Europe from the Crimea on a boat that docked in Sicily. It quickly spread into an epidemic that wiped out between a third and a half of the continent's population. So many died that, after the plague had run its course, the survivors inherited the property of the deceased and found themselves owning more assets than they'd owned before. Van Doren describes the last quarter of the plague-ravaged 14th century as "an epoch of burgeoning prosperity."

Among the goods left by the many who had died were clothing, bedding, and other items made of cloth. Rag paper, manufactured from all of this discarded cloth, had accumulated in surplus by the mid-1400s, at a time when interest in the classical knowledge revived by the likes of Petrarch and Boccaccio was reaching a state of genuine intellectual hunger.

These conditions—expendable wealth, surplus paper (the "bandwidth" of the age), and demand for knowledge—were thus in place when Gutenberg invented his printing press in 1450 (which mostly produced bibles; see Figure 1.6). Until that time, few people knew how to read, but fewer still could afford to own books, which were laboriously written, one-by-one, by scribes and monks. A handwritten book could cost as much as a small farm, so most knowledge resided in and flowed through the memories and hearsay of people, who passed it on the best they could to their children and fellow villagers by word of mouth.

After Gutenberg's contribution, the printing of books accelerated so rapidly that by 1500 there were more than 1,000 print shops in Europe, and all of the known handwritten books had already been put to print. As difficult as it might be for us to imagine today, book-wild Europe found itself suddenly with a lack

BENEFITS OF THE PRINTING PRESS

The development of the printing press, as with the development of the Internet centuries later, brought with it the following benefits:

- Provided a huge leap in available bandwidth
- Delivered more new information faster to more people than before
- Allowed more individuals to reach each other with their ideas
- Introduced more people to stuff they'd never heard of
- Stimulated conversation, debate, protest, and even war
- Facilitated widespread and local cooperation
- Supported mass propaganda campaigns
- Catalyzed the formation of new communities around ideas
- Supported local organization
- Accelerated education and the spread of literacy
- Hugely expanded knowledge storage

of new content. In 1490, Van Doren reports, "publishers bemoaned the success of the new enterprise, which seemed to have rapidly exhausted its product at the same time that it had opened up an enormous, hungry new market."

Many more people—the "knowing classes"—learned to read and write, but for most "nonknowing" people, *knowledge* continued to be defined according to what could be orally exchanged within their class and trade. There was little crossover between the written literature of philosophy and science and the practical skills that produced most of the goods and services for the majority of the people. The new medium for knowledge transfer had not found its footing as a practical means of sharing best practices in the industries that served the vast majority of the population. Advanced knowledge was a very top-down thing, whereas common knowledge continued to be a grass-roots thing.

Figure 1.6   A page of the Bible printed on Gutenberg's press. This new medium changed the course of history.

Courtesy of Universitaetsbibliothek Goettingen.

New Ideas and the Challenge to the Hierarchy

Van Doren, citing numerous historical examples, observed that "any change, for a tyrant, is for the worse." This had been a truism of rule since the earliest of civilizations, and it was still so as Europe passed through the Dark Ages and headed toward the Enlightenment. The lack of a mass medium for spreading knowledge had been a major handicap to changing society and thereby to challenging tyrannical rule. Once the printing press became a commonplace technology, absolute monarchs had to deal with many more well-informed and well-educated subjects.

The spread of new ideas in Europe was also held back, even in the Renaissance, by the rising political authority of the Catholic Church, which regarded the emergence of scientific theory and experimentation as a threat to its intellectual hegemony. In the classic case of 1633, Galileo, under threat of death, recanted his scientifically derived observation that the earth revolved around the sun and that the heavens were not, as had been believed since Aristotle, immutable and unchanging. Old beliefs, especially when espoused at the time by the Church, were defended to the point of criminalizing any challenges posed by the bold purveyors of young Science. As still happens in many modern organizations, entrenched beliefs of Renaissance Italy rose up to squelch the introduction and adoption of new ideas and knowledge.

The big headline of the Age of Exploration was Columbus's discovery of the Americas in 1492. Every European monarchy then entered the competition to claim territory on other continents, conquer their native populations, and abscond with their riches. Overseas exploration was the R&D (research and development) of the monarchy, though once the way to the colonial land rush was known, the research activities were given less attention than the development projects. Laying claim to land and bringing home the loot were more important to the ruling classes than learning from newly discovered cultures because competition depended on accumulated wealth. And besides, all of the new and exotic cultures were assumed to be inherently inferior.

Still, as sailors and missionaries returned, knowledge of the world and its diversity flooded what had been Europe's closed societies. Following and, in many cases, accompanying the adventurers, populations of refugees migrated to the colonies to escape religious persecution and poverty, draining Europe of much of its own creative diversity. And as the wealth of the New World was hauled back to Spain, Portugal, France, England, and the Netherlands, it trickled down to the growing middle class, which—being more educated and informed than ever before—began to question the absolute powers of their kings and queens, opening the Age of Enlightenment.

New ideas and knowledge of politics, religion, economics, and philosophy were incorporated into the platforms of the French and American Revolutions.

And once these two very different countries declared their freedom and independence from royal rule, it was only a matter of time before the rest of Europe would follow. But with the invention of the steam engine, a force even more powerful than political revolution was unleashed. Manual labor—a constant for thousands of years and the backbone of every human population throughout history—was about to undergo a revolution of its own.

Deskilling in the Industrial Age

In the preindustrial world, complex skills and trades were passed on from parent to child and from master to apprentice by direct demonstration and hands-on instruction. Schools and universities were attended by a relative few, even after books began to be printed. As nations came into being, guilds of skilled craftspeople drove the economies. Even the simplest farmer had to be a jack-of-all-trades in a very hands-on world. Beasts of burden helped with the heavy lifting, but few of them, beyond the horse and the hunting hound, could be described as "skilled." Human and animal power could only get so many units manufactured during a workday.

With the invention of the steam engine and the advent of the Industrial Age in the 19th century, people did more manufacturing with powered machinery. With the energy available from turning fire into steam, many more units could be manufactured by a given number of people. Steam and carbon-based power was obviously the best way to get things done in the physical world.

The comprehensive sets of skills and knowledge that had driven the preindustrial economy lost favor, in the eyes of business owners and managers, to the ability (and willingness) to perform more specialized tasks requiring much less subtlety, less training, less knowledge, and less creativity. "Repetition of simple tasks" became the prevalent job description.

Led by American industrialists, this change in labor needs became known as *deskilling*. Whereas a blacksmith required deep understanding of horses, metallurgy, and design, combined with hands-on expertise in the use of heat, iron, and tools, a line worker needed only perform the assembly procedures of a few premanufactured parts—a set of motions he or she would repeat all day long, day after day, for years (see Figure 1.7). Once those procedures were learned, there was little more knowledge to be acquired. Success lay in performing one's tasks as quickly and error-free as possible.

The goal of the company was to be superefficient, emulating the machinery that drove the manufacture of its products. Specialization also carried over into the bloated bureaucracies that supported the growing manufacturing companies. Governments expanded to provide services to the growing middle class and to regulate the increasingly large and powerful corporations.

Mass production meant getting the most possible work accomplished each day to serve growing mass markets. This became the driving goal of the organization,

Figure 1.7   Pass the auto frame, please! A factory worker tries to keep up with growing demand.

Courtesy of the Detroit Institute of Arts.

whether the end products were automobiles, shoes, or documents. To a great extent, today's organizations are still designed to seek efficiency above all. But with the rise of industrialization came further expansion of the middle class and the university system. Science extended into the social sphere, and people began to study the effects of the treatment of workers on productivity and on society as a whole. Social consciousness had, at long last, taken root in the workplace.

The Dawn of the Info Age

Beginning with our cave-painting ancestors, we arrived at the doorway to the 20th century with a considerable accumulation of human experience and recorded history. We'd transferred knowledge through voice, pictures, hand-drawn letters, parchment scrolls, and printed books. We'd shared knowledge between prophets, philosophers, tribes, cultures, city-states, kingdoms, empires, and nations. We'd recorded what we knew in numbers, murals, essays, poems, songs, plays, novels, and libraries. We'd managed to span deserts, seas, continents, and oceans with what our ancestors had learned.

With the dawn of the Information Age, we began to harness a technology that moved at the speed of light. Sparked by electricity, the last 100 years have propelled us into the future at an astounding rate. In many ways, we're still catching up to our technical miracles, discovering that the karma of wiring the planet has included many events that we hadn't planned on. Some of them have been good surprises, but others have been bad.

Management Goes Scientific

While mechanized manufacturing altered the face of work life, advances in transportation and communication set us on a path toward even faster change in the way we interacted with the world and with each other. Railroads and steam-powered ships shrunk the planet, and the invention of the telegraph and telephone made it possible for people to move information back and forth at relatively instantaneous speed. The ability to move goods and conduct business correspondence so much faster than before spurred the growth of industry and forced a reevaluation of the focus of management.

In the early 20th century, F. W. Taylor formalized the trends that began in the preceding decades into an approach he called "management science."[4] Based on "clearly defined laws and principles," it aimed to increase the productivity of modern industry by studying the tasks, the tools, and the incentives and then tuning them for best performance.

Knowledge of performance was gained by such practices as putting a stopwatch on workers and measuring the difference in output between those paid at different rates. Recommending optimum shovel sizes for moving various materials was a typical example of Taylor's theory put into practice. Ford Motor Company embraced his approach in making its assembly lines more efficient, though one result was that many workers could only stand the pace of such efficient production for a couple of years. This didn't seem to matter, though, as there were always many others willing to take their places on the line.

Management science was praised and criticized by conservatives and liberals alike because while it objectified work and made it easier for workers to produce more in a given timeframe, it continued to treat workers as if they were cogs in a machine, showing little consideration for their health, happiness, opinions, or recommendations. Business was still very far from supporting conditions that would foster conversational networking among workers. What collaboration did occur in the first half of the 1900s was among academics, who found the work environment a fascinating object of study and experimentation.

Taylor's pioneering work inspired others to elaborate on the science of management, putting more emphasis on planning, organizing, commanding, coordinating, reporting, budgeting, directing, and leading in the workplace. The concept of the *bureaucracy* flourished during the early 20th century to the point where tending to the organization became even more important than achieving its purpose. The Italian government became so enamored of the scientific management process that it had 20 bureaus studying how to cut out much of its unnecessary bureaucracy.

Anticonversational Attitudes

As the structure of the organization got all the attention, little mind was paid to the value of the individual worker. Informal conversation—spoken or written as intraworkplace correspondence—was regarded as idle talk: a waste of time that would distract the worker from performing the all-important assigned tasks and reduce output. With the rise of labor unions, talk between workers on the job was suppressed even more, being recognized as a threat to the company and a means for workers to organize and challenge the power structure. No one was ready to accept the possibility that conversation would lead to smarter, happier, more cooperative workers. And no one was asking whether the worker might have valuable contributions to offer to the usable knowledge of the company.

Executives and managers were hired specifically for the education and experience they brought in the door with them. The know-how they came with was considered sufficient to run the organization for years. There was very little, if any, emphasis on continuing education or new knowledge generation within the work force. So naturally, there was little incentive to learn, to teach, to support conversation, or to bring up new ideas. But that was "just the way things were" at the time, and few complained.

Workers as People Who Matter

Attitudes about management began to change when, in 1939, the Hawthorne Studies led by Elton Mayo[5] showed that *social factors* in the work environment influenced individuals and their performance. The studies also demonstrated that change within the workplace was likely to stimulate more change. The resulting new approach to workers and workplace led to improvements in working conditions.

After World War II, studies revealed that no single management approach was appropriate to all business situations and that the social and technological elements within a company were interdependent. These "discoveries" might seem self-evident to us today, but notice that they took quite a while to be accepted and ingrained into what was taught in business schools. Relevant to this book is the conclusion that *the structure of an organization is closely tied to the information systems it uses.*

In the 1960s, Edgar Schein[6] proposed that management theories that looked at people from the economic, social, and self-actualizing perspectives were still too simplistic. People are complex, he wrote, as are the organizations in which they work. Schein recognized that no single management style can succeed in improving the performance of all workers and that the motives of an individual worker are liable to change over time. He also pointed out that high satisfaction alone does not necessarily lead to higher productivity.

This increasing focus on the individual and the motivating factors that lead to higher productivity was a distinct departure from the viewpoint of scientific management. The worker could no longer be treated as a mere cog in the machine if maximum productivity was desired. Consideration had to be given to what would drive the worker to perform best over the long haul. In the 1980s, the idea of collective decision making entered the picture as part of the new school of Business Process Reengineering. More worker *empowerment* would lead to a greater sense of responsibility, smoother workflow, and less load on the management layer.

Fixing the Organization

Reengineering got its name from the very process that it recommended: reorganizing the way that the organization functioned from top to bottom. In principle, it appeared straightforward. Companies had to change their management philosophies and restructure themselves to reflect that change. In practice, the change process itself began to suck up the time and resources of the company to the extent that the benefits of the change were often lost. As was true about managing the growth of bureaucracies, the purpose of the organization was sidetracked into the reengineering process. The individual worker ended up even more confused than before, and productivity suffered.

The role of the individual within the organization was certainly evolving, but knowledge networking activity remained limited in terms of who participated, the consistency of its practice, the means of communication, and the availability of information. Technology has since had an impact on all of those limitations.

The Emergence of Computer Networks

From here on, the history becomes more familiar to most of us. The advent of the Information Age began rather ponderously with room-sized mainframe computers like the one shown in Figure 1.8, accelerating decades later with the introduction of desktop personal computers and computer-mediated networks. These systems quickly evolved in sophistication and speed, penetrated the office and the workplace; and people—thousands and then millions—began to use them from their homes.

The earliest adopters of networking technologies were, naturally, the populations that designed the systems and had the systems designed for them. These included engineers, programmers, scientists, the military, and academics. As we track in more detail in Chapter 2, "Using the Net to Share What People

Figure 1.8   Not a desktop model, ENIAC (Electronic Numerical Integrator and Computer) was designed to help aim the big guns of World War II.
Courtesy of University of Pennsylvania.

Know," they invented the first communications applications such as email and conferencing, and they set the stage for what was to happen once networking advanced beyond its initially limited accessibility. To a great extent, they modeled the first online knowledge networks. The design of computers, software, and the Internet were all collaborative efforts that piggybacked on existing stages of technology to plot the improvements for the succeeding stages.

In the 1990s, as the Internet became accessible and user-friendly to regular citizens outside the workplace, the inadequacy of the management science approach and its derivative theories became very clear. Information could be produced, transferred, and distributed to thousands. It could be stored and retrieved not only by the specialized "data drones" and the upper echelons of the organization's hierarchy but also by everyone who had access to the tools and the networks. The hierarchy was still essential for commanding the work force and for dealing with peers in other similarly structured organizations. However, it proved to be slower in moving valuable knowledge around than allowing employees to directly network with one another and with the exploding volume of information available on the Net.

As the Web opened to the world, information began zipping around from so many sources to so many destinations in such volume and at such speed that management was forced to admit its limitations in keeping up with it. Information, which various pundits insisted "wanted to be" both free and expensive, had escaped and was acquiring other qualities, mixing truth and fact with rumor, error, and deliberate lies. Companies founded specifically to work through the Web led the way in fitting its capabilities to their business needs, while large established corporations sweated out the possibility that they'd missed the boat and might be displaced by progressive new competitors.

Outside the organization, the old knowledge-sharing traditions of conversation, direct demonstration, and storytelling were being reborn through the Net. The toolmakers and the tool users found a common communications ground for enabling widespread distribution and discovery of fresh information and ideas. Organizations were no longer leading the technological revolution. Those organizations not formed around the Net were finding that their ability to find and exchange information was simply too slow to keep up.

The Knowledge Explosion

Some businesses, especially new ones that could move without the leg irons of legacy beliefs and practices holding them back, joined the technical subculture to find the information they sought and to communicate with the people who possessed it. Encyclopedias and libraries "went live" on the Web, forced to evolve quickly in an environment that seemed perfectly suited to their core purposes of storing, cataloguing, and retrieving information. Organizations—handicapped by procedures and practices that had worked when employees had few opportunities to communicate their ideas to each other—recognized the widening gap between their internal operations and this new network of free-flowing information. They found themselves trapped in closed systems while, outside, their customers were conversing, criticizing their products, lambasting their services, trading ideas for improvements, and inventing new companies and methods to outdo them.

The business world's first reaction to these rapid changes was to better organize its operational information using the networking technologies of its closed internal systems. To move faster—to counter the speed of the Internet—businesses attempted to improve the flow of information within the company by identifying their most vital facts and figures, making sure they captured and stored them, improving systems to retrieve them, and instructing their managers and employees to contribute whatever they knew to a database of total company know-how and experience. The totality of this practice became known by a term that many now consider an oxymoron: *knowledge management*.

Summary

Human history contains most of the lessons required to build successful online knowledge networks. We have learned to be natural knowledge sharers, both as individuals and as members of tribes, trading networks, and cultures. Our brief historical review has demonstrated how the essential principles of knowledge networking have been developed and preserved over thousands of years.

The natural knowledge-sharing behaviors of early civilizations were influenced by the forms of governance and the media that developed through the ages. Hierarchical structures felt threatened by the open flow of new ideas, but powerful media such as writing, paper, and printing served to increase the flow and distribution of ideas. As organizations formed to do business, managers had to learn to deal with governance issues and the value of knowledge in the workplace. Gradually, our natural tendencies to share knowledge have been recognized as important to the organization. Just as innovation was vital to early communities, it has become vital today in business competition and organizational readiness. Knowledge sharing is a key to that innovation.

CHAPTER 2

Using the Net to Share What People Know

Knowledge sharing is an ancient and adaptive behavior, but history cautions that the emergence of new ideas—spread through new media—is often resisted by The Powers That Be. That was the case in most organizational cultures until the 20th century when industrialization generated the need for more scientific management practices, which in turn led to more perceptive techniques for internal analysis. Using those techniques, organizations over the past 50 years have identified *information handling* as the great challenge heading into the 21st century. In this chapter, we describe how knowledge management theory has responded to that challenge and how the subject of this book—online knowledge networking—has developed, since the invention of the computer, as a valuable practice for uncovering and applying knowledge. Throughout the chapter, we provide examples of groundbreaking and current state-of-the-art knowledge networking applications.

Managing Knowledge

As we mentioned at the end of Chapter 1, "Knowledge, History, and the Industrial Organization," some claim that *knowledge management* is an oxymoron, which Dictionary.com defines as "a rhetorical figure in which incongruous or contradictory terms are combined, as in a *deafening silence* and a *mournful optimist*." We're not so sure that knowledge management fully qualifies under that definition, but we recognize the shortcomings of a term that implies that knowledge can be managed.

David Skyrme, a respected British consultant, calls the two words "uneasy bedfellows."[1] He points out (and we agree) that real knowledge—based on experience and practice—lives in the human mind and defies external management. Indeed, some say management can *kill* knowledge, and the history we reviewed in Chapter 1 includes some supporting evidence that kings, pharaohs, and popes have often attempted to suppress the advances that come with new ideas and intellectual exploration.

New knowledge tends to incite change, and entrenched rulers (which include many managers of successful companies) tend to steer clear of adventure, risk, and surprise. Knowledge cannot thrive where its emergence is overcontrolled. But as Skyrme also observes, "knowledge is increasingly recognized as a crucial organizational resource that gives market leverage. Its management is therefore too important to be left to chance." So there must be a happy medium between allowing the wild and random exchange of ideas and opinions and prohibiting any crosstalk among people in the work place. This happy medium can be attained by establishing clear goals and purposes for the exchange and identifying the people who should (and must) be included in the conversation.

A functioning knowledge network does not manage the knowledge. Rather, it manages the structure and composition of the networks that exchange the knowledge. This book provides instruction for building and populating effective online networks that fill an essential role under the broad conceptual umbrella of knowledge management.

Knowledge as an Object

The knowledge management approach was originally developed to meet two looming challenges recognized by large businesses as they sought a competitive edge in an expanding and information-intensive marketplace. One was to get a better handle on the runaway growth of useful information by somehow taking control of the sources of that information and not losing information that had been located and captured. The other was to manipulate information to answer vital business questions in an increasingly complex and fast-changing world.

This was the origin of what some call the *knowledge as object* path. Its goal is to gather key data and configure them in ways that tell the organization how to proceed toward whatever it defines as success. It starts with data collection, storage, and management and applies the searching and parsing skills of virtual librarians and economists to the various data streams associated with purchasing, production, sales, marketing, and human resources.

This path has led to the development of increasingly sophisticated and "intelligent" software platforms—some are called *expert systems*—that can weave the various data streams together into systems that bring more efficiency to labor-intensive and complex business processes. Today, sophisticated platforms exist for supply chain management, customer-relationship management, hiring, sales forecasting, and resource location, all of which are based on capturing and storing essential information for internal reporting. Suppliers and service providers now employ systems that are compatible with their buyers and clients so that, for example, UPS can interface its delivery system with its customers' supply chain management system, saving time for the customer through greater convenience.

The first waves of knowledge management (KM) theory treated knowledge as *content,* and the first technologies to implement the theory could best be described as elaborate digital *containers* and *decanters.* But just as the cave walls at Chauvet contained information that none of us today can interpret, the information many organizations collect is often beyond the interpretation abilities of their own employees. The tools that store and report the information have to somehow provide (or be used within) a context that gives *meaning* to the information. Information without context is not truly knowledge.

Knowledge as a Process

Treating knowledge as an object—to be captured, stored, and retrieved through intelligent reporting—was (and still is) a powerful lever for organizations, but the approach has practical limitations. It fails to take advantage of the communications capabilities of the Net, and it cannot uncover, store, or distribute the human intelligence possessed by the people in the organization. This *intellectual capital* is much more fluid and accessible through person-to-person interaction. The facilities of email and online conferencing systems, running on the same digital networks that serve the knowledge-as-object software, allow knowledge sharing to take place on a deeper and more customizable basis.

The management focus of *knowledge as process* is on people and how they communicate rather than on information and how it is handled. People are more complex and more difficult to manage than information, so it's easy to understand why most organizations have spent more money, time, and resources on developing their capabilities for information handling than on developing those for interpersonal collaboration.

People may be natural knowledge sharers, but within organizations there are competing motivations between loyalty to the organization, loyalty to the team, and loyalty to one's career. There are many different contexts for collaboration depending on the structure of the organization and the task at hand. There are cultural issues, professional issues, and when we're considering online networking, technical competence issues, all of which will be discussed throughout this book.

The knowledge-as-process path is a continuation of the long history of human knowledge sharing. Its leaders and proponents tend to be sociologists, organizational development experts, and anthropologists rather than programmers, executives, and MBAs. Its most enthusiastic participants tend to be the people who actually own the know-how within the organization and who resist the idea that their intellectual assets can be controlled or condensed into pages of data.

Knowledge management was formalized to some degree in the early 1990s, but the roots of both the as-object and as-process paths go back to the very invention of computers and the networks that joined them. The problem recognized then, at the end of World War II, was the same one that prompted the focus on knowledge and information 50 years later.

Roots of the Knowledge Network

Only two generations ago the Digital Age was science fiction. The evolution of hardware, software, communications technologies, and interactive techniques is still in its infancy today, but we've come a long way since the idea of storing information and connecting people electronically was conceived, half a century ago. And though we make much of the fact that knowledge networking is an underutilized practice within organizations, the natural tendency for people to want to communicate inspired the earliest visions of what computers could be.

Blazing the Trails

The first description of the modern knowledge network was published on July 1945, at the end of World War II. Dr. Vannevar Bush, director of the U.S. government's Office of Scientific Research and Development, wrote an article in *Atlantic Monthly* titled "As We May Think."[2] He lamented a situation where, in spite of the many great scientific advances that had been made, the organizations of his time were stuck using obsolete methods for dealing with their fast-growing stores of information.

"The summation of human experience is being expanded at a prodigious rate," he wrote, "and the means we use for threading through the consequent maze to the momentarily important item is the same as was used in the days of square-rigged ships." His solution to this outmoded knowledge access situation was an imagined device he called a *memex* "in which an individual stores all his books, records, and communications, and which is mechanized so that it may be consulted with exceeding speed and flexibility."

Inventing Tools for Collaboration

Bush was visualizing the desktop computer. After several generations of technical evolution, the first computer-mediated networks appeared as ARPANET, built by the Advanced Research Project Agency during the 1960s. Initially funded by the Department of Defense, the distributed hub model of ARPANET, in which no single communications node was essential to its operation, was intended to preserve its functionality in case of a nuclear attack. The design proved to be valuable for other reasons, too. It was easy to add nodes, and its nonhierarchical structure encouraged innovation. But the incremental adoption of institutional and academic networking that followed over the next 20 years could only advance the technology so far. These networks were not commercial, and the population using them was very limited. The mainframe computers of the era, which filled large air-conditioned rooms and were accessed through dumb terminals, were prohibitively expensive and slow compared to even the first generation of desktop PCs.

The earliest networks allowed their users to share data files. An operating system named UNIX, which allowed multiple users to share and work simultaneously on files located on a single computer, was invented in 1969. Email was invented in 1971, and many-to-many conferencing through Usenet became a reality in 1979. But these tools served only the relatively few professionals and university-connected users who had access to mainframe computers at the hubs of the various educational and government-sponsored networks that grew out of the ARPANET model. The use of these networks—BITNET and EDUNET were among the most active—served the purposes of scientists and academics seeking to collaborate over a long distance.

Dr. Bush's vision of a personal computer was finally realized in the late 1970s, and with the introduction of the first Apple computers and IBM PCs, commercial multiuser systems like CompuServe, the Source, Genie, and the WELL—all of which relied on modems and telephone dialup connections—introduced new populations of early adopters to the practice of what came to be called *virtual community.*

The Birth of the Special Interest Group (SIG)

A plethora of *bulletin board systems* (BBSs), each with its own dialup numbers, served the wide range of hobbyists and *special interest groups* (SIGs) operating from their homes. People paid good money for access to one another's knowledge, and by the late 1980s, the denizens of BBSs and those of the commercial dialup communities discovered each other and began comparing notes on their technologies and cultures.

Connecting people who shared the same interests was the central business proposition of the pre-Web online world. During that time, computer networks were rarely used to support central business processes and internal communications. With few exceptions, computer applications in business were limited to calculating, accounting, and building customer databases, even after the personal computer became commonplace in the office. After all, the software program that most stimulated sales of IBM's first PC was not a communications interface; it was the spreadsheet Lotus 1-2-3.

The Slow but Steady Adoption of Groupware

But almost a decade before the IBM PC, early computer programmers had recognized the possibilities for using their primitive networks to help them improve the software they were writing for nonprogrammers. PLATO was created to share knowledge,[3] but in what we'd think of today as a customer-service application.

PLATO TO NOTES: A LINEAGE OF DIGITAL KNOWLEDGE EXCHANGE

True knowledge sharing software probably began with PLATO Notes, a creation of the Computer-based Education Research Laboratory (CERL) in 1973. Originally created to help users inform programmers of where they found bugs in software, it evolved for network use into PLATO Group Notes in 1976. As Notes.Net describes, it allowed its users to:

1. Create private notes files organized by subject
2. Create access lists
3. Read all notes and responses written since a certain date
4. Create anonymous notes
5. Create director message flags
6. Mark comments in a document
7. Link notes files with other Plato systems
8. Use multiplayer games

Most of the team that developed PLATO Group Notes went on to design what became Lotus Notes, first released in 1989 and still the most widely used internal corporate messaging system. Now owned and marketed by IBM, Lotus Notes continues to evolve with market needs.

Its features and foundation inspired the next generation of collaborative software interfaces. Notes, in its PLATO and Lotus forms, was the idea framework around which other software applications were designed to support teams involved in projects, programming, and design. Peter and Trudy Johnson-Lenz were two inventive researchers who had used and helped design special applications for such software, which they christened *groupware*.

Groupware was typically categorized along two dimensions:

1. Whether the members of the group worked together at the same time (*real-time or synchronous work*)

2. Whether the members of the group worked together in the same place (*collocated or face-to-face*) or in different places (*noncollocated or distant*)

The resulting 2×2 matrix described the kinds of software applications and collaboration that were appropriate to the various combinations of time and place.

	SAME TIME	DIFFERENT TIME
Same place	Voting, presentations	Shared computers
Different place	Chat, videophones	Email, conferencing, workflow

To help design the software that would fit these various needs and situations, a field of study called Computer-Supported Cooperative Work (CSCW) developed. The people working in this field represented many different aspects of the work-place experience. According to the Usability First Web site: "The field typically attracts those interested in software design and social and organizational behavior, including business people, computer scientists, organizational psychologists, communications researchers, and anthropologists, among other specialties."[4] The resulting design was more than a mechanistic set of tools to meet the needs of cooperation and work; it was a carefully orchestrated suite of capabilities and options that considered the importance of aspects like competition, socialization, and play.

With the invention of the personal computer, the evolution of design toward greater support of CSCW seemed to reverse itself, but within a short time, the local area network (LAN) was invented to link mainframes, PCs, and computer peripherals as shared resources. Groupware development moved to the local Net. By the late 1980s, LANs could interconnect with the larger geographical networks that were then merging to become what we know as the Internet. The seemingly overnight emergence and adoption of the World Wide Web interface made the Internet more useful, more user-friendly, and consequently, more attractive to a generation raised using PCs.

The Web attracted a user base counted in the tens of millions, and many corporations began to carefully integrate Web compatibility into their planning. Lotus and IBM, the owners and developers of Notes—at one time the definitive model of groupware—were conspicuously absent from the first wave of Web-based collaborative software. Fully occupied as they were serving lucrative standalone networks for their clients and enterprise-level customers, they underestimated the degree to which the Web protocol would be adopted and the influence it would have on internal system design. The Web had lifted off without them, and its groupware vacuum had to be filled.

From its very beginning, the idea of groupware made perfect sense, but its adoption by organizations had been slowed by bad experiences, typically where design and implementation—the CSCW stage—had resulted in poor matches between social and workplace realities. Workers didn't use the tools, or if they did initially, they were likely to abandon them.

In retrospect, it's not surprising that organizations still in the early stages of companywide computer literacy found it difficult to be both laboratory guinea pigs and end-user customers of experimental software. The Web altered the game board of collaborative software design by providing designers with millions of eager guinea pigs and a gigantic test bed for online group interaction.

The Web Breakthrough

The Web's explosive growth moved the question of Internet integration into the corporate fast lane because new channels of contact had been opened with so many of the right kinds of customers. And because millions of those potential customers were interacting regularly with one another, interest in the adoption of groupware was promoted from an esoteric curiosity to a mainstream business consideration. Which is not to say that most companies then joined the groupware revolution, but they at least gained a passing familiarity with chat, message boards, and other manifestations of online group collaboration.

What is most important here is that the Web's user-friendly technology and its adoption by the masses drove its acceptance by business. The Web's simple utility generated a *network effect*, which the dictionary at Marketing Terms.com describes as "the phenomenon whereby a service becomes more valuable as more people use it, thereby encouraging ever-increasing numbers of adopters." [5] If someone's friend, business associate, or family was on the Web, that individual was more likely to get on the Web, too. This applied, likewise, to customers, partners, and competitors.

Surely, if so many were jumping at the chance to buy the equipment and learn the techniques required to connect to the Web, its methods deserved attention within the company. But even in companies where the executives remained ignorant of the Web's growing influence, workers, who surfed the Web from their home computers, launched guerilla marketing campaigns within their companies. Years of effort had gone into spreading the groupware gospel, but it took the Web, with its public demonstration of diverse and widespread group interaction, to seize the attention of most organizational decision makers.

Design for Attracting Users

The best of the Web-based collaboration tools were originally designed for use by masses of individual consumers, not by the staffs of organizations. Web ventures expected the industry's primary source of revenue to come from advertising dollars. People hooked on online conversation—clicking daily to new pages (and banner ads) with every new exchange of messages—offered the potential of a user-powered perpetual money machine. The Globe was one of the Web's early examples of online communities centered around an easy build-it-yourself homepage kit. It gained over 600 percent in share value on the day of its initial public offering (IPO) because investors assumed that its *sticky* social content and conversation would attract a captive, self-categorizing audience for high-value advertisers.

People, relationships, prefab home pages: The rush of users signing up to immerse themselves in the Web was described as doubling annually with no end in sight. But in the Web's stratospheric boom, overoptimistic marketers failed to see that such rabid infatuation with the Web's amusement park-like novelty would eventually wear off. Investors didn't realize that people would tire of clicking on banner ads or that, in the midst of interesting online social activity, they would simply ignore ads altogether. But that's exactly what happened, and the dreams of ad-supported interactivity died along with many other Web-based business models.

Today, The Globe is history, and the days of overblown expectations for commercial online communities have passed, but the tools developed to support group interaction on the Web are still widely used. Many chat room and message board interfaces are being overhauled and upgraded by their developers to serve a marketplace where organizations, rather than individual Web users, are beginning to express demand for powerful, flexible, collaboration-supporting online environments.

The idea of groupware has merged with the battle-tested, practical design of software meant to attract communities of special interest. But well-designed and robust technology is only part of the knowledge networking formula. How we behave as social creatures in electronic environments may be more important than the technology, as some experimental communities discovered in the pre-Web years.

Lessons of the Pioneers

A community is made up of people with common interests who communicate, form relationships, and establish shared history. The community is a basic social structure that we all recognize in our lives but often have a hard time describing. Try to name the specific communities you are a part of. Try to describe their boundaries and what defines them as communities. What does it take for someone to join your communities or to lose membership in them? Like us, you probably define them according to your feeling of membership. "If it feels like I'm part of a community, then it must be a community."

Communities have historically been defined by their geographical location because people needed to be in the same place to communicate. This is no longer the case. People can communicate very well using the Net, and since the first email messages were passed over the early ARPANET, communities have formed in its virtual space. Scientists working together on projects exchanged messages regularly over long periods of time, extending their limited opportunities to meet face to face through the use of electronic connections.

When the first publicly accessible electronic networks were launched in the late 1970s, the founders and first customers were people who once had access to the government-sponsored networks, usually as students or instructors on university campuses. They'd had a taste of the Net's utility and were willing to pay hefty hourly fees to use similar technologies through private networks. As the populations of these online gathering places grew, more people began to practice the art of informal knowledge networking. Changes in societal patterns, such as increased mobility and decreased involvement with local social activities, were also making the advantages of online communication more valuable as a means of staying in touch.

Computer-Mediated Communications (CMC)

Howard Rheingold wrote *The Virtual Community*[6] in 1993 and exposed his readers not only to a new concept of social interaction but to the wide variety of people, ideas, and types of interaction that had been mixing for years through, around, and within the scattered experiments with *computer-mediated communications*. The stories in his book illustrate the overlap of friendship, intellectual stimulation, and professional interaction that characterized the early research and commercial networks. Rheingold states that people used CMC to "rediscover the power of cooperation," describing how their interaction represented "a merger of knowledge capital, social capital, and communion."

Murray Turoff built what Rheingold calls the "great-great-grandmother of all virtual communities" in 1976. Named Electronic Information Exchange System (EIES), it was funded by the National Science Foundation as "an electronic communication laboratory for use by geographically dispersed research communities." EIES served as a test bed for the use of online conferencing in problem-solving applications, and through people who spent time using the system, EIES got the word out among many students of organizational development about the useful potential of multiuser online conferencing.

On a separate track, Tom Truscott and James Ellis developed Usenet News in 1979 as a program to support ongoing *stored-and-forwarded* message-based interaction among users of computers that ran the UNIX operating system. Because it cost so much to connect to ARPANET, Usenet was created to be the "poor man's ARPANET." Usenet newsgroups began circulating among college campuses and other installations a year later, but distribution grew slowly.

The newsgroups were originally meant to be a discussion platform for questions and answers about UNIX and its technical administration. There were many UNIX enthusiasts and pioneers at AT&T Bell Labs, so the organization helped Usenet however it could. AT&T benefited from participating in Usenet newsgroups about improving the operation of internal email. Digital Equipment Corporation (DEC) adopted Usenet and UNIX to help sell their UNIX-based computer systems. Usenet became the central knowledge base for discussion of the operating system that would eventually be the basis of the Internet and the model for all other multiuser, multitasking operating systems.

No one owned Usenet, and no one was in charge of the system that expanded faster and more widely than its creators had expected. It grew as much around a culture as it did around a technology. The original intention had been to provide a forum for mutual self-help among people facing similar technical problems, but the subject matter of newsgroups diversified quickly as Usenet got connected to ARPANET and, eventually, to the Internet. As Michael Hauben writes in a chapter of *Netizens: An Anthology*:

> The number of sites receiving Usenet continually increased, demonstrating its popularity. People were attracted to Usenet because of what it made possible. People want to communicate and enjoy the thrill of finding others across the country (or today across the world) who share a common interest or just to be in touch with.[7]

Its popularity forced its loyal users to develop a code of rules for posting messages to newsgroups, with an entire category or *domain* of newsgroups devoted to orienting the newcomer to the virtual culture. The culture attempted to take care of the commons by instilling itself in its new members. It accomplished this through what Hauben calls the "contributed effort" of the people who donated content and the site administrators who maintained the systems required to run, maintain, and distribute news from their local Usenet installations.

Through its first decade, Usenet was available only to those who, through their school or workplace, had access to computers that could move newsgroups through modem connections or the ARPANET itself. But once habituated to Usenet, people who lost their access upon leaving a school or workplace were quite willing to pay for a connection to the growing collection of networked minds and ideas.

Paying to Participate

The first pay-for-access online discussion system was the Telecomputing Corporation of America, which *Reader's Digest* bought in 1980 and renamed "the Source." CompuServe was founded by H&R Block soon after. Joining either of these systems required an initial membership fee and hourly fees that varied with the time of day. An hour-a-day habit could easily cost hundreds of dollars per month, but thousands of people joined, even when the fastest modems ran at only .005 the speed of today's 56-kilobit-per-second (Kbps) modems.

Communities on these text-based systems formed around professional interests, hobbies, humor, current events, general technology, and most significantly, around the specific technologies of the systems that made the conversations possible. These self-tuning activities fascinated us at the WELL, and their practice is one of the great underappreciated assets of online discussion communities.

Using a collaborative interface, a group can learn through experience how to make its environment more conducive to achieving its needs and goals. Like Usenet, the subscription-based online communities showed that where members valued the online interaction they would, if allowed to, actively work to improve the system's design and operation.

A Knowledge-Swapping Community

People who describe themselves as "knowledge workers" are especially at home in the environment of the Net. The authors were privileged to be associated with one of the prime examples of grass-roots knowledge networking: the Whole Earth Lectronic Link, better known as the WELL.

The company was founded in 1985, and working as part of the WELL's small staff for 6 years convinced us that valued relationships could be developed and maintained purely through online communication. WELL members, like those of the Source and CompuServe, paid a significant amount to converse with a diverse selection of learned people on a wide variety of subjects.

There was always plenty of disagreement and some fairly spectacular feuds to spice up life in the virtual village, but most people logged in to find friendship and intellectual stimulation, not conflict. Many individuals separated by hundreds or thousands of miles became loyal friends and even professional partners exclusively through their online conversations and email. This took place at a time before people could build graphical home pages to describe themselves and their interests in minute detail. Instead, they made themselves known through their typed responses in online conversations.

Building Relationship Bandwidth

WELL members occasionally referred to the *bandwidth* of relationship, meaning the amount of information that could be transmitted about each other's personal qualities through the medium of slow PCs and slow modems. Having only words on a screen to work with, and lacking pictures or sound to fill out one's description, we sought higher bandwidth through other means. One was the sparing use of symbols to convey emotions—the so-called smileys that employed punctuation marks to represent facial expressions. Another was the development of a local style of writing that included jargon and shorthand for adding personality and efficiency to messages. But the two most effective means for getting to know people were parties and a far-ranging selection of conversation topics.

Beginning in its second year, the WELL began holding monthly office parties open to members and their friends. These Friday night gabfests served as an excuse for in-person meetings with characters previously known only by their written words. Face-to-face (F2F) encounters raised the reality level of relationships, providing vivid mental referents for future online interactions.

Though many WELL members lived too far away from the San Francisco Bay Area to attend the parties, it was important for the WELL's overall community stability that as many people as possible got to know each other F2F. The WELLers who actually knew and trusted each other formed the *core* of the community, a social flywheel for interaction that could carry the soul of the community through difficult times.

The diversity of the WELL's structured online social environment was an equally important factor in establishing trust and familiarity between individual members. Well-rounded relationships could be based on the varied interaction that members shared around hobbies, family, personal life, entertainment, and world events.

The structure of the WELL's knowledge space was based on the *conference*: a collection of conversation *topics* with a common focus. Like a newspaper, the WELL had sections devoted to politics, sports, movies, and many of the area's local neighborhoods. It also had conferences for single people, married people, parents, writers, journalists, and computer geeks. It had a jokes conference, a future conference, and a sarcasm free-fire zone called Weird. The network of conferences permitted WELLers to build *multidimensional familiarity* with each other.

Joe might find Sue to be an obnoxious adversary in the politics conference but a compassionate advocate in the parenting conference. They might give each other helpful tips in the cooking conference and agree on the strengths of the latest mouse design in the Macintosh conference. But Sue might find Joe's jokes in Weird to be very strange and troubling. They might never meet in person, but they could at least know a lot about different aspects of each other's personality—enough to establish trust, if not to be the best of friends.

The Knowledge Pool

The WELL was founded on the groundbreaking publishing model of the *Whole Earth Catalog*, which intentionally blurred the boundary between publisher/writer and consumer/reader. The catalogs had, for over a decade, invited readers to submit recommendations and reviews of products and articles about intriguing subjects. Such amateur authors were compensated modestly for their submissions, but many proved to be competent experts in their fields.

The WELL took this model online in a conversational format where members would submit the benefits of their experience and education to the curiosity of others. The voluntary sharing of knowledge fed on itself over the years, persuading members that if they gave freely of what they knew, they would get back at least equal value in kind.

The rewards from fellow WELL members might come in the form of useful facts, humor, moral support, advice, or opinion. They might come from someone for whom they'd provided help or from someone with whom they'd never interacted at all. Rather than just being a space for person-to-person knowledge barter, the WELL became a *knowledge pool* to which everyone gave and from which everyone could draw. It was both a knowledge marketplace and knowledge collective.

One of the community's earliest topics was called "Experts on the WELL." Today, more than 16 years after it was first started, the Experts topic is still active in its umpteenth incarnation. In Experts, a member posts a question and another member posts an answer. There's always a response and most of the time a definitive answer, though it often comes from a combination of people and pointers.

In Figure 2.1, a simple plumbing question elicits a straightforward suggestion and then a pointer to a source for what could be the comprehensive remedy. Experts is an informal and general resource. During the same period when this question about plumbing was posed, other questions addressed the molecular

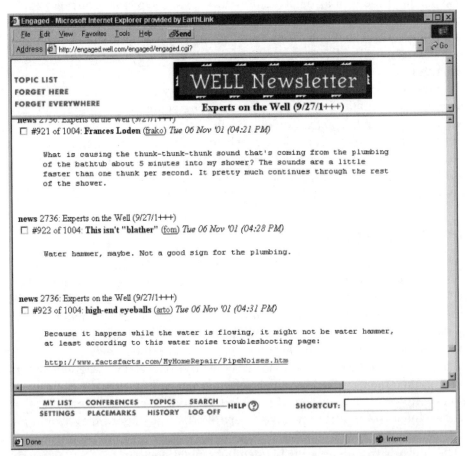

Figure 2.1   Screen shot from the Experts on the WELL, where groupthink provides the answers.
Courtesy Salon.com

properties of different types of alcohol, a problem with Microsoft software that turned out to be a virus, the schedule of monarch butterfly migration to Big Sur, tenants rights laws in Marin County, and how to relight the pilot light in an oven. All were answered thoroughly and cooperatively. The catch on the WELL is that each question is likely to trigger an entire conversation, which by its volume makes the answers difficult to find later using the WELL's rudimentary data retrieval tools.

Familiarity and Trust

To reach such fluency in exchanging valuable and often hard-won knowledge, a large majority of WELL members had to trust each other. Most never got the chance to meet in person, and it took some time for interactions across a variety of conferences to build the level of familiarity that would allow members to "know" each other. Two years into its existence, Howard Rheingold and another community leader founded a conference named "True Confessions." Its purpose was to be a space for people to describe themselves through autobiographical stories. As it turned out, True accelerated the coalescence of WELL culture.

In Chapter 6, we'll include more about the effectiveness of stories in opening people up to each other and to new ways of thinking and generating knowledge. But suffice it to say that after people had posted true tales about their upbringing, about their adventures growing up, about their parents and siblings, or about how they found their life's work, membership in the WELL began to evoke feelings of living in a real-life village. When the Loma Prieta earthquake struck the Bay Area in 1989, the postquake support and caring reached an almost familial level.

It must be pointed out that the WELL's purpose was not to get work done. It was a small business that best described its mission as "selling its subscribers access to each other." It was in the relationship business more than the technical business, and to make the business work, the staff had to foster and maintain an overall atmosphere of trust. There was no common allegiance to a company to hold our members together, and many refused to trust certain other members even after True Confessions, the earthquake, several deaths in the family, and the passage of many years. But for the majority of people and the majority of relationships, the WELL's discussion space felt safe, open, and supportive.

Rules, Customs, and Culture

Governance in the WELL's community was based on some simple guidelines. The first ground rule was "you own your own words," which meant that as a business the WELL would not be responsible for anything that any member posted on its site. Another founding principle was the distribution of power to responsible members who volunteered (or were appointed) to be *conference hosts.* Hosts presided over the hundreds of interest-based discussion locales of the WELL and qualified for their privileges through a combination of expertise in the subject, reliable presence and participation in their conference, and—we would always hope at the outset—responsible behavior as good representatives of WELL culture.

Hostship, with its power and responsibility, was awarded to almost as many people as volunteered to accept it. Hosts were empowered through the software to control and edit the content of their discussion areas, even to delete messages and entire conversations posted by their participants. Their powers to do harm through overcontrol were regulated by the cultural perception that censorship was a last-resort evil. Good hosts were assets to the business because they helped keep paying members interested and active, improving the quality of the WELL's content.

Hosts were rewarded for their help with free access to the system—a custom that was, for many years, the standard way that all online businesses managed their communities. This arrangement worked as long as online communities charged hourly membership fees, but when the business model changed to monthly flat fees in the mid-nineties, the rewards of free access became much more limited and AOL's volunteers challenged the legal fairness of being compensated with a mere $30 per month for many hours of valuable work. Good online discussion hosts deserve fair compensation, and within organizations good online hosts and facilitators are worth training and hiring for the difference they can make in knowledge-sharing discussion communities.

The WELL's one rule concerning bad behavior was conceived in response to actual experience. It outlawed intentional harassment and threatened any member who persisted in bothering another member with expulsion from the community by denying them further login privileges. As much as possible, WELL management encouraged self-governance and a sense of shared ownership and pride in the system, a strategy that seems to have worked more than it didn't.

The WELL is still active, with many of its early members still participating, even after 17 years. It has not grown steadily like AOL, which was founded around the same time, but the WELL was not built on the same business model, with the same motivations. It is a stable and persistent community, while there are very few such social entities living on AOL. The WELL's longevity has demonstrated the value of history in an online culture that, while not created to serve the knowledge needs of an organization, has enriched its members (and overall Net culture) in many ways.

Inside-Out Design

One of the WELL's founders contributed its first central computer, six modems, a hard disk loaded with the UNIX operating system, and a software program called Picospan to support its online discussion. Picospan was a *conferencing system*, which put it in the category of *asynchronous message boards*. Members read the messages left on the system in its various *boards* or conferences and, when motivated to do so, wrote responding messages for others to read. *Asychronicity* means that WELL members didn't have to be online at the same time to converse. A response to a message might come in the next minute or the next month. A conversation might be displayed on the WELL for years. In fact, some historical conversations from 1986 can still be read today in the WELL's Archive conference.

Because members were permitted access to the operating system—the software layer that supported Picospan—the WELL was considered an *open* installation, where members with programming skills could build features and utilities for their own use or for the benefit of the community as a whole. Thus, the more the system was used, the more its users were able to improve upon its original features and operations.

One member wrote and donated the first user's manual. Another built the equivalent of today's instant messaging tools, allowing members who were logged in at the same time to communicate in real time, lending a greater sense of presence to their conversation. Another built a tool that allowed members to blank out or ignore the messages posted by other members who irritated them in some way. Called a *bozo filter*, its availability improved the perceived quality of online life while having a deterrent effect on behaviors intended to be abrasive. Thus, the environment of the WELL could be customized to fit the needs of its users, making it more useful, more appealing, and more consistent with the ways they managed relationships in the F2F world.

The WELL's example of user-driven software improvement is significant from a cost-management point of view. Any organization making decisions about software to support a knowledge network should consider that a flexible and easily customizable interface is better able to meet the evolving needs of the communities that use it. Buying a platform with rigid features—custom configured in advance of its actual use by "experts"—can freeze the community into processes that it finds neither natural nor comfortable. In Chapter 5, "Fostering a Knowledge-Sharing Culture," we'll describe some of the platforms that offer the design flexibility required by new conversational knowledge communities.

Organizational Knowledge Networking

These early prototypes of knowledge-generating networks, pioneered by research communities and commercial providers, were like petri dishes, demonstrating the possibilities of using technical conversation interfaces for a variety of purposes and populations. Though some aimed to make large profits, many were satisfied with just breaking even or getting funded. All sought to stimulate activity and involvement.

The managers of these systems were focused on learning how to make their untried models work. They regarded their systems as full-time focus groups, testing the process of group problem solving in virtual environments. They listened for direction in refining their online interfaces to fit the specific needs of their communities. They involved themselves in conversations about governance and manners. They openly asked for advice and appreciated getting it. The relationship between management and customer was symbiotic, and this solid trust was needed going both ways.

The interaction on these systems resulted in many positive and surprising outcomes. One of the most fruitful by-products was the *cross-pollination effect* of different internal cultures brought together electronically. Groups whose physical paths might have never intersected were able to interface and integrate in a new knowledge nexus. In the most classic example, when technical people and nontechnical people communicated across the early networks, the alchemical combination provided a steady driving force for better product design.

The WELL was a tossed salad of professional writers, techno-geeks, counter-culture veterans, journalists, Gen-Xers, futurists, scientists, musicians, artists, and fans of the Grateful Dead. These different communities met through the years under a variety of contexts: as cohorts, fellow parents, witnesses to disaster, seekers of discourse, observers of the world, business associates, concerned citizens, and attention seekers. Our conversations, at their best, were far ranging, witty, and passionate. At their worst, they were infuriating, depressing and passionate. All of this social and intellectual involvement made the community an always-open marketplace for hard-earned knowledge, hearsay, and opinion.

The Learning Organization

Pioneering systems like the WELL learned that certain hassles came with the human territory. Misunderstandings happened. Arguments and hurt feelings happened. So did feuds and fits, social sabotage, accusations, and the occasional rebellion or mutiny. People could be relied on to flip out from time to time as individuals or as groups. In many ways, both good and bad, social reality was plainly the same online as it was in the so-called *real* world. But some social games proved easier to play in virtual space than sitting across the table where one's nose might get punched.

Through using the tools of online group interaction, the community manager was able to learn in actual practice how to do a better job and produce a better product. But even *that* had to be learned. The immediate feedback that networked communities generated was a revelation to organizations that had not yet begun to use the technologies. The idea of the *learning organization* did not arise directly out of online discourse, but it was yet another response of the pressures of the Information Age.

Royal Dutch Shell, the global oil company, was among the first businesses to change emphasis from long-range planning to "the microcosm (the 'mental model') of our decision makers."[8] Peter Senge soon became the lead proponent of the idea of the learning organization, describing it as one "in which you cannot *not* learn because learning is so insinuated into the fabric of life." The people who comprise a learning organization are, he wrote, "continually enhancing their capacity to create what they want to create."

For the most part, the early online knowledge networks were informal exchanges among users with shared focus, compatible backgrounds, and enthusiasm for using the technology available to them. Their activities needed no official approval by the boss or company. People took part either on their own time or in pursuit of solutions for problems that they'd encountered in their workplace.

The idea of bringing such collaborative learning interaction into the organization was being tried only by a few companies. The concept of the learning organization was not originally framed around any technology at all. If the value of the company centered on learning, then whatever practice or technology could advance that value was likely to be pursued. Computer networks, as it turned out, fit many of the needs of the learning organization.

Communities of Practice

Few of the early virtual communities were assigned to do the organization's work. Some did generate knowledge that was used internally by the companies that sponsored them. But people didn't participate with the boss looking over their shoulders to see if they were affecting the bottom line. Informality was an advantage because their members felt free to say what they thought and to float new ideas even if they were off the wall. Informality took their collaboration out of the box.

One thing these experiments showed was that the most productive communities, from a business or organizational point of view, are those made up of people who communicate about what they do: their practice. Communities formed around common skills and knowledge are perhaps the most natural of associations and group identity beyond the family. One leading expert in applying the idea of communities of practice (CoPs) is Etienne Wenger, who got his Ph.D. in artificial intelligence and now works full time developing intelligence within groups of people with similar experience.

Wenger's definition of CoPs encompasses, "your local magician club, nurses in a ward, a street gang or a group of software engineers meeting regularly in the cafeteria to share tips."[9] Like workers in Japan and Korea, he equates knowing with doing. "Knowledge," he writes, "is an act of participation." Many of the earliest uses of computer networks were by communities of practice—the programmers who were building on the very networks they used as their primary meeting places. Now Wenger applies his principles to the situations of multinational corporations. We'll draw from his work in our discussion of the relationship between culture and technology in Chapter 7, "Choosing and Using Technology," and in some of our guides to knowledge network implementation in Chapter 8, "Initiating and Supporting Internal Conversation," and Chapter 9, "Conversing with External Stakeholders."

Not all virtual communities within the organization are CoPs, nor should they all be. Homogeneous communities of practice are valuable for their members, but cross-pollinated communities formed around diverse practices can create different types and hybrids of knowledge for the organization that can break new ground and discover novel solutions.

Tech Companies Take the Lead

After the programmers, academics, and researchers pioneered the virtual meeting space, the next community of practice to blossom was that of customers—notably customers of some of the first personal computer products. This was a population of early adopters who found nothing more fascinating than the potential uses of these new tools and their operating languages. As soon as it became possible, they jumped on whatever manifestations of networked communication they could reach, from dialup BBSs to Usenet News. A new kind of relationship was being formed between companies and the people who used their products, and it wasn't the companies that initiated the relationship.

User Groups

Apple computer was one of the earliest examples of a company whose customers used its products to communicate with each other and with the actual product designers and developers. According to the lore found on the Applefritter site,[10] Joe Torzewski started an Apple I users' group in 1977. Communication among fellow users and with Apple Computer initially took place through letters sent through the mail. Once the Apple II was released, the still-small company stopped supporting the Apple I and Joe, the customer, became Apple's main contact for supporting its first machine and its software.

The development of the Macintosh, in combination with the availability of modems and earlier Apple computers, spurred the growth of online user groups. The Stanford University Library's Macintosh history site[11] reports that user groups distributed software for the early Mac when commercial software companies were still in their formative stages. The groups circulated news and shared advice before Apple was ready to perform those duties. Enterprises for supporting the Mac grew out of the interaction and incubation of the user groups. The groups' newsletters also served as records of members' "dealings with the Macintosh," exposing bugs, tips, tricks, and shortcuts and reinforcing the cult status of the revolutionary new computer.

User groups also sprang up for other early computers and operating systems such as the Radio Shack TRS-80, the CP/M operating system, and the Atari. The users themselves began developing software products that could be used with these systems and made them available as "freeware" or at minimal prices as "shareware." Indeed, the customers were driving the knowledge marketplace around the PC revolution just as hard as the companies that were producing the hardware.

But it took a while, even after modems became commonplace, before the companies themselves joined the conversations directly. Of course, you were liable to encounter key developers of products (from Apple, at least) on the user group BBSs, but it wasn't until the common connectivity and common interface of the Web that the support function of the user communities had its counterpart within the company.

Product Codevelopment

In late 1999, one of the authors of this book began a consulting engagement with Cisco Systems, helping them prepare to open a Web-based conversation with the networking professionals (NPs) who installed, configured, and maintained Cisco's equipment on customer sites. Cisco realized that there was plenty of room for improvement in its ability to support these thousands of technicians in the field, even though it already had one of the most advanced and sophisticated customer support operations anywhere. Cisco presented itself to the world as the leader of the migration to the Net. Its marketing slogan was, "Are you ready?" So it figured it needed to make itself readier by learning and applying the practice of virtual community.

The original vision inside the company was to provide a space where NPs could meet, share war stories, and suggest solutions for problems not covered in Cisco's extensive online documentation. Often, the problems encountered in the field were unknown to the customer service representatives who answered email and phone queries. The people using the equipment in unique situations were the sole owners of knowledge about how to resolve those situations. The NP community site would establish a space where those people could meet as a last resort and find the elusive answers to their questions under Cisco's URL.

The NP community was not meant to be a place to ask Cisco support questions. But Cisco's customer support staff, on hearing the idea, recognized it as a potential learning resource for them. They could learn from conversations between Cisco equipment users how to improve the company's documentation and support. The team working to develop the community interface and processes began to see how the conversations among expert users of the products could serve as a valuable pipeline into the minds of the customers for all of the company's product developers and marketers.

The community launched in the summer of 2000 and within a year had grown to such a level of activity that other divisions within Cisco asked to adapt the community software, management training, and design template for their own communities of practice and use. The evolution from a helpful service and a branding enhancement to an integral part of the service design process had taken root even as the company endured a brutal pounding in the marketplace.

Other technical companies such as Sun Microsystems, Hewlett-Packard, and Adobe had provided and supported online discussion communities with their customers for years. They still do so, not only as add-on services to their core products but also as a means of learning from some of the smartest and most relevant people they know: the customers who use and depend on their products.

Building the Extranet Bridge

These communications and information resources—reaching through the company firewall, extending from the internal networks that had been there for many years—were the first *extranets* made practical for many companies by the Web protocol. Here, too, technical companies took the lead, putting to use the very products they were developing.

For a company like Cisco, every useful application of networking justifies the purchase of their switches and routers. For Sun, every envelope-pushing idea for connecting the company with its customers is another clear example of why a network based on Sun servers and software would be worth buying. With technical products, the reasoning was clear. It was not so clear, though, to companies whose customers were behind the technical curve, without the connectivity or skills to participate online with their suppliers. The standardization of the Web interface has changed all that.

Extranets now connect organizations with the various communities defined by the buyer/seller relationship, information technology managers from companies seeking to make their systems compatible, and customers and their customer support teams. Extranets are used not only to coordinate data flow for transacting business, but they also provide meeting spaces for the kinds of knowledge that should be shared between the different links in the business chain. The implications of extranet-supported knowledge communities will be considered further in our chapters on culture (Chapter 6, "Taking Culture Online," and Chapter 7, "Choosing and Using Technology") and on external knowledge networking solutions (Chapter 9, "Conversing with External Stakeholders").

Portals Simplify Navigation

In 1995, the term *portal* was first used to describe a Web site. One didn't refer to them as Web *companies* because they had yet to prove themselves as viable businesses. But at about the same time, Yahoo, Excite, and Lycos began developing the idea of a single arrival page from which a user could find almost anything else on the Web. The site wasn't meant to be a final destination; it was designed to be a pass-through—a portal. For almost 3 years, these three leaders in the Web portal derby set the pace for stock valuation.

They had earned the status of Web companies for sure, but once the advertising model fell out of favor, their values deflated precipitously. But not before enterprises saw, in the portal model, an answer to their problems with trying to make complex information stashes more useful to their employees. The solution was a single starting point, with links to all the important people, forms, and information—a gathering place for the essentials that even a technophobe could deal with.

Emulating the Web

By the mid-nineties, intranets had connected the desktops within most large organizations, but in a slapdash manner. As new generations of software were introduced and new applications were added to the organization's internal systems, they were installed or upgraded and made available to the workers who needed them. But each new addition required new training for the workers and integration by IT. It seemed that the more powerful the company made its information systems, the more useless they became to the people who needed the information they contained. Email was available, but it was completely separate from the information systems. Online tools for continuous group interaction were rare or weakly supported, and few companies had the means for groups to view information together and discuss it through the intranet.

The Web protocol and the portal model offered new options to eliminate the chaos that intranet users had been experiencing. The challenge for IT, as the nineties came to a close, was to migrate intranet tools to the Web protocol. As we'll explore in Chapter 4, "The Role of IT in the Effective Knowledge Network," IT knew that life for them and for the organizations they supported would be easier if a common platform lay under all of the disparate internal applications and under the applications shared through the extranet as well. Once this conversion had taken place, the experience on the worker's desktop could be made more attractive and easier to use.

The New Intranet

The modern intranet is now almost seamless with the Web. Of course, there are firewalls between it and the Web's wide open spaces, restricting who can get in and what can get out, but the user experience is consistent across the boundary. Hyperlinks open other pages or launch programs. Files can be exchanged and downloaded. Email can contain HTML. And conversation spaces can be imbedded within or proximate to the information that is relevant to them.

By bringing the Web into the organization, the possibilities for what can be accomplished through the intranet expand tremendously. Once this stage has been reached by IT, more than half the battle of knowledge networking has been won because the knowledge-as-object and knowledge-as-process approaches can be integrated. Content can be produced and moved around. Conversation can refer directly to content. Conversation can also be converted into content. Information can be put into context via discussion. People can be found by their skills and the knowledge they bring to the table. Communities of practice can meet and invite people with complementary skills to cross-pollinate their knowledge pools.

Maybe the most significant improvement is that power and responsibility can be easily distributed to the different realms of the intranet. Web-based interfaces allow department-level content production and interaction. New protocols like XML allow Web pages to exchange data with non-Web applications. And the flexibility of group conversation tools allows many configurations for meetings and support for working relationships within and between departments in the company. The intranet is no longer a bothersome system to use but has the potential of being a vital network for the entire organization.

The new intranet is presented as the primary foundation for building the knowledge network through the remainder of this book. But it's not the only format for generating and exchanging knowledge over today's Internet. Other software solutions and social configurations are becoming more important as organizations spread out geographically and simultaneously tighten the purse strings of their travel budgets.

Online Events

Companies have more experience in producing face-to-face events than virtual ones. Gatherings called "knowledge fairs" have become one increasingly popular way of bringing the various departments, divisions, and teams of the company together in a physical space to catch up on who's doing what, which practices are working, and which discoveries are worth sharing in the mutual interest of the organization's success.

The time-and-place limitations of meeting face to face compared to meeting online are clear, as are the relationship bandwidth advantages of meeting in person. A consistent theme of this book is the trade-off of advantages between physical copresence and virtual communications. It's always important to combine and balance these two approaches in optimum proportion to fit organizational needs and budgets and to optimize knowledge-sharing relationships.

Events differ from ongoing conversations in that they are defined by beginnings and endings. Some events last only an hour; others go on for days or weeks. They take place through the Web, intranets, extranets, or special interfaces that run over the Internet. Some require high bandwidth connections, whereas others work over relatively slow modems. Events, like F2F conferences and meetings, have purpose and a focus. The handy thing about conducting these get-togethers online, aside from saving the time and cost of travel, is that they can be preserved, visited, and searched later through the wonders of digital storage technology.

Virtual knowledge networks make good use of the event format as a complement to the day-to-day exchanges that go on in message boards, email, and other more open-ended communications formats. Events provide opportunities for introducing new products, colleagues, and strategies. They attract attention and generate interest and enthusiasm around new knowledge networking communities. We'll describe the techniques for producing successful events in several formats in Chapter 8, "Initiating and Supporting Internal Conversation," and Chapter 9, "Conversing with External Stakeholders."

Virtual Meeting Interfaces

The current prospect of a slow economy combined with terror in the air has forced companies to reduce their travel budgets for attending meetings and conferences. Even staff located in different buildings on the corporate campus find it time-consuming to get together in person. More companies than ever are trying real-time video conferencing and groupware as the means for holding meetings.

Companies, such as Webex and Placeware, "rent out" online meeting rooms to organizations by the event, by the week, or by the year (see Figure 2.2). They offer to provide online "facilitators" to manage the meetings, which can include slide presentations to the group and comments exchanged through text or simultaneous telephone conferencing.

Participants must be present to participate in such meetings, though they are usually recorded and can be played back when convenient for those who miss them or need to review them. Because some of these presentations include video feeds of the attendees, they provide the social bandwidth that many people appreciate (and some people dread.)

Like F2F meetings, these require coordinating schedules and, as companies become more international in scope, careful planning to include people across many time zones and local cultures. They answer the need for group communications that are direct and immediate in spite of the distance between participants. But in their limited timeframe, they do not encourage or support the kinds of thoughtful responses that can be composed in email or in asynchronous discussion boards, which are kinder to those with more problematic scheduling needs.

Celebrity Access

AOL has hosted online "celebrity events" since the early 1990s to build traffic and attract new members. Where else could one have a chance to ask Michael

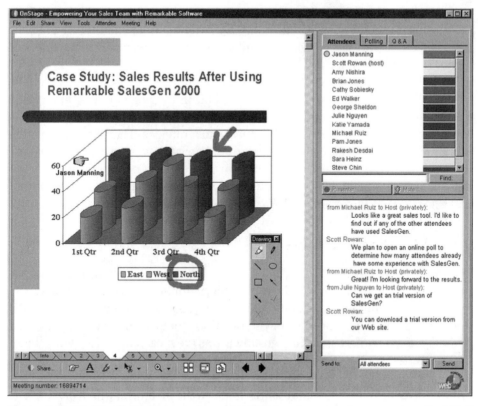

Figure 2.2   Webex allows a group of remote attendees to see and comment on the latest case study.

Courtesy of Webex, Inc.

Jackson a question without leaving one's bedroom? Where else could 377,000 people simultaneously attend a live chat about the release of President Clinton's scandal-related tapes?

As soon as the first commercial chat interfaces were designed for popular use on the Web, they were modified to include features—variously called *auditoriums* or *forums*—that allowed more than the usual number of chat attendees, while shielding designated special guests from direct contact by audience members. Questions and comments were sent through a moderator to be filtered and then relayed to the guest, who then responded directly back to the audience. Members of the audience could chat with others in their same *virtual row* but not with people in other rows. The celebrity event worked very well as a marketing technique, so naturally, companies that were not networking entertainment giants like AOL also began to try it in different formats but with the same intentions of attracting an audience.

The Corporate Showcase

The ability to hold virtual meetings—where audiences could be addressed by and interact with special guests—fit into the marketing needs of wired corporations once enough of their customers, partners, and investors were found to have access to the Internet. This became even more important and valuable when SEC regulations began to require public companies to share information equitably for all of their investors. The corporate "conference call" could now include audiences numbered in the thousands.

Product rollouts, demonstrations, training sessions, and press conferences can all take place now completely online, attracting people who never would have gone out of their way to attend a live promotion event in a hotel ballroom in their hometown, much less in another city on the other side of the continent. The knowledge networking aspects lay in the ability to reach a wider audience with current information and to gather feedback immediately or within a limited timespan.

The quality of response when the audience is able to carry on a give-and-take dialogue with an authority is much higher than what can be gleaned from polls and surveys. But showcase events tend to be asymmetric in the amount of information going out to the audience compared to the amount coming in. For real learning over a limited timespan, more conversational formats can provide better results.

Virtual Seminars and Conferences

The *online conference* is another type of knowledge-sharing event. It employs asynchronous tools—which, for clarity sake, we refer to generically as *message boards*—and lasts longer than the real-time meetings just described: from a full day to a month or more. These formats are used widely in the e-learning sphere, where students tend to have full-time jobs and can only participate when their busy schedules allow. Interaction takes place over time, and students are often required to post messages and responses as evidence of their engagement in the learning process. Where the context is not formal education but organizational learning and knowledge exchange, the format is similar, but one's participation is "graded" in other ways.

Lisa Kimball is a veteran in producing group events. Her company, Group Jazz, combines the use of online tools and F2F interaction with the practical skills of facilitation and virtual teamwork. Group Jazz produced Mathweb 2000, a professional conference with sponsors such as PBS and the National Council of Teachers of Mathematics. It also produced Online Social Networking 2001 (see Figure 2.3), which Kimball describes as "an online conference to help companies understand why and how to organize, lead, manage, value, and sustain internal online social networks for teams, communities of practice, learning cohorts, and other mission-oriented groups."

Such formats—where experts attend online and "speak" on their specialties and where the ensuing discussions blur the lines between experts and people seeking to learn new skills—are applicable to communities of practice, internal training programs, and marketing-focused conferences. We'll elaborate on the techniques for producing virtual seminars in Chapter 8, "Initiating and Supporting Internal Conversation," and Chapter 9, "Conversing with External Stakeholders."

IBM Learns from Its Work Force

In May 2001, IBM held an online brainstorming extravaganza that it called WorldJam. Over the 3 days of the event, 52,000 of its 320,000 employees logged in and contributed over 6,000 ideas and opinions about the operations, processes, products, and organization of their employer. The end result of this

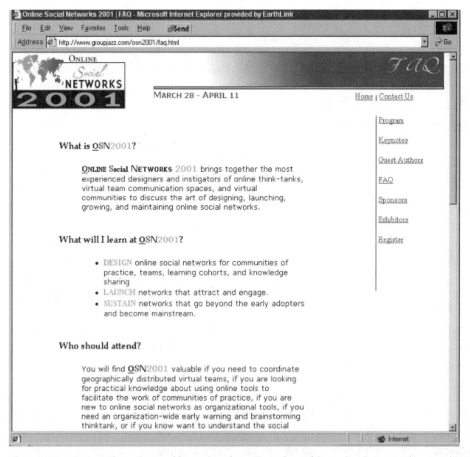

Figure 2.3 Description of a weeklong virtual event on the subject of online social networking.
Courtesy of Group Jazz

invitation for workplace input was an archive of comments that continued to be visited heavily by employees in the days immediately after the event. It was, at least, an occasion for global IBM visibility, but the internal analysis of the shared knowledge and its application went on for months, reportedly yielding enough useful information to justify its costs.

Though it was certainly a large event in terms of intentional participation, its perception as a success was tempered (for us at least) by the seemingly low worker response, which in itself could be a valuable indicator of employee sentiment. IBM's figures report that, given the advance invitation and opportunity over 3 days, only one of six IBM employees bothered to log on. Those relative few contributed only 6,000 proposals and comments.

Does this mean that IBM is an organization whose workers feel no incentive to take advantage of a risk-free opportunity to sound off or communicate with fellow employees about improving the company? Or does it simply demonstrate that over 80 percent of the employees think everything is as fine as it can be? It's hard to say, but it's clear that a culture for using online communications has not yet permeated IBM.

For comparison, we can look at a system that one of the authors managed for over a year. The estimated 20,000 active members of the Table Talk online discussion community on Salon.com posted over 6,000 new messages almost every weekday in 1999. These people had little, if any, stake in the success of Salon.com as compared to the workers who most definitely had a stake in suggesting improvements to IBM. Yet, WorldJam stood out at the time as the most visible and spectacular demonstration to that date of the use of the Net as a channel for gathering internal input to a large organization. Maybe many of IBM's employees felt it safer to refrain from posting their 2-cents worth, whereas Table Talk's members stood no risk of being fired or demoted no matter what they posted.

The greatest immeasurable benefit to IBM of WorldJam may have been a boost in employee perception of the company. As distinguished from the usual secrecy (or disdain) with which feedback from the workplace is treated by management, the open nature of WorldJam's forum may have demonstrated something significant to IBM's employees: that the company was willing to let the world know that it welcomed widespread input and that it trusted the medium of the Net as the channel for that input. Whether the company keeps the communications channels open for continuing conversation and whether the employees make greater use of those channels will determine, in our eyes, the real and lasting impact and success of the event.

Generating External Knowledge

Much key knowledge is also held outside the organization in the minds and opinions of customers and constituents. It's still a sad fact that most Web sites provide a *contact us* link to which no real person is assigned responsibility to respond as the *us*. But customers on the Web—now accustomed to the immediacy of online communication through email, chat, instant messaging, and online discussion—are more eager than corporations are aware to offer their feedback and suggestions as long as they believe it will have some effect on the company to which it's directed. Some businesses have begun to seek this input directly from customers on the Web, with or without the customers' prior knowledge.

Touring Customer Hangouts

IBM let the world know of its active listening through dedicated chat rooms, message boards, and surveys. Other companies do their listening more surreptitiously—not in dedicated message systems and communities but in public discussion spaces across the Web, where people who are likely to fit their target demographics tend to log on regularly and converse. Some companies train and assign internal employees to this task, and others provide the service under contract and send in regular reports of customer feedback and commentary to their clients.

A *USA Today* story[12] told of a man, calling himself "the Starwood Lurker," who would troll the Internet, dipping into frequent-traveler electronic bulletin boards to check the postings about his employer, Starwood Hotels & Resorts. The lurker scanned for comments about big hotel chains operating under Starwood's corporate umbrella, which included Westin, Sheraton, St. Regis, and W, and when he found such comments, he'd respond to them, usually through email. The reaction from frequent travelers (according to the company) was almost always positive as travelers appreciated the concern and the customer service outreach.

Most companies consider this kind of activity—whether they have an employee do it or hire a specialty service to scan the Web for comments about them—to be more in the realm of customer relationship management (CRM) than knowledge gathering. But this is where the lines blur between the two intentions. Learning about customer attitudes builds knowledge that can lead to happier customers and better customer relationships. But the company doesn't have to go lurking around the Web or send a Web clipping service out on its behalf. It can instead create a dedicated space for customers to gather and interact, not as a focus group, but more like a customers' think tank.

Providing Customer Hangouts

Hallmark greeting cards decided that it needed to know more about how its typical customers lived to understand the kinds of products they needed and were willing to buy. Instead of asking customers directly about their preferences, they invited a group of their female customers to join "Idea Exchange," an online discussion community where they would be encouraged to get to know each other and interact informally over time.

There was no schedule or set of topics to follow—just a group of women talking online about their lives, their concerns, their joys, and their challenges. Hallmark unobtrusively, and with the participants' full knowledge, listened in and learned. As *Business Week* reported: "Many say they love tuning into their own soap opera every day. They sign on when they have a moment, chat among themselves, post pictures of home decorations at Hallmark's prompting, and answer the company's questions about products and ideas."[15]

From the interaction, Hallmark discovered new opportunities for products that stood a good chance of selling because they met consensus needs of these 200 women. It was relatively cheap to pull off, and it achieved a depth of meaning that gave the input far more impact than that of a focus group or survey.

Competitive pressures to provide better customer service and develop improved customer products are forcing companies to use the Web as a research tool for learning more about how their customers think, behave, and make their buying decisions. It's the kind of knowledge that can translate directly into business success.

Summary

The Information Age brought new technologies and new needs to organizations. The technologies gave birth to new methods for bringing groups together around common interests. People communicating through electronic networks were able to collaborate on improving these networks and thus work more effectively as communities in the new meeting space of the Net. Early pioneering systems established precedents and spread practical ideas for dealing with social realities in environments where people were not physically together. Now these ideas and practices are being integrated into the wired organization.

The vanguard in putting networks to social use was made up of early adopters who were most ready to deal with the new technology. Similarly, the leading groups in populating organizational networks are likely to be people most familiar with communicating online and most motivated to go through the adjustment and improvement period that comes with every new online application. Groups that work together for mutual benefit, like the user groups in the early days of personal computers, will push knowledge networks ahead.

There are now many options for creating and designing online group interaction, and they all have different strengths. The organization today can talk to itself through its workers; it can talk with its customers and with collaborating partner organizations all through the uniformity of the Web protocol. There are software solutions for use in intranets and extranets to share information and knowledge in many formats, and the pioneers of the past years have been making use of the ubiquitous Web interface to learn more about their customers and workers.

There are many solutions and promising new techniques, but there are still many questions to be answered and predictable problems to be dealt with in every attempt to form conversational communities for generating knowledge. The next chapter describes these challenges and the solutions and attitudes that can be applied to counter them.

CHAPTER 3

Strategy and Planning for the Knowledge Network

Three factors position today's organization for building a strong and vibrant knowledge network. First is our historical human predisposition to share knowledge where it serves mutual interests. Second is the widespread acknowledgment that access to the most current knowledge is now a requirement for success. And third is the diverse and sophisticated selection of tools available for exchanging knowledge through electronic networks.

Organizations that naturally converse and share knowledge among their various cultures will find the migration to the online environment less difficult than those that must adapt both their communications habits and their leadership practices. Most of the companies cited in this book as good examples of knowledge networking practice have already embraced the internal sharing of knowledge as a core value. Those that haven't would be wise to prepare carefully before launching online networking efforts. This preparation takes place on two dimensions:

- Strategy, where the practice of knowledge sharing must be woven into the long-range goals and cultural evolution of the organization

- Planning, where answers to initial design and budgetary questions clear the way to approval, funding, and implementation of the pilot phase of the project

Even organizations that emphasize the free exchange of knowledge among their cultures may be disrupted by the movement of important conversations to the online environment. But those that refuse to change because they fear the impacts of such a movement will be less able to keep pace with the rapidly changing global marketplace of ideas.

This chapter presents some common organizational challenges to starting effective online knowledge networks. It also offers basic, experience-based suggestions for meeting them. Subsequent chapters will provide guidance for implementing strategies and plans, fostering knowledge-sharing cultures, and integrating the technologies to make them work.

Strategy and Change

Building an online knowledge network will have long-range impacts on the organization at several levels:

- At the level of human resource management, it will impact job descriptions and incentive structures.

- At the practice level, it will require new training, job evaluation, scheduling, and day-to-day task-management processes.

- And at the cultural level, it may profoundly influence the way the company is organized and branded.

Purposeful online conversation affects the company's relationship with the marketplace and with the online public. If the company prepares well, these changes will work to the company's advantage. The risks of taking no action to improve the flow of knowledge and information within the organization and with its customers are becoming too serious to ignore.

Change is a constant, but change today is more certain, swift, and unpredictable than ever before. The most direct way for an organization to keep up with external change is to use internal change to its advantage. It must increase its intercommunication by putting out as many feelers as possible to bring a collective view of the constantly shifting situation into the organization.

Reporting the Surprises

A current and comprehensive perspective of the marketplace has become a strategic necessity, but the means for gaining and maintaining such a perspective challenges old management models. The decentralized, self-organizing social communication structures required to efficiently gather and circulate the knowledge that individuals learn and develop don't fit gracefully under the hierarchical, centrally controlled structures that still rule most organizations.

Steven Johnson founded an online literary magazine called *Feed* that unfortunately succumbed to the downturn in Web advertising. In that role, he pioneered some revolutionary improvements in collaborative Web publishing interfaces. Based on his studies and experience, he recently wrote a book titled *Emergence: The Connected Lives of Ants, Brains, Cities, and Software.*[1] In an interview on *Salon.com*,[2] he commented on the phenomenon of self-organizing systems that learn to take care of themselves without central control. He pointed to ant colonies as the best examples of leaderless but extremely productive organizations. "They look like they should be planned from above, but in fact they are entirely organized by local rules and local interactions. *The catchphrase is that the whole is sometimes smarter than the sum of its parts.*" This, we believe, should be the strategic goal of the modern organization.

ANTHILL COMMUNICATION

Scientists used to believe that ants communicated through a kind of insect semaphore—wiggling their antennae in an understood code to exchange information about danger, food, or the need to protect, rebuild, or move the colony. Recent research indicates, instead, that exploring ants bring back and share their experiences in the form of scents that tell the colony of food found or enemy ants encountered. The stronger the scents, the more wildly the communicating ants wiggle their antennae.

Knowledge-sharing communities are similarly motivated by the strength and significance of their members' discoveries and contributions. The greater the impact of the knowledge, the greater the resulting motivation and activity in the community.

Most organizations are looking for ways to make their wholes smarter. They are changing their information strategies to keep up with the velocity of the Net and to keep up with, or preferably overtake, their competitors. A growing percentage of businesses now practice some form of e-commerce—whether it be selling over the Web, communicating with customers online, or managing business relationships with supply chain partners through compatible software—and that, too, is having an unavoidable effect on their strategic thinking.

Yogesh Malhotra is a recognized expert in the fields of knowledge management and business innovation. In an article published in the online periodical, Brint Institute's *Online Book on Knowledge Management*,[3] he describes organizations as moving their knowledge management focus "from *information processing* to *knowledge creation.*" He also maintains that today's organization must recognize that its most limited resource is no longer information; it has become *human attention*—the ability to deal effectively with the growing volume and speed of information.

In Malhotra's recommended knowledge strategy for today's fast-changing e-business world, information manipulation is replaced by processes that emphasize the "renewal of archived knowledge, creation of new knowledge, and innovative applications of knowledge in new products and services that build market share." The *new* is what matters most here, and the strategy must seek to home in relentlessly on what is most emergent and relevant.

Organizations no longer operate in a stable business environment where the future can be predicted by what happened in the past. Business strategy, Malhotra warns, must change from "prediction" to "anticipation of surprise" because the emphasis of the 21st century organization has moved from "structure" to "the edge of chaos."

THE NEW PURPOSE OF KM

Knowledge management caters to the critical issues of organizational adaptation, survival, and competence in the face of increasingly discontinuous environmental change.

—Yogesh Malhotra

Leading the Moving Target

In both skeet shooting and football passing, the shooter or passer must aim not where the target is but where it is going. Strategy must anticipate where the organization's target goals will be by the time a product gets to market or a project is completed. The trick today, Mr. Malhotra warns, is that the strategy must also anticipate surprise.

In skeet shooting and football, the clay pigeon and pass receiver are far more predictable in the timeframes of their seconds-long trajectories than the marketplace is in the timeframe of the business cycle. A clay pigeon travels in a smooth arc. A pass receiver runs an agreed-upon pattern. Only the exceptional skeet shooter or quarterback can compensate for the sudden wind gust or improvised pass pattern.

Rigid, top-down strategizing has always assumed fairly predictable futures, but such an approach breaks down when the future is highly speculative. An intensively communicative and flexible organization—like an ant colony—is better able to detect sudden changes and to communicate appropriate adjustments in preparation or reaction. Effective strategy today must account for surprises in both the short and long terms.

Nimble Strategy for Short-Term Surprises

The emergence of the PC, the explosive growth and standardization of the Web, the rise and fall of the dot-com business model, a volatile economy, and most recently, the unpredictable tragedies and global repercussions of September 11 have forced organizations to adjust as quickly as possible to changing market conditions, changing consumer moods, and changing knowledge needs. With instability in world politics and potential environmental threats like global warming looming on the not-so-distant horizon, there's no reason to believe that the accelerating forces of change will let up.

LITTLE DID THEY KNOW ...

Surely the following facts and figures, compiled in a *Business Week* article in December 2000,[4] were not considered in the strategic planning of the dot-com business leaders or their suppliers:

- Ventro, once one of the leading "online exchange" builders, had traded at $244 a share in March. It was trading at $1.09 a share in December.
- By December, 35 percent of the publicly traded Web companies were worth less than $2 per share.
- By December, 31,000 dot-com workers had been laid off.
- Web advertising rates per 1,000 page views had plummeted from $2.50 to 50 cents.

The good news? The pundits quoted in the article didn't think it could get much worse. Surprise! It did.

There's no way that an organization can anticipate an event like September 11, but well-supported strategies from now on must assume that the outrageous and unexpected could happen at any time. This is where the advantages gained from functioning knowledge networks will be crucial. The ability to distribute current knowledge, preserve relevant old knowledge, and generate new knowledge as insurance against unforeseen events and trends is a strategic asset that no organization can afford to be without.

Evolutionary Strategy for Long-Term Trends

Surprise and chaos make an active, well-organized, and responsive knowledge network a critical asset. Certain demographic and technological trends provide further justification for enabling fluid online conversation within the organization. With every year, a greater percentage of Americans continue to use the Internet. The dot-com bomb may have wiped out many businesses and their revenue models, but it did not halt the trend of increasing presence on the Net as the following statistics indicate:

- A report published by the National Telecommunications and Information Administration and the Economics and Statistics Administration found that 143 million Americans (54 percent of the population) used the Internet in September 2001. That's a 26 percent increase over August 2000.[5]

- According to *eMarketer*, there were 445 million people online worldwide at the end of 2001, of which 119 million, or 27 percent, were located in the United States. By 2004, there will be 165.5 million U.S. Internet users, accounting for 23 percent of the global total.[6]

- Nielsen/NetRatings reports that in the fourth quarter of 2001, 24 million people worldwide gained Internet access at home. The rate of growth of the global Internet population in the fourth quarter was nearly double the third quarter's 15 million new at-home users.[7]

- Projections by *Commerce Net* show Internet usage in the United States rising to 75 percent of the population by the year 2005.[8]

Those numbers represent a steady increase in the number of Net-literate workers, consumers, and customers, many of whom will be conversing through online channels. Any intelligent business strategy must come to terms with the trend that more people and more of their communications will be moving online.

GROUP CONTACT THROUGH THE INTERNET

The *Pew Internet & American Life* Project[9] found the following facts about U.S. Internet life:
- 84 percent of Internet users have contacted an online group
- More than half of those said they'd become active in a group after connecting with it through the Internet
- 60 percent email their group and 43 percent do so several times a week

---

The use of networked communication tools in the workplace also continues to rise as more workers are given access to the Net from their desktops and as their home-use experiences influence their workplace activities. Companies must mold their strategies around the reality that their workers will tend to innovate on their own when they have access to the Net.

As Jupiter Media Metrix reported in November 2001, "the number of unique users of instant-messaging applications at work increased 34 percent, from 10.0 million in September 2000 to 13.4 million in September 2001."[10] The total amount of time spent using instant-messaging (IM) applications at work increased by 110 percent!

Such adoption and use of Net-based communications tools like IM are often done independently, without the support or leadership of management or information management or IT departments. They clearly demonstrate the network effect described earlier—where people begin to use a tool because it provides them instant access to valued associates who already use it. These trends of increasing use of the Internet and the tools that allow groups to communicate will prepare more people to become knowledge networkers within the organization.

The Agile Culture

A company's extended strategy must also take into account the sometimes stressful cultural migration it will go through as it moves from its information-based past to its knowledge-based future. This transformation will deeply affect its core values, image, and identity and will influence its incentive structures and job definitions. Companies tend to avoid disruption, preferring more graceful and controlled change, but the realities today are forcing organizations to accept disruption and to learn how to change both quickly and gracefully.

Cross-pollination—the exchange of knowledge between different departments and divisions within the company and with different organizational cultures outside the company—is not only possible, but it is an asset of growing importance for competition and intelligent decision making. The broader the conversational matrix, the wider will be the organization's vision and pool of options.

CROSSING THE ORGANIZATIONAL BORDERS

As Stephen Denning puts it in *The Springboard,* changing to a knowledge-sharing strategy "entails a shift from an organization that has operated vertically and hierarchically to one that will operate horizontally and collaboratively across organizational borders."[11]

Within the definition of its strategy, the company must recognize whose knowledge is (and will be) of critical value and worth deeper tapping. In planning for the future, company leadership should anticipate the synergies that will be realized through fostering conversations among specific people with high-value knowledge and how those synergies will help the company achieve its strategic goals.

The Change-Embracing Organization

Strategy for a knowledge-sharing company assumes that change itself will become an internalized value all up and down the work force. The company, as a collective organism, will become adaptive and toward that end will *invite* contrary viewpoints and criticism rather than ignore or deflect them. It will *encourage* the generation of ideas that lead to intelligent change rather than resist it. Stability will be found in its core values and mission statement rather than in the predictable comfort of routine practices.

The new strategy will accept the growing likelihood that the company will be working out of multiple locations or will need to work with partners located in different places. The connectivity and communication needs of the offsite or traveling worker will become more important. The wired workplace will be pumping current news and information to the desktop at faster speeds, and competition will increasingly depend on converting that news and information into immediate action and redesigned products.

What the Company Wants to Know

In their book, *Working Knowledge,* Thomas Davenport and Laurence Prusak emphasize that "intentions are important: a firm needs to know what it wants to have a good chance of getting it."[12] The key to assigning a strategic purpose to a knowledge network is the clear description of its goals; the company must know the kinds of knowledge its network is meant to discover and how that knowledge will advance its overall strategy.

As an example, in 1999 Cisco Systems specified a list of strategic purposes for its online community-building initiative. (Cisco resists using knowledge management terminology, but in fact their online communities serve as meeting places for knowledge exchange.) The Internet equipment giant had decided to enable online conversations among a segment of its customers—the *networking professionals* who install and maintain Cisco equipment for its clients and partner companies.

It undertook this effort primarily to enhance its Internet leadership position: to meet the public expectations set by an advertising campaign that asked the world, "Are you ready?" Cisco sought to demonstrate that as the leading equipment provider, it was making full use of the Internet's communications power.

CISCO'S ORIGINAL STRATEGIC GOALS FOR ITS KNOWLEDGE EXCHANGES

- Strengthen partner relationships and capture information
- Maintain Cisco brand integrity
- Maintain Internet leadership
- Respond to competitive threats
- Build an ecosystem of partners and solutions
- Drive increased sales for both Cisco and Cisco partners

As the initiative moved toward the design of an appropriate Web infrastructure, the importance of responding to competition and building what they called "an ecosystem" for diverse knowledge exchange came to the fore. The internal business units collaborating on the project began to recognize that the strategic value of knowledge-sharing conversations could prove even more crucial in a shifting marketplace than branding, customer relationship management, and sales enhancement.

Cisco needed to know what its networking professionals were learning. In the community space Cisco provided, they would exchange their homebrew solutions to operational or compatibility problems. They would complain to each other about shortcomings in equipment design or documentation. Occasionally, they would expose unsolved problems that only Cisco could address. They would share their wish lists for new features or products. They would reveal, in their conversations with each other, ways that Cisco could earn their continued business and respect. These were the nuggets of reality that Cisco desperately needed to know to maintain a dominant position in the industry.

Different types of organizations and businesses will naturally have different knowledge needs. Companies whose businesses revolve around the introduction of new products and services will require knowledge related to research and product development. Those that rely on marketing will need knowledge that helps set pricing, design effective promotion, and locate their products in the marketplace. Some companies will need more knowledge from and about their customers, whereas others will seek knowledge about cutting-edge consulting techniques or about specific client behaviors and habits. The key is in identifying the knowledge needs that will make the most difference in the organization's success.

Knowledge of Maximum Leverage

Once an organization begins seeking the knowledge held by its employees or customers, it may find that there's more knowledge than it can deal with. Knowledge glut can be as much of a problem as knowledge starvation, so needs must be prioritized and some means of filtering must be put in place. This is a strategy-level problem in that procedural and cultural practices should be ingrained early to set the filtering strategy on the right course.

Questions must be asked at the outset of strategy formulation. What specific types of knowledge will be of most benefit? What essential knowledge is missing today, and what essential knowledge will be consistently necessary? What kinds of human resources will be in demand now and in the future? How will the organization use conversation—online and F2F—to augment its ability to find answers to specific critical questions?

An organization's strategy is like a map into unknown territory. Historical knowledge and scientific theory combine with best guesses (and some prayer) to plot a route toward a destination, but there are plenty of blank stretches on the map that can only be filled in with newly acquired knowledge. Somehow, the strategy must take into account these unknowns and transform them into knowns as soon, and as reliably, as possible. To do this, the company needs to focus on discovering the current and future knowledge that will make the most difference.

Setting and Maintaining a Focus

Success in motivating people to engage in online conversation can be counterproductive in a knowledge network if certain natural human tendencies are allowed free rein. Once the goals of participation, trust, sharing, and relationship building have been met, people become more willing to explore and wander into

---

CUTTING THROUGH THE FOG

Mark Monmonier, a distinguished geographer, wrote the following: "Not only is it easy to lie with maps, it is essential … . To avoid hiding critical information in a fog of detail, the map must offer a selective, incomplete view of reality."[13]

Gathering knowledge for strategic purposes can result in a "fog of detail" that hides the critical information from the organization. The strategic knowledge map must be selective, if incomplete, to be a useful guide to smart, responsive decision making.

---

subject areas that are further and further removed from the organization's intended focus. This can be both good and bad. Good because it is evidence that the group has become comfortable with conversing through the medium. Good because it raises the possibility of serendipitous discoveries and out-of-the-box thinking. Bad because it can result in too much extraneous information and too much time spent in activities that are not helpful to the organization.

Informal conversation is often the source of key knowledge nuggets that don't come to the surface when the conversation is tightly controlled. But a strategic plan for knowledge networking must include provisions for prioritizing activities that answer the organization's most pressing needs. The design of the interface and the organization of its content, combined with the training and assignments of knowledge community leaders and editors, should provide sufficient guidance to prevent the knowledge network from becoming a home for trivial chat and wasted time in the workplace.

STAYING ON POINT

Software features can help an organization maintain focus in its knowledge network. A World Bank-sponsored partnership of organizations called the Global Knowledge Portal (GKP) uses an interface called Simplify as an exchange space for its communities of practice.

A case study of GKP[14] notes that "quality control and content management are of critical importance," and it describes how subject matter *editors* are empowered, through the software, to filter incoming content for relevance and to reroute it to editors of other subject areas to prevent the dilution of valuable content.

The original focus for the networking activity should be set on knowledge that provides maximum leverage for the sponsoring organization. As the network generates the desired knowledge, the focus can be expanded, and other related networks, with their own focused priorities, can be spun off or initiated.

A knowledge network without a clear strategic purpose and overall guiding hand can become an aimless liability in terms of infrastructure investment, human resources, and technical maintenance. There can be value in unstructured and unfocused brainstorming activity, as we described in the WELL's aggregating a diverse knowledge pool. But especially in the startup phase of an online knowledge network, it is vitally important that a focused strategic definition of the knowledge needs of the organization guides the conversations that ensue. You'll find a guide to formulating such a definition in Chapter 8, "Initiating and Supporting Internal Conversation."

The Right Leadership

A purposeful knowledge exchange community depends on reliable and exemplary leaders for its unity and trust. These leaders may be the founders and initiators of the activity, or they may emerge from the activity once it has started. If an organization expects active participation by the people who hold (and will generate) the knowledge it requires, its leaders at all levels must themselves support and practice online conversation.

These company leaders don't necessarily have to demonstrate expertise, but they should strive to demonstrate proficiency in the use of the technologies and should devote themselves to improving their mastery of the knowledge networking practice. If company leadership doesn't set a good example, it can't expect the work force to lead the charge on its own. Most people rely on guidance, clarity of mission, and good role modeling in deciding how much and how deeply they will commit themselves to adopting new practices.

The value to the organization of a knowledge-based community will increase with its longevity and continuity. Although leaders will naturally rise up from within the community ranks as it learns about itself, ongoing strategic guidance will be necessary to achieve long-range goals. Strategic leadership originates at the executive level and can be reinforced by expert consultants brought in to provide the organization with objective assessment of its evolving knowledge resources, performance, and needs.

Executive Wisdom

If a knowledge network is functioning within an organization—even if it is an informal one, originating in grass-roots interaction among the workers—the CEO should know that it exists. If the network is productive in generating original ideas or solving problems that otherwise might go unsolved, the CEO should at least be familiar with its focus, its participants, and its product. If the network has become productive enough to affect the decision-making processes of the organization, the CEO should be directly involved with it, even to the point of being part of its conversation.

Effective knowledge management systems depend on total buy-in from the top level of the organization. The communication that makes knowledge networking effective requires more than simple approval and support; it requires involvement and understanding that engender trust among the network's participants.

WALKING THE WALK

Management that pays lip service to the value it attaches to knowledge sharing but rewards employees who hoard knowledge will not create the level of trust needed to make the knowledge market effective.

—Thomas Davenport and Laurence Prusak[15]

Trust building must be integral to the company's overall knowledge strategy. Top-level management bears the responsibility for fostering the cultural values and practices that will encourage workers immediately and in the future to participate in the exchange of what they know and think. Since many companies are still catching up to the New Economy, their managers—still accustomed to old models of management practice—may find it especially difficult to make the jump to leading roles in the flattened hierarchy of a knowledge-sharing culture.

As Davenport and Prusak describe in *Working Knowledge*, the organization must strive to build a *knowledge market* where individuals and teams can shop for the know-how and information they need and where any individual might possess high-value knowledge to sell. Management must help define and sanction this perspective of interaction and content management, and to do that, management must, more than other levels within the organization, understand how the social dynamics work in a knowledge marketplace.

Executives, especially, must understand at the gut level that the interaction among workers, customers, and partners in today's economy has become a much greater factor in strategic planning. Quality interaction through the Internet and the intranet has become an asset. Understanding how people behave in a knowledge marketplace is now a prerequisite to leading them into strategically productive modes of behavior. But even the executive, surveying the activity in this new marketplace from a lofty perch, can lose the objective perspective required to keep a knowledge-networking strategy on track.

The Role of Consultants

One of the risks of implementing a knowledge network is that the executive will lose control over its organic and decentralized development by focusing more on the process of extracting knowledge than on the type of knowledge that is being distilled. In the executive's effort to collect and manage as much as possible of what people have learned from the past, the high-leverage knowledge can easily be missed—lost in the "fog of detail." The company depletes its knowledge management resources in the act of enthusiastic gathering, leaving too few resources for filtering out the critical information and putting it to work.

The consultant, who remains uninvolved in the social interaction that stirs up wild knowledge from within the work force or customer base, provides the fresh and objective viewpoint that can help internal leadership regain its rele-

HERDING THE KNOWLEDGE CATS

Knowledge is wild, but wild knowledge is a necessity. Here are five principles for leading a wild knowledge network to success:

- ■ **Participate.** Be an active member; stay in touch; help guide its development.
- ■ **Maintain a knowledge market perspective.** Provide incentives for high-quality content.
- ■ **Bring in the consultants.** Do regular "sanity checks" on where the network and its attention are headed.
- ■ **Drive iterative improvement.** Direct the network's wild energy to debugging its own design.
- ■ **Adapt leadership culture to the online meeting space.** Look for emergent leaders in the virtual communities.

vance bearings. In a knowledge-networking context, consultants need to maintain distance from the organization to be most useful. A good consultant is a leadership asset not only as a distanced observer of the organization's attempts to maintain focus but in other roles as well.

An experienced online facilitator, for example, can help the company discover (or rediscover) its knowledge-sharing personality by guiding online conversations that stay on point and reach satisfactory resolution. Outside viewpoints are especially valuable when the organization is in the midst of confusing cultural change. Good consultants also bring in external knowledge gained from their engagements with other client companies that may have gone through similar processes and situations. Competent outside consultants help the company regain its perspective of the knowledge forest by *overlooking* the trees.

Leadership Culture

Leadership culture is more style than substance within the organization. People tend to follow leaders they respect, regardless of title. All companies have leadership cultures based on a combination of their organizational chart, company values and mission, and the role-modeling standards that guide behavioral and hiring practices. This culture is established primarily through communications in the workplace. In the strategic sense, leadership culture will change significantly as the company moves more of its communications online because the online environment is a very different space than the meeting room, office building, or telephone call.

In the online communications space, both the boss and the frontline customer support representative have user names that appear in identical form on the screen. You can't see, from these names, how fancy or simple their respective offices are or whether they're wearing power ties or T-shirts at their desks. You can, of course, find a descriptive profile of each of them (and you should know the boss by name when you see her online), but in the interactive arena, the effective leaders are those individuals who are reliable in showing up regularly in the online space. They are the ones who use the technology well to organize and prepare conversation and content for the rest. They are the clear communicators and sensitive conversationalists who set good examples of efficient writing and editing. They are the social facilitators who help guide the online interaction to its most productive end.

Strategy involving online knowledge networking will take into account the changes in how leadership will emerge and be demonstrated in the workplace. The more reliant the company is on its virtual meeting place, the more important this new leadership culture will become to the organization. Leadership in Cyberspace is earned through online performance rather than through position on the org chart. The organization must anticipate the change of having its new leaders emerge based on their demonstrated skills and mastery of online communication and content management.

Planning and Cost Issues

Strategy is the big picture. Planning brings things closer to home; this is where the organization finds its starting point and, with a strategic eye to the future, decides how to build the knowledge network and the supporting culture that will achieve its goals. In this section, we cover the two major challenges of the planning process:

- Designing an integrated technical platform and social practice that will serve the network in both its startup and expansion modes

- Justifying the costs of implementing the pilot stage of the design

Proposals to build a knowledge network also require planning for growth. Fortunately, online knowledge networks do best when allowed to grow organically and incrementally. Members of the network will collaborate to identify the best direction and pace of expansion and how to improve their systems. Good planning at the outset will produce networks that can perform their own growth planning as they gain experience and group intelligence.

Designing the Network

The challenges of knowledge network design do not, as you might expect, revolve around technology. That comes later and will be dealt with in our chapters on information technology (Chapter 4, "The Role of IT in the Effective Knowledge Network") and on the relationship between the technology and the knowledge culture (Chapter 7, "Choosing and Using Technology"). Once the knowledge community and its needs are specified, the appropriate technology can be chosen and configured. The initial design revolves instead around some issues that have already been mentioned: identifying the knowledge that the organization needs the most and identifying the people who should be included in the network to develop that knowledge.

A knowledge network requires phased implementation, and phase 1 is the pilot project where best guesses are tested with live participants on a scale that minimizes risk of failure. A knowledge network is also more than simply a means for online conversation. It is an integrated platform for conversation and managed content that can be used not only as a space for group process but also for individual research. Thus, it requires people skilled in both discussion facilitation and online content editing. The software tools that support these coordinated activities will be presented in later chapters.

THE INTRANET AS A COLLABORATION TOOL

Interface guru Jakob Nielsen comments on trends in his "The 10 Best Intranet Designs of 2001":
We saw a greatly increased emphasis on the intranet as a collaboration tool that lets employees exchange information through *discussion groups* and other features. The intranets also emphasize communication by encouraging departments to post *news* and other information of interest to different groups.[16]

Although the initial network coming out of the pilot phase may be provided for a single team or department, the design process should be inclusive and contain representatives from different parts of the company as potential users of the knowledge-sharing system. Chances are that after the top priority knowledge community has blazed the trail, other divisions and business units within the organization will want to form online communities of their own, adapting the existing design to their own needs. Thus, the overall organizational culture should be involved in specifying the capabilities and extensibility of the system. Planning will include this projection of possible expansion and scaling.

And finally, design must take into account the organization's need to define parameters for assessing the success of the networking activity. How will managers decide when change is necessary? How (and to whom) will they report the gains realized through use of the network?

Seeding the Knowledge Community

Ideally, the starting point of the knowledge network is like a seed that will send down roots, grow, and spread like a rhizome to extend the network throughout the organization. Thus, it's important where and how this seed is planted. Just as you would in trying to get a garden started on unfamiliar ground, you choose a place and time that give the seed its greatest chance to thrive. And to take the seed metaphor one step further, it should be planted where it is most likely to germinate quickly, send up its shoots, and start using the soil and sunshine that make up its immediate environment.

In knowledge terms, this means providing the resources to the people who will be able to make the best use of it in the shortest amount of time, significantly improving their effectiveness and job performance by sharing knowledge. Based on this early success, participation will increase, and the organization will see good results that feed back into greater support within the organization for the young, sprouting knowledge network.

Often, the people most ready to use online conversation as a knowledge tool are those who have already begun doing so on their own. They may have discovered the utility of the practice in their home-based connections to the Internet or in their day-to-day email correspondence over the company's intranet. Maybe a relatively unimportant project in the office became a startling success because it was coordinated through use of AOL's Instant Messenger tool.

If a business unit or project team has figured out on its own how to marshal its knowledge resources toward accomplishing a task, it has eliminated the barrier that often slows adoption of new technologies, practices, and communications concepts. Often, when a company has identified a gap between what it knows and what it needs to know, the holders of that key knowledge have already been identified within the organization but have not been introduced to the tools and means of getting that knowledge to where it can make the most difference.

The company's business strategy should make clear the areas where knowledge networking is most needed. As we said earlier, companies that rely on the introduction of new products and services will need to develop their knowledge around managing research and product development. Companies that rely on strong marketing will focus more on knowledge about pricing, promotion, and product location. These define the most appropriate starting points for seeding the network.

Cultural Influence

The knowledge network should fit as gracefully as possible into the existing organizational culture if it's going to be attractive to employees and accepted by the leadership structure. The design should ideally be a coproduct of many stakeholders from different locations within the organization so that it will ultimately serve them all when they are ready to use it.

Groups within the organization that already practice some form of knowledge networking should be identified. This can usually be accomplished by issuing an invitation to all parties who are interested in discussing the subject of improving knowledge exchange. Expect a large turnout because most people feel an acute need to know more and to improve the flow of (and access to) missing knowledge.

CISCO'S COMMUNITY BUSINESS ORGANIZATION

Five separate vertical businesses were operating within Cisco Systems in 1999, with numerous lines of business (LOBs) working under them. When several of these LOBs found that they were separately investigating the idea of online communities, they joined forces to form what they called the Community Business Organization, or CBO.

Through meetings of the CBO, they formulated enough of a shared vision of needs to hire consultants, first to help write a strategy document and then to begin implementing a pilot program that would serve the community deemed most ready to make use of an online discussion system.

As this pilot, the Networking Professionals Community, launched under the Enterprise Marketing LOB, the rest of the CBO was kept informed of its progress and learning. Once initial bugs had been eliminated and key processes had proven themselves, other LOBs and communities of practice within Cisco began adapting the design to their own needs.

An assessment of the existing culture's flexibility—its willingness to change—will help locate points of resistance. Understanding resistance and the reasoning behind it is necessary in designing systems that can respond to and neutralize the fears and habits that are incompatible to knowledge exchange over the Net.

If the company is unwilling to change because of entrenched belief systems or hierarchical rigidity, it may not be a good candidate for building a knowledge network. The same level of assessment must be applied to leadership in the organization. Unless the top people are supportive of the idea and are willing to accept the changes likely to come through open knowledge exchange, the initiative won't get off the ground.

The Pilot Phase and Network Expansion

Cisco's Community Business Organization provides a good example of a company that identified a starting point, got most of its business units involved in the design, and was patient enough to wait for the pilot program to succeed before expanding the network in other directions. Initial design can't be a slave to future planning, but it should consider—in its choice of tools and organization—the need for flexibility and reconfiguration that will become apparent as it is used and critiqued.

Pilot projects are an important design specification wherever computer-human interfaces are being developed. They are even more important when those interfaces are interwoven with complex knowledge relationships within the company. The knowledge network should be planned for phased implementation, providing plenty of time for testing, evaluation, debugging, tweaking, and redesign.

As the network goes through its early stages, the rest of the organization should be kept abreast of its progress—including the good, the bad, and the ugly of its early attempts to reach its goals—and invited to observe, if not participate in, its activities. Setbacks as well as triumphs should be reported through an ongoing internal educational program carried in email bulletins and/or Web pages so that other groups, teams, and business units can prepare themselves to develop their own knowledge networks when the technology and business processes have proven reliable.

Defining Success

Planning should include the scheduling of regular periodic *health checkups* that include evaluations based on participation, satisfaction with the interface, assessment of technical performance, and comparison with set mileposts for progress and deliverables. Original goal setting is important but should not be used alone to determine success or failure because unanticipated benefits may emerge under actual use that make those goals less meaningful.

The fresh, outside perspectives of consultants are especially valuable in these early evaluations. Positive evaluations are, of course, more encouraging to other potential knowledge-sharing communities within the organizations, but negative evaluations done in a timely manner catch bugs while the design is still young and malleable.

SELF-IMPROVEMENT PLANNING FOR THE INTRANET

Jakob Nielsen emphasizes that in intranet design, management of user input is a key element to successful results.

Firstly, they must consider the usability of an intranet because if people can't use it to support their tasks the project has failed. Secondly, they must remember that an intranet project never stops. It is a process of continuous improvement. Humans are very creative creatures and if they get the chance they can easily upset an intranet project, but if you manage them carefully, that creativity can add further benefits to the intranet and it will continue to adapt and grow to meet the organisation's requirements.[17]

The ultimate goal of a knowledge network is to make the jobs of its users simpler, easier, and more effective. This will inevitably show up in productivity, but the most immediate evidence will be in the amount of usage it gets and the satisfaction expressed by its users. It's important for those in charge of its design and feature set to listen to those users constantly and to incrementally improve the network interface in response to their comments. That listening and responsive action, in itself, will be regarded as success by the users who recognize their role as codesigners of their own tools.

Cost Justification

Proposing any new practice within the organization—especially when it involves the installation, expansion, or reconfiguration of a technology—brings with it the challenge of funding. Evidence is required that the new idea will pay for itself either by bringing in more money faster or by slowing down the loss of money without reducing the effectiveness of the organization.

We've emphasized the importance of having the CEO on board for a knowledge network to succeed. The funding proposal is a first step in convincing the CEO that the network has been designed with the organization's ultimate success in mind.

Many of the flashy, enterprise-level knowledge management software solutions have promised a lot but have failed to deliver the kinds of return on investment that companies hoped for. The knowledge network doesn't have to be so ambitious in its design or in its costs. Investment in infrastructure development, training, and job redefinition can be justified because a well-designed knowledge network will start small and grow incrementally. Though there will most certainly be more costs per participant in the beginning than at later stages in the network's development and expansion, the incremental costs should be manageable.

WHY ROI ON KM IS OFTEN SO POOR

The KM technologies are suffering from poor return on investment (ROI), simply because the KM decision has been made by a CKO, who's a brand new individual, or an IT individual, and neither of them have ever consulted with human resources (HR), which knows how to motivate and compensate employees.[18]

—Nick Bontis, Ph.D.,
Director of the Institute for Intellectual Capital Research Inc.,
assistant professor of strategic management at the Michael G. DeGroote
School of Business at McMaster University in Hamilton, Ontario,
and chief knowledge officer (CKO) of Knexa.com Enterprises Inc.

The Cost Savings of Doing Smarter Business

If there hadn't been success stories from applying knowledge networking techniques, we would not have been persuaded to write this book. In fact, there is enough buzz around the idea to excite business leaders at all levels. Some of the better known examples of large companies that have begun utilizing their human intellectual capital are referred to on the AskMe site,[19] one of the Web's most creative knowledge-sharing oases. Here are some of these companies, the description of their knowledge networking activities, and the bottom-line results they reported from those activities:

Xerox	Access to technicians' lessons learned	5–10% savings on labor and parts costs
Ford	Access to best practices	$1.25 billion in savings

Buckman Labs	Allows employees to find colleagues with expertise and ask them questions	New product sales up 50%; response to customer inquiries down to hours from days
Texas Instruments	Access to best practices	$500 million gained in "free" fabrication capacity in 1 year
Hoffman-LaRoche	Capture and access approval-related knowledge	FDA approval time reduced from 3 years to 9 months
Honeywell	Create, capture, share, and use organizational knowledge	46% increase in proposal win rate; costs cut by 35%

Most of these companies developed their techniques in house and expanded them gradually and experimentally. Today, most companies are just becoming aware of their knowledge deficits and may not have the luxury of allowing knowledge networks to develop spontaneously from grass-roots initiative, but the basic principles we describe in this book still apply. Look for the most promising starting points and seed the network wisely.

BY-PRODUCTS OF THE KNOWLEDGE NETWORK

Though it's difficult to assign a dollar value to these benefits, they do eventually show up on the balance sheet. A knowledge network does the following:

- Preserves and uses existing assets
- Creates intellectual synergies
- Leads to smarter decisions and reduced losses
- Teaches the company more about its market
- Increases trust and loyalty
- Saves time

Typical indirect paybacks for transitioning to a knowledge-sharing culture will be measured in factors like employee loyalty and longevity, customer satisfaction, product development cycles, travel expenses, and overall productivity per employee. These improvements will be increasingly visible as the cultural transformation permeates the organization.

Minimizing Financial Risk

Many vendors are now marketing fully integrated knowledge management systems that claim to simplify the sharing of vital information across the organization. (This subject will be discussed more fully in Chapter 5, "Fostering a Knowledge-Sharing Culture.") Some of these offer obvious improvement in usability to large corporations whose various information-gathering applications—purchased from different vendors, installed at different times, and each treating similar data differently—have confused the unfortunate users of intranets built to tie the applications together. But such integrated solutions don't necessarily fulfill the needs of a conversational knowledge network.

The technical costs of starting a productive knowledge network can be quite modest. Message boards can be purchased or run on the vendor's servers cheaply, with small installation or setup expenses and incremental pricing based on the number of users and traffic that run through them. Email can be customized and used creatively to support group interaction. Even the platforms required for real-time event production, which were mentioned in Chapter 2, "Using the Net to Share What People Know," can be rented out by the event or for affordable periods of time.

Indeed, the initial investment for technology should be small during the testing and pilot phases of knowledge networking. The phased approach to implementation is most appropriate to building the practice and culture of knowledge sharing. Organic growth allows the organization to assess the success of the activities and make funding decisions based on observed success.

Jakob Nielsen, quoted earlier in this chapter, is a widely respected expert on interface design. In his evaluation of "The 10 Best Intranet Designs of 2001,"[20] he pointed to "iterative design" as one of the chief factors leading to designs that were deemed most useful, even at relatively low cost. One of the intranets chosen for his top 10 was built by graduate students at the Luleå University of Technology in Sweden. About it, Nielsen wrote, "Though small and lacking a lot of resources, this design team focused relentlessly on users needs and on simplifying their design through many fast iterations."

The costs of designing and starting the knowledge networking activities should be centered more on overseeing this iterative design process than on purchasing software that supposedly offers "all the features you'll ever need." The students at Luleå University took some of their features through 50 iterations before arriving at a design of optimal usability. This requires commitment and participation by a population of users and interface programmers that is aimed at arriving at a design that people will use because it is simple, straightforward, efficient, and well-mapped to their needs, habits, and culture.

In the following section, we will describe some of the software platforms that lend themselves to such an iterative, collaborative design approach.

Summary

Building a successful knowledge network begins with careful strategic preparation and planning. Strategic thinking is not only a reason for fostering a knowledge-sharing culture; it benefits from the internalization of knowledge-sharing values in the organization.

Trends toward more widespread use of the Internet and its group communications tools are making knowledge-sharing activities more commonplace both inside and outside the workplace. Companies should take advantage of these trends and form their strategies around them. And as the description of the worker and the typical company change, so must the strategies for collaboration and communication.

To increase the probability of success and to decrease the cost of the knowledge network, an appropriate high-leverage starting point must be identified. This point is defined by the highest priority knowledge needs of the organization and by the location of skills and existing groups of knowledge exchange within the company. Using this as a focal point, the knowledge network can be seeded to grow incrementally, finding its way to success and steadily improving design through the interaction and input of its founding members.

PART

Two

Matching Culture
with Technology

Among organizations, no two cultures are identical and neither are the technologies that best support their knowledge networks. There's a large and growing selection of platforms and interfaces claiming to meet the special needs of knowledge management, and existing software applications continue to be refined to better fit the way people actually work and interact with each other. The four chapters in Part Two aim to help executives, managers, and IT professionals understand the important and evolving relationship between technical infrastructure and workplace culture and, more specifically, how nurturing that relationship leads to efficient, well-utilized, and productive online knowledge networking.

Chapter 4, "The Role of IT in the Effective Knowledge Network," describes the role of the information technology (IT) manager and the IT department in supporting dynamic, self-guided knowledge networks. Chapter 5, "Fostering a Knowledge-Sharing Culture," is a survey of both the standard tools and the cutting-edge software products that enable the coordination of online conversation and relevant content publishing. Chapter 6, "Taking Culture Online," describes the vital characteristics of a knowledge-sharing culture and how relationships formed and maintained online can color the overall cultural values and strategic choices of the organization. In Chapter 7, "Choosing and Using Technology," we bring the technology and culture together and, using actual examples, demonstrate the productive interplay between the design of the networked interface and the values of the organizational culture. This is, in essence, how the organization learns to improve itself—constantly and efficiently.

The Role of IT in the Effective Knowledge Network

The theme of this chapter is the need for simplicity in choosing and implementing technology. It is tempting to think in terms of choosing or designing software that will do more work and thereby increase human productivity. However, there are important reasons for at least beginning with the simplest tools that will enable measurable improvement in knowledge exchange. One reason is cost. Another is in facilitating the building of a good working relationship between the IT department and the people looking to build the online knowledge network.

The overarching purpose of information technology (IT) is to increase productivity in the workplace. To that end, as we've mentioned in previous chapters, IT departments now assemble complex systems of specialized hardware and software applications to serve the varied and distinct information needs within the company. Some of these applications are designed to work together or to share standard interfaces, but many are not.

Once adopted, these applications and their software structures become indispensable to the company or business unit in direct proportion to the amount of information they hold. So in a busy business, as the information and knowledge needs of the company change, its rigid *legacy systems* become the weak links in the coevolutionary chain that would ideally evolve software in coordination with changing needs. Outdated and limiting features hold back the company's ability to adapt its technology to important aspects of its evolving business values and culture.

The twin preoccupations of the chief technology officer (CTO) today are overcoming the inertia of legacy systems and attaining greater interface flexibility, where the technology is able to adapt to meet the needs of the organization in flux. Knowledge networks, by their nature, seek change and discovery and are likely to bring demands for more change to the technical environment. This makes the relationship between IT and the concept and culture of knowledge sharing a critical one.

Until the technology in place can coevolve with the organization's changing business models and cultures, companies will go through periods where the design of the information interface is out of sync with operational needs. The use of information systems then becomes so cumbersome, nonintuitive, and inefficient that people refuse to use them, settling instead for less technical means to accomplish their tasks. This may be fine but for the fact that it sacrifices the potential efficiencies that well-designed technology can bring. For the technology of an online knowledge network to succeed, its members must choose to use it regularly as an essential part of their jobs.

This chapter focuses on the importance of the IT department's collaborative role in building the knowledge network. This role centers on its cooperation in the overall design of the networking environment, including tool selection and configuration, and the integration of features and functions appropriate to meet the needs of each distinct knowledge-based community. The role extends beyond the provision of tools to an active part in an ongoing relationship with the social network as it strives to improve its knowledge-sharing environment incrementally.

The professional and social relationship between the people implementing the knowledge network and the people in the IT department, which comprises a powerful knowledge network in its own right, is crucial. A close working relationship between IT and those leading the development of knowledge exchange systems will, in the end, benefit both groups.

IT and Knowledge Exchange

How do the people responsible for the information technology in an organization relate to the needs of those seeking to improve knowledge exchange and transfer through computer technologies? What issues consume IT's attention today, and how do those issues affect its ability and willingness to work with knowledge-networking advocates? It's important that we understand some practical and cultural realities about the people charged with IT responsibilities before we assume that the implementation of the right technologies is simply a matter of asking that they be done. IT is a busy place, and the technologies required by an effective knowledge network can be complex.

Our historical account of the tools and management models that heralded the arrival of the Information Age described email as one of the first applications created after the hardware, software, and networking protocols were made available to support it. The information technology community became the first working online knowledge network.

As technology was subsequently adopted and embraced by large businesses and organizations—and then customized to meet their growing information-handling needs—emphasis switched from group communication to more sophisticated ways of inputting, organizing, storing, and retrieving the burgeoning mountains of data. And as these information-processing organizations eventually connected to the Internet, the challenges and problems faced by the person in the role of CTO multiplied.

Now emphasis is swinging back from data storage and manipulation toward interpersonal communication as the most effective means of exchanging knowledge. How do the priorities, activities, and culture of IT—with its information-based worldview built in the 1990s—relate to the needs and culture of the interactive knowledge network? There are many ways in which IT inherently understands the model of the knowledge network and may be able to save itself some work in the long run by helping to establish strong technical bases for them.

The CTO's Growing To-Do List

In most companies, the work of the IT department is forever a work in progress and never without crisis. Consider just some of the department's responsibilities. Most IT departments must do many, if not all, of the following:

- Provide the most up-to-date tools and connectivity for internal system access to every desktop

- Configure, maintain, and upgrade the software used by every employee

- Select, secure, install, and fix all of the company's computer technology

- Provide system security, backups, Internet access, firewall configuration, and virus protection

- Evaluate and approve the selection of new technical tools for new needs

- Program in-house solutions to business problems

- Work with outside technical consultants on a wide variety of projects

This is, of course, only the tip of a very complex iceberg. When all of this has been systematized or accomplished, IT is expected to integrate all of these components and requirements into a seamless system that can serve a long list of different and changing needs throughout the organization.

IT AND THE ENEMIES WITHIN

As if there weren't enough threats to IT from outside the firewall, the results of a study by KPMG show how even internal relationship building can impact security:

79 percent of senior management executives polled by KPMG in 12 countries wrongly believe that the biggest threat to their e-commerce system security is external. . . . In reality, disgruntled or former employees, or external service providers who have a long-term relationship with the company, are most likely to commit an attack, or cause a security breach.[1]

This would be a full plate under any circumstances, but the emergence of and connectivity with the Web have added yet another dense layer of complexity to IT's tasks. Among the many facets of that layer, IT must now account for a much greater volume of independent and collaborative online activity by the average worker. No longer is the individual at the PC simply the destination point of an information query's response or the source point of input for a page or stream of information. Now, every individual, both local and remote, is a potential correspondent, contributor, and editor in an interactive network of ad hoc publishers and readers. There is an ever-increasing volume of information passing back and forth across the last bastion of internal company security: the corporate firewall.

Since 1997, the Web interface has become the lingua franca of commerce over electronic networks. This level of standardization has simplified many interface challenges. However, IT managers still face an imposing array of incompatible software platforms with no accepted standard for integrating the many different applications now accessible through this global Web protocol. Such standards, now referred to under the umbrella label *Web services*, are under feverish development (and are described more fully later in this chapter). Yet there remains the question of whether the Web-using world, so accustomed to incremental grass-roots innovation, is ready to accept standardization and thereby change a culture with roots going far back to the original days of collaborative technology *hacking* in the sixties. Until that question is resolved, the major challenge to IT, especially from the knowledge management point of view, will remain the integration of disparate sources of information and knowledge through the shared interface of the Web.

The Daunting Task of Integration

Referring to software as a *legacy system* makes it sound as if it's been around for a long time. But these days, any system that has been installed and has become essential for a core function in the company is, de facto, the legacy system. The costs of replacing it can be prohibitive, so other upgrades or links between it and new applications adopted by the company must be designed to work with it. The products provided to build bridges between noncompatible applications are sometimes referred to as *middleware*. However, the more applications needing to be made data compatible with each other, the more geometrically complex becomes the integration, and the less reliable the final results. In Chapter 5, "Fostering a Knowledge-Sharing Culture," we'll describe some middleware products and products that attempt to remove the need for middleware by integrating applications directly through the top-level user interface.

Application integration directly addresses knowledge management problems. The purpose for taking on this daunting task is to make the knowledge contained in various legacy information troves more accessible and useful across the company. Customer relationship management should be able to use information from the order control system. Stock control systems should be integrated with accounting. The software designed for these different applications has, historically, been provided by different vendors, so merging or integrating their formats into one that made sense for the end user has required translation.

Such data translations have been done in the past by programmers, who wrote the code that glued the applications together. The more applications requiring translation, the more consultants and programmers needed to be hired or assigned to work on the task. Return on investment often became the determining factor as costs rose, and for that reason, the relatively new genre of *enterprise application integration* (EAI) products has appeared to reduce the need for expensive programming. But EAI brings its own unintended consequences of complexity and expense.

GETTING REAL ABOUT THE PROMISE OF EAI

So everyone has come back to earth in terms of their expectations and what the technology can do. It doesn't promise everything, and it doesn't cost three million bucks.[2]
—*Erik Swan, CTO of CommerceFlow, referring to the promise of a "nirvana," where enterprise application integration (EAI) products would solve every company's information problems*

The CTO has huge problems to solve, even as interoperability standards like XML (Extensible Markup Language) attempt to fill the solutions gap. The knowledge network is made smarter by the availability of information from the many applications at work in the company, and it has its own needs for application integration in the technologies of online conversation and content management. But the promise of integration standards and of new middleware solutions that can automatically standardize the input and output of a variety of software applications has yet to be fully realized. Companies are finding that the work involved in installing and applying these solutions can be unexpectedly difficult and expensive. This is a chief reason for our recommending a *phased* approach to implementing knowledge-networking systems.

The technical fixes needed to improve *knowledge management* (KM) which relies on the manipulation and integration of information-handling applications, is more complex and expensive than the technologies required for interactive *knowledge networking* (KN) which provides online facilities for managed conversation and the sharing of relevant content. In that respect, KN should be simpler to implement than KM, but the more socially driven aspects of the knowledge network and its technical needs make it important that some intercultural issues between IT and KN be examined.

IT Culture in the Organization

Although we, the authors, work with technology and information, we don't think of ourselves as "IT people." Yet having worked cooperatively with them over many years, we've come to understand how IT professionals work, how they think, and the language they use. In our roles as online community builders, we have served as bridges between the users of the community-supporting interfaces and our associates in IT who managed the servers, operating systems, and software applications. We recognize a distinct difference in culture between the tool *makers* and the tool *users*—between the technicians who build and maintain the digital and hardware infrastructure and the people who use it as one of their primary social communications channels and thereby discover flaws that they can't fix. One culture is dependent on the other, and that asymmetry can lead to less than optimum collaboration.

Most information technicians learn their science first in the classroom, removed from the realities of organizations that must react to opportunity and competition. Once on the job, technicians follow learned standards in building systems that have been proven over time to work. They face constant demands to expand and modify those systems to meet new and unique needs presented to them by the CEO in response to the often-competing needs of various departments. Two key goals of their work today are *integration* (making all of the internal systems compatible with each other) and *scaling* (configuring technical systems to expand to meet growing demands).

The population of users in most organizations is unsophisticated in its understanding of technology to an extent not fully appreciated by the technical culture. Often, the highly trained people of IT incorrectly assume that the technology, as provided and configured, is easy for untrained people to use when in fact it is not. Often, IT will assume that the applications are delivering the required solutions when they are not. And often, IT will overlook the importance of and need for training in the use of the tools they provide.

Still, as we've pointed out, IT has strong knowledge-sharing roots. Its culture has formed over the years around attention to detail, faith that there is a technical solution for every problem, the shared assumption that a technical system is never truly complete, and a united feeling that, were it not for the soldiers of

IT, the company would grind to a sorry halt. IT is the original digital knowledge culture because it has traditionally depended on the free exchange of ideas, discoveries, and credible rumors for its collective learning and advancement. To the extent that proprietary standards and technologies are now becoming more prevalent, IT as an open, knowledge-sharing culture that traditionally spanned the loyalty boundaries of competing companies is changing. But within each organization large enough to support an IT department, the local IT culture usually remains a microcosm of the knowledge-sharing tradition.

People who work day in and day out with network technologies develop their own viewpoints of best approaches to system design and development. But we know many IT managers and departments that have worked cooperatively and collegially with their internal colleagues, building close consultant-client relationships. The best keep an open mind and go out of their way to understand the needs, values, and strategies of the departments that depend on them for making optimal use of the technical platforms and facilities. These managers serve as the communications liaison between the technicians and the nontechnicians in the company, helping to translate needs into tasks and reducing misunderstandings and communication disconnects. This level of cooperation is critical to the implementation of knowledge-sharing technologies and to meeting the unique challenges they bring.

IT Culture and Knowledge-Sharing Culture

Knowledge sharing is about dynamic information exchange and communication. Its technical challenges have to do with interaction, the retrieval of stored information, and the constant gathering of new information. The key players, who may range from specialized teams to cross-discipline experts to entire departments, must be enabled to interact through the network with one another and with information resources. As part of that process, these knowledge-sharing communities must be able to produce new collections of information—based on their interaction, conversation, and the content they create and gather—that can be categorized, searched, and retrieved.

For IT managers, knowledge networkers are a special class of client. People who rely on the availability and regular maintenance of online meeting places will have different relationships with IT than those who deal only episodically with the software and the data it carries. The direct conversational involvement of knowledge networkers with their supporting technology can lead to frustration with IT, or it can serve to build unique working relationships with individuals in IT. The social nature of the knowledge-networking community should ideally become an asset in forging strong alliances with the IT community by building active and well-nurtured communication links between the two.

TOP IT NEEDS OF A KNOWLEDGE-SHARING CULTURE

1. A distinct virtual space for knowledge exchange
2. Content publishing tools that can be managed locally
3. Group communications tools appropriate to the culture
4. Gateways to control access to the space
5. Technical support and tools for local reconfiguration of the interface
6. Application integration for ease of use

Unlike most user populations served by IT, knowledge-sharing communities spend time "living in" the company's technical environment. They treat it as a malleable resource just as they would a physical meeting room where the furniture can be rearranged to facilitate conversation and where various audiovisual tools can be requisitioned and operated to present information to the group.

Self-determined local control over incremental improvement to the interface is important for both the knowledge community and IT. The ability of community managers to respond to needs and suggestions of their members without having to get approval from IT is both convenient and empowering. And with the right software setup, IT can be relieved of the responsibility of making every minor (in terms of system resources) interface-level change in software configuration.

Knowledge sharers converse *through* the technology and *about* the technology because they recognize together how improvements in interface design and content delivery can help them discover, exchange, and use information and conversation more effectively. More than with other technical clients, IT can expect the members of a knowledge culture to be well informed and involved in identifying needs for their own changes and modifications. When those experience-based changes are specified directly by the tool users, as shown in Figure 4.1, they are more likely to be appreciated and used productively when implemented. The rising quality curve in Figure 4.1 shows how suggestions made by the community to improve the interface are followed by small jumps in the quality of the online interaction. As the community adapts to the interface changes, the quality curve flattens until the next suggested improvement brings another jump in quality.

What IT managers most need to know about knowledge culture is that, like programmers and system administrators, people conversing through the Net about their special interests are likely to be experimenters and explorers. They fill disk space with their discourse, their writings, relevant documents, and with the information they gather and collect as the basis of their shared work. Through their activity, they discover the needs for new software features, changes in the design of their online work environment, and the composition of their online teams. The idea is to put knowledge directly to work, and the best way to do that through the Net is to establish a trusted communications loop between the knowledge network and the IT resources that support it. Figure 4.2

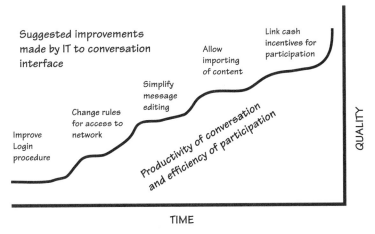

Figure 4.1   Incremental advances in conversation quality with technical improvements.

illustrates how the members of the knowledge network discover what is lacking in the technical interface, pass that information along to IT or the parties qualified to improve the interface, and then receive the benefits of those improvements. These improvements often serve to make use of the interface more convenient or more specific to the knowledge network's needs.

To establish an ongoing relationship between the knowledge exchange community and IT, a phased approach to implementation is most economical and productive. With each phase of technical improvement, as shown in Figure 4.3,

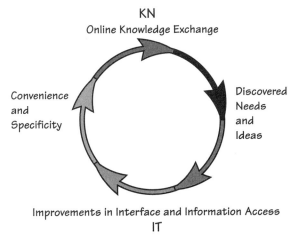

Figure 4.2   The ongoing feedback loop between IT and the knowledge network.

the communications between the two communities can be refined and made more efficient. IT can assess its practical capabilities, assign resources, and work with the knowledge community to define the goals of each phase of implementation. The feedback process of technical design and actual use of the technical changes can be made smoother, with time set aside between phases for reevaluation of needs and capabilities.

The knowledge-sharing community, for its part, must be sensitive to the practical capabilities and limitations of the IT department and thereby minimize inappropriate demand. Communication between the two communities should be defined by an agreed-upon process, with identified liaisons on either end. IT departments prefer *trouble ticket* systems that keep complaints and bug reports in order and track responses to them. IT should provide training to the knowledge exchange community in how to obtain its services most effectively.

Teams representing the expressed needs of the knowledge community should meet, between build-out phases, with teams representing the relevant skills and responsibilities in the IT department. As Figure 4.4 shows, an uncoordinated barrage of individual requests and trouble reports from an active knowledge community can force a busy IT support team to shut down its intake. Orderly systems for reporting technical bugs and suggested improvements help preserve good relationships between an IT department and its clients. Uncoordinated communications can confuse technical fixers and cause them to avoid responding to a deluge of redundant or conflicting requests.

The mutual interests of knowledge exchange and IT serve to (1) keep solutions as simple as possible, (2) arrange efficient and steady communications about

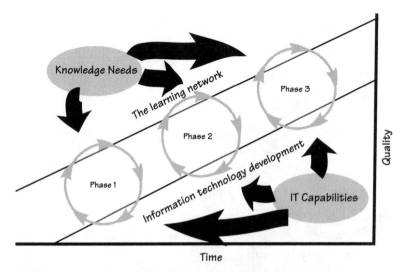

Figure 4.3   The relationship between the knowledge network and its technical resources should be active and ongoing.

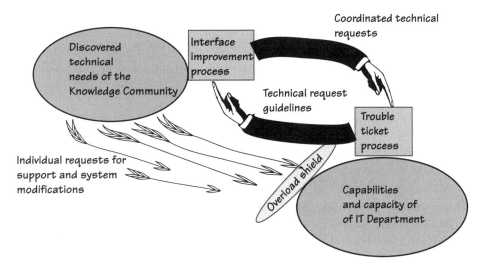

Figure 4.4 Coordinated and orderly communication with a busy IT department brings better results and relationships.

needs and capabilities, and (3) make the most positive difference for the company for the least cost in terms of time and technology. With so many software integration solutions reportedly running way over already high budgets, the knowledge network should be technically managed to make the company smarter through the collaborative creativity of the knowledge sharers and the technicians.

IT and the ROI of Knowledge Networks

A constant drumbeat in the technical press today is the heightened need for CTOs to work within ever-tightening budgets. Return on IT investment has become more important than at any time in the past decade, and the need to justify every dollar spent has forced CTOs to find better ways to evaluate in advance the return that can be expected from every purchase. So many intangibles affect those returns that accuracy and certainty are impossible. Costs may be easy enough to estimate, but returns can be affected by a range of unknowns such as the strategic fit of the technology, levels of customization required, and the possibility that a competitor's change in strategy will somehow devalue the investment.

Knowledge networks don't necessarily require the scale of expenditure that many other IT projects do because their objective ROI assessments can be based more on the cost and resulting revenue impact of basic online communications tools and integrated interface design. However, improvements in online knowledge sharing tend to lead more indirectly to greater revenue returns. Thus, the ROI assessment of those improvements must be done more subjectively than in situations where changes directly affect costs of production or net profit on sales. Some experts have confronted this situation and have devised several useful approaches.

Jakob Nielsen, the widely respected user interface guru, in considering how ROI assessment could be achieved for improvements in the interface design of a company intranet, recommends "measuring the productivity gains and seeing how it improves the employee's ability to undertake their tasks."[3] He looks for *objective* criteria for assessment, achieved (in the specific case of intranets) by having "study groups of ten, twenty people being monitored in their tasks to see the gains they are making." Organizations, he says, should "list a number of key metrics right at the start of the project" and work toward defined goals to realize the cost savings that technical interface improvements can and should bring. But for many technical improvements, objective measurements of ROI are tricky.

HOW CULTURE AFFECTS ROI

People are often looking for a panacea, some magic computer program. The answer is usually inside their organization. They have to have a clear process for decision making and a clear articulation of how we account for certain costs and benefits.[4]

—*Pat Harker, professor of operations and information management at the Wharton School of Business, commenting on the relative value of finding and using hard numbers in determining the return value of technology investments*

A joint study by Intel and the Wharton School of Business[5] recommended more subjective evaluation of IT investment as one way to avoid purchases based only on objective (but speculative) revenue numbers. The study also emphasized the concept of *revenue distance:* how far the software or hardware proposed for purchase is from the collection of actual revenue.

Unlike technology acquisitions that can be used immediately and directly by buyers of the company's products, most knowledge-related applications have large revenue distance. Their use leads to clearer thinking in strategic planning more often than to immediate effects such as higher sales. But combined with subjective evaluation, an investment in improving knowledge transfer can bring greater overall long-term benefits to the company. Further combining these evaluative approaches with the objective observation of actual changes in employees' efficiency in work patterns recommended by Jakob Nielsen can provide reliable metrics for ROI assessment.

Another approach to economizing through the technologies and practices of knowledge networking is in improving "management leverage metrics."

Through the wise use of online communications, the number of employees reporting to a manager can be increased. Even a slight increase in this metric, multiplied across a company with thousands of employees, can pay for the investment in technology in a short time.

Of course, for the knowledge network, this level of analysis should be part of the initial strategic planning. Combined with phased implementations that employ basic and economical software solutions rather than elaborate and expensive ones, the CTO should be able to justify the initial phases of the knowledge network's technical infrastructure. The solutions we recommend in Chapter 8, "Initiating and Supporting Internal Culture," and Chapter 9, "Conversing with External Stakeholders," will provide further ideas for ROI assessment.

Technical Approaches to Managing Knowledge

As we emphasize throughout this book, a knowledge network is a technosocial entity requiring a good match between the tools supporting conversation and the organization of the conversationalists. Without the involvement of humans and their social concerns at all stages of strategy, planning, design, implementation, management, and development, the technological components can do little to advance the spread and use of knowledge in the organization. And without the correct technology, selected and implemented with the wisdom of IT, many opportunities and conveniences for sharing knowledge and generating new knowledge will be lost.

Technology can only do so much, and it can be deviously simple to provide what look like the right solutions only to find that they don't fit the process needs, work habits, or social culture of the people meant to use them. However, there are several areas where technology can provide tremendous leverage, and IT, in collaboration with the planners of the knowledge network, should prioritize the fulfillment of needs in the following areas:

1. Integrating knowledge resources

2. Organizing relevant information

3. Providing the most appropriate basic tools to support the knowledge exchange conversation

Limitations of Technical Solutions

Knowledge is not like inventory items that can be stored by description in distinct bins on assigned shelves. A 6-millimeter hexagonal brass nut with standard threads, for example, is not subject to different interpretations. In contrast, a story about how a salesperson learned to understand the needs of a customer might be stored, presented, and understood in many different ways by different people because it has many subjective characteristics.

Knowledge is so dependent on human perception and context that one can't depend on a purely technical, automated solution to meet the learning needs of a group or a company. The group must involve itself in the design process of its technical knowledge-sharing environment. That effort is, in itself, a knowledge-sharing activity. The ideal role of IT in that process would be as the group's technical advisor and consultant.

JUST BECAUSE THEY CAN DOESN'T MEAN THEY WILL

Companies install e-mail or collaborative software and expect knowledge to flow freely through the electronic pipeline. When it doesn't happen, they are more likely to blame the software or inadequate training than to face a fact of life: people rarely give away valuable possessions (including knowledge) without expecting something in return.[6]

—Thomas Davenport and Laurence Prusak

This collaborative design process for knowledge-networking technologies distinguishes it from the more top-down implementation of many knowledge management technologies. Knowledge networks, by definition, are to be used as part of the daily work process. They require the participation of their members in their strategies and design. As the big consulting firm KPMG concluded, after a large-scale analysis of the realized benefits of knowledge management systems reported by 400 companies: "These responses confirm the fundamental flaw in viewing KM as a technology issue: It is not the technology that is holding organizations back but a lack of strategy and a failure to build KM in the organization's day-to-day operations and its culture in order to encourage end-user buy-in."[7]

What good is technology if it is not used? An online knowledge network does not exist without its technical tools, but it must wisely choose tools and design interfaces that are appropriate and will actually be used because they answer real needs. The base-level tools that one knowledge group requires will almost surely differ from those required by other groups. Some kind of technology will certainly be necessary for online knowledge exchange, but unlike KM systems, the most important exchange activity will not be in the retrieval of well-organized information. It will be in the active give-and-take between people through the communication and content delivery systems provided by IT.

FAILURE TO DELIVER: PROBLEMS WITH KM TECHNOLOGY

KPMG analyzed 400 firms and their use of knowledge management systems. In answer to the question, "Why do you think the benefits failed to meet expectations?" they got these responses:

1. Lack of user uptake due to insufficient communication: 20 percent
2. Everyday use did not integrate into normal working practice: 19 percent
3. Lack of time to learn or system too complicated: 18 percent
4. Lack of training: 15 percent
5. User could not see personal benefits: 13 percent
6. Senior management was not behind it: 7 percent
7. Unsuccessful due to technical problems: 7 percent

Of the firms whose systems were fully set up, 85 percent reported that the KM system failed to meet their expectations.[8]

Integrating Knowledge Resources

According to the technical dictionary site WhatIs.com, "a *kludge* is an awkward or clumsy (but at least temporarily effective) solution to a programming or hardware design or implementation problem."[9] In the pursuit of higher productivity per worker, many IT departments, lacking sophisticated solutions or strategies to guide them, have built kludges to provide access to different applications from a single location on an intranet. Although usable, the resulting online gateways have not really solved the interface compatibility problem, and the resulting confusion with incompatible interfaces presented in a common window has often eroded or reversed the very gains they were meant to achieve. Users refuse to use the confounding gateways, and their productivity is not improved. Thus the emphasis in IT on improved integration: the technical conversion or reconfiguration of data and interfaces from different software applications into single, unified, comprehensible "consoles" that users are more likely both to understand and employ on a regular basis.

ALL-IN-ONE OR KNIT-TOGETHER SOLUTIONS

The predominant goal of software vendors is unifying and automating the entire e-business operation. There are, roughly speaking, two ways to achieve that goal: deploying a suite of products that offer "all-in-one" e-business functionality or knitting together "best-of-breed" digital tools into a unified platform.[10]

—Katherine C. Adams

The conversion of business theory to the knowledge management approach brought greater focus on two things: (1) delivering specific information to specialists who needed it and (2) avoiding the unnecessary duplication of the same tasks within the organization. To those ends, specialists defined the knowledge resources that needed to be made more conveniently available to them. Depending on the business unit or department being served, these may have included records of client transactions, stored proposals and project histories, and locators for expertise and current related activities within and outside the organization. Different applications created and stored these resources, and IT provided kludges to tie those different applications and their databases together. Recognizing a clear opportunity for improvement, software providers began offering packaged products that claimed to serve the same purpose, saving time for IT and providing solutions that were more elegant and intentionally designed.

Whether or not the company's integration solution consisted of knitting together best-of-breed software applications or purchasing these ready-made all-in-one applications, one great obstacle to utility remained: the inappropriate manner in which the content of the databases was selected and stored. IT would create and set up the information storage process, but without the essential advice and consent of non-IT experts, who represented the knowledge needs and perspectives of the end users and internal clients. Thus, the stored information did not go through the essential processes of editorial selection, categorization, and filtering provided by the people most familiar with the content and how it would ultimately be used. The results of providing application integration without the involvement of the end users of the information can be something like granny's attic, where piles of articles related to the family history have been stashed expediently over the years. There they sit, gathering dust in their random heaps, until a family member with a desire to do genealogical research (and plenty of spare time) finally comes along to make sense of the chaos. Without including some systematic and meaningful ordering of content as application integration takes place, the knowledge held by the organization becomes, for all practical purposes, useless.

Web Services: A New Approach to Integration

In the pursuit of simpler application integration, the latest trend as we write this book is toward the creation of standardized "Web services." It's too early to be sure that these will fulfill their early promise, but there is no doubt that companies desire what Web services claim to deliver: the ability to mix and match utilities from different providers to build full Web applications for use in both internal and public networks. Web services would eliminate the shortcomings of both kludged integration and all-in-one solutions because they could neatly bring together the best-of-breed solutions for various functions in customized, internally consistent Web interfaces.

The software standards being bandied about go under different acronyms such as UDDI, WDSL, and SOAP. Through widespread adoption of a Web service standard, programmers hope be able to assign "agents" that can go to specific Web sites to accomplish specific functions such as integrating various programs. For a knowledge network, this opens the possibility of selecting a variety of applications from different Application Service Providers (ASPs)—message boards from one, news feeds from another, supply chain management from yet another—and integrating them into one seamless Web site. Here all of the required applications follow the same formatting and functionality rules, thus eliminating the need for cutting and pasting data from one application to another.

The greatest barrier to the widespread adoption of any one Web service standard, as we noted earlier, is the Internet's history of incremental grass-roots innovation and its tendency to resist the freezing-in-place effects of standardization. Microsoft (no surprise) is one of the leaders in bucking the resistance, offering its "Net" standard for Web services. Through its alliances with eBay, CNBC, and its own Carpoint site, Microsoft has been able to demonstrate its protocol in action. Its allied companies can, through the Web, send custom alerts to their customers containing auction updates, stock prices, and real-time auto-related news tidbits. Customers can receive these alerts by way of email, cell phone, and personal digital assistants (PDAs).

Because of Microsoft's huge installed base of PCs and servers, there would be widespread compatibility with its standard. That would be a good thing for many companies, but the groups advocating competing standards maintain that there would be unacceptable interoperability problems with systems based on other operating systems, notably the very popular UNIX. UDDI also provides a list of applications that, under its UNIX-based standard, could be linked together into integrated products.

As of year end 2001, the Web service standards issue remains unresolved. IT managers not concerned about compatibility with external systems managed by other companies might be persuaded to adopt any one of the standards internally to gain its application integration benefits for building out their intranets. But should they make a decision now, they might regret it later if an important partner or market turns out to be using a different Web service.

Besides compatibility problems, a secondary hurdle in the adoption of Web services across applications could be the assignment of responsibility for problems encountered in integrated systems. Suppose a company employs Web services to deliver an online product to customers or clients through integrated applications provided by five different companies. If a customer encounters problems with output from the system, who takes the blame and provides the support? The application provider or the application integrator?

Internal knowledge networks can benefit greatly by adopting Web service solutions. It's only when the networks extend to outside the organization—as in applications where customers on the Internet are involved or where partnering companies become members of a knowledge-sharing extranet community—that the hard questions about choosing a standard must be answered.

Knowledge Organization

Knowledge networks rely on the organization and contextual availability of content to support their conversations and their work. Likewise, they need to quickly store the content they produce with the same quality of order and with the same level of availability. IT must provide the tools that allow this customized information flow.

The need to assign order to knowledge resources led to the development of taxonomies and categories as far back as the Library at Alexandria in Egypt. In today's world of knowledge, categorization helps match information with the tasks, projects, and departments that create and need to retrieve it. Editors and archivists, representing the focus of the knowledge community, are essential in making the best use of static and dynamic information as it flows between conversations, new content, and stored databases. IT provides the technical facilities, and the knowledge network provides appropriate human intervention for using them. As Figure 4.5 illustrates, a librarian or archivist fills an important role in any online knowledge-based community. Categorization must address the special needs of business units, teams, and communities where new information is being generated constantly.

To meet this need, automatic taxonomic software programs, which file information according to embedded or assigned keywords or by the context of its

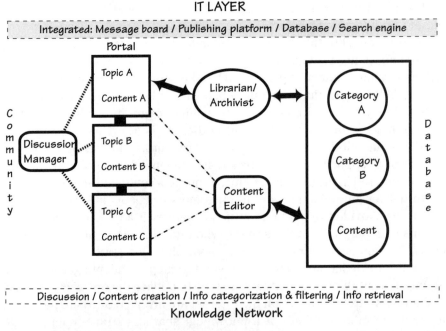

Figure 4.5   Essential elements for online integration of discussion and content resources.

creation, are becoming more common. IT may recommend these as solutions for the knowledge community, but they are only as effective as the active involvement of their human users makes them. Automation of knowledge organization may help prevent the granny's attic scenario, but human involvement and evaluation are necessary to determine what knowledge is truly worth saving and in what context it should be saved.

The categorizing functions of a knowledge network should have an online home that, through its location, provides some context and access to the people most likely to use it. This is an important integration point for IT, where it can bring such services to users in immediate online proximity to the conversations that will make use of, and contribute to, the contained subject knowledge. Such an online location would be the *knowledge portal*. In our discussion of portals later in this chapter (see *The Knowledge Portal*), we describe how knowledge communities can perform taxonomic functions through the portal interface.

Basic Tools of the Knowledge Network

Conversation and content are the basic building blocks of knowledge exchange. Putting the process online creates the need for basic tools to support the wide range of conversation styles and structures and the wide variety of content formats and shelf life. We emphasize the wisdom of starting small, following a phased implementation, and basing that implementation on an overall strategy. Thus, in this brief overview of the basic tools, we focus on technical products that are inexpensive to install, easy to scale, and simple to customize and manage. Chapter 5, "Fostering a Knowledge-Sharing Culture," provides a view of knowledge-networking software that expands beyond the basics.

BASIC RULES FOR APPLYING TECHNOLOGY

David Snowden, of IBM and the Institute for Knowledge Management, says that three assumptions about humans and what they know determine whether a technology will work to help spread knowledge.[11]
   1. Knowledge can only be volunteered; it can't be conscripted.
   2. People always know more than they can tell and can tell more than they can write.
   3. People only know what they need to know when they need to know it.
   He also advises, "Use the simplest technology you can for the purpose at hand."

The IT department's involvement in these tools will begin with evaluation and approval and can extend from integration into the company's intranet interface to full administration of the platform on company servers. In most cases, some level of support will be required for ongoing improvement and evolution of server-side integration and for support of the Common Gateway Interfaces (CGIs) and Java applications now a part of most software.

Email

This oldest, most basic, and most ubiquitous software application is recognized as the one "killer app" that, more than any other, justifies the existence of the Internet. It is also the most abused of applications, as everyone who must delete junk email constantly or who has received misdirected messages (or sent them) understands.

Email was, and is, the channel of most communication between individuals and groups. As a means of participating in mail lists, Usenet newsgroups, and now, many commercially designed online message boards, it serves as the interface to group communications. Through its many user interfaces, it permits the sharing of files, links, and graphics.

For IT, the existence and maintenance of mail servers are some of the most basic elements of their installation. Their involvement is necessary in configuring special mail lists and aliases that allow defined groups to circulate announcements and participate in conversations. Where email is used as a means of participation in online message boards, they may need to be brought in or at least consulted about the configuration of the program and its interaction with the company's mail servers.

The most vexing problems of email (besides the unending task of filtering junk) are user overload and the security risks of transmitting viruses to internal systems. The more groups or lists people subscribe to and the more alerts and updates they ask to receive, the more likely they are to begin ignoring those messages as time goes by. IT can only do so much to help relieve the email burdens that people put on themselves in their pursuit of the right knowledge and information. As to security, most competent IT departments have active virus-filtering programs in place and use firewalls and policies to minimize risk.

Instant Messaging

Email is asynchronous; two people corresponding don't have to be online, writing and reading at the same time, to carry on a conversation. But there is a different quality to communication when the medium is synchronous, like the telephone or instant messaging (IM), as America Online calls their Instant Messager technology. The immediacy of response when people communicate in real time is much closer to the experience of talking face to face or on the telephone. For many people, that immediacy makes the communication more intimate, more exciting, or more social. It's a very popular way of communicating, as was demonstrated when a company called ICQ offered its instant messaging client over the Web several years ago and, without any marketing, had 14 million people download it over the course of a year.

Today, IM software is available primarily from two sources: AOL (even for non-AOL members) and Microsoft (and the many distributors and servers of its technology). Although compatibility problems still exist between the two main standards used by AOL and Microsoft, the use of IMs within businesses has been skyrocketing because of its convenience for supporting teamwork.

The problem for IT is one of IM security, as noted in a report by the Gartner Group.[12] With up to 70 percent of enterprises expected to be using IM for various purposes such as customer support and workplace collaboration, the use of what Gartner calls "free" instant messaging clients opens the door to the interception of messages, transmission of computer viruses, and intrusion through nonstandard system ports. New enterprise-level secure instant messaging applications are now on the market.

Discussion, Conversation, and Conferencing

Online message boards and conferencing interfaces allow groups to engage in organized, moderated conversations that serve as both a means of meeting in virtual space and a content-generating activity. The main strengths of these platforms are that they offer the opportunity for participation and involvement at the convenience of people whose schedules may not allow them to attend real-time online meetings, and their interfaces allow conversations to be built on planned structures as an aid to organizing knowledge communities and their projects.

These systems are available to support conversations in two main formats: linear and threaded. Linear conversations begin with a title and topic *header* and proceed with messages that are added one after the other in a linear progression. As each participant reads through the list of messages and adds his or her own, it becomes the last message in the list. Threaded messages permit a participant to respond directly to any message posted after the topic header instead of only to the last one. Thus, any message responding to the topic header can, itself, become a topic header for a new conversation or *thread*. Which is best for a given knowledge community depends on the preferred format of conversation, the amount of participation, and the purpose of the individual conversation. Some products permit the use of both formats, with the participants able to choose their preferred view and use of the interface.

Message boards can run as licensed applications on the company's own servers or can be used for activity-determined fees as run on ASPs. The preference of the IT department and its need for security or to customize the interface will determine a given company's approach. Different products provide different levels of control over customized interfaces, degree of organizational options, and the extent to which different users can be assigned permissions and powers for administrative control over levels of interaction.

For example, a system may be used to conduct ongoing meetings for four related work teams. Each would need its own set of conversation topics, and each would want to have its own conversation manager with powers to start, end, edit, and organize topics. An overall community manager would be empowered, under the software's tools, to set up these lower level administrative capabilities.

The best of these products also permit the integration of content through their Web interfaces, making them hybrid platforms for conversation and relevant content publication. They may also permit the integration of other software applications such as email (for posting messages or for receiving new messages posted to selected conversations), real-time chat or IMs, and groupware tools such as collaborative white boards and copublishing interfaces such as *wiki*, which we'll describe in detail in Chapter 5, "Fostering a Knowledge-Sharing Culture."

The Peer-to-Peer World

Peer-to-peer, or P2P, applications are the rebellious youth of the organizational software world. They permit peers (that is, individual computer users) to collaborate directly over the Internet without the direct use of intermediating servers, which are the domain of control of IT. In fact, one of the reasons P2P applications are being developed is to circumvent the limitations and rules imposed by IT on users of its systems. Many people would prefer to configure their working interactions according to the needs of the moment rather than wait for approval, clearance, and possibly unsatisfactory results coming from the requirements of IT's involvement in the process.

P2P is truly the ultimate vision of the Web in that it gives equal power to every individual with a connection and a computer. Yet, as Eric Woods states in *KM World*,[13] "it has yet to make a significant impact on the corporate IT world." The reason he gives is that the prospect of people in the corporate workplace all doing their own technical thing "is the stuff of nightmares for most IT managers. Their systems—and their lives—are complex enough without adding new layers of connectivity and interaction."

That said, there's not much more for us to write about it in this chapter about IT, but we'll write more about the exciting possibilities of P2P in the knowledge-networking realm in Chapter 5, "Fostering a Knowledge-Sharing Culture".

Content Management and Publishing

Providing timely and relevant content through the Web to working knowledge communities is just as important as supporting their conversations. In fact, as we've pointed out repeatedly, those conversations often become the stuff of content—as edited transcripts of the actual interaction, as quotes extracted from dialogues, and as stimulators for new writings and documents that become available to the group.

There are many products available for enterprise-level content management, and most enterprise-level companies now have at least one installed for publishing to their intranets, extranets, or customer-facing Web sites. Many of them can be adapted for use in combination with the interactive interfaces described earlier. And as we mentioned, some message board interfaces provide at least limited content management capabilities.

All of these tools, of course, need to be integrated into a common, useful online space where the knowledge community can gather and share what it knows in the context of specific projects, goals, and practices. In the next section, we describe two approaches to bringing it all together into knowledge-sharing environments on the Net.

Online Environments for Knowledge Sharing

Though any of the foregoing Web-based tools can serve the needs of a knowledge-sharing community, they are more likely to be used and to make a difference in the productivity of that community if provided through an online facility meant to serve the entire organization. Such facilities have been available in many organizations since the late 1980s, yet they are still in their infancy in terms of design and utility. Application integration is only one of their shortcomings, and IT is usually given most of the responsibility for designing and creating them. However, it would be unfair to expect IT to understand the human engineering dimensions necessary to fit them to all of the possible uses that different groups within the organization will have for such resources.

The first attempt to bring useful services and resources to the desktop of employees was called the *intranet* because, unlike the Internet, it was meant only to network within organizations rather than between them. Intranets, as we've pointed out, suffered in their acceptance from poor design and limited integration and standardization. Only the most skilled or curious employees made good use of them. And though much has been written about them as knowledge management resources, their most telling limitation was in their lack of actual use. People simply chose not to devote the time necessary to learning how to penetrate their confusing interfaces and formats.

GIVING UP THE SEARCH

IBM reports, "white-collar professionals spend a rather consistent 20%–25% of their time information seeking."[14] Independent of the apparent information intensity of the job domain, when the amount of their time devoted to seeking required information approaches 20%, knowledge workers appear to *satisfice*—to consider the solution they've found in that time satisfactory if not optimal.

Knowledge networking depends for its success on participation. When the members of such a network find that they must devote too much of their time to searching for information, learning to use the tools, or establishing a connection between the conversation and its supporting content, they will give up and make decisions based on whatever information they can find before frustration sets in.

Thus, good design in the online environments that support employees and, in our case, knowledge communities is important. Companies are learning from their failures in early intranet design, and the examples set by Web pioneers like Yahoo! have demonstrated the value of building sites that provide access to many complementary resources, the so-called Web portals.

These can be key resources for knowledge exchange, so we will devote some pages to them in this chapter, where we'll concentrate on the IT department's role in providing good ones. In Chapter 8, "Initiating and Supporting Internal Content," and Chapter 9, "Conversing with External Stakeholders," we'll provide design and management tips for making these environments a good fit with the needs and goals of knowledge networks.

The Productive Intranet

In the 1990s, corporations began building intranets to give their employees access to commonly used information resources. These included directories of personnel, information from human resources about benefits, 401(k)s and stock option plans, online forms (also used by HR), and general news about the company. Some companies used their intranets as gateways to different databases of business-related information maintained by the company. These were accessible in their raw data formats and were not presented through user-friendly interfaces. As Jakob Nielsen described most intranets through the 1990s, they were "lacking interface design standards, unified information architecture, and task support for collaboration and other activities."[15] Employees weren't motivated to use them because their designs were confusing and difficult.

As the Web became more widely used and as its technology and more standardized interface features penetrated the internal design sensibilities of these organizations, the options for what could be provided through the intranet expanded, as did the capabilities for more integrated interfaces. Their original purpose—to enhance employee productivity through convenient access to often-needed information and resources—hadn't changed, but the ability to motivate their use by making them simpler and more attractive to use had.

People who study intranet utility now regard simplicity and adequate training as the best ways to entice employees to use them. Once the work force has become accustomed to intranet use as a normal part of the daily routine—checking shared calendars, company bulletin boards, paycheck stubs, and daily management announcements—its use for purposes beyond those administrative and HR-related tasks is more likely to be adopted. Groups seeking to share knowledge will begin to recognize the utility of taking their activities online and, following the design examples of simplicity and utility, will drive the building of their knowledge networking environments.

Figure 4.6 shows the design of an intranet page chosen by interface guru Jakob Nielsen as one of the best of 2001. Simple design and navigation with emphasis on a "community" feel and intracompany communication are among its strengths. But intranet design must address the needs of the communities using them. This one, assembled by an intranet specialty company called silverorange (www.silverorange.com), meets Nielsen's design criteria and implicitly supports the values of knowledge sharing. However, it does not provide the specific utility required by a specialized knowledge network. Instead, it serves as an informative bulletin board for an organization.

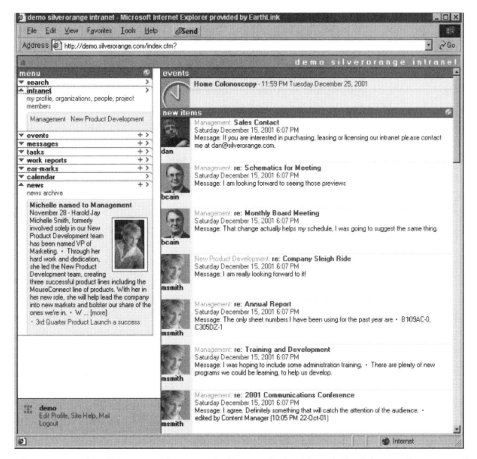

Figure 4.6   The silverorange intranet design was judged by Jakob Nielsen to be among the best of 2001.

Good and useful intranets should be designed by the people who will actually use them. Following the theme of this chapter, IT should serve in the role of consultant to the client design team to make sure that the end product is something that will answer real needs. The resulting product should make it easy for people to innovate: to create new pages, post new content, and collaborate with colleagues. The people who would use the intranet to find information should be able to find what they're looking for without *satisficing*—making do with unsatisfactory results. Eric Hards, a senior designer for Lockheed Martin's intranet, recommends redundancy: "You need to give users as many ways as possible to find something."[16]

IT'S PART IN THE INTRANET

In an article in *Fast Company* magazine, Phil Sandoz of Anadarko Petroleum describes how their successful intranet works: "Think of it this way," says Sandoz. "Our IT team maintains the trunk of the tree. But each department is in charge of maintaining its own branch."[17]

To ensure that the design will work, IT must implement and then go through testing phases with the design team as focus groups and beta groups use the initial design and evaluate its usability, navigability, and searching capability. Subsequent improvement will need to be made, and where needed, training resources will need to be provided. Once the intranet is launched, IT will maintain the basic structure while providing an interface that is under direct control of the various groups, including knowledge-exchange communities, who make use of it.

The Knowledge Portal

Portals are like intranets in that they provide online interfaces that bring a variety of resources together in one place. One difference in definition between intranets and portals is that the intranet is a system provided to all employees of the company, whereas the portal interface is a Web page devoted to serving the needs of more specific interest groups. Portals are often accessed through the company intranet.

Sometimes referred to as enterprise information portals (EIPs), portals have the same purpose as the intranet: to improve the productivity of employees. The best of them provide access to a range of services from company history and policy to training resources and detailed product information. They bring together all of the tools we've described in this chapter—conversation interfaces, content management, access to information databases—and they can be administered locally by leaders of the teams that use them.

Well-designed portals can reduce IT costs by distributing administrative responsibilities to the people who are most likely to understand the changes needed in them and are most able to respond promptly to the expressed needs of portal users. That effectively removes a time-consuming task from the support loop and spares IT the responsibility of making technical changes that are within the expertise of less skilled (and often, less expensive) people.

Not all portals are limited to internal access, as are, by definition, intranets. The broad definition of portals applies to Web interfaces that invite access and participation by customers and partners, fitting within the definition of *extranets*. In their support of knowledge exchange among customers and between customers and the sponsoring company, they serve as knowledge networks.

All of the divisions of responsibility and design we described for intranets apply equally to portals, the difference being that organizations that support portals are likely to have more than one of them, with corresponding teams designing and managing them. This creates the need for some restructuring within the IT department to serve what may be a whole new category of support under the IT umbrella rather than a single point of contact for intranet administration.

As with intranets, we will explore best practice solutions for portals as a powerful tool in the knowledge-networking process in Chapter 8, "Initiating and Supporting Internal Conversation." We'll revisit portals as an extension of the knowledge network into the realm of customers and interbusiness collaboration in Chapter 9, "Conversing with External Stakeholders."

Summary

An online knowledge network depends on the active support of the IT department for the creation and basic maintenance of its working environment. For that reason, it's important that a well-understood working relationship be established between the leadership of the knowledge community and the appropriate people in IT. The knowledge network is a dynamic entity that discovers better solutions for its needs through its internal conversations and exchanges. It requires an attentive ear in IT just as it needs software tools that it can modify at its own discretion.

Simplicity is the primary criterion for technical solutions both because of costs and the need for members of a knowledge network to adopt and use them. Beginning with the most basic of interface tools for conversation and content management will bring greater participation and a smoother path to incremental improvement of the interface. The role of IT should be to aid in tool selection, initial installation, and the maintenance and integration of relevant information applications within the company that will support the pursuit of knowledge.

Knowledge-exchange communities are most productive when provided with complete online environments that include current relevant content, appropriate conversation tools, and the ability to customize their virtual workspace as needed. Intranets are one approach to building these environments, but portals fit more of the criteria of meeting spaces specialized to the focus of distinct knowledge networks.

Fostering a Knowledge-Sharing Culture

Conversational knowledge sharing can (and will) only take place in a supportive social atmosphere. Such an ongoing environment is what we have come to call "culture." An organization's culture should be aligned with its values, mission, goals, and strategy, but the culture doesn't have to be defined by them. Different subcultures can exist in alignment with each other within one organization or even across different organizations.

The knowledge network exists first within the organization's greater culture. It may grow out of a more local subculture such as an area of expertise or a functional division within the organization. And it will probably develop its own unique subculture once it goes online. An online knowledge-sharing culture requires certain conditions and nutrients just as an orchid can grow only within certain ranges of temperature, humidity, and soil conditions. Yet unlike an orchid, an online knowledge network can adapt to changing conditions through its conversations and technology.

In this chapter, we describe these ideal cultural conditions. We discuss how how to create or migrate to them. We also elaborate on the *nutrients* that are necessary to start and grow a healthy knowledge-sharing culture within an organization: the analysis, the motivation, the leadership, and the trust. For most organizations, deliberate knowledge sharing is a new direction, and supporting it will entail some cultural change. So we also spend some pages on the change process and what it entails.

Creating the Ideal Conditions

If a knowledge-sharing community is like an orchid, how do we create the right temperature, humidity, and soil conditions for its healthy growth and spectacular bloom? Some cultures might already offer the ideal conditions. Specifically, consulting firms—created for the express purpose of sharing internal knowledge, findings, and generating new knowledge, and packaging and selling that synthesized knowledge—are natural knowledge networks. Most organizations are not, though. This is especially true where individual specialization has always been rewarded and collaboration has not.

Taking the knowledge sharing online, which is the focus of this book, adds yet another cultural hurdle in the way of providing the best conditions for germination and growth. There is no prescription for an ideal culture that can fit all organizations, but there are certain values that must be honored in a culture if its members are going to feel free and motivated to share what they know and to collaborate around their shared knowledge.

THREE ESSENTIALS OF A SHARING CULTURE

Trust: What I share will not be exploited or used against me
Tolerance: What I contribute will not be criticized unfairly or bring personal attack
Reward: I will benefit from the exchange if I contribute to it

---

Trust, as we've mentioned numerous times, is essential. If people think that, by telling others what they know, someone else will take credit for that knowledge or that an expressed opinion will somehow get them in trouble, they will not participate. Trust in an organization means that the stated rules and policies for using the network are clear and fair. It means that any incentives for contributing to the network provided by the organization will be real.

Tolerance is important as people begin to use new systems to take part in new formats of interaction. The online knowledge network is an arena where people bring their ideas, feedback, opinions, experiences, and questions. Its members must sometimes walk the fine line between being frank and being rude. In a virtual environment where facial expressions and tones of voice are lost, that line becomes even finer. The organization must be receptive to criticism and encouraging to truth. Knowledge does not always come neatly packaged, and in an active and open knowledge network, it may sometimes be presented in unsettling forms.

An assumption of mutual reward answers the key question, "What's in it for me?" Communities are places of exchange, where members expect to get things (not necessarily material things) of value from each other. They are not places of one-way contribution where members give to some greater entity in return for nothing. There must be satisfaction in participation, or people—even if they are being paid for it—will not contribute knowledge of value.

The Sense of Place

A characteristic of every enduring virtual community we've ever heard of has been *a sense of place*. It was vivid to us after our first months of participating in the Whole Earth 'Lectronic Link, better known as the WELL. Even though we were in the office or at home, sitting in front of our computer, we had a sense—as we read people's words and typed our responses to them—that we were actually somewhere else, where these other people were, in a space that was really nowhere specific. Our minds reacted as if we were "talking" to people in a room rather than typing in a "topic" in a "conference" on a "system."

In an ideal online knowledge-sharing culture, people will be able to find that sense of place. It is a product of trust and openness because the members of such a culture need to drop some of their defenses to participate at the level where they will tell each other the essence of what they know in a spirit of helpfulness and collaboration. A conversation requires that its participants return regularly to follow up. It requires *engagement*, which in turn requires a perspective of "going back to the place where conversation happens."

Informality is an important aspect, especially when moving social relationships online. The difference in format between face-to-face and virtual communication is enough of a challenge, but if interaction is kept rigid and businesslike without offering the opportunity to hang out and schmooze in the same environment, the trust, tolerance, and rewards will be hard to come by.

In his book *The Great Good Place* (Paragon House, 1989), Ray Oldenburg emphasized the importance of the *third place*, apart from home and work, where people feel free to socialize and relax outside their usual roles. Throughout human history, people have created such informal places to fill an important niche in their lives—the tavern, the town center, the bowling league, the church. The knowledge network is definitely part of the workplace, but within each organizational culture, there should be an opportunity to get to know one's co-workers and to interact in trust-building ways separate from the business process. Later in the chapter, we'll touch again on the subject of communities of practice and how they fit within the cultural framework of the organization.

The Thirst for Knowledge

The motivation to learn is the most powerful force driving participation in a knowledge network. Although all organizations have needs for knowledge and for the social networks that share, acquire, and generate it, few of them do a good job of recognizing and describing those needs in a motivational way. On the contrary, many organizations have cultures that inhibit knowledge sharing in one way or another.

Part of the motivation to learn must exist within the individual, and part must be motivated by the organization just as schools are meant to motivate their students. Schools motivate students for the good of the students, whereas organizations motivate employees for the good of the organization, but the cultural approach is similar; ultimately, the individual learner stands to benefit.

If the employees in an organization are looking to learn something important for the overall good of the organization, a knowledge-networking culture will serve them well. Their practical needs will help to build that culture. But the organization must take a role in supporting it, even where the employees are self-motivated. It must be okay for people to communicate and exchange what they know. The section on leadership later in this chapter will revisit this idea.

Analyzing an Organization's Culture

If one can "sense" a culture, how does one describe or evaluate it? How does an organization know what it's got, even when it thinks it has described its culture in a list of values or in a mission statement? An organization that aspires to have a knowledge-sharing culture might need to make some significant changes, or it may only need some minor adjusting. How does it know how far it needs to go to expect knowledge sharing to have an effect on the bottom line?

The Elements of Culture

In their book, *Built to Last*,[1] James Collins and Jerry Porras examined 18 of what they called "visionary" companies to find out what made them successful and enduring. It turned out that exceptional leadership and business plans were not a common characteristic. Instead, they identified *core values*, *clear purpose*, and *internal alignment* as the elements that kept their exemplary companies steady as they adapted to a changing world.

"Those who built the visionary companies," they write in the introduction to their paperback edition, "wisely understood that it is better to know *who you are* than where you are going—for where you are going will almost certainly change." So an organization's understanding of its own core values and purpose is important in establishing a strong foundation from which the organization can move. If values, purpose, and internal alignment are unstable—changing with the winds of each new business trend that comes along—the organization's culture has little integrity.

Culture is a complex social characteristic of human groups. In addition to those values, purposes, and internal alignments, it includes *structured relationships*, *language*, *etiquette*, and *history*. Culture is built over time, through both deliberate and unconscious practices, and must be learned by newcomers to the organization if they are going to work effectively within it. Although culture is difficult to describe, its presence in an organization is undeniable and powerful, influencing—and in many cases, determining—behaviors and decisions as well as power structures and role definitions.

As we mentioned in Chapter 1, "Knowledge, History, and the Industrial Organization," Edgar Schein studied people and management in the workplace, observing that, since people are complex beings, no single management approach aimed at increasing productivity will succeed for all workers. Schein, as a social psychologist, also has done extensive study of organizational culture and cultural change. Two of his conclusions in this area are particularly relevant to us in this chapter:

- Organizational culture exists on three levels

- Within an organization, there are likely to be conflicting cultures

In Figure 5.1, the three levels of culture are represented. An organization's culture manifests on a visible, material level as *artifacts*. How it is taught to its employees represents a less visible level as *espoused values*. And it works to influence employees and their behaviors on an ingrained, *unconscious* level. These levels, though closely related, are not always consistent with each other. What you see on the visible layers of a culture may not reflect what's happening on the attitude and assumption layers.

Cultural Conflict

Poor leadership and external forces can cause change and slippage in unconscious values even when the outward evidence of company culture remains constant and the values written into the company's charter go unedited. The

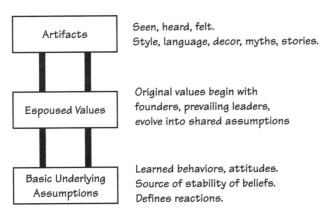

Figure 5.1   Culture exists on three distinct levels.

Internet has imposed a challenge on all organizations based on rigid hierarchical management by exposing their employees and customers to the nonhierarchical natural communications flow of the Net. This exposure puts pressure on established chain-of-command cultures because people begin to use their electronic networks to communicate in ways that ignore the existence of the hierarchy. Underlying assumptions about "how things work" change before espoused values in the company can catch up.

As to conflicting cultures within the organization, the culture of a sales department, where commission-based incentives motivate internal competition, is going to be very different from the culture of an engineering department, where collaboration leads to higher productivity and better products. A sales culture may promise customers high levels of support that engineering can't afford to provide. A service culture that is open to conversing with customers may be at odds with a legal culture that fears company liability and the escape of proprietary information.

In some large organizations, entire departments compete with each other to serve the same customers, sometimes without even being aware of it. Cisco Systems sells its products through certified partners but also does direct sales to customers, often in direct competition with its partners. Sales and service teams have been known to stumble over each other in their attempts to communicate with customers. These situations indicate not only a lack of coordination but also the kind of misalignment in values that could be eliminated through more effective knowledge sharing.

The Importance of Values

When you work within a culture, much of it eventually becomes invisible to you, shoved into the area of unconscious assumption. An outsider often is more able to sense the deeper, unconscious aspects of an organization's culture than someone who has been immersed in it. A new employee may find the established ways of relating within the workplace to be wonderful, strange, or a baffling mixture of the two. Of course, certain of the espoused values will be made highly visible, or part of the company's mantra.

At Hewlett-Packard, the "HP Way" has been described and applied to employee behaviors since the early days when the founders still ran the company. Hewlett and Packard began a tradition they called "management by walking around" in which managers spend time having informal chats with employees in the workplace to get feedback and develop close ties. These are *artifacts* that help maintain the visibility of a culture—from managers walking around, to the company logo, to local jargon, to the décor of its offices, and to the dress codes that determine how people present themselves.

In the end, though, it's how the company—through its executive officers and managers—treats its workers and customers that is the most powerful mani-

DAVID PACKARD'S 11 SIMPLE RULES

Hewlett-Packard's culture is a legacy of its founders. The following list (slightly altered here for today's standards of gender equity) was part of a speech delivered by David Packard in 1958.[2]

1. **Think first of the other person.** This is the foundation of getting along with others.
2. **Build up the other person's sense of importance.** When we make people seem less important, we frustrate their deepest urges.
3. **Respect the other person's personality rights.** Respect as something sacred the other person's right to be different from you.
4. **Give sincere appreciations.** If we think someone has done a thing well, we should never hesitate to say so.
5. **Eliminate the negative.** Criticism seldom does what its user intends, for it invariably causes resentment which will rankle, to your disadvantage, for years.
6. **Avoid openly trying to reform people.** Every person knows he or she is imperfect, but they don't want someone else trying to correct their faults.
7. **Try to understand the other person.** When you begin to see the whys of another person, you can't help but get along.
8. **Check first impressions.** We are especially prone to dislike some people on first sight because of some vague resemblance to someone else whom we have reason to dislike. Follow Abraham Lincoln's advice: "I do not like that man ... therefore, I shall get to know him better."
9. **Take care of little details.** Watch your smile, your tone of voice, how you use your eyes, the way you greet people, the use of nicknames and remembering faces, names, and dates.
10. **Develop genuine interest in people.** You cannot successfully apply the foregoing suggestions unless you have a sincere desire to like, respect, and be helpful to others.
11. **Keep it up.** That's all, just keep it up.

festation of its culture. Practice, far more than ideals and values, slogans, and furnishings, describes the explicit culture of the organization. The criteria for hiring, compensating, and promoting people demonstrate the real-life priorities of ownership and executives.

So it's critical, when considering a change to (or an increased emphasis toward) a culture of knowledge sharing, that the changes go beyond the level of words and intentions. There must be real incentives and demonstrations of faith in the new cultural direction. The espoused core values must be made appropriate, and the culture must become aligned in the knowledge-sharing orientation across the entire organization.

To change an organization's culture so that it can, and will, effectively exchange knowledge as a regular part of its operations, the organization's leaders need to understand where its culture stands in the present. To reach that level of understanding, it should undertake two studies: a *cultural assessment* and a *knowledge audit*.

Cultural Assessment

An organization should understand its current culture and the culture it aspires to before it begins the deliberate change process. A *cultural assessment* provides that understanding. This book doesn't pretend to be a definitive work on organizational culture, but we will cite here some widely recognized techniques used by specialists in the area of change management. Three popular and complementary approaches are *gap analysis, goal alignment,* and *individual-organization fit.*

Gap analysis is a term widely applied to environmental conservation. In that context, it identifies species that are not represented in current plans as "gaps" in conservation coverage. In the context of cultural assessment, gap analysis compares an organization's current cultural practices and assumptions with *ideal* practices in a desired culture, highlighting gaps between the two. The purpose of the analysis is to identify where the greatest gaps exist as well as where little or no gap exists. Thus, change efforts can be concentrated on where they are most needed, reducing the perceived task from one of total revolution to incremental or focused change. This saves cost and minimizes disruption within the organization.

Gaps can be measured along parameters associated with the three levels of organizational culture we discussed earlier in this chapter:

- The visible evidence of the culture

- The espoused values of the culture

- The unconscious assumptions of the culture

Surveys administered to employees and analyzed according to their departments and positions can provide a good overview of what the people recognize as their culture or of their distinct microcultures. The ideal might describe the attitudes and assumptions that would be expected to exist in a knowledge-sharing version of the organization. It could be that the company already believes in open exchange of what people know but that it doesn't buy in to the value of taking its conversations online. Maybe its reliance on the decision making of a single leader or management team has made employees apathetic about collaborating to find new solutions. If the ideal is a culture that values open conversation, and analysis reveals a culture in which people feel intimidated when they speak openly about company issues, a critical gap has been identified.

Goal alignment addresses the problem of conflicting internal cultures. It first identifies different microcultures within the organization—whether they are defined by divisions, management levels, project-oriented teams, or geographically separate offices—and finds discrepancies in assumed goals between them. By understanding these different perspectives of the organization and its goals, efforts can be made to bring them closer together so that cross-company change can be smoother.

Goal alignment may not be as critical where the organization has chosen to lead its change efforts with a *pilot* subcommunity, beginning with the team or division that is most ready to adopt the new technologies and practices of knowledge exchange. In such cases, the vanguard group serves as the test case or as the cultural change *role model* for succeeding subcommunities, and the realignment happens incrementally as the new model proves its success. In any case, if the ultimate common goal is a knowledge-sharing organization, there will eventually be social pressure for distinct internal microcultures to come into goal alignment so that the knowledge exchange can take place not only within them but also among them.

Individual-organization fit looks primarily at placement and hiring practices and affirms that as the organization reorients itself toward its ideal culture, it is putting people in place who fit with its new direction rather than with its old one. In this way, new values can be imported to help push the transition from old, entrenched assumptions. For example, bringing in new people who are comfortable with using online media in group communications situations can break the ice in companies just beginning to move their interaction to the Net. In addition, recognizing where valuable individuals are being challenged in migrating their communications to message boards or email helps define the need for new training programs.

Objective cultural self-assessment is difficult for organizations because it exposes inbred subconscious attitudes and often unearths unpleasant formative histories. Some people, particularly in leadership positions, don't like to be reminded of failures and errors made in the past that remain embedded in current operations and culture. But if a company is to make itself amenable to change—as all companies should be in this fast-changing age—then it must begin by understanding what keeps it from changing. Bringing in a qualified organizational change consultant at this stage is a good idea.

The Knowledge Audit

Carl Frappaolo, executive vice president of the Delphi Group Inc. in Boston, says that for what he calls "knowledge harvesting" to be productive, there must be an *environment* where people are comfortable with sharing knowledge. To find out what defines such an environment for a given organization, a *knowledge audit* needs to be done. This, Frappaolo explains, is "a benchmark of where the organization is from a *technical* standpoint, a *leadership* standpoint, a *work habits* standpoint, a *cultural* standpoint, a *communication pattern* standpoint and a *team structure* standpoint." [italics ours] The results of the audit "will give insight as to whether the whole process of knowledge harvesting is going to be perceived as beneficial."[3] In other words, if people don't recognize any gains from knowledge exchange and harvesting in their jobs, they simply won't use the systems provided.

From a technical standpoint, the organization may not be providing the tools necessary to exchange knowledge effectively. As we emphasize throughout this book, the ability to converse and to share information through electronic networks broadens the possibilities for people who are not physically able to meet but who have access to the Net. The selection of online tools, as we'll describe in Chapter 7, "Choosing and Using Technology," also determines to a great degree the amount of knowledge exchange that can take place.

Company leadership (which we've covered before and will cover again later in this chapter) is another powerful determinant in the organization's willingness and motivation to adopt knowledge-sharing practices. Though many "bottom-up" initiatives instigate change, they require their own styles of local leadership—and ultimately, the support from the top—to be truly effective.

Work habits and communications patterns can be difficult to change. Where the mindset is such that an employee sees "knowledge" as only being of interest to the "intellectuals" in the organization, that employee is likely to resist working or communicating in ways that more openly share what he or she knows. This resistance may be rooted in a reluctance to expose one's intellectual property or from an inability to use the available means to describe one's knowledge eloquently. Either way, it's helpful for the organization to understand that these habits and patterns exist so that it can address them, on a case-by-case basis if necessary.

Because so much of an organization's culture, especially if it has a long history, is below the surface level and unconscious, assessment and auditing should be done with the aid of consultants who don't share that history. Fresh viewpoints—unsullied by skeletons in the closet and old axes to grind—are valuable here, as is an understanding of the special needs of knowledge-sharing cultures. Companies such as Denison Consulting (www.denisonculture.com) and the Hagberg Consulting Group (www.hcgnet.com) specialize in this field of assessment and evaluation.

Denison invented what it calls The Denison Organizational Culture Survey, which measures an organization's culture according to four traits: *adaptability*, *mission*, *involvement*, and *consistency*. Surveys administered to employees build scores on the evaluative tool that can be compared to benchmarks of other companies and correlated to other measures of company performance such as customer loyalty and sales. This is a kind of gap analysis. The tool also highlights conflicting tendencies within an organization, such as values for consistency of practice that may limit the organization's adaptability to changing circumstances.

Conversational Tendencies

An organization's overall culture influences the behaviors of all of its employees regardless of the microcultures in which they work, but most employees are more aware of their membership and allegiance to smaller communities within the larger one. Different motivations drive those smaller groups, and some—defined by their interests and practices—are much more likely to engage in conversation than others.

Online communities demonstrate these different tendencies very clearly. Communities come together around the common interests of their members, but the Web has provided a continuum of examples. At one end of that continuum, communities of people are comfortable convening around one-way content. They flock to the sites of celebrities or of products or news, and though they don't interact with each other, they direct their attention toward the same content. At the other end of the continuum, people are driven by a need to interact about their shared interests. People, and the varying degree of focus they bring to their communities, are represented in Figure 5.2. The degree of focus, represented by the variation from big ball to little ball, depends on the perceived importance and relevance to the group of its *core interest.*

For a project team, the focus will be large because the team members must devote their time and attention to achieving a common purpose within a given length of time. For a department in the organization, there may be many scattered foci, from attention to ongoing projects to the routines of departmental administration to the social planning for staff birthday celebrations. Because the attention of workers is split among them, none of these interests will be as important as the product is to an engineering design team or as raising customer satisfaction numbers are to the CRM team.

Many intranets serve communities of people who share interest in the information provided but feel little need to converse with each other about it. Instead, they may contribute to the content of the intranet by submitting ideas and suggestions to IT, the Webmaster, or to the intranet administrator. The communication flow is like a one-way broadcast with a contributing but silent audience. Figure 5.3 shows members of an organizational community all paying attention to the huge ball of relevant and essential content—company news, employee directories, policy statements, and HR forms—with some of them bringing their own offerings in the form of announcements and updates from the workplace. Conversation is not a priority when the content provides the sought-after knowledge.

Figure 5.2   The varying importance of core interest (or focus) in community relationships.

Figure 5.3   A community focused on content of common interest such as a corporate intranet or Web site.

In an organizational culture, the content of the intranet is important as a shared database of information available to everyone. It is an important organ for imparting cultural values and communicating knowledge about the company itself. Separate areas of the intranet may serve the informational needs of the different divisions of the organization. Documentation of important cultural artifacts, such as the mission statement and company values can be referenced there along with profiles of fellow employees and their specialties.

On the opposite end of the continuum are communities with little in the way of shared interest but with a desire to socialize. Many of these formed spontaneously on the Web as chat rooms and message boards proliferated beginning in the mid-1990s. They are likely to form internally if the organization provides open, unrestricted opportunities for employees to communicate with each other through its intranet or if employees start their own internal email groups. Think of these as the *third places* in the knowledge network.

Conversations in such situations (see Figure 5.4) happen around topics, but the topics themselves are not as important to the participants as the contact and interaction itself. Though there is certainly some time-wasting potential in seizing these opportunities, they can effectively introduce people to the concept and practice of online conversation and allow people to get comfortable with new interfaces without the additional stress of forcing their conversations to be goal-oriented. However, even in a goal-oriented online community, it's important to provide some "free space" where informal conversation can take place.

Figure 5.4   The social interaction itself, rather than the knowledge gained from the conversation, may be the prime focus.

Most online conversations that take place within organizations happen in the context of some shared interest or purpose, with relevant content being at the center of discussion, as in Figure 5.5. This is the realm of project teams and communities of practice, which we discuss in more depth later in the chapter. Communities that form around shared interest in a subject—and have the means to interact—can reenergize their central focus with new collaborative ideas.

People in these arrangements discuss what is important to them in the workplace: their shared goals and the work that is at hand. The balance between interaction and content creates a kind of equilibrium, and both of our previous examples—where content was everything and where conversation was everything—will tend to gravitate toward this more balanced dynamic. Where people point their common attention toward content, they will want to discuss it more, and where people simply talk, they will tend to form communities of shared interests—requiring supportive content—as they discover commonalities.

Along the continuum from content-focused communities to interaction-focused communities, the middle ground, where content and interaction feed each other, is the most stable and rewarding, especially given the flexible toolset of the Web. Cultural migration can be leveraged by developing the organization's intranet to move employee participation from wherever it is along the continuum to this more balanced state of involvement, communication, and focus.

Tapping the Mind Pool

As we've pointed out, understanding its *current* culture can be an imposing task for an organization, but our main concern in this book is in describing the *destination* cultures that will value (and participate in) online knowledge sharing. From wherever a company is, it needs to arrive at a culture that encourages the smooth flow of knowledge and experience from where it exists to where it is needed. And as always, the most fluid, current, relevant, and usable knowledge resides in the minds of people both within and outside the company.

Figure 5.5   The big ball of context stimulates conversation and serves as its focus.

To get that *mind flow* going, some companies are proactive in developing practices and compatible technical systems that attract and support participation. Others are more reactive, following the spontaneous leadership examples of entrepreneurial employees who make use of whatever technologies are available to exchange knowledge and make their jobs more productive. The two sidebars describe these very different approaches.

MONSANTO'S KNOWLEDGE MANAGEMENT ARCHITECTURE

Led by CEO Robert Shapiro, Monsanto Company modified its culture by reorganizing. The company made itself "small and connected," subdividing its 4 business units into 14. Its Knowledge Management Architecture (KMA) allows the units to communicate and build *maps* for learning, information, and knowledge, leveraging employees' human abilities to "make sense" of available information that computers could only store and organize.

Director of Knowledge Management Bipin Junnarkar says, "we're attempting to change organizational culture by sharing and learning from each other so that the core values of individuals and organizations overlap ... ."

Using clearly defined roles in self-directed teams, Monsanto is attempting to understand and optimize the interactions between people so that its workers can become "analysts and thinkers," providing the company with "tremendous competitive leverage."[4]

(Monsanto's KMA will be described in more detail in Chapter 8, "Initiating and Supporting Internal Conversation.")

Tacit knowledge is held in the mind of every employee. But not every employee is able to put that knowledge into words. As they address their workplace responsibilities, they develop skills and expertise that, through repetition, become almost instinctive. They become more productive but may not be able to describe the subconscious elements of their skills.

The company relies on tapping into this deep experience to more quickly bring other workers up to the same level of productivity. Often, the only method for doing so is visible demonstration, which can be a time-consuming approach. Yet, through the give-and-take of conversation—online or face-to-face—such ingrained techniques can usually be explained, coached, and transferred to others.

The key to unlocking such tacit knowledge is in motivating employees to participate in transferring their experiential knowledge to others. A companywide value in openness and sharing is more likely to motivate an individual than a culture that rewards workers for hoarding their experience to enhance their individual prospects. If workers are rewarded for revealing the secrets of their productivity rather than keeping those secrets, the benefits can accrue to the company's bottom line as well as to the individual's.

If a practice of knowledge harvesting is put in place, then everyone within the organization must be open to having his or her individual knowledge

GUERRILLA KNOWLEDGE SHARING

David Weinberger is a consultant, analyst, and coauthor of *The Cluetrain Manifesto*. He observes what really goes on in the business world and emphasizes that groups are making effective use of technical capabilities in ways that the so-called leaders of their companies don't always "get."

In an interview with *CIO* magazine,[5] he pointed out how spontaneous, task-focused subcultures develop through internal networks, often in spite of established protocols.

"Businesses are taking on the structure of the web—decentralized, messy, self-organizing."

" … motivated, intelligent, committed hyperlinked teams keep the business closer to the customer."

" … many businesses are devoted to maintaining the org chart through everything from disciplinary action to body language, so hyperlinked teams route around org charts."

" … these teams constitute a second life of the organization and the place where the most valuable work is getting done."

sources tapped. Everyone must be able to benefit in some way from the sharing, and everyone should have access to the resulting bounty of explicit knowledge or conversation. These and more concrete incentives are important because when the most generous are rewarded, the least generous will eventually get the point and follow.

Often, leadership from the top levels of the organization is hesitant to upset the delicate balance of the status quo by initiating new cultural practices or marshaling change within the organization. In such cases, individuals who understand their own needs and the capabilities of the technology available to them are likely to take some leadership into their own hands and tap into the minds of colleagues who can serve as their personal knowledge resources. This was the original "hackers' model" of innovation, dating from the early days of computer networking. We see more and more evidence of cultural change being initiated in this manner, where grass-roots models are built and executed before top-down cultural initiatives are able to get off the ground. But top-down leadership and example are crucial if core values are to change across the breadth of the organization.

Leadership: Energy from the Top

For emphasis, we repeat: Unless the top tiers of the leadership hierarchy recognize the importance of knowledge exchange in the culture, there is little hope that grass-roots efforts will transform the entire organization. Some individuals in the company may pursue learning from each other, but knowledge as a driver of success and change throughout the organization will not be significant.

The CEO, of all people, should understand and represent the purpose and goals of the organization and how its culture relates to achieving them. This is more than a managerial relationship; it is a social leadership role that directly transfers to the behaviors and communications that happen all across the company. If the success of the company relies as much on generating and exchanging knowledge as it does on product development, production, marketing, and sales, then it is essential that the CEO make sure that its culture, at all levels, remains aligned with knowledge sharing, even if it has to change to do so.

Buckman Labs, a medium-sized chemical business in Memphis, is recognized as one of the leading examples of the knowledge-sharing organization. Its vice president of knowledge transfer, Victor Baillargeon, emphasizes the necessity of having buy-in by the "top brass." As he stated in an interview, "It takes clear leadership to set the culture and change it, and the leadership must remain involved. It's an ongoing battle. The challenge is to make it so that there is value in participating."[6]

Titles and Terminology

We use the word *knowledge* endlessly in this book, but in the real world of the workplace, knowledge is less used and widely misinterpreted. Few people consciously seek knowledge in their daily jobs. Instead, they seek *answers*; they try to learn from each others' experiences; they look for records and histories that tell them what has been tried and what has succeeded. They attempt to contact people who understand the goals they are pursuing and the difficulties they are encountering. They hunt for experts and advisors. Rarely do they think in terms of knowledge gathering per se.

We use the term to represent all of the foregoing, but within the organization's culture, there may be other terms that are more appropriate and better understood. Cisco, which has for years deliberately shared know-how through its Web site, intranet, and extranet, rarely uses the word *knowledge* on any of these sites. Instead, you see many references to *solutions, training, e-learning*, and *guidance.*

The CEO may also think in general terms of improving knowledge management throughout the company or in specific business units, but his or her directives must describe the actual needs that must be fulfilled, whether they are to increase the speed of innovation or to generate more new ideas. It is up to the CEO to understand the organization well enough to know whether or not a senior manager needs to be assigned or hired to oversee the development of knowledge-sharing resources and practices and whether that person should bear a title such as chief knowledge officer (CKO) or, as we just described, VP of knowledge transfer.

Some cultures may need that titled person to oversee the cultural transformation, leading the organization from the assessment stage to the software design stage, through the implementation of new knowledge-sharing practices, and into the production phase where operations are monitored for success. Other cultures may find it more appropriate (and the change smoother) to allow workers to develop their own systems for sharing knowledge and, as Dave Weinberger suggests, to have the VPs and senior managers get out of the way. "It's not your job to create conversations, to create voices," he says to those titled leaders. "It's your job to listen to the conversations and voices already there."[7]

Patience, Patience

In leading transformation to a knowledge-sharing culture, it's unwise to expect change to happen overnight or even over the span of a year. For many people accustomed to other ways of doing things in the workplace, it may require several business cycles to recognize the improvement and get used to the new tools and techniques. That sense of place and culture may not arrive until some time has been logged actually exchanging knowledge.

As Victor Baillargeon described his experience leading change at Buckman Labs, "The first year they think you're crazy. By the second year, they begin to think it can work, and in the third year, they buy in."[8] You can get more buy-in by demonstrating incremental success, even if it's only in one small sector of the organization, than by promising that success will come for everyone at the same pace. The cultural assessment and knowledge audit should have identified the divisions or teams within the company with the most promise of improving through use of knowledge exchange. It is through watching the development of those high-leverage *seed communities* that new cultural values will gain a credible foothold within the organization.

The danger, as we've seen over the years in our own initiation of online communities, is that the CEO and board of directors will demand to see direct improvement on the bottom line in the short term rather than allowing the new practice to mature and catch hold. Social practices, especially those taking place virtually, rarely work that quickly. They must be permitted to find their way through some trial and error before they "click" and build a critical mass of participation and exchange. But leadership can and should define goals toward which teams can strive as motivators for advancing the use of their knowledge-sharing systems.

Performance as a Motivator

The building of a knowledge network begins with a perceived need to know more and to know it sooner. That need not only justifies the expense of reorganization, technology, and new leadership positions, but it drives the buy-in by employees who must participate in the network to make it a success.

A study by the consulting group McKinsey and Company[9] identified *performance* as a prime motivating factor in knowledge cultures. By setting goals and mileposts to measure improved performance in teams and business units, the need for attaining and circulating new information—for learning—becomes more valuable and urgent. Workers see the importance of extracting from each other all relevant knowledge and experience and of seeking the same from other people within the organization and outside the organization. Thus motivated, they innovate new practices using the communications tools available to them and look for ways to improve those tools to better fit their needs. Motivation and purpose, stimulated and set by senior management, spur innovation and collaboration. Where a relationship with IT has been established, that innovation moves smoothly into the area of creative interface configuration to shorten the time between stating the purpose and achieving it. Members of the motivated working group become conscious of any inefficiencies in their process and seek whatever means are available to streamline their activities, thus learning and implementing as one fluid and collaborative activity.

Organizations that define themselves as *performance-oriented* cultures push the development of the networking tools that enhance that performance. The role of knowledge network leaders (including the CKO and senior managers who may be closer to the specific projects or lines of business) is to provide the perspective and overview that spots inefficiencies and facilitates connections between people and the resources they need to eliminate those inefficiencies. This focused leadership serves as the liaison with IT and with the CEO whose purview must remain broad and long range.

Listening as a Motivator

Some leaders emphasize that workers should be careful with what they say and to whom. Thus, fear dominates the message that they send into the workplace. The result is an underground communications culture that protects itself and its conversations from the prying eyes and ears of management. If management gives the impression that it would rather not hear what workers have to say, even in the form of constructive criticism, then the idea of a knowledge-sharing culture has little hope of reaching fruition.

Former Intel CEO Andy Grove wrote a book titled *Only the Paranoid Survive*.[10] As the leader of one of the world's largest and most successful companies, he was not meaning to write a prescription for survival in the workplace but was describing his perspective from a key position in a company that was subject to the crises and sudden changes that occur in the modern world and, subsequently, in the marketplace. The aftereffects of 9/11 are only our latest example, but Grove's book was written 5 years before that event and puts paranoia to work recognizing the subtle evidence of approaching change that allows good leaders to avoid the industry-shattering changes that may follow.

Grove is considered by many to have been a great business leader. He writes of how leadership must relieve workers of the fear of change by recognizing the need for change far in advance, before it reaches the crisis stage. He describes the dangerously narcotic effect of the "inertia of success" and welcomes "Cassandras" who announce rumors of potential cataclysms. He also praises "free flowing discussion" and "constructive confrontation" as important to keeping management appraised of employee attitudes and concerns. Though his paranoid mindset is rumored to have trickled down into the engineering layers of Intel, he does at least talk a good game and describe what would be a good role model for a knowledge-focused leader.

Such a leader is a good listener, both inside and outside the organization. By doing that knowledge-gathering task on behalf of the workers, an attentive leader can steer the company along a successful path, motivating workers to contribute what they know and think by demonstrating to them that their knowledge and opinions are being put to use for their benefit.

The ideal results of good leadership and effective motivation are what Junnarkar at Monsanto describes as "an ongoing upward spiral" of converting information into insight and formalizing new roles for people who make sense of information. And as we described in earlier chapters, the people active in the knowledge network will continue to refine its tools and techniques to make the exchange process all the more natural and productive for them.

Self-Organizing Subcultures

Another key motivator for circulating knowledge among employees is intellectual stimulation. By engaging in conversation with people who have experience and information about topics of shared interest, one is exposed to new ideas, different perspectives, and the personal enhancements that people give to the things they know. When an organization gives its blessing to—and provides opportunities for—such interaction, people are likely to participate with enthusiasm. Where the topics of their conversations have some relationship to business goals, these *communities of practice* (CoPs) can actually help advance one's career.

As Etienne Wenger[11] describes them, CoPs are conversational communities convened around passionate interests. Participation in them is voluntary, driven by personal motivations, and they are completely self-organizing, requiring nothing from the organization except the access to online meeting tools or F2F meeting places. CoPs don't exist without motivation, for motivation is what creates them in the first place.

Organizations are just beginning to understand that by sponsoring and supporting CoPs in the workplace, they get to harness the most creative energies of groups of workers without having to devote management resources to organize and oversee them. When the focus of the CoP is related to that of the business, the business stands to benefit in ways that are unpredictable but potentially profitable.

An article about CoPs on the Intelligent KM site[12] suggests examples of these extracurricular but relevant communities, such as "multimedia application development at a software company, herbal remedies found in the Amazon rain forest at the National Institutes of Health (NIH), or aerodynamic automobile design at a car manufacturer." In all of these cases, hobbyists would come together to share resources and attempt to answer each other's questions while advancing collective knowledge. Often, a CoP coalesces around an acknowledged leader in the field: an expert or *master* who helps train eager *apprentices*. Members of the community bring new knowledge to it and, through cultural osmosis, into the sponsoring organization.

Because CoPs are more concerned with learning and innovation than execution and productivity, they may seem to run counter to the priorities of the businesses that sanction them. Yet they can add value to those businesses by serving social and research functions that the business may not feel at liberty to perform. And being relatively cheap to administer—requiring only the use of email, message boards, or simple group communication tools—they aren't a liability to management.

Members of CoPs must be aware that their time spent in the community is not company time or, if it is, that the community must give back to the company in some form. The most successful CoPs seem to be those that exist specifically outside the work environment, where their members are free to explore and experiment without concerns about the value or cost of their explorations to the company. Only under those conditions can their passions truly run free.

The most important side benefit of CoPs is that they allow employees to experience the potential of open collaboration and innovation. Having gotten a taste of that kind of interaction, many will be motivated to bring the same kind of energy, relationship, and collaboration into the organizational culture. And by being allowed to participate in CoPs under the company's approval, they may be less likely to leave (with their knowledge) for greener pastures.

A more centralized approach to motivating innovation in knowledge exchange has been practiced by the aforementioned Buckman Labs. By fostering communication and collaboration among people across the entire company, the scientists and technicians at Buckman are able to realize *serendipitous* benefits. They describe an example where scientists in their microbiological control division were stumped in trying to control the growth of an organism and were given the solution by an employee in another division who had learned to control the growth of a similar organism while practicing his hobby of brewing beer.

Self-organizing conversational communities are not inherently about control; in fact, most managers would find them frustrating to oversee. But as Dave Weinberger says, "You have to learn to love messiness—although messiness has been the sworn enemy of information management professionals." He gives the example of the employee database that tells all of the essential facts about the person but leaves out personal observations such as "that Sally is wickedly funny, that Fred is really creative but many of his ideas are bad, that Carlos is a great initiator but is weak on follow-through, and that Wanda is a great person to travel with."[13]

Roles within the Network

At the WELL, we learned through trial and error. The role of *host* was created at first to provide a level of autonomy to the WELL's members, allowing them to apply their interest and expertise to managing a diverse selection of conversation topics. Over time, though, certain individuals added other qualities to the host's definition. They not only brought some subject matter expertise to their conferences, but they also began practicing facilitation and social counseling, keeping conversations on-topic and resolving arguments and disputes among participants. Some provided information resources and organized "field trips" for members of their interest groups into the physical world. The best hosts attracted loyal communities who showed up daily almost as if they were voluntarily instructing classes at school.

In a conversational knowledge network, there are similar roles that need to be filled. And just as hosts became an essential part of WELL culture, these knowledge facilitation roles will become identified with the knowledge culture in an organization. At Monsanto, Bipin Junnarkar emphasizes the importance that roles play in the successful conversion of information into insight in self-directed teams. Because these teams work within the context of an organization, their level of performance is more important than in the less formal interaction of the WELL. Thus, the team leader must keep an overview of how the team is achieving the goals of knowledge creation and exchange. The leader must keep track of what lessons have been learned and feed those lessons back to the team.

It's not an easy role to fill, as Junnarkar admits. "It is a very new concept for the entire organization. We look at creating value at the level of the individual, to improve the capability of each person. And we're attempting to change organizational culture by sharing and learning from each other so that the core values of individuals and organizations overlap, which represents a change from the classical way of interacting."[14]

Across the Firewall

Another self-organizing subculture is that of *the customer*. Increasingly with the availability of the Internet, the public is able to get a more detailed impression of corporate culture. Web sites, more than most advertising, provide insight into the values and purpose of organizations. Customer service and support—all of the elements of customer relationship management—are now being provided through the Web. Hence, whatever the company's internal culture, it must take into account the public's exposure to it.

Customers now "talk" to one another online about the companies they buy from—what some have called "word of *mouse*." They want to connect with people inside of the companies they buy from, too. As Dave Weinberger says, "Customers want to talk with the crazy woman in your back room who actually comes up with all the good ideas as well as tons of bad ideas. They want to talk with the designers of the interface or of the controls. They want to talk with everybody who's involved with the product."[15] Those customers share a passion for the product with the company's employees, especially with the product's designers.

The knowledge community should extend beyond the firewall to the customers who care enough to provide feedback and try to connect with the company. This inevitably requires some cultural adjustment because the assumption in most companies for decades has been that there would be minimal interaction between the workplace and the customer. Today, through sophisticated customer relationship management (CRM) interfaces and innovative customer contact practices, the boundary between company and customer is becoming more and more transparent. But if the company wants to do a good job of conversing with its customers, it had better learn to converse internally first.

The Challenge of Change

For many organizations, the change to a knowledge-sharing culture will be slow and at times difficult. It will cause disorientation and disruption because people are used to working in a certain way, within a certain organization, using certain tools. New skills will need to be developed and, as we've pointed out, different skills will be valued. Good writers and explainers will gain prominence; fluent users of technical interfaces will excel. Those accustomed to developing their specialized skills and to being treated as high-prestige local gurus will find themselves being asked to share their expertise openly with many others. People who have the social skills to entice others to reveal their knowledge through artful conversation will be recognized in new roles in the company.

The organization as a whole will need to emphasize values that may long have taken a back seat to profit and market share. As Victor Baillargeon said of Buckman Laboratories, "We have a code of ethics that is the firm's cornerstone and that contributes to building a climate of trust and respect." Shareholders may have to understand that to build for profits over the long haul, the organization has to adapt to the realities of the knowledge economy of the future where profit may only come to companies that understand the importance of trust and respect.

Buckman Labs' status as a leader in companywide knowledge sharing was not gained easily or quickly even though it concentrated on deliberate cultural transformation. It took 3 years for its employees to "buy in," Baillargeon admits. "I advise companies contemplating it to take a bite and get started. As you prove it works, you can grow it and migrate it into other parts of the company. You need a unifying technology that will be a good tool for your people."[16] And with that admonition, we move on to discuss some of those good tools in the context of the cultures that may be using them.

Summary

An organization that wants to share, exchange, and generate knowledge must have a culture that is aligned with the values that make such open transfer possible. Building or migrating to such a culture requires deliberate analysis of the starting point and the desired end point of the culture-changing process.

Different parts of the organization may have different cultures and ingrained habits that make them easier or harder to move toward the ideal knowledge-sharing culture. The company's leadership must clearly describe that ideal and make the call as to which of its diverse subcultures will lead the way in moving toward that ideal. This change can be accomplished by planned companywide reorganization and technical revolution or by allowing small, self-motivated, self-organizing communities of practice to serve as role models for the more formal divisions of the company.

A company's culture is increasingly transparent to customers, so it's even more important today that the company align its culture with the needs and expectations of those customers. The knowledge sharing can extend through the corporate firewall into the Internet where mutual learning can take place. The intersection of interests between the company and its customers is in the shared passion for products and in the use of common communications technologies.

Taking Culture Online

People and their cultures are adaptive; that has been the story of the human race, and we constantly see evidence of it all around us. The personal computer, the Internet, and the Web have made us invent new ways of seeing and interacting with the physical world through our new virtual world.

We humans have proven over time that we can adapt to almost any condition or situation, and we use technology to make our adaptation easier. We've developed clothing to keep us comfortable in hostile environments. Our cars have eight-way adjustable seats and smart climate controls. We devise ways of interacting with technical gizmos as if they were human. Now we can design online environments that allow groups to communicate in Cyberspace in ways similar to those they use in the physical office space.

Our first five chapters were mostly about people, organizations, and culture because they are in fact the most important factors in the success of a knowledge network. This chapter introduces the relationship between those human entities and the interfaces that allow them to practice knowledge sharing in Cyberspace. We follow this chapter with one focused on the technology tools that work best as components in a knowledge exchange interface. The technical choices and design are important to the flow of information between people. They can block or inhibit that flow just as easily as they can make it possible or even improve it. But we begin by emphasizing a point we've hinted at in previous chapters: Keep the interface as simple as possible.

Unnecessary complexity should always be avoided. Change for the sake of change is often counterproductive. Interfaces with which a culture is already comfortable should be leveraged. This chapter is full of cautions and descriptions of pitfalls. There are many choices for online conversation tools available, and software producers are constantly hawking new "knowledge management solutions." If we have anything to recommend beyond keeping it simple, it is to avoid dead-end solutions. Use tools that can be adapted to new needs as they arise.

Cultures and the environments in which they function evolve together. People adapt to their environments while modifying them, where they can, to fit their needs. The human-computer interface is a special case because humans have created it *for* humans to be further changed *by* humans. Knowledge exchange is a special case of *this* special case because people who use virtual interfaces to learn are more likely to notice how the interface helps or hinders their learning. The interface, the culture, and the learning are tightly linked. This chapter describes those links and how an organization can smooth the adaptation of a knowledge-sharing culture to its online meeting place.

The Medium Is Part of the Message

When Marshall McLuhan wrote "the medium is the message," he was exaggerating somewhat to make a point. The medium is certainly not the entire message, but it can be a major component of the total impression made by the message being transmitted.

The medium does, indeed, make a significant difference in communication. A stage performance of *A Few Good Men* does not impart the same experience as the movie version. Seeing a football game in person is qualitatively different from seeing it on television. And a conversation that takes place in a conference room does not leave the same impression as one that takes place through an online message board. The difference between any two media conveying the same content is experienced not only by the recipient but also by the sender. Compare, for example, standing up and speaking at a meeting with sending an email message to the same audience.

This medium-message effect applies just as powerfully to cultures as it does to individuals, which is important to keep in mind when selecting and designing the interface through which a community will converse. An online interface will force its users to alter their customary ways of communicating. Replacing face-to-face interaction with online interaction requires a period of adaptation during which individuals adjust their work habits and, in some sense, the way they project their personalities.

As individuals adjust to communicating online, their group culture also adapts. Most organizations and their cultures tend to resist change, so the end results of any change to social expectations must be justified. The key incentives to a group's going through adaptation to the online social environment are the need for effectively exchanging and generating knowledge and the faith that the new approach will deliver more knowledge faster and more efficiently than the face-to-face technique.

Another element that must be preserved in any transition to a new conversation environment is trust. If use of the interface erodes the participants' willingness to trust one another, which is a risk in any virtual communication, the credibility of the knowledge being exchanged will likewise be eroded.

The Postocracy

Effective use of an online interface requires technical skills and social skills that are not emphasized in face-to-face conversation. Table 6.1 lists some of the differences in valued personal qualifications between the two meeting contexts. The differences may affect the membership, values, and productivity of the group. When a culture first goes online, part of the apparent medium-message is that certain members have suddenly become more visible, more active, more persuasive, and more competent than they ever have been in person. People with no prior experience conversing online find themselves lagging behind the veteran users in their ability to communicate clearly and convincingly or in the amount of their presence in the conversations.

An online discussion community is what we call a *postocracy*, where those who post their messages and opinions have more de facto influence than those who don't. A cultural hierarchy originally based on good in-person conversation and presentation skills may be turned on its head when taken online. People who have logged time on Web communities demonstrate their fluency in this new environmental language and assume the leadership roles in the digital conversations.

The more complex the new conversation environment, the greater this cultural disruption is likely to be. But even in the most basic online conversation environment (email), the change from standard office interaction is significant. Email affects the *velocity* of group communications. People expect immediate response to their email messages. They also feel increasingly overloaded by the volume of email they receive. Email, when used regularly, seems to try to force more communication into a day than is possible to deal with. At least in person, one is able to engage in only one conversation at a time. Email asks that we be engaged in dozens of exchanges simultaneously.

This hurry-up effect is even more pronounced when using the aptly named instant messaging tools, where real-time interaction is assumed and a failure to get an instant response from someone may be interpreted as a deliberate snub. People who structure their workday around checking email and keeping an instant messaging window open on their screen are more prompt in responding; thus, they are more visible—and probably more influential—in the online communities of which they are members.

Table 6.1   Comparison of Technical and Social Skills in Online Communication vs. Those in Face-to-Face Conversation

IN-PERSON SKILLS	ONLINE SKILLS
Different:	
Eye contact	Typing accuracy
Tone of voice	Spelling
Handshake	Formatting
Posture	Description
Timing	Responsiveness
Facial feedback	Choice of words
Similar:	
Sense of agreement	Sense of agreement
Manners	Manners
Brevity	Brevity
Eloquence	Eloquence
Persuasiveness	Persuasiveness
Insight	Insight
Synthesis	Synthesis
Originality	Originality
Tact	Tact

John Suler, a clinical psychologist who studies online group behaviors at Rider University in New Jersey, affirms that different genres of networked communication media enhance different aspects of our social experience. Being online and communicating with people who are online at the same time, he says, creates a sense of "presence" that conveys *commitment* to the group. Showing up regularly for a scheduled chat reinforces *cohesion* in the group. And he emphasizes that no matter how sophisticated the interface, there is no substitute for in-person encounters, which "help seal the relationship and make it seem more 'real'."[1]

The message conveyed as the by-product of any chosen medium must be considered in the context of its purpose and the culture it is meant to support. The tradeoffs of any virtual medium—for example, more convenience for less intimacy—must be taken into account. Rarely will the fit between technology and culture be perfect, and where it is not, the adjustments that will need to be made, either in the technology or the culture, should be acknowledged from the beginning.

Matching Environment and Culture

The online world is an environment just as surely as are one's physical surroundings. It has different characteristics from the world of trees, sky, walls, windows, and air conditioning, but its features and rules are just as influential on the human activity that takes place within it. In the online world, software defines the virtual environment, and our human faculties interpret what we experience.

Some virtual places may "feel" like library stacks, others like auditoriums, and others like classrooms. The software, the site design, and the culture of the users are components of these electronic social environments. Many factors, including the following, help define the social experience when a group goes online:

1. Availability: how simple it is to access and navigate

2. Appearance: its colors, layout, design, and clarity of purpose

3. Complexity: the number of choices the user has to make

4. Synchronicity: the degree of immediacy in the communications

5. Richness: the amount of information contained in the communication

6. Population: the number of people who can and do use it

7. Depth: its number of layers of content and activity and their searchability

8. Rule structure: the policies in place for using the system

9. Interactivity: the extent to which users can affect its content

10. Privacy: the extent to which access is limited and secured

The results of a cultural assessment and knowledge audit—two evaluative approaches described in Chapter 5, "Fostering a Knowledge-Sharing Culture"— can identify traits that indicate how important these factors are to the people who use the interface. The *artifacts* of a culture—its symbols, language, and stories—can be represented, employed, and conveyed through the tools and design. The *espoused values* of the culture can be supported in the implementation of the technology and in the rules and policies put in place to regulate participation. Even cultural assumptions at the *unconscious* level will be reflected (and affected) as people adapt to working and communicating in the virtual environment.

In Chapter 5, we described the three main aspects of a cultural assessment: gap analysis, cultural alignment, and the fit of individuals to the organization. Here are some simple examples of how the interface might relate to each of these:

Gap analysis. Many gaps in knowledge-sharing values can be closed through the choice of appropriate software and design of the environment. If people are unaccustomed to logging on to a virtual meeting room to engage in conversation with colleagues, an interface that regularly delivers the latest conversational updates to them via email will engage them in a more convenient way and motivate them to gradually increase their participation.

Cultural alignment. Subcultures within the organization can become better aligned through the use of common interfaces and access to shared content. Each subculture may have its distinct conversation area, but some conversations may be shared between groups or across the entire organization so that differences can be aired and the useful cross-pollination of ideas can take place.

Fit of individuals to the organization. This can be improved as the culture goes online by hiring and training people for competence in the use of conversational interfaces. The introduction of new environments for conversation can, in effect, give a culture a fresh start by providing a new context for gathering and interacting where new histories of interaction and new relationships can be built.

Organizations often attempt to replicate established cultural practices when choosing their technologies, but this is not always the best idea. For example, many businesses that before 9/11 were accustomed to holding regular face-to-face meetings among people from geographically distant offices now save on travel time and expense by arranging virtual meetings using videoconferencing interfaces to provide a rich face-to-face experience. Instead of flying across the country, spending the night in a hotel, and sitting together around a conference table, the attendees assemble in special conference rooms in their home offices and converse with one another's video images.

Michael Schrage, of MIT's Media Lab, says such decisions respond to a "substitution imperative" and warns that in these cases simply "throwing bandwidth" at a problem to minimize change in social convention may not be the most effective solution.[2] Though it's cheaper than actual travel, it's still far more expensive than the lower bandwidth solutions of text communication, and the technique used in most cases does not address the real purpose of the meetings. Most video projections focus on the participants' faces yet surveys about the use of videoconferencing reveal that participants would prefer to see more of the *information* that the meeting is about.

Many management surveys through the years have shown that meetings, regardless of their format or environment, are considered by most workers to be the biggest wastes of company time. We've all spent too much time sitting in rooms and waiting for every person to finish talking about subjects that may or may not be relevant to the work we need to get done. Spending money on a video hookup to reproduce the same result seems to be not only inefficient but also unwise, except for the fact that it provides an opportunity for people to make brief (but virtual) eye contact with one another.

superbookdeals.com

Thanks for your order!

We value your business. Now - you can select a **FREE** Book as our "Thank You" gift.*

It's easy - just 3 simple steps!

And - **a Great Selection** to choose from!

(Selection changes *daily*!*)

Get your **FREE** book TODAY!*

Absolutely NO Catch

NO Purchase Necessary

3 Easy Steps

And - it's FREE

3 easy steps

① Go to - www.superbookdeals.com/nocatch

② Fill out the form

③ And your FREE book will be on its way ...

www.superbookdeals.com/nocatch

We recommend that rather than select technologies based on their ability to replicate in-person work practices, leadership should encourage the culture to adapt to technologies that bring maximum efficiency and effectiveness, even if they force some change in cultural habits. It is important to design the interface to serve established cultural traits and needs. However, it is equally important that the design exceeds what is possible in person and provides the culture with a meeting environment that can be customized to its new needs as they arise, which they most certainly will.

Collaborative Design

The best way to select software and design an interface for online collaboration is to get thoughtful input from the culture that will be using it, involving key members early in the process. Including actual users in the initial discussions of the knowledge network allows them to identify and prioritize their knowledge needs while describing their customary communications processes and the structure of their working groups, project teams, or communities of practice.

No one knows better what will work in an online environment than the people who are meant to use it for a purpose. As we've pointed out in previous chapters, the relationships of the user community to IT and to the interface designers are very important to the success of the technology. This involvement should begin early and should be maintained.

If a new interface needs to be designed, interviewing members of the user groups through *use-case surveys* should be part of the predesign process. Through these surveys, individuals describe the tools and capabilities they require and how they will use the interface in a variety of situations. Members' responses are analyzed by interface designers, Web masters, and IT professionals to compile a list of required features, assemble a blueprint for configuring the various software programs, and draw a map showing how various resources—such as the discussion space, information library, and member profiles—will be organized in the knowledge-sharing environment. As iterations of the design are built and made available for testing, the target group then serves as the guinea pigs, trying out the new design and providing input for *tuning* the interface.

The next stage of user involvement comes when the design is final enough to create training programs for its use. Input from future users at this stage identifies gaps in skills and experience that must be addressed through training. This is also the time to bring in representatives of other key areas of expertise within the organization, notably IT and Legal. Their involvement is essential to answer critical questions about security, technical feasibility, and policy considerations for the upcoming online interaction.

Early involvement of a community in the design of its future virtual meeting environment helps ensure that it will be used actively and effectively. The right features will be there, and the members will be prepared. But more important is the fact that such involvement motivates the community to make its project succeed. By helping to build the interface, members have a *sense of ownership* in it. That buy-in will carry forward as the group continues to innovate and customize its knowledge-sharing environment.

Bringing Simple Conversation Online

In the early days of computer networking, email was invented to answer the needs for sending and receiving messages. By 1980, groups were able to exchange similar messages and read them in the stored format of online conversations. These were the Usenet newsgroups. New and unique social conventions grew up around these interfaces *because they were so simple* and because people used only the most basic of the available commands. One could correctly say that a culture formed around the use of the Usenet interface. It was one of the first examples of the computer interface and the culture becoming intertwined.

Leadership and Human Intervention

Before the Web, people coming online for the first time had to adapt their activities to the limited available features rather than expect the interfaces to serve all of their interactive needs. The conferencing interface used at the WELL beginning in 1985 was only slightly more advanced than Usenet's. But the simplicity of a primitive interface is not necessarily a weakness. Simplicity is often the key to adoption of a technology because by presenting the user with fewer choices it requires less learning. Indeed, the *people who lead* the social use of any technology are more influential in the adoption of an interface than the features that are missing or included.

The WELL provided a simple tree-structured environment of *conferences*—grouped-by-topic, text-based collections of conversations, each administered by a so-called *host*. These hosts were entrusted with privileged access to technical tools that allowed them to manage the conduct and content of their conferences. They could freeze a conversation if they decided that everything that could be said had been said. They could remove a conversation from visibility if they thought it had served its purpose. And they could remove the contents of a posted message if it violated their local ground rules for participation. The capabilities of the software determined, in part, the social structure and ethics of the WELL culture. No host, for example, could remove a member's message without a notice appearing that the erasure had taken place. That feature guarded against a host surreptitiously censoring someone's message without any notice or explanation—a clear abuse of power in our freedom-of-speech culture.

Writer Thomas A. Stewart tells a story of how a consultant in the firm Price Waterhouse (before its 1998 merger with Coopers and Lybrand) joined with some colleagues to create a network where they could, in their words, "collaborate so as to be more innovative."[3] To that end, they set up an email list on

Lotus Notes with "no rules, no moderator, and no agenda except the messages people send." Though the list was originally set up to serve a small group, it was open to any other employee. As of the writing date of the article, it had grown to 500 members and was considered the premier forum for knowledge sharing in the company. Lotus Notes has no advanced features for administering large email lists or for searching their contents. It's not an "ideal" platform in terms of design. Yet, the simple email list works because the right people use it, its use requires no training, and as the article points out, it's *demand-driven*.

The WELL's user community collaborated with its management in making improvements in the interface, but it was never the software that determined the culture. The social interaction and collaborative debugging of the conversational process made the WELL distinctive and attractive. There's no doubt that the PricewaterhouseCoopers group could benefit from some additional features for managing its growing volume of messages and participants. There is a place for appropriate technology if the users have a part in its selection and design.

The WELL had a slogan: "Tools, not rules." Wherever possible, the company would respond to customers' suggestions by creating a technical feature (or accepting an already created one from a technically adept customer) that would add to convenience or serve as a form of social mediation. Some of these tools allowed customers to configure their use of the WELL according to their social preferences. These tools also relieved management of some onerous and time-consuming responsibilities as social mediators and enforcers.

We tried hard to keep written rules to the absolute minimum, believing that fewer rules meant less inhibition and more creativity. In fact, our most effective methods for regulating the community turned out to be neither tools nor rules; they were setting good examples, selecting good hosts, and using public diplomacy. But *personalization*—the ability for the individual to tailor his or her online experience—can definitely eliminate some irritants from the use of an interface and can encourage people to participate more fully in online communities.

Conversation Filtering

Tools that allow the user to personalize the online experience do eliminate the need for some rules. For example, most interactive group discussion interfaces now include a feature that allows individual users to *filter* the content presented to them. In some cases, they can choose to filter out messages posted by specific people. At the WELL, we called such a tool a *bozo filter* while other interfaces refer to it as the *Ignore* feature. In many interfaces, users can rate messages based on their helpfulness or quality and can choose to be shown only messages rated higher than a selected level. Still another filtering feature allows users to *subscribe* only to the conversations they want to be shown each time they visit.

These are all, in some sense, time-saving conveniences, but they also serve to improve the user's overall *qualitative* experience of the environment. If the quality of the perceived experience can be improved in terms of convenience, relevance, utility, and interpersonal compatibility, the user is more likely to be a regular participant. Such filters map to the social techniques people commonly employ for in-person interaction, where they selectively pay attention to some people (and some conversations) and ignore others. Some cultures may choose not to have filters because it's important to them that every member be exposed to everything and to everyone else.

As we'll describe in the next chapter, there are many different products available to support online conversation. Many different aspects of a culture may determine the features that are most appropriate and effective. These include the size of the population, the duration of its task, the kind of work that needs to be done, and the physical locations of its members. But the *style and protocol* of its interaction and conversation are the most important criteria for choosing the software that it will find most useful.

Tools and Their Configuration

When computers and software were used only to crunch numbers, interface design was simply a matter of making input and output as simple as possible. Once networked computers became broad-based environments for communication and information sharing, their inadequacies for replicating in-person or even telephone interaction became obvious. The virtual social experience, though always advancing, will probably never be indistinguishable from physical presence.

Yet, as computers have improved at a rapid rate, the software that exploits their increased power and speed has brought us closer to providing options for reproducing the different ways we naturally communicate as humans. Not all of our conversations are the same. Some are one-on-one, others take place in a group, some are brief, and others are extended. Some are all business, and others are casual. So how do these translate to the capabilities of software? Consider the following choices, many of which overlap in their capabilities with each other.

The Genres of Online Conversation

In Chapter 7, we will provide some detailed descriptions of specific software programs and interfaces that support knowledge-sharing conversation. But in the context of their effect on social interaction and culture, we present the following descriptions of the main categories of those technical tools:

Email is, well, like mail: written correspondence, except it doesn't take days or weeks for an exchange to take place. It was the original online communications tool and is still the most widely used. One can send a message to an individual or a group that can be received almost instantly. A message can contain text, graphics, Web pages, animation, video, audio, or software. One can easily respond to any or all of the other recipients of a received message. Email client programs can be configured to filter and organize one's email to prioritize and keep track of numerous ongoing conversations. Email lists can serve as newsletters or as ongoing focused discussions. They can be moderated to reduce the noise-to-signal ratio, or their contents can be sent out in daily or weekly *digests* to reduce the clutter of individual messages.

Discussion is like meetings conducted through text. *Discussion* is our umbrella term for any asynchronous interface where multiple separate conversations can take place. Just as with email, the participants don't have to be using the system at the same time, but if they are, their exchange with each other can be almost instantaneous. Again, one can be involved in multiple conversations simultaneously, but in this case, all of the conversations are available in the same form to all of the participants, and those conversations—accessible through the same Web address—are easier to navigate than a collection of email folders.

Discussions can be open to all members of a community or privately accessible to only a few. Most discussion environments provide descriptive *profiles* of participants and tools for managing the contents of the discussion space. Old conversations can be retired and archived, and duplicate conversations can be merged. Completed conversations can be closed to new responses, and profiles can be searched at least by names.

Chat is conversation with time-based *presence*. Participating in a chat exchange is analogous to sticking one's head into a coworker's cubicle and asking a quick question or just making social contact. Chat (and instant messaging) happen in real time, unlike email and discussion where one can leave a message that might not be seen for hours or days.

In chat, there is a sensation of immediate engagement. Two people or a small group can carry on a very productive public or private conversation in a real-time environment. The conversation can be archived and reviewed, just as in email and discussion. But the immediacy of the interaction doesn't encourage deep thinking and the composition of long, careful responses, as do the asynchronous interfaces.

P2P, or *peer-to-peer* interfaces, are decentralized in that they are meant for communicating and sharing information between the personal computers of two or more correspondents without going through a hub or server. Instant messaging (IM) programs are similar to P2P programs because they connect individual peers using the same client software programs, but most IMs depend on central servers to coordinate communications.

True P2P programs directly connect client programs on individual personal computers to share documents, send and receive messages, and maintain shared schedules. They replicate the ad hoc arrangements that people make to collaborate as small groups on projects or interests without being slowed down by the central bureaucracy of the organization.

Video transmits the animated true-life faces and voices of participants. In its high bandwidth, most natural looking mode, videoconferencing is expensive. There's some question that, after the introductions, what people really want to see in such meetings is the faces rather than the information being exchanged. If the content of the meeting is better portrayed as numbers, charts, or Power Point slides, a phone call combined with some simple file transfers or email attachments will serve just as well for much lower expense.

Document sharing media are included in some groupware solutions that will be described in the next chapter. These may include coedited documents and virtual whiteboards or Web pages that can be worked on collaboratively by remote team members. These usually augment voice or text conversations and may be included in the Event genre that follows. Software is also available that allows groups to follow a leader's tour through Web pages, a sort of "guided Web surfing."

Event environments seem to fit better into most organizations' needs and budgets these days with their increased restrictions on business travel. They permit the presence and immediacy of a true meeting format, including slide presentations, shared documents, and virtual whiteboards, while concentrating on synchronizing voice communications with those transmitted presentations. Chat conversation also can be coordinated with the information displays.

A powerful intranet can provide access to most or all of the foregoing communications options through specialized portals. Only P2P solutions stand alone, outside the context of the intranet. But each of these media, if used exclusively as the sole communications method for a knowledge community, will shape the format of the community in some way. Again, this can be beneficial; forcing change in communications practices often can bring out more of a group's communication potential. But if the wrong tools are chosen, or if adoption is rushed, the group may resist and become even less communicative as a result.

Fitting Diverse Subcultures

The challenge of matching interface with culture is simplified if there is a single, homogeneous culture in the organization. If communications methods and social networks are well established and stable, choosing the appropriate tools from the preceding list may not be so complex, especially given the flexible, multigenre nature of many products (which will be described in Chapter 7).

On the other hand, if an organization is large and diverse enough that distinct subcultures exist, each with different needs and habits, then the selection of tools and overall interface design must account for those differences. In the interest of economy and efficiency, the organization will want to avoid building completely different interfaces for each subculture but will still want to serve their differing styles of communication. If at all possible, a base or *platform* should be assembled that can be adapted, through custom formatting, to the unique needs and preferences of the various subcultures within the organization.

Building a replicable platform was the approach in designing for the initial customer community at Cisco Systems. The technical and business teams assembled tools and features—for conversation, content production, event calendars, and event presentations—at the *portal* level for the pilot project: the Networking Professionals Community. All of the components of that portal could be replicated to build other portals, and anyone in the company, regardless of their line of business, would be able to navigate to any specific knowledge portal on Cisco's intranet or extranet. There, they would find tools that were familiar though distinctive in their presentation.

Such an arrangement offers economies of scale in terms of software, engineering, design, and employee training because the one platform, with slight modification, can be used across all of the different internal or customer-facing communities. One training program can be adapted to serve all community staffs and stakeholders. A database and searching tool can gather and find knowledge that crosses business disciplines and departments. These original goals were realized in the creation of new knowledge-sharing community portals a year after the original community was launched. Yet there were important lessons learned in the design and implementation stages.

The Impact of Format on Conversation

How a communications tool is formatted can significantly affect culture by restricting the way people are able to interact. Here is one common example with a long history where a discussion interface offers two different options for configuring conversation: *linear* and *threading*. Though they both support group interaction using text, these two very distinct structures determine the order, continuity, and responsive style of a conversation and can strongly influence the direction a conversation takes and who will participate in it.

Linear Discussion Format

As Figure 6.1 illustrates, a conversation in a linear format is simply a series of *responses* following from the *topic header*, which serves as the title and intro-

THE USE-CASE PITFALL

Although use-case surveys are meant to describe all of the possible features and choices the eventual users will want to have in an online environment, experience in designing Cisco's initial customer community showed how bad surveys and insufficient research can lead to poor results.

A technical consulting company was contracted to build the interface in conjunction with a business process team. The company selected a well-known and widely used software program for supporting online discussion. Their responsibility was to conduct use-case surveys of prospective users to determine the configuration and feature set required in the discussion interface. Unfortunately, they had no experience using such software and did not appreciate the importance of certain features.

As a result, they did not include certain essential options in the use-case surveys. People taking the surveys, not being offered those options, did not ask for them, so they were not included in the first iteration of the discussion interface. The first usability tests rejected the interface as clumsy and confusing.

The lesson: When installing new interface tools, bring in experts with experience in the use of the tools to make sure all of the configuration options are understood and included in use-case surveys.

ductory message for the ensuing conversation. The order of responses reflects the order in which people log on and post them. Sometimes the central topic of the conversation is interrupted (Response #3). This can lead to *topic drift* (Response #4) unless an attentive *moderator* (Response #6) brings the discussion back *on topic* by suggesting that the drift initiator start a new topic about his or her tangential interest. Using linear structure, this would be the most appropriate method for accommodating new linear topics.

A linear conversation is most useful when the reader can scroll up and down on the computer screen, navigating to different responses or conversational passages to get the context of the discussion. This is a more natural way of following a coherent conversation as opposed to the alternative approach of viewing only one response per screen. The best software gives the user the option of having the entire conversation displayed as one scrolling document or of breaking it up into page-sized chunks.

Threading Discussion Format

A similar conversation portrayed in a threading format is illustrated in Figure 6.2. Note the difference in terminology. The ability to respond directly, and separately, to a *message* (A) means that there is no need for a moderator to bring the discussion back on topic: Each thread becomes its own topic, which readers are free to follow or ignore as they wish. The main *spine* of the topic (B) continues on where participants respond directly to the header. But with no

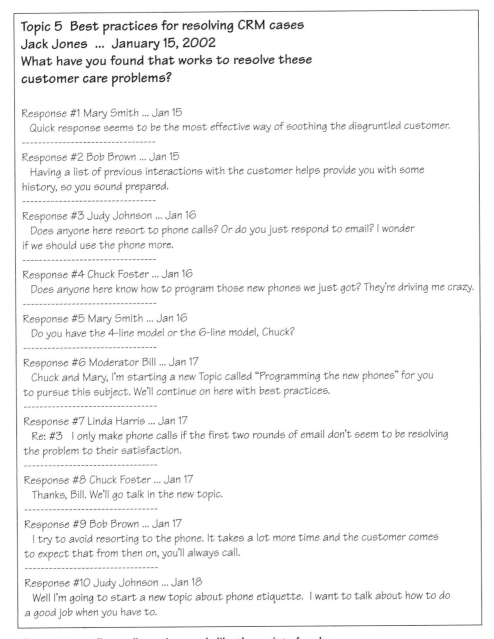

Topic 5 Best practices for resolving CRM cases
Jack Jones ... January 15, 2002
What have you found that works to resolve these
customer care problems?

Response #1 Mary Smith ... Jan 15
   Quick response seems to be the most effective way of soothing the disgruntled customer.

Response #2 Bob Brown ... Jan 15
   Having a list of previous interactions with the customer helps provide you with some
history, so you sound prepared.

Response #3 Judy Johnson ... Jan 16
   Does anyone here resort to phone calls? Or do you just respond to email? I wonder
if we should use the phone more.

Response #4 Chuck Foster ... Jan 16
   Does anyone here know how to program those new phones we just got? They're driving me crazy.

Response #5 Mary Smith ... Jan 16
   Do you have the 4-line model or the 6-line model, Chuck?

Response #6 Moderator Bill ... Jan 17
   Chuck and Mary, I'm starting a new Topic called "Programming the new phones" for you
to pursue this subject. We'll continue on here with best practices.

Response #7 Linda Harris ... Jan 17
   Re: #3   I only make phone calls if the first two rounds of email don't seem to be resolving
the problem to their satisfaction.

Response #8 Chuck Foster ... Jan 17
   Thanks, Bill. We'll go talk in the new topic.

Response #9 Bob Brown ... Jan 17
   I try to avoid resorting to the phone. It takes a lot more time and the customer comes
to expect that from then on, you'll always call.

Response #10 Judy Johnson ... Jan 18
   Well I'm going to start a new topic about phone etiquette. I want to talk about how to do
a good job when you have to.

Figure 6.1   A linear discussion reads like the script of a play.

moderator present, a thread's subject may wander far from the original intent of
the topic (C), confusing readers who depend on the topic header to inform
them of its contents.

Topic 5 Best practices for resolving CRM cases
Jack Jones ... January 15, 2002
What have you found that works to resolve these customer care problems?

Message #1 Mary Smith ... Jan 15
   Quick response seems to be the most effective way of soothing the disgruntled customer.

Message #2 Bob Brown ... Jan 15
   Having a list of previous interactions with the customer helps provide you with some history, so you sound prepared.

Message #3 Judy Johnson ... Jan 16
   Does anyone here resort to phone calls? Or do you just respond to email? I wonder if we should use the phone more.

A --Response #1 Linda Harris ... Jan 17
   I only make phone calls if the first two rounds of email don't
   seem to be resolving the problem to their satisfaction.

   --Response #2 Bob Brown ... Jan 17
   I try to avoid resorting to the phone. It takes a lot more time
   and the customer comes to expect that from then on, you'll
B always call.

Message #4 Chuck Foster ... Jan 16
   Does anyone here know how to program those new phones we just got? They're driving me crazy!
   --Response #1 Mary Smith ... Jan 16
   Do you have the 4-line model or the 6-line model, Chuck?

      --Response #1 Chuck Foster ... Jan 17
      I think they work the same, Mary.

C --Reponse #2 Judy Johnson ... Jan 17
   I liked the old phones. At least they were easy to use.

Message #5 Linda Harris ... Jan 17
   I keep a contact list of people in engineering, inventory and shipping to help me answer questions and get replacement authorizations quickly.
   --Response #1 Bob Brown ... Jan 18
   How did you find someone in engineering who would talk
   to you?

Figure 6.2 A threading conversation invites interruption and the branching off of threads from the main spine of the topic.

For coherence, each person who posts in a threading topic should first understand how to use *messages* as opposed to *responses*. If a user posts a message in response to another message, the conversational pattern breaks down and confusion results.

Note also that in threading software interfaces, there is often no scrolling display for conversations. Readers must click separately to open and read each message. Reading such a fragmented conversation is distracting, like listening to people talking over CB radio where every comment is followed by "Over" or "Back to you." For busy people, screen-by-screen participation in a conversation can seem laborious and inefficient.

Certainly not all groups are drawn to the long and extended conversations that are best supported by linear formats. When people are more interested in getting direct answers to specific questions—often provided by one experienced person rather than a group—the threading interface is considered easier to use and quicker to enter and exit. However, when people are more interested in posting their opinions rather than engaging in discussion, a threading format is more appropriate.

Regardless of the format, the members of an online conversational culture need to be *considerate* in the way they use their interface. Clarity, brevity, proper use of the conversational structure, and attention to staying on topic all make for more productive and effective communication.

Appropriate format is important, but the selection of appropriate tools should also consider the *social* characteristics of the groups that will use them. These aspects are especially relevant when the participants are new to meeting online, which is why some analysis of these cultural tendencies should take place before designing and formatting the platform for the group's virtual meeting place.

Through our years of working with online communities, we've developed a methodology for analysis that helps us to frame the interface needs of a conversational group. Such groups differ in ways that can be described along three overlapping dimensions, which describe their tendencies to converse, define common interests, and identify with each other.

Three Dimensions of Collaboration

In the previous chapter, we described three different relationships between people and content. These ranged from groups that interacted without concern for other content to groups focused entirely on content of common interest. Between the two extremes were groups that interacted about shared content. Now we'll describe three dimensions along which groups can be distinguished from each other in terms of their style of collaboration. These dimensions help picture the balance of conversation and information that needs to be served in a group's ideal online environment. We refer to these dimensions as *interactivity*, *focus*, and *cohesion*, and each of them is considered along a continuum ranging from high to low.

The Tendency to Interact

Some groups thrive on interaction. It is required as part of their community definition. We described these groups in Chapter 5, "Fostering a Knowledge-Sharing Environment," and showed them yakking away with their small bubbles of focus floating about. Members of these groups are driven to check in often with their fellow conversationalists to discover and share the subtle tacit knowledge that they hold. Their purpose may be professional or social, but in either case, they exchange a lot of information and are constantly building trust and relationships as they converse. In a normal online session, they will spend 80 percent of their time in email, chat, or discussion rather than searching for information or viewing content.

Groups at the other end of the continuum couldn't care less about interaction. They are interested only in the information that will quickly answer their immediate questions, be it in documents, statistics, news, or graphic files. Members of these groups spend a minimal amount of time answering the obligatory email about the subjects that tie them together.

Most groups depend on a combination of interaction and content, with one complementing the other. They may converse intensively for a week, put together a research plan, then spend the next week assembling a library of documents and reading them. They may divide their online time constantly between interaction and content, or they may go through cycles of intense interaction and relative inactivity.

Serving High Interaction

How a group naturally behaves along this continuum can define which genres and feature sets of the online interfaces will best serve its purposes. For a highly interactive community, feature-rich conversation tools are essential. For a barely interactive community, a good online publishing system and database combined with email may suffice.

The immediacy of the communication required also determines the kind of tools that are needed. Teams hard at work on a project may require secure instant messaging to share knowledge that can be put to use in the moment. Groups that are learning collaboratively without hard deadlines will be served well by message boards or email lists.

Where interactivity needs are high, a group may require a structured interface (for organizing and preserving their conversations) and tools for moderating conversation (to guide and facilitate efficient discussion). Hosts require software tools to fulfill their online social leadership activities.

The technical interface, in communities of high interactivity, must also provide searchable, descriptive *member profiles* to inform people of each other's skills, backgrounds, and interests. In a social network, such personal context is just as important as the information that fills the core of the group's common interest. In a knowledge network, all participants will have a credibility factor associated with the experience and know-how they bring to the conversation.

A community's tendencies toward interactivity and conversation may evolve, of course, once they have access to the means for conducting online conversation. For a group that is geographically scattered, shared access to a message board may be its first opportunity to initiate discussion and continue communicating day after day. The online discussion space may provide the first chance for natural group leadership to emerge and motivate wider participation in the dialogue. That leadership can be at least as important as the interface in stimulating interaction, but poor interface design can frustrate attempts to conduct effective discussion.

The Degree of Focus

Communities naturally come together around common interests. For some, those interests are vital and concentrated, but for others, they are more casual and diffuse. Most of us identify with many different communities, with our focus ranging from intense involvement (raising kids, immediate health concerns, a current job) to amused curiosity (the football rankings, lawn care techniques, Hollywood gossip).

A highly focused knowledge community, such as a project team with a hard deadline, will have agreed-upon goals, acknowledged experts, concentrated information needs, and aligned motivation. In an office setting, these people would talk to each other frequently, hold a standing reservation on a conference room, schedule regular meetings, map out and follow a work process, and set mileposts for establishing their progress.

Focused communities are the best populations for leading online pilot projects because their inherent motivation to solve common problems helps them clearly recognize and agree on their communication needs. Their members participate with enthusiasm and are aware of how the interface slows them down or inhibits their collaboration. They help debug initial attempts at platform design so that subsequent communities, which may not be so unified and focused, will have a smoother time using their versions of the platform.

Groups with no common focus don't really qualify as groups at all. But a realistic other end of the focus continuum would be people in the organization who primarily work on their own but share interest in company news and resources provided through the intranet. Their interface needs are no more special than any other member of the organization.

Serving High Focus

In the context of serving high focus through online interfaces, the main differences between groups are in how much of their time is spent in the online environment pursuing their focused activities. Those activities probably include lots of conversation and access to common libraries of information. Access to their online area may be restricted to maintain high levels of expertise and continuity.

High focus also adds to the list of requirements a higher level of expert leadership. Knowledge sharing and learning usually put a group's focus into the higher range because of the specificity and immediacy of the knowledge being sought. But focus, as we all know, is difficult to maintain.

The longer a focused community remains intact, the less focused it may become. It won't look that way from the outside, but within even the most narrowly focused group, the diversification process is at work. A project to design a single product soon breaks into many subprojects for organizing the many pieces of design and production. A team brought together to plan an event is soon involved in many different conversations about the various aspects of planning, security, lighting, sound, parking, publicity, and so forth.

A population with little in common, provided with the ability to meet and converse, will tend to organize and form many different communities of focus. Most public community sites on the Web began by attracting random Web surfers and evolved into collections of small online neighborhoods formed around a wide variety of subjects: people from California, libertarians, NASCAR fans, singles looking for dates, people with diabetes, and so on.

The previous two paragraphs illustrate that group focus at either end of the continuum seems not to be a stable situation. In our experience, the focus of most groups tends to oscillate around a middle point, being more intense at times about some subjects and less intense at other times about different subjects. This leads us to believe that the tools for serving knowledge communities should be able to support a wide range and that designing for the high-focus needs is the best practice for most groups.

The Effects of Group Cohesion

Very loyal groups—those with a high level of internal identification, commitment, and significant history—behave differently from those that have only recently come together or that recognize few common interests. Cohesion is different from focus in that it is based more on trust, whereas focus is based more on topic. The interpersonal relationships in cohesive groups are strong. They can endure difficulties, even inadequate interfaces and the technical problems that periodically prevent members from connecting.

Cohesion doesn't drive communities to learn or meet deadlines. High cohesion builds familiarity and shared knowledge over time. Cohesive groups understand which members know what and have established practices for interaction and collaboration. They may have formed before they had access to an online meeting space, but their social ties are solid and serve as incentives to bring all members into whatever meeting environment is agreed upon.

Less cohesive communities might fall apart because of such problems as interface difficulties, internal disagreements, miscommunication, absence of strong leadership, and the occasional breakdown in group connectivity. They require much more technical reliability and better custom interface design to keep them together.

Interactivity, Focus, Cohesion, and Interface Design

The three dimensions for evaluating a group's collaborative tendencies are closely related. We can imagine groups that are very interactive, very focused, and very cohesive, yet few actual communities fit that description all of the time. Most groups that can benefit by conversational knowledge exchange are high in only one or two dimensions and then only some of the time. A highly interactive community may not be very focused. A newly formed community won't have much cohesion, though it may be very interactive. A community with intense focus may not feel compelled to interact at all, preferring to have common access to content that is kept current and detailed.

In Figure 6.3, we show four examples of communities with different profiles along the three continuums of interactivity, focus, and cohesion. Each profile describes different interface needs.

Profile A, a short-term project team, calls for an interface that all members can access and use quickly, with minimum need for training or technical integration. With no group history and a short group lifetime, simplicity of use is the most important factor. Email may be sufficient if there is no need for organizing numerous parallel conversations. A basic message board with access limited to team members would permit some helpful organization of project-related discussions. A content publishing component would permit team members to post documents and to share project management timelines.

Profile B, a stable department within an organization, needs an online meeting place for certain administrative conversations and content but is driven more by routine than deadlines. It has the time to learn how to use and manage its space on the intranet. It can benefit by preserving certain conversations as a record of interaction. A basic message board that can send out the latest postings in email will serve to involve employees who don't voluntarily log on to the site. Such staffers receive digests of online conversations on a regular basis, inviting them to participate but not forcing them to spend much of their time in the virtual meeting environment. The environment serves as a gathering place for shared knowledge and a conversation space for sharing knowledge when it is required.

Profile C is a group of workers who lack the time to get online regularly but who hold valuable knowledge about their hands-on skills and experience. Regular daily or weekly reports or involvement in periodic online debriefings may serve as the means to harvest their knowledge and allow them to tap into the knowledge of

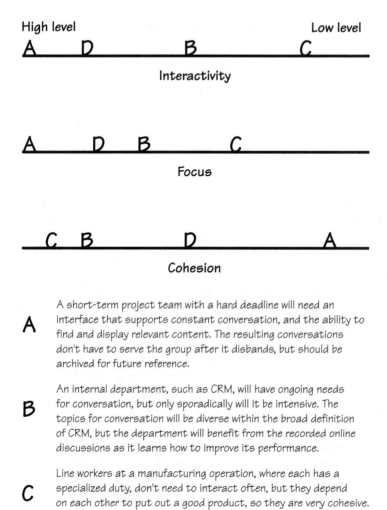

Profiling Group Relationship

High level   Low level

A   D   B   C

Interactivity

A   D   B   C

Focus

C B   D   A

Cohesion

A   A short-term project team with a hard deadline will need an interface that supports constant conversation, and the ability to find and display relevant content. The resulting conversations don't have to serve the group after it disbands, but should be archived for future reference.

B   An internal department, such as CRM, will have ongoing needs for conversation, but only sporadically will it be intensive. The topics for conversation will be diverse within the broad definition of CRM, but the department will benefit from the recorded online discussions as it learns how to improve its performance.

C   Line workers at a manufacturing operation, where each has a specialized duty, don't need to interact often, but they depend on each other to put out a good product, so they are very cohesive. They can enter reports weekly or whenever they encounter problems that need to be addressed.

D   A community of practice, where employees communicate about a shared interest outside of the work environment, is focused and interactive, driven by personal motivation. Yet, since it is not strictly work-related, it is only as cohesive as its members spare time allows.

Figure 6.3   Four group profiles and the implications for their most appropriate interface design features.

other resources in the company. Because they spend so little time online, their interface to the Net should be as simple and quick to use as possible. Online surveys and email might be the most appropriate way to gain their participation.

Profile D is an ongoing, focused population that interacts for enjoyment. The knowledge generated in their conversations may or may not be of direct value to the company, but their relationships do offer the potential of releasing valuable knowledge and experience indirectly available to the company. Communities of practice are cohesive as long as their members work for the organization and have time to participate, but their motivations are powerful for making the best use of whatever tools are available for group communication. As we'll describe in Chapters 7 and 8, communities of practice differ greatly in their needs for technology. Their motivating focus makes them more adaptive than communities that are formed more artificially to accomplish work-related tasks.

Initial group tendencies, as we've pointed out, are not deterministic; they are likely to change and fluctuate. But as a group takes its first steps into the online meeting space, it's worthwhile to address these natural tendencies for collaboration with the intention of making its early experience as nondisruptive as possible. Forcing cultural change by trying to fit square-peg cultures into round-hole interfaces has a low probability of success. But once accustomed to working through an online interface, the square pegs can change their shape and adapt to interfaces that they find more helpful to their reaching goals.

Knowing the People and the Policies

Besides the software that enables conversation and content publishing, there are two other key elements that can make or break an online knowledge-sharing network. One has to do with the people who are considered members of the network, and the other has to do with the rules that apply to use of the network. Both must be available through the interface if effective communication is going to take place.

The Power of Personal Profiles

Most intranets provide space for their users to describe themselves to varying degrees of depth and detail. Some companies provide only name, title, and contact information, but others permit users to post more elaborate descriptions including personal histories, information about hobbies and family, and even entire Web-based home pages.

In a knowledge-sharing community, it's important to know with whom you're communicating, and to be able to find people with whom you need to communicate. Such professional and experiential information is often posted in what are called *yellow pages* directories, searchable from within the intranet or specific portal used by the community. Many discussion software programs also provide fields to be filled in by each registered user that can be accessed by other users from within the interface. Ideally, though, the profile page should be customized to the needs of the specific knowledge community, with access to some field restricted to that community.

Detailed personal profiles, even with photos and other graphics, can fill the same need for rich content that some believe can be obtained only through in-person presence or high-bandwidth videoconferencing. Appropriate profile design can elicit well-rounded descriptions of community members that engender trust—the gold standard in knowledge exchange.

Policies and Guidelines

A knowledge-sharing community's culture combined with the features of its online interface describe most of its style and process, but policies and guidelines clarify its boundaries, manners, and ideal behaviors. Just as appropriate tools and interfaces are important to implement on the technical side, *appropriate use* is important to define on the social side.

Policies generally align with an organization's internal values and legal limitations. Examples of policies relevant to online conversation are to not share company secrets with outsiders and to be courteous with customers contacted through the Net. There may also be policies describing who in the company has access to which portals and information directories.

And by now, every company should have a very visible and comprehensible privacy policy on both its internal and public-facing Web sites. Where the population has any questions about personal privacy in an online community, a policy should be spelled out for that purpose. Information entered in one's professional profile should not, for example, be distributed publicly without the owner's consent.

In some companies and situations, people with ideas, suggestions, or complaints to offer for the benefit of the company are reluctant to post them online under their true names. A company must decide whether or not to allow anonymous participation in online exchange or how such anonymous contributions can be made. Of course, the ideal is to have sufficient trust in the organization that fear of reprisal is not a factor, but few organizations of any size engender such openness.

Policies regarding entitlement—who has access to what portal or conversation space—can have a great effect on culture. Restricting access to conversations can keep them more focused, increase trust, build cohesion, and make them both more effective and more efficient. But restricting access also can block valuable complementary or critical voices from being heard or prevent the cross-fertilization of useful ideas from diverse viewpoints and other communities.

Guidelines, as distinguished from policies, are more proscriptive, suggesting interactive habits that are supportive of interaction and would be good for community members to develop. One useful guideline for posting messages in almost any online conversation is to divide messages into small paragraphs for easier reading. Another reliable guideline is to keep messages as short and concise as possible. And of course, welcoming newcomers to an online meeting place is not only good manners, but it leads to greater overall trust and participation.

An online community's policies and guidelines should provide a pretty accurate reflection of its culture. Guidelines may differ among an organization's subcultures. Policies generally come from the top level of the organization, though a cohesive community of practice may have its own policies for membership or submission of new content. In the interest of preventing too much irrelevant conversation, a focused knowledge community might also have its own policies limiting the range of topics that can be addressed in its online forum.

It's often through guidelines, which gradually grow into a compendium of good practices discovered in actual interaction, that online cultures become established and evolve. Guidelines, in some sense, reflect the folk history of the community and incorporate its distinct jargon. Guidelines should be open to expansion and modification by the members of the community and should be made prominently available to prospective and new members as they join.

External Collaborative Communities

So far, we've been looking at culture almost exclusively in the context of internal communities and knowledge-sharing activities. But increasingly, organizations are communicating with external communities for a variety of reasons. Carrying on knowledge-sharing and knowledge-seeking conversations with customers, vendors, partners, and consultants requires a *cultural interface* between that of the organization and that of the group on the other end of the communication.

Companies increasingly use the Web to learn about the people they do business with. Marketplaces are increasingly showing themselves to be conversations. The terms of those conversations are increasingly escaping control by the company, even when it provides the conversational interface. The customer is often more seasoned in use of the Web than the company providing the service. The customer is in the driver's seat.

The implications of these truths to this chapter are that the company must learn to be as sophisticated in its use of interactive technologies as the people it is trying to serve. Instant messaging may not be the most compatible communications format for an organization's culture to use internally, but it may be the necessary format for responding to requests for support from customers pushing its online shopping carts through a confusing Web-based catalogue. An online discussion community provided for users of the company's products cannot become a forum for argument about the company's sales return policies. The company's presence in the public forum of the Internet marketplace must be as a member of this new relationship, this new culture where the common interest is high-quality product and service. We'll focus on some best practices in knowledge sharing with external communities in Chapter 9, "Conversing with External Stakeholders."

Summary

There is an undeniable link between the elements of a culture and the environment in which the culture exists. When the environment is Cyberspace, that link is even more significant because the technical world lends itself to relatively simple customization. Communication in a virtual space requires new skills and rewards different aptitudes from those that work in the face-to-face world. And each different medium and format for conversation in the virtual world adds its own distinct context to the communication that takes place through it. For those reasons, it's important to understand those contexts and to understand the elements of a group's culture before choosing and designing its online meeting place. Simplicity of design and minimal disruption in routine communications methods are often more effective for encouraging knowledge exchange than elaborate software solutions.

Cultural assessment and knowledge auditing help match groups to compatible technical features as a culture takes its interaction online. Evaluating a group's propensities for interaction, focus, and cohesion is important in selecting appropriate software and designing the knowledge exchange space. Software and portal designs have identifiable strengths and weaknesses that can make the transition from in-person to virtual communication smoother or, if choices are made carelessly, disastrous. It pays to design the virtual destination right the first time because bad experiences become disincentives for making second efforts.

Well-designed online environments are malleable and likely to be changed once a culture begins using them. The environment affects the culture just as the culture should be able to affect its environment. An organization must decide, as it begins building a virtual space for knowledge sharing, whether that space is dedicated to only one of its subcultures or is meant to serve as a template for use by others of its subcultures. Tools that can be formatted to meet diverse needs and cultural habits provide the economy and flexibility that allow the organization and each distinct subculture to customize them and adapt them to fit different purposes and styles of communication.

It's important to remember that a culture's tendencies can and will change with time, after the transition to the virtual meeting space. Carry QueRY to pages]Initial design for that space should not be set in stone but should be compatible enough with the group's current habits to motivate its members to use it with as smooth a transition as possible. Appropriate policies and guidelines will further smooth the transition.

Where the virtual meeting space is to be shared between internal and external cultures, design needs of the external groups should have top priority. They are, after all, the guests in the conversation. Only if they are satisfied enough to participate can the company learn what it needs to know from them.

Choosing and Using Technology

Physically scattered groups that need to converse have many options today. This chapter describes some of the networked technologies that can be used to fit the descriptions and serve the purposes of different teams, business units, and populations. These technologies are, indeed, tools that must answer the needs of the groups and their individual members if they're going to be used by them. Knowledge networks exist to get things done, and once they have set their goals and agreed on their common motivation, they need the conversation-enabling tools that will best fit their particular needs.

The tools that support group conversation on the Net fall into familiar genres: email, chat, instant messaging, message boards, and the more recent arrivals of real-time meeting interfaces and peer-to-peer (P2P) applications. Intranets and portals are the underlying technical structures through which these communications tools are often provided within the organization. It's through intranets and portals that access to relevant information is also provided. The tools we describe in this chapter will be used in combinations. They will be configured differently for different groups. They will be customized by individuals, and as more power comes to portals and P2P applications, they will be adapted constantly to the changing needs of their user populations. Our descriptions here are but snapshots of a fast-evolving marketplace of communications software.

Any one of these genres of conversation-supporting interfaces can serve a wide range of circumstances. Our experience tells us that the dynamics and interface needs of conversational groups vary most according to their *size* and the *duration* of their conversations. You may be seeking technical solutions for an entire company or for a small project team. The duration of your needs may be only until the project is completed or lasting well into the foreseeable future. Customers may be directly involved in the conversations, or the members may be participating as students, learning new skills. There are many dimensions for evaluating the technical needs of your group, and we've considered several different approaches to organizing this chapter. We've chosen to order it by the genre of the technology, in each case commenting on the effects of the size and duration of the knowledge-sharing group on the implementation and configuration of the specific online interface.

We mention specific products here, but not necessarily because we know them to be the best of their breed. There is a large market for online communication and knowledge networking tools, and some are better in a given situation than others. We include specific products because they help us illustrate features that serve various knowledge-related purposes. Our descriptions of these tools focus on their ability, in combination with good management and social practices, to achieve the purposes of the knowledge networks that employ them. Our goal in this chapter is to help you in your search for the right tools for the right job.

Tools for Every Purpose

First a caution: When all is said and done, knowledge networking is not really about the technology. A poor choice of tools for conversing online is less likely to undermine the success of your efforts than your lack of a common purpose and a clear reason for conversing online. If your group agrees on its purpose and is motivated to get something useful out of its knowledge-sharing conversation, even the most rudimentary online interface will be sufficient at least for starting your conversations.

Getting a good start is, after all, the best you can do. If the conversation happens and the community is actively learning, it will begin to figure out its own best way of interacting. That is almost certain to drive changes in the technology that supports the conversation. So, as we emphasize throughout this book, it's important to *select technology that can be modified as simply and inexpensively as possible*—software that comes with an assortment of potential features that can be implemented or withheld by the group's software administrator based on the group's changing needs.

Simplicity and Power

Of course, no online interface will ever provide the experience of sitting in a room together. There will always be room for improvement in the virtual meeting place, but an amazing amount of knowledge can be exchanged through the use of even the simplest level of email. Texaco's knowledge management guru, John Olds, said, "Use the simplest technology you can for the purpose at hand."[1] We would say complex technology is fine as long as the complexity provides power for experienced users, but make the basic user interface as simple as it can be to get the knowledge flowing.

Simplicity is good primarily because it lowers the barriers to adoption. Email is a fine starting place for knowledge networking because it's a familiar and frequently used technology. But the purpose of your knowledge network may be hindered by the limitations of a simple email list. For example, it's difficult for even as few as 20 people to be actively engaged in coherent conversation in a single email list. When the single conversation thread of the email list is forced to accommodate several different conversational threads, each one identified by a different Subject line, the labor of following all or even a selection of the threads can overwhelm the participants. People frequently drop out as the interwoven conversations become confusing. Email has proven to be a less productive interface as the number of correspondents and the intensity of the conversations increase.

Each of the technologies we describe has a *simplest* configuration. To the extent that they are new technologies and don't behave just like email, even simple programs can present challenges to new users adapting. People are understandably averse to having to learn a new computer program unless they're sure it's going to help them in their jobs. So always offer "the simplest technology" to people just beginning to converse with others online. And wherever possible, provide upgrade paths to more features, more convenience, and more power once people have become accustomed to the entry-level interface.

Choosing Tools to Fit Circumstances

The following graphic depicts the two major variables of time and place and the kinds of communications that fit the four possible combinations. It's a 2×2 matrix, but its message is really too simple. Yes, people will work together online because they are in different places, but just because they are in the same place at the same time does not mean that they will be communicating by making presentations. Nor does it mean that two people sitting in cubicles 20 feet apart don't communicate with email.

	SAME TIME	DIFFERENT TIME
Same place	Voting, presentations	Shared computers
Different place	Chat, videophones	Email, conferencing, workflow

People working in the same location generally collaborate online because it's a shared, orderly, and manageable way to get work done together. Information can be found and shared faster online. Records of interaction can be kept. Contact lists and shared calendars can be maintained and accessed. And one can engage in multiple conversations, with time to think about one's responses, more gracefully in Cyberspace than in most in-person meetings.

The choice of tools for your knowledge network is definitely affected by the time and distance variables. The greater the time difference, the more difficult real-time communication can be. The less opportunity there is for physical meetings, the more work must be done on building familiarity and trust. If the entire group is located in the same office, tool selection will be influenced by the amount of time spent in face-to-face interaction. Your network may consist of scattered individuals, each working in a separate office but forming a virtual team through the technical interface. Their only shared office space may exist online.

So in describing and evaluating these tools, we will address their suitability for different circumstances, with suggestions about how they should be configured or matched with other technologies to fit the needs of groups in those circumstances. Such information also can be culled from our chapters on culture (Chapter 5, "Fostering a Knowledge-Sharing Culture," and Chapter 6, "Taking Culture Online") and from both Chapter 8, "Initiating and Supporting Internal Conversation," and Chapter 9, "Conversing with External Stakeholders."

Every computer-human interface and technology has its limitations. Some have too few features, others have too many, and some have features that don't meet the needs of the group using them. The first duty of the person selecting technology for a group or organization is to understand the people who make up the knowledge network: their culture, their experience with technology, the time they can devote to participation, and their commitment to helping adapt and improve the interface they use for knowledge sharing.

Matching Technology with Purpose

Circumstances define the choice of technology as the knowledge network begins and gets up to speed. The longer range considerations of the technology are tied to the purpose of the knowledge network. What must it accomplish and over what time period? What tools will be required for it to achieve its goals?

Knowledge networks exist primarily for learning, but they have many other purposes. They are formed to manage and complete projects, to generate new ideas and innovations, and by educating and inspiring their members, to stimulate more productive activity in the workplace. Software design is becoming increasingly specialized to serve a wide variety of specific interactive and collaborative purposes, and though many companies include their products under the broad banner of "online community tools," they all lean toward serving certain types of group needs over others.

Etienne Wenger, introduced in Chapter 5, devised his own categorization scheme to describe how a variety of platforms relate to the varied needs of communities of practice (CoPs). Although we don't equate all knowledge networks with CoPs, his approach to matching software purposes with group purposes is useful.

As our adaptation of his scheme in Table 7.1 shows, he identifies four continuums along which these purposes vary.[2] The emphases of groups and technology differ along these four dimensions: conversation versus content (A), serving social structures versus exchanging knowledge (B), getting work done versus learning (C), and ongoing versus fleeting interaction (D). Of course, these are fuzzy categories—continuums that don't have hard boundaries between one another—but as such, they accurately reflect human social behavior.

Wenger is concerned with the needs of the ideal community of practice, which lie at the convergence of these various purposes, where all purposes are served equally well. Our approach in this book is a bit different in that our purposes are more focused *on conversation*—specifically on supporting the most productive online conversation for sharing knowledge. Although we recognize the distinctions Wenger describes, CoPs as social groups define only one corner of the world of knowledge networking. Groups form around many other interests beyond those of common practice and profession—such as project management, strategic brainstorming, customer relationships. Wenger's categorization, though insightful, is of limited use to us here because the success of online conversation for effective knowledge exchange depends on social dynamics: how much knowledge can be passed and absorbed among a group of people.

Table 7.1   Etienne Wenger's Categories of Community-Oriented Technologies

	COMMUNITY PURPOSE TO BE SERVED	CATEGORY OF TECHNOLOGY
A	Enabling conversation	Discussion groups
	Storing and providing documents	Knowledge bases
B	Supporting social structures	Web site communities
	Facilitating knowledge exchange	Access to expertise
C	Getting work done	Project spaces
	Providing structured instruction	E-learning spaces
D	Supporting ongoing integration of work and knowledge	Knowledge worker's desktop
	Making best use of fleeting interactions	Synchronous online communication platforms

Technology, Group Size, and Duration of Activity

Differences in size and social composition of a knowledge network are more significant differentiators for us, with our focus on conversation, than the purposes listed by Wenger. Many specialized technologies for supporting collaboration come bundled with interfaces for online conversation. All of the major portal providers include message boards. Many include chat and some are even bundling IM capabilities. Yet those interfaces aren't necessarily the best ones, or even suitable, for every group's conversational needs.

We've been involved in online communities of all shapes and sizes for many years. We've observed that the size of a group in conversation and the accepted duration of the conversation are the two factors that most influence the choice of appropriate technology. We provide a simple depiction of how this works in Table 7.2.

How Many Participants?

Email will be used by individuals within groups regardless of the group's effective online size. But when looking for the best technology for a knowledge network, the scale of its usage makes a difference. A conversation can contain only a certain number of participants. When an organization expects hundreds or thousands of conversations to be going on among hundreds or thousands of people around many different subjects, the choice of platform and its configuration options become even more critical.

We define small knowledge networks as having from 2 to 20 people. That's about the maximum number of participants that online community managers have discovered are able to converse effectively and coherently in a single thread of online conversation. A chat room's size limit is usually set to 20 active

Table 7.2 Appropriate Conversation Technologies for Knowledge Networks

COMMUNITY SIZE, DURATION	MOST USEFUL TECHNOLOGY GENRES
Small, spontaneous	Email, IM, chat, message board, P2P
Small, project focused	Email, IM, message board, P2P
Department level, ongoing	Email, message board, portal
Department level, transitory	Message board, portal, real-time event
Cross-organizational, transitory	Message board, real-time event
Cross-organizational, ongoing	Email, IM, message boards, portals

participants or less for the sake of order and coherence. This also applies to email lists and conversations in message boards. Active small networks easily can outgrow the entry level of technology and often will move to message boards where they can "cluster" around a wider diversity of discussion topics.

What we call department-level knowledge networks are defined more by a common culture than by numbers, for at this level, there will be many simultaneous conversations happening. The fact that the group has some boundaries around it and commonalities within it means that its members will benefit from using a common conversational interface. There may be tens, hundreds, or thousands of people in these loosely tied communities, but the technologies they use allow them to support many effective knowledge networks at the same time. Email and the portal tie the overall population together by informing members of current projects and directing them to the various subgroups operating within its network. The scope of the conversation is widened by the ability of individuals to circulate among the various specialized knowledge networks.

What we refer to as cross-organizational communities are really networks of knowledge networks that span the breadth of a company. These federations of networks are united more by the shared organizational strategy than by any specific common practice or interest. On this level of numbers—with perhaps thousands of people conversing in hundreds of separate knowledge networks—the greatest need is for good portal design and scalable online discussion boards.

Cross-organizational groups encompass departmental-level groups and the small groups as well as cross-departmental and multigroup knowledge networks. The organization's purpose in providing online conversational technologies is to stimulate knowledge exchange and cross-fertilize ideas from one side of the company to the other. The key to success is integration because, depending on the size and location of the company and its offices, the technology needs to be able to distribute knowledge from a wide variety of sources available to a wide variety of internal stakeholders.

How Long Will the Conversation Last?

Some knowledge-sharing conversations may last only an hour or two or a day or two. Others may last a week to a month. They are opportunities for people to gather online and exchange what they know with people who aren't part of their usual knowledge network. They may be called classes, conferences, online knowledge fairs, or seminars. They can take place through asynchronous communications interfaces like message boards or even email. In their shorter formats, they are conducted through synchronous interfaces like chat and real-time event facilities.

The shorter the duration of the conversation, the more appropriate are the real-time interfaces. Once you get beyond several hours, the scheduling dynamic changes. Rather than set aside two specific hours to meet online with live voice, messaging, and possibly video interaction, attendees are more likely to prefer participation over the course of several days in a message board, scheduling their participation time according to their own convenience.

When message boards are used for what we call time-bound events, they function identically to their usage in ongoing community discussion. The difference is more in how they are administered and hosted and in how their content is organized and rolled out. The technology for real-time events is hosted on remote servers, managed by the vendors in coordination with administrators from the organization or knowledge community. The most important criterion in choosing the configuration of these tools is the amount of bandwidth available to all of the participants. Even the fastest modem connection through a basic phone line won't provide a satisfactory experience if audio or video streaming is involved.

The Importance of Familiarity and Participation

Besides size and duration, another community variable, not included in Table 7.2, is *cohesion*, which in some cases describes the level of *familiarity* among participants. Communities of practice have inherent cohesion in the commonality of their members' skills, but not all CoPs begin with people who know each other well. When starting a knowledge-sharing community, certain technical features can speed and smooth social mixing. For example, online *profile* pages that describe members in the context of the common interest of the community are helpful in striking up conversations and relationships.

When people are familiar, initial communications problems due to faulty or inappropriate interface design can be transcended and solved more smoothly. People who don't know each other and encounter technical problems before they've established working relationships have less social incentive to make the learning curve worth climbing. If reaching the social incentives requires first overcoming the technical barriers, the best approach is simply to lower the technical barriers. Either keep the interface simple where unfamiliar participants are involved, or you'll need to motivate them to participate in other ways.

Your primary goal in providing conversation-supporting technology must be to build early and then regular participation. We've seen some very sophisticated interfaces go to waste because no one showed up to use them. Motivation and a sense that something important will get done are powerful attractors to a working group. With motivated participants, the interface receives plenty of practical critique toward improvement in design and function. If the interface gets in the way of productive interaction, the motivated group will detect immediately what needs to be changed. This is where, as we described in previous chapters, a good relationship between the leaders of the knowledge network and their IT liaison can be called on for promptly making the required changes.

Who Forms the Group?

Another tool selection criterion and differentiating dimension of online conversation is the origin of the group itself. It matters whether the group was formed by its members in direct response to a commonly recognized need or if the group is an already existing business group moving its activities online because the organization has just provided it with the interface to do so. The first case is an example of a bottom-up network, and the second is an example of a top-down network.

Say Group A decides to begin sharing what each member knows about a particular problem their company faces. They work in different parts of the company but have a common interest in finding a solution based on their complementary skills and experiences. They look at their communications options and find an appropriate medium—email or instant messaging or one of the new generation of P2P clients—and form their own ad hoc knowledge network. They have formed what we call a *spontaneous community*.

At the opposite end of the continuum, Group B is put together by a middle manager and assigned to use the company's message boards, found through the corporate portal, to coordinate online conversation among product designers to speed innovation. We call such communities, initiated by executives and managers to serve the growing needs for better knowledge distribution in the company, *strategic communities*.

The third type of conversational group, *transitory communities*, are similar to the conversations of short duration we described earlier. They may be formed spontaneously or produced with strategic purposes, but once they have served their purpose, they are usually disbanded.

All of the factors that affect the choice of technology for supporting knowledge networks and their conversations—the immediate circumstances, the purpose of the group, the number of participants, the duration of their interaction, their familiarity and roots—should be considered. We know from experience and largely from hindsight how these factors influence the social activity that is at the core of knowledge sharing. The tools must serve the people, not the other way around.

We always recommend that you seek input from some of the users and potential users before selecting the technology you will provide for them. Allow them to test the technology and make their own suggestions for what will work best. Regardless of which technology you choose, make sure it has enough flexibility, expandability, and customization options to adapt to the changing needs and growing populations of the knowledge networks that use it. Pay attention to those spontaneous groups who already are engaged in online knowledge-sharing conversation in your organization before you dare to change the technology they are using. They may have discovered valuable knowledge about what actually works with the tools they are using.

Technical Autonomy

One important factor in selecting technology for your knowledge network is the amount of autonomy you will have in managing the application and your group's use of it. As we described in previous chapters, it's important that a community formed around learning and sharing knowledge be able to keep its communication environment evolving at the same rate as its communication needs. A close tie with IT is the minimum requirement for ensuring fast turn-around of requested changes in the conversation interface.

When you need (or are provided with) an application that must be run on your organization's servers, your IT friends must be relied on for most of the changes and fixes related to that application. Even with your cooperative arrangement with IT, there are going to be delays as your important interface tweak sits at the bottom of the priority list behind much larger scale projects.

Local Interface Control

Fortunately, the trend in groupware is toward providing customers and clients with more power to self-configure their own interfaces. Most of the platforms we describe here can be modified and adapted to meet changing group needs without the direct involvement of IT. Most community-oriented applications now come with built-in customization tools that can be manipulated by administrators with minimal technical skills.

Figure 7.1 shows part of the "sysop control panel" that comes with the widely used community interaction platform called Web Crossing (www.webcrossing.com). The screen shot shows a small part of the control panel where the "sysop" can change the appearance of the interface—the header and footer at the top and bottom of each Web page in this case—using simple text windows. The sysop (whoever has the password as the site's Web Crossing administrator) also can modify the text that greets new members, format the messages people post, control the process for member registration, set the options provided to members, and manage both the membership and content of the community. In the increasingly rare case that Web Crossing is installed on your company's server, IT's responsibilities for maintaining it may be limited to running back-ups, making sure you're provided with sufficient disk space, and setting up its email-related functions.

The ASP Way

Most of Web Crossing's customers "rent" the application, paying to use it as it is run and maintained on Web Crossing's remote servers. Like many modern software companies, Web Crossing is an *application service provider* (ASP). More organizations choose to run more applications in this mode because it reduces the installation, configuration, and maintenance loads on their IT departments

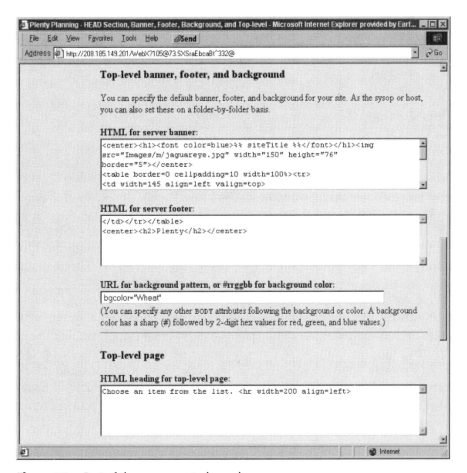

Figure 7.1 Part of the sysop control panel.

Screen shot of the authors' message board using WebCrossing ©SociAlchemy

and raises the quality of maintenance of the applications. The system administrators at an ASP do one thing and they do it well: maintain their application servers. An IT department with perhaps dozens of different applications to manage won't have the application-specific expertise of the technicians at the ASPs.

As we explained in Chapter 4, "The Role of IT in the Effective Knowledge Network," some organizations, especially the largest companies, will continue to install applications on centralized systems managed entirely by their IT departments. They will do this because they feel it gives them more control over their software environment and because there are still complexities involved in integrating ASP-provided services with their centralized systems. But it's also a simple matter of efficiency, standardization, and economics. A standard companywide interface reduces the "per seat" cost of the collaborative platform, minimizes the complexity of supporting multiple platforms, and cuts training costs. The downside of installing one online conversation platform for use by the entire organization is that a one-size-fits-all solution won't provide the most appropriate and productive tools for all of the organization's diverse internal groups.

The Peer-to-Peer Wave

The groups frustrated by the inadequacy of available online collaborative options are most likely to look for better solutions to their unique communications problems. This motivation to bypass the centrally controlled servers and put the choice of appropriate communications interface in the hands of the end user is what inspired Ray Ozzie to develop Groove, the most widely known of the new wave of peer-to-peer (P2P) applications. Ozzie had noticed the trend in organizations to more decentralized decision making, a change indicated by more workers communicating and collaborating with each other through email and Lotus Notes, his original contribution to software design.

Peer-to-peer communication eliminates the need for the third party, namely IT. A population of workers equipped with a program like Groove quickly can assemble interconnected teams and virtual workplaces without having to wait for approval, implementation, or the clearance of backlogged work on the server. Knowledge networks operating through Groove clients can work together across the corporate firewall, communicating PC to PC. Groove, which we'll describe in more detail later in the chapter, is the most high-profile example of what may be the most appropriate knowledge-sharing solution for our networked future.

Tools, Their Features, and Their Applications

The rest of this chapter is a guide to the selection of conversational interfaces for knowledge-sharing networks. We introduced the general features of these interfaces in Chapter 4, and here we present more detailed descriptions. We not only suggest appropriate interfaces for specific groups and circumstances, as we described in the previous section on *Tools for Every Purpose*, but we also provide suggestions for appropriate configurations of tools to meet some of the more common needs of knowledge networks.

We don't attempt to address every possible situation, and we stick to the focus of this book: online conversation. Every group has its own unique needs for handling information and content, for dealing with collaborative utilities like shared calendars and coauthored documents, but in terms of media for supporting their conversations, the choices we present are limited but infinitely configurable. Message boards can be integrated with a myriad of features and other applications for enhancing their knowledge-sharing power. So can email and the latest P2P clients. Even instant messaging is being beefed up to transfer files and behave like a cross between email and asynchronous discussion.

The tools we describe in this chapter range from those that provide only a single interface and format for online group conversation to those that provide multiple formats for conversation—asynchronous message boards and synchronous chat—plus capabilities for sharing files, managing content, and collaborating on activities like project management and calendars.

Our descriptions begin with the simplest application, email, and move through chat and instant message to message boards. We devote a section to Groove as the representative P2P application in the knowledge-sharing world and finish with a description of portal software and how it can contribute to the effectiveness of knowledge networks and online conversation.

The Dimensions of Email

We assume that you have used email for many different reasons and purposes. You have learned through experience of the strengths and weaknesses of basic email. You've probably been involved in lengthy conversations and innumerable short exchanges. You love its convenience and you hate its spam. You've probably lost many an important message and mistakenly sent a few embarrassing messages to unintended destinations. Email is far from a perfect, secure, and orderly conversational medium. But it's ubiquitous and you can reach almost anyone through it.

Over half of all Americans use email, spending almost half an hour per day tending to it, according to a 2001 report by Forrester Research.[3] Practically everyone who uses the Net understands the basics of email, which is the main reason it's such a powerful piece of the knowledge-sharing toolkit. There's a lot you can do with email besides send text. Today's email can contain Web pages and hyperlinks to Web content. It can carry attached documents and graphics. It can be used for one-to-one conversation or many-to-many communication.

But as powerful as it is, basic email was never meant to do all of the tasks it is now used for in such a populous and commercial environment. People working in organizations now use it routinely to send proprietary information across the Internet, where a simple mistake in forwarding a message can result in a competitor or journalist receiving information that can be more than embarrassing; it can be quite damaging. As people's use of email grows, ongoing threads of conversation grow to be hundreds or even thousands of messages long. Important work-related contents get lost in stuffed email folders and force users to engage in desperate searches.

It still may be the killer application of the Internet and a wonderful convenience for people looking to share knowledge with minimal muss and fuss, but it is far from the ideal tool around which to build a robust and expanding knowledge network. Nevertheless, it serves an important role in getting new knowledge-sharing communities off the ground and can serve as the basic foundation for new applications that take advantage of its global familiarity and status as the one application that every Internet-connected person uses.

The Email List

Email lists, also called *listservs*, are powerful group communications tools. They are easy to set up, involve simple, reliable technology, require minimum bandwidth, and can reach large populations quickly. They can be run in broadcast mode as electronic newsletters or in interactive mode as ongoing conversations. They can be *moderated* by human editors who trim extraneous or off-topic information from the content they then pass on to list members.

Members of an email list can choose between receiving all individual messages submitted by others and receiving *digests* of messages bundled together on a daily or weekly basis. Many people prefer to get the digest to reduce the clutter of many separate messages. Others find messages in the digest more difficult to respond to than those received separately.

Again, email lists work best when no more than about 20 people are engaged in ongoing conversations. Even with that number, the interaction can be hard to follow if more than two or three different topics are being discussed at the same time. A good facilitator can help keep a busy email list coherent, but when the traffic in the list grows beyond the ability of members to keep up, dropouts are inevitable. Filtering messages requires manual perusal of Subject lines and many people find that to be too labor intensive.

If your group is small and focused, your members can't meet in person, and prefer to have the messages come to them rather than having to remember to log on to message board, an email list may be an appropriate and sufficient platform for your conversations. An exemplary mail list that serves members of the online learning community is Learning-org, which has been running since 1994. Richard Karash, host of the mail list, describes its function as "a flow of messages over the internet. There is a list of subscribers and all subscribers receive all the messages. Our robot keeps track of subscribers and distributes the messages. To add your contribution to the flow, you send a simple e-mail message to our address and the robot takes care of everything else."[4]

Etiquette Makes Email Effective

Because email list hosts like Karash have paid attention to the social amenities of groups using the medium for online conversation, they have been the sources of written guidelines for the considerate use of email. These guidelines are part of the overall online social code known as *netiquette*, and their practice makes a positive difference in conducting productive email conversation.

Consideration of others helps build trust and brings mutual respect to online discussions that might descend into divisive argument and debate. A conversation carried on through email requires a lot of manual involvement, from opening each message (or the digest) to the act of sending each response. It's not a lot of work, but email conversation relies more on the responsible participation of each individual than does the next step up in technical organization of asynchronous conversation, the message board.

The importance of the Subject line in an email message is too often overlooked. It tells the reader what the message is about without forcing the reader to open it. The tendency of many is to put more value in the Subject line when receiving a message than when responding to it. A message may arrive with the Subject line reading, "Linux expertise needed," and as people respond in turn to the subsequent interaction, the Subject line is left as is. Meanwhile, the actual content of the messages evolves from Linux expertise to the Linux operating system and then to the cost of Linux boxes. The final messages in the thread rant about the flaws of Windows XP and the cost of Bill Gates's house. List members coming in late expect to see a deep conversation about Linux and feel cheated to have opened nine messages about something else. It's not a lot of wasted time, but these little inconsiderate actions add up in the frustration they cause when people are looking for helpful knowledge in their email.

As a responsible email correspondent, you should be clear about whom you are addressing and what specific parts of the message you are responding to. An email list is but one thread of messages that can only be kept coherent by judicious use of the Subject line and by the conscientious use of its members. It's considerate to "sign" your messages with your name at the end, and including your email address allows other people on the list to respond directly to you, rather than through the list if they want to pursue a side conversation.

Annotation and the use of embedded correspondence are also important in email-mediated conversations. When people reply to a message and the contents of that message are included in the reply, it serves as context for the response. As the correspondence continues, its entire history may be carried in each message. This soon becomes unwieldy for readers and, where messages are saved, can occupy significant disk space. Good etiquette is to copy only the part of the message being responded to that is relevant to your response.

Social etiquette varies between mail lists, but it usually recommends that people introduce themselves in the list when they join. It's a way of saying, "I'm here" because most people don't check the member list very often. Introducing yourself is also a way of telling others why you've joined, what you know, and what you hope to learn. Your position in the organization and any projects you're working on will be helpful, as will a little story about your relevant experience.

Every list needs some policies, though the associations may be so loose within your organization that internal communications policies are understood to transfer to the list. But members should know, for example, if the list is moderated or not. They should be informed clearly of who holds responsibility for words posted to the list (each member should, but in some cases, the sponsor of the list claims copyrights on all contents). There should be emphasis on mutual respect and avoidance of personal attacks as useful ground rules for interaction.

A mail list also needs clear instructions to its subscribers as to how to get on and off the list. Every list has an "owner" who serves as administrator and intermediary between members and the software that controls the list's automated functions. Figure 7.2 shows some typical instructions for an imaginary mail list for fans of koalas. Those shown here are for joining a list run on the widely used (and free) Majordomo list management software.

Email on Steroids

Because email is the most widely used Internet application—the one most people open first when they get to work and close last before they leave—it should be

```
Our list is run by a program called Majordomo.
No humans are involved in list maintenance,
but Majordomo only understands certain commands.
Follow these instructions carefully:

1) To subscribe to receive individual messages,
send an email to:
        majordomo@hypothetical.com
The Subject line is ignored. Begin your message
with two lines:
        subscribe koalabears
        end
2) To subscribe to a daily digest of messages,
send an email to:
        majordomo@hypothetical.com
The Subject line is ignored. Begin your message
with two lines:
        subscribe koalabears-digest
        end

        Any additional text in the msg body
        (e.g. your sig) will be ignored. You
        will be added to the list and will
        receive a Welcome message including
        this info file.
        Please, please, please...
        keep the Welcome message
        for future reference!!
```

Figure 7.2   Clear instructions for joining an email list.

Based on documentation for Learning-org email list. © SociAlchemy leveraged to do as much work as possible. After all, so many people know how to use it. Most people don't need additional training or motivation to check their email, and they are comfortable with tending to their regular email work habits.

A company called Zaplet (www.zaplet.com), founded in 1999, provides an application called Appmail that turns the normal email message into a dynamic group workspace. The company aims its products at Fortune 1000 companies where it hopes its buyers will install it on all desktops as a new way to get people to interact and work together online. Basically, Appmail integrates collaborative tools into email messages and turns those messages into ongoing shared workspaces.

Arriving in your Inbox looking like a normal email message, an Appmail message acts like a window into data stored on the Appmail server. Once the window is opened, the recipient is invited to use any of the applications that are involved in the message. There may be a document to open and fill in or a live feed of data from an accounting application. When recipients reply to an Appmail or update any information on the server, the existing message gets "recycled" and pops back to the top of your unread messages list. An active Appmail does not sink to the bottom of your constantly growing Inbox list. The Appmail server also keeps an audit trail of every message.

Appmail messages don't contain proprietary data that are at risk of getting into unintended hands; those data sit on the secure servers. Business rules can be applied to Appmail correspondence, assuring that messages and requests flow to the right people at the right time. Different applications can be integrated into an Appmail network so that members can use the system like a *miniportal.*

Like Groove and several other products we describe in this chapter, Appmail is an example of the kind of software hybridization that takes advantage of the Web's ability to adapt to existing and changing work habits and business models. Though Appmail is expensive to purchase and implement (costing up to seven figures for a site license"), it shows how an application that is used habitually by millions can be transformed into a much more powerful tool for collaboration.

Real-Time Communications: Chat and Instant Messaging

The most distinguishing characteristic of real-time online communication is *nowness*. Chat enables people to send messages to each other in group settings, and IM is used primarily for two people to connect. Real-time communications on their own have limited value for ongoing knowledge exchange, but they are important to knowledge networks for two main reasons:

- They are valuable tools for maintaining social ties

- Once a social tie has been made with a knowledge source, questions can be asked instantly

Chats take place in *chat rooms*, where groups of virtual attendees can gather and exchange responses that roll up and out of the chat window as they are added. Although any number of people can be in a chat room, the live interaction can become difficult to follow if more than about 10 people are responding to one another immediately. As happens in conference calls, people tend to talk to one another, and the messages—who is talking to whom about what—can get confused.

PROS AND CONS OF CHAT

Pros

- Its use is intuitive, and most chat platforms on the Web are similar enough in look, feel, and operation that newcomers adapt to them quickly.
- Navigation to a chat room is usually quite simple if you are in the online community environment. You either get an "invitation" and click on it, or you create the chat room yourself and send the invitations to others.
- There's a sense of presence, spontaneity, and actual conversation in chats. Responses to your comments appear as you watch.
- Transcripts allow review of interaction by participants and those who could not participate but are interested in what was discussed.

Cons

- The interwoven conversations of a busy chat room can be confusing to follow.
- Serious or sustained discussion can be difficult if people are constantly interrupting one another.
- Long posts, stories, and explanations don't lend themselves to the short response format.
- If you and your friends are online at different times, forget chatting with one another.
- The same is true of live online events; if they don't fit into your schedule, you can't participate.

Chat is often included in live online events, where content and live interaction (typically between a moderator and guests) are broadcast to an audience over the Web. The audience is invited to submit questions and comments to the moderator and to the special guest or the panel of experts who are the focus of the event. Some working teams use chat for quickie meetings when getting together in person is not possible but the entire team is available online. Chat is often bundled with message board software or included in portals.

Instant messaging, which gained its initial popularity on America Online and then became the rage on the Web when over 11 million copies of the ICQ messaging client were downloaded, is both a convenience and comforting online social companion. With an IM window open in the corner of your monitor, you are alerted whenever any of the people you keep in your *buddy list* are online with their compatible IM client active. You may choose to send them a message or just be aware that they are available in case you have a question or something to tell them. Your IM client gives you a sense of presence—a feeling that you're not completely alone at your keyboard or on the Net. IMs can support group conversation, allowing their users to open chat rooms windows and invite fellow IMers to join a conversation.

Some software platforms include a feature that Web Crossing calls the *Web Tour*. When you join a Web Tour, you enter a chat room that features a framed window that the host of the chat can use to move from Web page to Web page as the tourists post their comments. The potential uses of such a tool include pushing content, classrooms, and staging conference events. It's an alternative to the more prevalent slide shows that are presented in most live online events.

Chat Tools

The technology of chat has become almost a commodity except for the new field of *secure chat*. Chat requires a server-side installation but no longer requires a client permanently installed on the PC side. Most chat is run today using Java applets that download and fire up quickly, although these can be a problem if run across firewalls. Secure chat applications require that client software be installed on the PCs of participants. Chat comes bundled with most asynchronous message board software and can be enabled at the discretion of the community.

Some platforms display a listing of existing, open chat rooms that can be visited or of chat rooms that are currently active. Chat can also be integrated into company portals. There are many sources for chat software, including secure chat for business networks. A good site for finding an updated list of sources and resources is Messaging Software Solutions at www.messaging-software.com.

Options available in chat applications include:

- Ability to participate in HTML rather than Java mode to avoid compatibility or firewall problems

- Private chat rooms that don't show up on the public menu of open rooms

- The ability of individual chatters to send private real-time messages to one another

- Support of anonymous users

- Validation of logons to restrict access

- Icons or colors for identifying roles of participants: chat host, special guest, staff, and so on

- Single logon: participants are not required to log on to chat separately once they are logged on to the portal or community environment

Chat Etiquette

Like email lists, chat is a single-threaded conversation interface. As such, it requires cooperation on the parts of its users if conversations are to be useful. Chats usually begin with the participants greeting each other and, if they are not familiar, introducing themselves. When leaving the chat before its scheduled ending time, it's good to announce that you are logging out. Don't try to enter long messages in chat. Take a breath between parts of your message by ending them with ellipses (three dots …), waiting to see if there are responses or comments, and then continuing with another chunk of your message.

The role of chat facilitator, like that of email list moderator, is important when there are more than a few participants in the discussion. Restraint in posting messages allows all participants to read and respond to each other in an orderly and logical fashion. A facilitator can recognize and call on people who signify that they have questions or comments to submit. One protocol is for participants to post a question mark if they have questions and an exclamation point if they have comments. The facilitator keeps a queue list and invites people, in order, to post their questions or comments.

The more a group uses chat, the more effective it will be in conducting productive meetings. When entering a chat in progress, it's recommended that you scroll back to see what has been said before jumping in and repeating a previously made point. The use of abbreviations can make the real-time interaction move along more smoothly. The following are some typical and frequently used chat abbreviations:

- BTW = By the way
- IMHO = In my humble opinion
- BRB = Be right back
- LPFN = Last post for now

Chat can be a powerful tool for knowledge sharing, but it works best as a complement to other communications tools and interfaces for sharing information. Some people aren't comfortable using chat; they feel hurried in the interaction and prefer the more relaxed interaction of asynchronous technologies like email and message boards. If possible, provide a variety of alternative communication venues to accommodate people's different styles.

Asynchronous Discussion: Message Boards

In asynchronous discussion platforms, participants read and post responses that remain on the system when they exit. Variously called message boards, conferencing systems, and forum environments, these conversation interfaces do not require participants to be logged on simultaneously. That can be a great advantage when people have busy schedules that don't allow them to attend scheduled conversations. And because there is no short time limit on the duration of the conversation, they can spend more time reading what others have written and composing their own messages.

Message board interfaces differ in their structure and in the options they offer to administrators and participants. Later, we describe some of the more important features relevant to knowledge networks. We consider message boards to be the most useful platforms for knowledge networks because they combine conversation with the Web's presentation of content. An online conversational thread in a message board is not only a social interaction, but it is also a document containing valuable information in context. The content can be searched, and with some platforms, it can be integrated into the organization's companywide database. This is not possible if the platform comes with its own proprietary database product, as does Web Crossing.

PROS AND CONS OF MESSAGE BOARDS

Pros
- Convenient for people to participate according to their own schedules and free time
- Require no clients or Java applications to be downloaded and run
- Responses remain available for a while; each discussion has some history
- Variety of available conversation topics
- Responses can include Web links, HTML, and file insertions
- Participants have time to think about and compose their contributions

Cons
- Navigation becomes complex as discussions accumulate and diversify
- Less sense of presence than real-time communication

Message boards are also multithreaded. While email lists and chat rooms only permit one thread of conversation to go on among the group, a message board interface allows members of the group to participate in many different conversations that may or may not be related. Social activity can be segregated from work-focused activity or discussions dedicated to knowledge sharing. And because the conversations take place along a more extended timeframe, there is more time for a facilitator or discussion manager to intervene and keep the conversations well ordered and on track. Content can be provided to accompany or stimulate conversation in a knowledge-sharing environment, and many message board platforms can be extended toward portal-like functionality, integrating both content and other specialized tools into and around the actual discussion space.

The Organization of Discussion Environments

Most message board products organize their conversations according to the nested folder metaphor. Thus, when entering the environment, the participant will find folders or discussion areas dedicated to different groups, topics, or interests. Within those areas may be another layer of folders or even a combination of conversations and folders that allows a deeper level of distinction between conversations.

The interaction within different folders may be formatted differently. As we will describe, some may be formatted as *threaded* conversations and others may be in *linear* conversational format. Some folders may contain chat rooms and collaborative tools, whereas others are pure asynchronous conversation. You may choose to segregate different teams and special interest groups while providing a common area for all members of the knowledge network to mix and converse.

To Thread or Not to Thread

In Chapter 4, we described the differences between threaded and linear discussion structures, noting that threaded structures—where participants can respond directly to a message rather than to a general discussion topic—are best for situations in which quick question-and-answer interactions are most valued. Linear structures support more conversational interaction where the participants address a specific topic or area of interest. Some message board interfaces provide only one of these structures, but many allow the group or even individual participants to choose threading or nonthreading according to their preferences and needs.

Web Crossing permits its users to choose the format in which they view a discussion as either threaded or linear (which they call *chronological*). The group using the platform can choose to enable or disable the threaded option, and users may have the option to use or not use the threaded option. This flexibility can lead to some confusion. To better illustrate this, we provide Figures 7.3, 7.4, and 7.5—three different views of the same online conversation.

In Figure 7.3, we see what looks to be a linear conversation, with the header introducing the topic and the responses following one after another as the reader scrolls down the page. Note the time signatures on the responses; they are in chronological order. This viewpoint is from the perspective of a user, Joe, who does not have the threaded view enabled. Often, even when the option of threaded structure is not available, linear online conversations get scrambled as different people drift from the main topic into side conversations. The reader is forced to decipher which messages are responding to which side conversation, and writers must learn to include references in their messages to indicate which side conversation they are responding to.

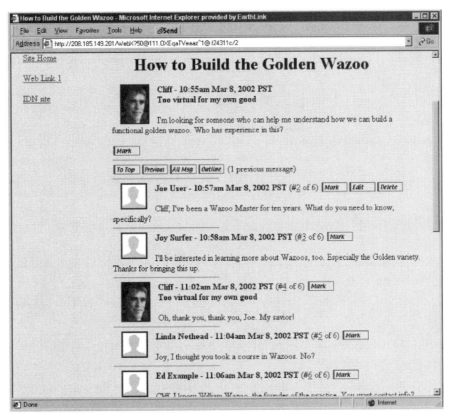

Figure 7.3   A discussion viewed in linear (also called "chronological") format.
Screen shot of the authors' message board using WebCrossing ©SociAlchemy

In Figure 7.4, we show a schematic view of the actual threaded structure of the conversation. Although the participants are all talking about the same topic—building Golden Wazoos—there is actually more than one conversational thread happening. This view can be seen by users who have activated the threaded view in their personal configuration option. Indents show the parent-child relationship of messages and the responses made to them. The layout portrays the actual interaction that has been prompted by the topic header. This user can click on any response and respond directly to it rather than to the main header. But in this view, though navigation is simplified, you can't tell what the content of each post is. It serves as an overview of the conversations that have begun based on Cliff's search for the secret of the Golden Wazoo.

For participants who have the threaded option enabled, the view shown in Figure 7.5 reveals not only the content of each message—displayed in what appears

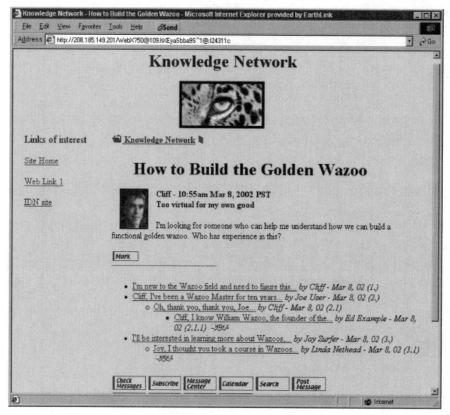

Figure 7.4 The outline view of the same conversation in threaded format.
Screen shot of the authors' message board using WebCrossing ©SociAlchemy

to be the more readable linear format—but also the context of the threaded conversation. Note that the time stamps on the posts are not in chronological order and that the symbols to the left of each message show which are responding to the conversation header (small rectangles) and which are responding to messages (arrowheads). The reader can see that there are subconversations happening about knowledge of Golden Wazoos, but the overall conversation is made readable by the linear, scrolling arrangement of the messages.

We should add here that we don't recommend that this particular option be made available in all situations because, as Figure 7.3 showed, when some people are responding to messages and some are responding to the overall topic header, the results may be less coherent for both groups. It's better if every participant in a conversation treats it in the same way, as either threaded or linear.

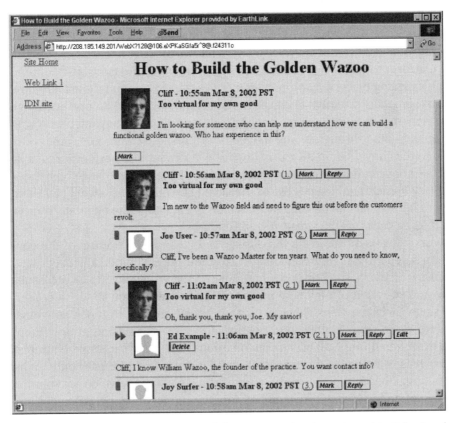

Figure 7.5   The threaded structure of the conversation is portrayed in this view by the symbols to the left of each message.

Screen shot of the authors' message board using WebCrossing ©SociAlchemy

Features That Affect Participation

People participate in message boards based not only on their interests in the subjects of conversation and the other participants but because their participation helps them to be more productive in their work. That feeling of productivity can be lost if the use of the message board is too complicated or tedious. As the content of a discussion environment grows, it forces participants to make more choices about their use of time. It's easy to begin with involvement in a few conversations that soon branch off into a few more conversations that include more people, more comments, and yet more conversations until a daily allocation of 1 hour in the message boards grows into a daily obligation of 2 or 3 hours just to keep up. This is where interface options for filtering and prioritizing content become important in retaining the interest of valuable members of the knowledge network.

The personalized view of a message board allows the user to configure the use of the platform to his or her needs. The first thing that the user must contend with after logging on is navigation; which conversations are of interest and how to get to them most directly? The user finds those with titles that look attractive and joins them. For most message board products, to *join* a conversation is simply to open it, read through it, and maybe post a response in it. For some products, to join a conversation means listing it on your member preferences list as one of the conversations you are engaged in. All of the best message board systems allow members to keep a list of preferred conversations—we'll call them *Favorites* here—that can be visited conveniently each time the member returns. Web Crossing calls this the *subscription* function.

Web Crossing users can click the Subscribe button at the bottom of the conversation screen to add that conversation to their Subscription List. Users who are *subscribed* to five specific conversations can log on, click a Check Messages button, and see a list of new responses that have been added to those conferences since their last visit. They can then proceed directly to those conversations and, when done reading and posting, leave the discussion area without having to search through all of the conversations that are of less or zero interest to them. This is a quick and convenient way for users to participate only in the conversations that fit their immediate interests. It's a way to avoid the common syndrome of online community membership: the sudden disappearance of time. Online conversations among interesting people make interesting reading, but in spending hours following them, they don't always help you get your work done.

Another feature that aids many people in staying involved in message board interaction is the ability to be notified by email when a new message has been posted in a Favorites conversation. Figure 7.6 shows an example of an email notification of a new post in the conversation about Golden Wazoos. When I get a message like this, it first of all reminds me that I am engaged in this conversation. It may give me an incentive for logging on to the message board and responding. But unless I follow that incentive and visit the conversation, the automatic emailer won't send me any more notifications about this particular conversation.

Some platforms send every new post to members who choose to receive them. Others send accumulated digests of posts on a schedule set by the user. Some permit the user to send messages and responses to be posted in the conversations. Email notification of new messages draws participants back into the message board and reminds busy people of their engagement in the ongoing conversations. Email posting allows members who are not able to log on to the message board to continue participating. When more people are participating via email than directly through the message board, the resulting conversations can begin to resemble unwieldy email lists as messages come in out of chronological order.

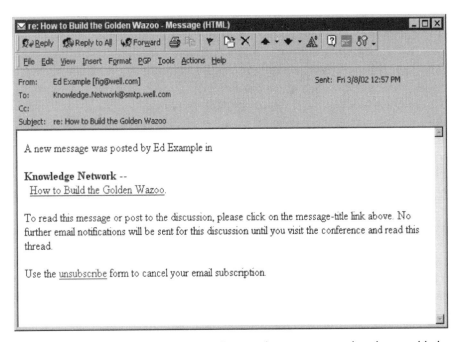

Figure 7.6   This email notification tells me that a message has been added to the discussion I started.

Screen shot of the authors' message board using WebCrossing ©SociAlchemy

Instant Messaging and Presence

If the Net is our workspace, we should know who else is sharing the workspace with us. The notion of *presence*—that the Net is a populated space rather than just miles of wires and silicon pulsing with electrons—may affect your motivation and the way you interact online. *Notification of presence* can have a direct effect on your productivity. If you know your partner on a project is on the Net when you are, you can connect and communicate. When people are logged on to a network, the network knows they are all there. When the network informs the users of who else is logged on at the same time, people know who they can contact for live conversation.

We see more applications all the time that provide presence notification. For us, it began with the UNIX operating system which could, through the WELL, provide a list of members currently logged on for anyone who typed the command *who*. Early in the WELL's history, a friendly programmer made a tool that let logged-on members send real-time messages back and forth. He called it *send* and later created the add-on *huh* to repeat back to you the sends you missed the first time.

We saw presence notification next on AOL, when it implemented its first instant messaging tool. The IM had a feature called the Buddy List in which you could put the *screen names* of other people on AOL you might want to IM with if they were logged on. IMs and an endless supply of open chat rooms were responsible for much of AOL's phenomenal early growth.

It was teenagers who really made instant messaging popular—teenagers working on their homework, with IM windows open, gossiping with friends, and collaborating on their assignments at the same time. That's multitasking productivity, and it's productivity that has brought IM into the workplace.

Since Web-based messaging clients became freely available, enterprising workers have been downloading them from AOL.com or MSN or Yahoo! so that they could stay in more immediate contact with important coworkers. There has been so much demand for them within businesses, and so many of these free clients are now in use behind firewalls, that some serious security concerns were raised. Messages sent through these consumer-level clients could be intercepted. Messages coming in over the firewall could carry viruses. The demand shifted to the need for industrial-level secure messaging systems that would operate within virtual private networks.

Jabber (www.jabber.com) is one of the leaders in developing the new generation of business-ready instant messaging and what it calls *presence management* systems. Instead of a Buddy List, Jabber provides a Roster. But Jabber is more than a secure IM client. The company claims that Jabber's advantage is "its ability to embed streaming XML data into other applications, devices, and services."[6] Jabber, in the same vein as Zaplet's Appmail, aims to make a popular personal communications interface into a virtual workspace. It's but one of the competitors in this new market niche.

Peer-to-Peer Knowledge Nets

Immediacy and local control are increasingly valuable to the wired worker. Even the delay of sending messages through intermediating servers can be an irritant in the era of the instant message. When Ray Ozzie conceived of Groove, he wanted to give more autonomy not only to the individual worker but also to the collaborative team. He wanted to connect workers and their computers as directly as possible, which meant removing the applications they used from the centralized servers and putting them instead on the actual machines that needed to communicate. Groove connects people like email does and like messaging systems do, but unlike them it does not rely on a server to transfer and relay the messages.

John Udell, an expert consultant in the field of groupware writing at OpenP2P.com, says of Groove: "Presence, in Groove, is exquisitely granular. You know when your message is delivered, when it is received, and in some cases, even when it is read."[7] Given the uncertainty of receptivity in spam-stuffed email inboxes, such surety is worth a lot to many people. And again, there is the need to provide the shared virtual workspace, but with P2P, there is also the flexibility to rearrange the workplace as the nature of the work and working team change. One arrangement is shown in Figure 7.7. A brainstorming application dominates the main window, but surrounding are communications tools including IM, chat, conferencing (message boards), and voice options. Tools can be added when needed by the group. Different configurations can be created on the same Groove installation for working with different groups. In the peer-to-peer network environment, the peers serve as their own network administrators.

The members of a Groove network, like those of any P2P network, are the designers, administrators, and users at the same time. They can build very responsive knowledge-sharing systems to support very communicative relationships. Figure 7.8 shows what might be Figure 7.7 five minutes later, with the MindManager chart displayed and the fellow peers present in a group brainstorming chat. Interactive Groove sessions and communications don't have to go through a central server, but the program provides a high level of security, even when crossing the company firewall. John Udell understands how the rigidity of centrally designed systems can stall creativity. Using a system like

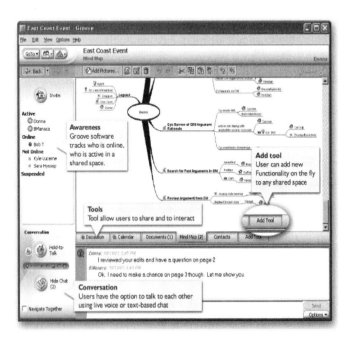

Figure 7.7 One of many possible configurations of a shared workspace using Groove.
©Groove Networks Inc.

Groove, the casual IM exchange with a coworker that leads to a full-blown project can be accommodated quickly by the flexibility and control of the client software. In such situations, Udell writes, "you can capture the exchange in a shared space and bring other tools to bear—a browser, a threaded discussion, a file archive. This effortless transition from casual to more formal interaction is the singular genius of Groove."

Our main focus is online conversation, and almost all of it happens through either the asynchronous platforms of email and message boards or the synchronous platforms of chat and instant messaging. Even in Groove, the descriptions we've provided about the use of tools in this chapter apply. But the prospect of knowledge networks operating through direct connections between individuals and their personal computers or digital devices is different enough from the server-centered communications environment that we are fascinated by the capabilities of this new approach to collaboration.

This may be the future of online knowledge networking, but the current drawback of P2P software like Groove is the need for the individual user to install and learn to implement its capabilities. Today, the priority of IT is to install and support applications that go through the central server. That will have to change if Groove and other helpful P2P clients are to be used to build collaborative networks on a widespread basis within organizations.

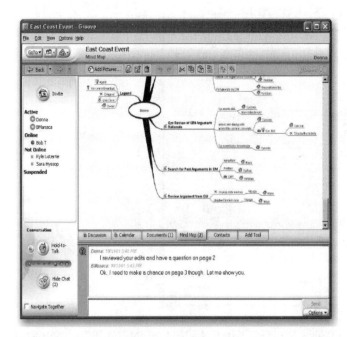

Figure 7.8   An abruptly called conference in the chat window.
©Groove Networks Inc.

Building Environments for Collaboration

An effective online environment is more than the sum of a few complementary tools. It's a combination of design, tools, and features carefully assembled to serve a community or culture. Most organizations are just beginning to recognize this but are hampered in their efforts by the challenges of application integration and their own lack of understanding of how an online community works.

In our study of Hallmark's use of consumer communities, which you'll read more about in Chapter 9, "Conversing with External Shareholders," and Chapter 10, "The Path Ahead," we got to see the work of Communispace (www.communispace.com), a company that combines its software design with community insight to provide appropriate solutions to businesses. Its installation at Hallmark provides a home to groups of consumers who interact with each other and with Hallmark's product design and marketing people in an online community that is more fun than work. And though, as we explain later, the interface is helping the community become a major knowledge resource for Hallmark, we are using Communispace here to illustrate some of the smarter approaches we've seen to matching technology to purpose and culture.

Making Members Feel at Home

The community environment is a combination of personalization and consideration. It greets the returning member on the home page as shown in Figure 7.9. In the most visible spot on the page, the Idea Exchange—an online community of mothers with young children—lets the member know what has happened in the community since the member's last visit. Other announcements are prefaced with the triple asterisks (***) telling members that they come from Hallmark rather than from fellow community members. Members of the community are able to post their own announcements on the home page. It's their community, after all. Helping staff members from the Resource Center are identified by photographs, and the menus in the left column are clearly identified by function.

Lower on the home page, shown in Figure 7.10, is the presence notification of Who's Online. Community facilitators are also identified by photographs, and members are invited to check out their profiles. Getting familiar is a big part of building the trust necessary to get consumers to open up to each other and to Hallmark. Yet Hallmark takes care not to be overbearing. The members themselves are empowered to post the links to timely message board conversations—in this case, on Easter-related topics.

Learning from the Conversation

The purpose of the Idea Exchange is to generate ideas for Hallmark, but as you can see in Figure 7.11, the conversations in its message boards don't look like

Figure 7.9 The home page of Hallmark's Idea Exchange community.
©Hallmark & Communispace

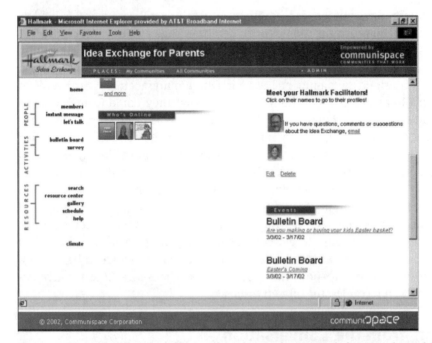

Figure 7.10 Who else is online at the Idea Exchange and the members' highlighted conversations.
©Hallmark & Communispace

those of a product design brainstorming team. Members are encouraged to use the community informally, creating relationships and conversing about their daily lives, challenges, and joys. In this community of moms with young children, they talk a lot about their children and home life. In the process, they not only bond with the community and the site, but they also provide insight into the values of a huge part of Hallmark's market. And again, we see in Figure 7.11 that members are invited to start their own discussions. In fact, most of the conversations are initiated by the members, not by Hallmark. What members choose to talk about is also useful knowledge for Hallmark's creative staff.

The message board for the Idea Exchange has been customized by Communispace for Hallmark's needs. In responding, members designate their messages according to the type symbolized by the icons in Figure 7.12. Knowing whether a message is a question, answer, idea, experience, or opinion not only helps Hallmark track the reasons that people post messages, but it also helps the members themselves quickly recognize the nature of each post. Note that agreements and disagreements are also included in the options. Using them, Hallmark can run quick polls using the message board interface where members hang out rather than ask them to use a different tool. Members are also allowed to make anonymous posts, an important option to offer if you want people to speak out on issues even when they'd rather not identify themselves.

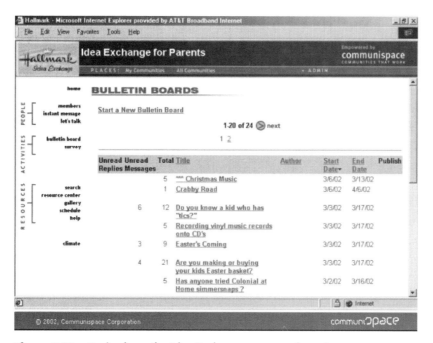

Figure 7.11 Topics from the Idea Exchange message board.
©Hallmark & Communispace

The interface also offers members a list of keywords they can associate with their posts. A dropdown menu lists keywords entered by Hallmark and community members. Associating keywords with messages can help in the analysis of the community's interests.

Hallmark and Communispace, which are learning as much from this project as their client, monitor the activity in the community through a measurement they call climate. Whatever members do in the Idea Exchange, the software tallies it. Figure 7.13 shows a 6-week record of *participation* and *contribution* by members. Participation counts the number of individual logons by members in a week, and contributions measures the total of messages posted on the boards, surveys taken, and visits to chat rooms. In this case, the higher the ratio of contributions to visits, the better.

This is but one instance of the Communispace software and design consulting put to work. On other sites with other companies, it may look and function very differently. But in this case, they provide us with a valuable teaching tool for applying a good balance of technology and social insight. To achieve the purpose of your knowledge network, you need more than powerful tools. Yes, we keep saying that, but it's worth repeating.

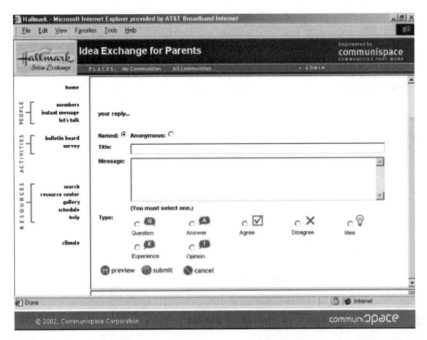

Figure 7.12   Icons describe the nature and purpose of messages posted to the Idea Exchange.
©Hallmark & Communispace

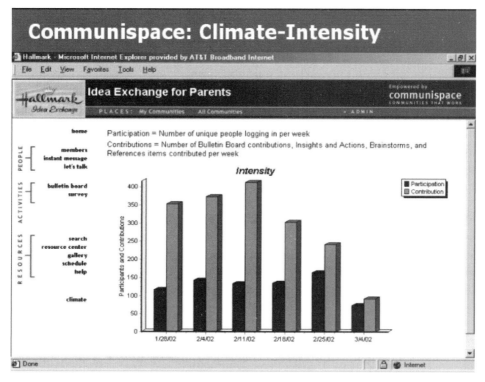

Figure 7.13   A 6-week record of activity and involvement in the Idea Exchange.
©Hallmark & Communispace

Tools for Transitory Conversational Events

There are many situations and occasions when a permanent and ongoing conversational environment is neither required nor appropriate. Many of these fit under the heading of education and instruction, but increasingly, coworkers who are geographically separate simply need a way to meet, collaborate, and share knowledge. These time-bound meeting opportunities can be conducted either asynchronously over a period of days or synchronously over the span of an hour or two.

Asynchronous conferences use message boards for their conversations, with chat an option for allowing attendees and experts to connect or maybe to hold *classes* or Q&A sessions in real time. When the event is better served by bringing people together in live interaction, many organizations and groups now use the technical services of companies like Placeware (www.placeware.com), Centra (www.centra.com), and Webex (www.webex.com) to produce their online meetings.

Asynchronous Conferences

We've participated in and managed asynchronous online conferences and seminars that have lasted for a week to 10 days using message boards and content posted on a Web site. People have paid to participate in some cases and have been invited to participate for free in others. These formats are useful for engaging communities of interest in conversation around a topic, issue, or event. They require meticulous preparation and comprehensive *hosting*, which includes marketing the event in advance, handling signups, creating original content, recruiting thought leaders and experts, managing the interaction once it begins, and providing transcripts or digital copies of the interaction to attendees after the event.

To provide rich experience, the online conference needs the same amount of attention that one would put into planning a face-to-face conference. Instead of renting rooms, preparing nametags, arranging furniture, and providing audiovisual equipment, the virtual conference planner must provide an online meeting area with access restrictions, a clear Web layout of content and community links, informative online profiles of attendees, and technical facilities for presenting a changing menu of interesting content.

Although the conversational platforms used are the same as those used in permanent conversational communities, they must be managed with the pace of the meeting in mind. Conferencing managers must be agile in recognizing the need to wrap up online conversations that have run their course, and in starting new conversations that serve the fast-changing focus of attendees.

In place of keynote speeches, featured experts provide written essays that lead into open online discussion. Attendees are directed to Web pages that also serve as a focus for conversation. And perhaps most important, the "hallway conversations" that serve as the most productive opportunities for knowledge exchange in nonvirtual conferences must be provided in the virtual conference, too. Forums for informal interaction and searchable directories of attendees and their specialties are a requisite feature of the asynchronous seminar.

In 1997, we coproduced a 14-day conversational community around IBM's staging of the chess match between then-world champion Garry Kasparov and IBM's most powerful thinking machine, Deep Blue. We recruited chess grandmasters, chess teachers, chess historians, and programmers of chess-playing computers to serve as our experts and play-by-play commentators for the six chess matches of the contest. We provided a phalanx of experienced online facilitators to be present around the clock in serving the global audience. Hosting activities were coordinated in a private "backstage" conversation area, with one crew shift updating the next as the event proceeded. IBM provided the content—about technology, chess, and the human brain versus silicon intelligence—on their part of the site.

What was evident from Kasparov versus Deep Blue was that an interesting topic can be made even more interesting by providing a wide range of relevant expertise and by active hosting that keeps the conversations lively and encourages attendees to jump in and participate. Knowledge flows best where it is fed and stimulated in the online environment. The chess match was a win-win event: a great marketing success for IBM that provided the thousands of people who signed up and participated in the online conversations with an educational and exciting experience.

Producing Live Events

AOL, which first popularized instant messaging, also pioneered the production of large audience online events with their *auditorium* interface. Inviting celebrities and providing typists to transcribe their responses, AOL allowed thousands of members to attend and submit questions to a moderator who would choose and pass along approved questions to the special guest. The experience of at least having the chance of interacting online with a Michael Jackson or a Billy Graham was compelling enough to the public that AOL realized huge gains in membership and online usage from their presentations. Now the Web has technologies that allow small-to-large groups to meet and exchange questions and answers in much the same way, but with an expanded selection of interactive tools.

Most companies don't have their own internal systems for providing the level of service they can get through specialized companies like Webex. Their need for such services isn't great enough (yet) to make it worthwhile to develop their own in-house system. Thus, they pay companies like Webex to provide the tools and connectivity through which their company can conduct its meetings to serve whatever its immediate needs happen to be. Because of the cost and inconvenience of post-9/11 travel, more companies are making use of these options to conduct business meetings between people in distant offices. Some companies use these real-time events for marketing or to address investors. Some use them to connect professionals around projects, problem solving, or product development. They may be expensive to use, but long-term contracts can be arranged that reduce the cost of a single event to a reasonable level. As the technology matures, costs also should come down.

With all events, planning and orchestration are important. Content must be prepared and submitted to the service provider, and because these events are usually planned with hard schedules, even rehearsal may be necessary when the purpose is addressing a given amount of information to an audience. When these technologies are used for collaboration within teams and knowledge networks, the combination of tools they provide can be quite powerful. In Figure 7.14, Webex is being used by salespeople and product managers to discuss sales strategies. A slide is presented, a chat window is provided, and a list of attendees is displayed. Using the platform's collaborative tools, attendees can draw on the slide.

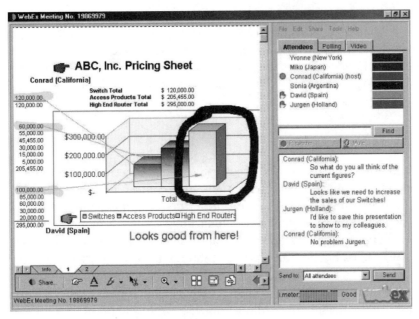

Figure 7.14   A collaborative meeting taking place through Webex.
©Webex

As organizations use event interfaces like Webex more frequently, they will become more familiar, routine, and affordable. We believe they also will justify their expense. As we described, a group of people connected peer-to-peer using Groove can accomplish much the same thing as groups using a platform like Webex. When such meetings can take place spontaneously, without the need for making arrangements ahead of time and scripting the interaction, the online knowledge network will be much closer to matching our natural human social tendencies and behaviors.

Summary

There are many new, powerful but complex technologies available for improved knowledge management, but online knowledge networks rely on the basic technologies that support conversation. These have not changed much in their functional formats for years. You still read what others have posted, and you post your message in a text window. Message boards and chat, though now wrapped in nicer designs and including new features, still work in much the same way as they always have. The same can be said for email, though even that old reliable technology has been expanded to become a carrier of files, data, and even other applications. Our descriptions in this chapter have been about the increased convenience and integration of conversational interfaces and how each interface has its own social characteristics.

Organizations and the knowledge-focused groups that exist within them must make their technology decisions according to the purposes they need to achieve. The aim should be to create an online environment that, through insightful application of technologies and management, motivates the users of the environment to behave in ways that fulfill the organization's purposes.

Though conversational interfaces are key to building the knowledge-sharing relationships, supporting technologies like content management, document coauthoring, and shared whiteboards must be provided to stimulate and support conversation. Software that measures participation and helps participants achieve their individual goals supplies incentives to the organization providing the conversational opportunity and also to the participants who spend their time making use of it. There is no one best solution, even within a single organization. Every organization's needs are unique as are those of every group within every organization. By starting simply and incrementally adding new technologies or changing technologies as the group's online needs become clear, the migration toward a best solution can be smooth and steady.

PART

Three

Practical Applications of Knowledge Networking

In this final section, we provide examples, best practices, and suggested applications for the ideas, tools, and techniques we've described in the previous two parts. We also provide some projections of where online conversation will take the practice of knowledge sharing in the future. Chapter 8, "Initiating and Supporting Internal Conversation," focuses on the use of networked technologies to support communities of practice and working teams in their efforts to make the organization smarter and more efficient. Chapter 9, "Conversing with External Stakeholders," describes how companies are engaging customers and consumers in conversations that reveal the thinking and preferences that drive product development and successful customer service. Chapter 10, "The Path Ahead," features cutting-edge ideas, technologies, and techniques being put to use by pioneering companies today that we believe demonstrate the direction of knowledge networking in the future.

CHAPTER 8

Initiating and Supporting Internal Conversation

In this how-to chapter, we apply the cultural and technical elements of the first seven chapters combined with best practice recommendations to describe a framework for devising, designing, and implementing knowledge networks. This is not a list of quick and easy recipes but a process of analyzing what you've got, clearly stating what you want to accomplish, and choosing from the available options to design the most appropriate social and technical structure.

Our technique is to present recommendations—based on our experience and the experiences of other experts in the fields of knowledge management and online community—for mobilizing and supporting internal communities that will benefit significantly by conversing through the Net. Our instructions will provide some shortcuts, but their main value will be in helping to avoid subtle pitfalls—the miscalculations in social assumptions or interface design that can significantly reduce the enthusiasm, participation, or creativity of a group. Participation is vital to successful knowledge sharing.

We preface our recommendations by reemphasizing that the culture must encourage people to converse with each other online. Our advice alone can't overcome internal resistance to taking conversation to the Net. Some groups working within rigidly hierarchical cultures are satisfied with creating isolated pockets of free knowledge exchange. That may be revolutionary, but it's not guaranteed to inspire a revolution in a resisting company. Fortunately, the trends are swinging in our direction, and more executives are recognizing that it's in their own and their companies' self-interests to support internal group interaction on their intranets.

Cultural Preconditions

We're about to describe the best ways to grow productive knowledge networks on a company's internal network. If we were growing productive tomato plants, we'd begin by making sure the ground—the growing medium—was well prepared for planting the seeds or seedlings. The ground in which a social network is planted is the culture in which it must take root. The manager of an online social network is like a gardener who must get the plants off to a healthy start and then nurture them to maturity and a fruitful harvest. A gardener, though, has more control over the soil conditions of the garden than a knowledge network manager has over the culture of the organization. And though knowledge networking will influence the culture of the organization once it's under way, its interaction will become productive much more quickly if the leaders of the organization assume part of the gardener's role.

In this case, we refer you back to Chapters 4, 5, and 6 where we explored the relationships of culture to organization and technology. Having those relationships in order is the preparation required for getting the most from this chapter. Four optimum conditions highlighted in those earlier chapters are described in Table 8.1.

With these four conditions fulfilled, the recommendations offered in this chapter stand a much greater chances of success.

Table 8.1 Four Optimum Conditions to Have in Place before an Organization's Knowledge Network Can Be Successful

CONDITION	WHAT IT MEANS
Supportive leadership	High-level support removes the resistance to online conversation that stifles participation. Patient support allows time for conversation skills to develop and knowledge benefits to be delivered.
A thirst for knowledge	Demand for online conversational opportunities and motivation for refining knowledge-sharing practices must be strong to bring together and launch an effective knowledge network.
Internet-savvy throughout the organization	To take full advantage of the available tools for online conversation, the organizational culture must be aligned with the realities of Internet communication and an increasingly innovative marketplace.
Collaborative IT department	Building effective online communities for knowledge exchange requires involved technical support that will collaborate with and respond to groups that are constantly learning how their conversation environment can be improved.

Where Consultants Come In

In certain situations during the planning, launch, and maintenance of knowledge-sharing communities, the advice and guidance of outside experts are well worth their cost. On these occasions, consultants can save the organizations time and expense and make significant differences in achieving goals and high productivity. Table 8.2 summarizes the authors' recommendations on this topic.

A consultant with broad experience in social networking, online community, and organizational development can help your company prepare for successful knowledge networking by providing expertise in the following areas:

1. **Cultural assessment and knowledge auditing.** Chapters 5 and 6 explained the impact of certain traits of internal culture on the choice of

Table 8.2 Degrees of Necessity for Consulting in Various Situations

STAGE OF DEVELOPMENT	NEED FOR CONSULTING	TO DO WHAT?
Cultural assessment	High	Provide objective perspective drawn from experience with previous client organizations and groups. Point out traits that will help or hinder adaptation to online conversation.
Proposal	High	Align design of knowledge-sharing project with goals of company and culture of community. Advise on cost justification.
Pilot project	Medium	Identify existing conversational groups that would make the most effective pilot communities.
Prelaunch	Medium	Train and coach leadership and facilitation skills, especially where accelerated learning is mission critical.
Design	High	Match traits and goals of the group with appropriate software, features, and environmental design.
Early conversation	High	Coach conversation leaders and content providers to achieve early success and identify potential core members of community.
Marketing	Medium	Advise on leveraging early activity to attract more members and expand concept within organization.

appropriate technology and the design of online meeting spaces. *Cultural assessment* and *knowledge auditing* are valuable techniques for identifying those traits and determining the formats of interaction that work best with them. A consultant with extensive experience working with diverse organizations with different cultural traits and knowledge needs, and who understands the shifting social dynamics that take place when taking a culture online, will have relevant advice to offer a company going through that transition for the first time.

2. **Identify potential pilot groups.** An experienced consultant can help *identify potential pilot groups* whose natural tendencies to collaborate toward company goals through conversation qualify them to lead the way into the new knowledge-sharing environment. The consultant also can help the organization find existing internal networks or communities of practice that can serve as guides and prototypes for replication within the organization. Not all existing groups are appropriate pilots or models. Some use technologies not adaptable for use by other groups; others have membership requirements too restrictive for other groups to emulate; some are too informal, making them poor models for networks meant to get work done. A qualified consultant can recognize existing opportunities for leverage within the company that may be invisible to managers and executives.

3. **Provide training and coaching.** A consultant who has worked with groups adjusting to conversational interfaces can provide valuable *training and coaching* in community management and facilitation techniques. Although many workers now connect to a local network from their desktop, and a great number of them can reach the Internet, their interface with the company may only take them as far as information access and the basic necessities of email correspondence. Stimulating active knowledge exchange through conversation and taking those conversations online require new skills and new practices that may take time to discover without guidance.

4. **Assist in appropriate interface design.** Appropriate *interface design* for the size, style, structure, and goals of a knowledge-sharing group or an entire organization's needs is an art. Subtle features of the online interface can have a disproportionate affect on the behaviors and reactions of the people using it. Navigational clues (for example, the absence of links to "discussion" on the top-level page of the portal) and wording (inviting people to "join the community" when "join the conversation" is what they'd rather do) can encourage or discourage people from participating. Confusion can result from poor labeling or bad placement of navigational buttons within a discussion environment. The best practice elements of

Web design are inadequate to cover the design of an online meeting environment. Most enterprise-level software products come bundled with limited consulting services or provide customer support through their corporate sites. But not even the software vendor has the cross-discipline expertise to make the conversation environment compatible with the community that a good consultant has studied and analyzed.

5. **Advise on internal marketing.** The best marketing method for attracting more people to an online community is the word of mouth of community members and exposure to the actual interaction of the community. Even the early stages of an organization's online conversations provide a foundation to build on. Someone who has experienced all of the life stages of virtual communities can help the organization *identify social assets* in the young online community. An experienced eye can identify participants who fill vital roles in social ecologies: leaders, facilitators, mediators, provocateurs, and initiators. A qualified consultant can help the organization respond to the suggestions and complaints that will inevitably come from the community as it gets used to its new virtual home.

Selling the Idea

If upper management hasn't initiated the idea of knowledge networking, it will probably need to be convinced that it's a good idea for the company. The job of convincing them is getting easier every day now that knowledge management is being accepted as an essential practice in most organizations. But there may still be resistance, especially to the more self-governing aspects and "out-of-control" perceptions of the conversational knowledge network.

In these days of tightened budgets, every proposal is likely to get microscopic scrutiny. New concepts, such as that of a knowledge network, will encounter even more skepticism because they haven't had the time to generate a lot of successful case studies. Even the cases where intentional, purposeful online discussion has demonstrably helped a company become more innovative or respond better to customers might be regarded as "not applicable to our situation."

In any organization contemplating a knowledge network for sharing information, one of two basic circumstances is true about the level of knowledge sharing in online conversations:

1. No organized online conversation is happening for the purpose of sharing knowledge. Whatever the company does, it will be breaking new ground for itself both culturally and in building new skills. It has no internal guides or "scouts" from whom it can learn.

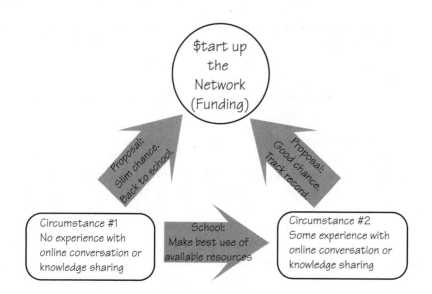

Figure 8.1   Leveraging experience to increase the chances of funding the knowledge network.
©SociAlchemy

2. Such conversations have existed historically or are currently going on. An organization has a base of experience from which it can learn and possibly some internal leaders for the expansion of the practice within the organization.

Which one of these is truer affects the process of selling the idea to decision makers.

Where the Practice Is New to the Company

Let's look at circumstance 1, where no employees are using online technologies in any organized way to share knowledge with each other. Email is available to employees; there may or may not be an intranet or portal with online discussion space. A team or work group has discovered (and agrees) that a more effective environment and process for exchanging knowledge would help them and the company excel.

In such a circumstance, we recommend minimizing the time required to propose and sell the idea and maximizing the use of available technologies and existing social agreements to begin the online knowledge-sharing process. Learn by doing. Demonstrate incremental success. Follow the recommendations made later in this chapter under *Spontaneous Conversational Communities*, and once the network has proven its value, point to that success in a more ambitious proposal. By that time, the group will understand the technical improvements it actually needs for more productive mutual learning and for putting its shared knowledge to work.

Your organization might be open to the idea of skipping these learning steps and diving right in to redefining itself as a knowledge-sharing company. This is a challenge, and we know of at least one company (Buckman Labs, cited in Chapter 5, "Fostering a Knowledge-Sharing Culture") that has pulled it off successfully and become a good example, but full acceptance and adoption of its new system and practices took 3 years. Two conditions must be satisfied for the strategy of skipping the incremental grass-roots learning phase to be a good bet.

1. **The CEO must be receptive to the idea.** This is most likely if there are problems in the organization that she attributes to slow or inefficient knowledge flow. The proposal for a system that increases knowledge exchange may be just the thing she's waiting for. In such a case, the CEO sees the knowledge network as being in perfect alignment with the company's strategy and as a good means for achieving that strategy. We describe such strategic communities later in the chapter.

2. **There is a base of experience in online conversation in the workplace.** People who have spent enough time engaged in online knowledge-sharing activities outside the organization and understand its utility can lead the organization to implementing internal communities without having to discover how it works through slow, incremental experimentation.

The cost of the interface does not have to be a major obstacle in getting approval or starting the network conversation. In fact, simplicity sometimes works in favor of the social interaction rather than against it. In our experience, we've witnessed higher cohesion and interactivity in online communities where the interface was not ideal and presented users with some challenges. In groups such as the early WELL, the early incarnation of Women.com, and in many email discussion groups we've managed and participated in, lack of features and sophistication in the discussion software and online environment forced people to try harder to communicate. They had to solve problems as groups to make the interface work. They were forced to collaborate to invent solutions and raise the quality of the communication.

In taking the cheap and simple route, there are trade-offs, of course; some people won't participate if the interface lacks certain features. Some of the creative energy of the group is used up in figuring out its online conversational processes. But there is something Darwinian at work when the interface selects for the most committed and innovative users. The filtering effect of what amounts to an *interface boot camp* is actually a good way to select participants for the startup stages for an online community when what you want are some willing pioneers to settle the new environment and *civilize* it for the later arrivals.

In sum, where the organization has not yet invested in leveraging online conversation, make the best possible use of tools and internal resources that are already available. Build a pilot network using email or available message boards and take the interaction as far as possible using technology that doesn't cost the company anything. Set reasonable goals, provide good leadership, document achievements, and demonstrate improvements over previous methods of collaboration in the performance of network members or of the group as a whole. The best way to sell an unfamiliar concept is to demonstrate its potential to change the organization in alignment with its strategy.

Where the Company Is Familiar with the Practice

Once an online conversational community has demonstrated its effectiveness within an organization, circumstance 1 is instantly transformed into circumstance 2, with experiential evidence to support the proposal. A track record and a functioning prototype will increase the chances of the proposal being approved.

The leap in effectiveness from conversations using email to conversations using a well-designed message board with content management can be significant depending on the group and the nature of its knowledge exchange. The proposal must outline how the current technology is holding the community back from achieving its potential. The specific gains that can be realized through better supported conversation must be detailed.

As described in Chapter 7, "Choosing and Using Technology," there is a wide range of software and platforms appropriate for knowledge networks. The scale of the conversational community must be large enough to justify the most expensive platforms by spreading out the costs over more users. There may be substantial costs for integrating the platform into the existing technology. There will be costs in training and refining the design once the platform is in use.

A joint proposal representing the needs of other groups within the organization stands a better chance of approval. There may be many other groups expressing the same needs to engage online through better software and wanting more training or more time to spend in online collaboration. The more groups that are allied behind the proposal, the more leverage there is for getting necessary funding. Be willing to compromise and accept software solutions that are less than perfect, at least as an interim concession. Different groups will have different visions of the ideal platform, but if the major features can be agreed on, all groups may benefit to a greater extent than any one of them could on its own.

Remember above all that it's the motivation and focus of the group, not the interface it uses, that is most responsible for the effectiveness of its knowledge exchange. It can be a blessing in disguise to be forced to bootstrap the community conversation from the ground up. If motivation and focus can carry the load in the beginning, the community will eventually earn itself access to better tools, and selling the idea will be relatively easy.

In summary, a group, community, team, or line of business that recognizes a need for more powerful online knowledge sharing should approach the appropriate decision maker with the following:

1. A proposal describing the needs and goals of the group that can be satisfied through online conversation

2. An explanation of the return on investment that the group will provide after it is empowered to converse online

3. A well-researched description, with pricing, of the ideal interface or platform that will fit the group's specific needs

4. Agreement with other groups with similar needs within the organization around a request for a shared platform that will serve them all for less cost than their respective ideal platforms.

Engaging the Stakeholders

Groups that seek to share knowledge may not be aware of how important their eventual success will be to other entities within the organization. These entities—individuals, other groups. or entire departments—are potential allies in all stages of development of the knowledge-sharing community; their knowledge needs intersect and overlap. They should be identified, contacted, and recruited to support the development of the network. As Figure 8.2 shows, there can be a variety of tight and loose ties between a knowledge network and established units and teams within an organization. In this case, we picture a product-related knowledge network that can gather and surface relevant knowledge to serve these relationships. The power of the online knowledge network is largely in its ability to easily involve people who have the knowledge it needs or who need the knowledge it has. These are what we call *stakeholders* in the knowledge conversation.

At Cisco, the original community of networking professionals was envisioned as a closed knowledge loop where individual users of Cisco equipment would meet with each other and share discoveries, experiences, and knowledge. Cisco employees would be involved only as discussion facilitators, encouraging people to participate and contribute but not serving as information providers. However, it was not long before it became obvious how important these conversations might be to other internal knowledge centers within Cisco's organization. Customer service could learn tips and solutions that only the actual users of its equipment had developed. Marketing could learn the strengths and weaknesses of Cisco's and its competitors' products in the language of actual users. Product design and engineering could learn what customers wished for in the way of new products or improvements in existing products.

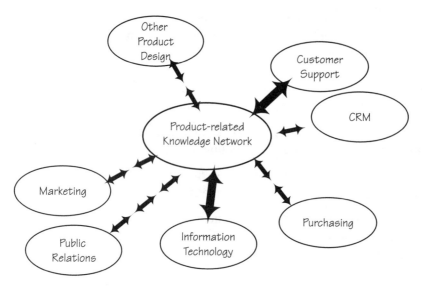

Figure 8.2 Linking in the stakeholders.
©SociAlchemy

When assembling the community, cast a wide net and consider who else in the company might be valuable members or associates, with interest in the knowledge being generated and with valuable knowledge to contribute. Consider who might stand to gain from the community's success. These groups not only help deliver the value of the knowledge network to the different arms of the organization, but they can also bring more leverage to proposals for upgrading systems and platforms. Engaging other stakeholders helps narrow the knowing-doing gap by providing more practical outlets for the knowledge being generated and exchanged.

Incentives to Participate

Return on investment in a platform to support online conversation requires *participation* by the people it is intended to serve. The conversation must not only offer knowledge and information that people will log on to receive; it must stimulate people to contribute that knowledge and refine it through discussion, debate, and collaboration. Many people have experience in online conversation, but it's safe to assume that most have yet to try. What kinds of incentives work to attract them to become productive members of an online knowledge network?

There are four main categories of incentives to join: personal, cultural, goal-oriented, and compensatory. Table 8.3 summarizes the motivating forces that characterize them. Note that there is plenty of overlap. A personal incentive may also have to do with compensation. Cultural incentives also have their goals in the company strategy and mission. A personal goal may be to get a promotion or land a job managing the online communities.

The thirst for faster access to solutions is a powerful force and can attract many people to a conversation where answers are revealed, traded, and created through collaboration. That thirst often is enough incentive for the people who commonly form the core groups in knowledge-sharing communities. No external motivations, carrots, or sticks are required to bring them in. In fact, they probably initiated the community.

But most online conversations initiated to develop knowledge must draw in other people from outside the core group who also hold essential bits, chunks, and piles of knowledge that are difficult to access in any form other than conversation. If they don't show up at the party, the party can't satisfy its attendees. The knowledge development loop remains small and limited in scope.

Table 8.3 Four Main Categories of Incentives to Join a Knowledge Network

TYPE OF INCENTIVE	EXAMPLES
Personal	I want learn from others. I want to help others. I'm curious about the topic or practice. I love participating in online conversation. I want to display my skills in online conversation. I want to be recognized as an expert in my field.
Cultural	Conversation is part of the company "way." Collaboration is the best way to get things done. Prestige comes with regular participation. To not participate is to be out of the loop. If you give, you'll get in return.
Goal-oriented	Online collaboration is the best way to get things done. The project team is meeting online, and that's that! The knowledge network is the most direct way to locate and contact experts. Conversing online saves money in our department's budget.
Compensatory	The company pays bonuses based on new ideas brought to the conversation. The company pays bonuses based on efficiency of operation. Promotions are partially based on regular participation in knowledge networks. New paid positions are being created for managing knowledge networks.

Eliminating Disincentives

Knowledge exchange won't happen online or off if there are cultural *disincentives* to telling others what one knows. If people feel that they will somehow lose opportunities, status, safety, power, prestige, or value in the company by sharing their expertise, their part in a knowledge-sharing conversation will be pretty quiet. A company may take pains to remove disincentives for contributing knowledge, but rather than rest at a *neutral* attitude toward sharing knowledge, there should be clear *positive* incentives for workers to join the online conversation.

Time constraints are a disincentive for many busy workers. One of the main reasons people refuse to adopt any new practice in an organization is the complaint of too little time. Their schedules are full, and asking them to learn and then participate in an activity that may cause them to fall behind in their other work is only going to anger them. Eventually, participation in the knowledge conversation will prove to be a time-saving activity, but there will be a transition period during which the employee has to make a choice: Should I drop what I'm doing and try this new thing or play it safe and keep delivering on my current responsibilities? Only management can make this decision easier and less risky for the employee. Some HR departments have begun allocating extra time for employees to spend seeking knowledge rather than reinventing wheels.

As we've described, an interface that puts barriers in the way of participation or that requires training and practice that consume valuable time can cause potential participants to lose interest early in the process. Using interfaces with which the population is comfortable, even if they lack key features for knowledge exchange, removes these early stage disincentives.

Rewards and Compensation

Financial incentives can be structured to reward individuals or to reward work groups, teams, and divisions. They can be offered as bonuses based on amount of participation in conversation, significant contributions to the knowledge pool, or effectiveness of leadership in a knowledge-generating community. There is little experiential evidence by which to judge the long-term effectiveness of such compensatory incentives.

Davenport and Prusak report that a large consulting firm "revamped its performance appraisal system to include contributions to the firm's knowledge database as an important part of compensation decisions."[2] This may work well in companies that sell knowledge but may not be as practical where knowledge is less central to the business strategy.

New software products record employee activities in ways that can be used to construct incentive reward systems. A product called "Clerity for Enterprise Knowledge Sharing" advertises that its "software and methodologies can create customized, automated incentive systems for your organization that can include points, recognition awards, linkages to human resource and employee review systems or other special programs."[3]

Reputation Enhancement

One of the most powerful and effective incentives is recognition by one's peers as an expert or holder of key knowledge in the group. Being invited to contribute to a conversation is like being invited to speak at a conference; even if you don't get paid, it feels good to be on stage as the center of attention. It feels good to tell people things that you know and they don't. Even being distinguished in the knowledge community's yellow pages directories can be satisfying.

For some, participation in a new or cutting-edge activity such as a knowledge network is reward in itself. The opportunity to be a big fish in a little pond or a pioneer in the company's newest project can be a great attraction. The opportunity to contribute to a community in a tangible way is refreshing to many people whose work seems to disappear into the ether with no response or feedback from its destination. In a conversational community, the likelihood of response is much greater.

Members of a community notice who contributes and whose contributions are most helpful. Reputations can be built in the online social context that may not be accessible in any other form to desk-bound workers. But reputations work in both directions. Those who exhibit selfish or impatient behaviors in a collaborative group can earn themselves social demerits. Redemption is fairly simple, though, because interaction is ongoing, and apologies and reparations are just as visible as offenses and insults. As we pointed out in Chapter 7, software that allows members of the group to rank each other's performance can inhibit participation in the early growth stages of the community. Use such features with discretion because they work best when people can't or don't take the time to form personal relationships.

Reciprocity

The nature of a knowledge-sharing conversation is that helpful information and ideas move in both directions: from the participant to the community and from other members of the community back to the participant. Once the reliability of the exchange has been established, contributors of knowledge are likely to return because they expect that they will be enriched in equal measure to what they have given. Reciprocity does not necessarily work throughout the organization. People don't have agreements to reciprocate, and they have limited opportunities to do so in their irregular encounters with each other.

In an online environment dedicated to the exchange of knowledge, it's easier to keep one's books straight on who has contributed and who has not. Because the transactional record is there for everyone to read, a sense of balance and fairness is apparent, at least to regular participants. Once the knowledge marketplace has begun working, members know that they can offer what they've learned and that they can learn from what others offer. The incentive to participate becomes part of the marketplace mentality. Marketplaces *are* conversations.

The Membership Effect

The most basic incentive to participate in any community is the sense of community that comes with it: the feeling of being part of something bigger than one's self. The social rewards of membership in a group can be compelling, especially if the group has a purpose and an agreement to collaborate civilly toward achieving common goals. Leadership and role modeling are important in establishing such cultural agreements, and mastering challenges together reinforces the bonds that make teams and conversational communities more efficient.

Thus, the founding members or central interest of a knowledge-sharing community may be the most effective incentives for participation by others. Communities of practice form around common interests, and their motivation to pursue those interests can overcome even powerful disincentives like lack of time and primitive conversational environments.

Learning to Tell Stories

Storytelling is as old as spoken language. As we related in Chapter 1, "Knowledge, History, and the Industrial Organization," it's the bedrock of knowledge transfer. In Chapter 2, "Using the Net to Share What People Know," we described how the WELL's True Confessions conference, with its autobiographical stories, was so influential in building trust within the community. Some people are natural storytellers, whereas others prefer to be on the receiving end of a good story. As a means of generating new ideas and explaining one's experience, stories are the ultimate knowledge transfer medium.

Story Power

To take it one step further, we recommend without qualification that people use the Net to tell stories to each other. This is no longer a belief held by an intellectual fringe; stories are now being adopted as the format for everything from organizational change to product branding. Storytelling is a skill worth learning and could become a distinguishing feature of leadership in a knowledge-oriented culture. People react to stories; we seem to be wired internally to follow from beginnings to middles to ends and to interpret deeper meaning from the tales we hear. Stories elicit emotional responses in us and awaken the human part that wants to connect with others. And some stories make us think.

Within an organization, especially one driven by business values and profit, the humanizing effect of sharing experiential stories builds trust. Trust, as we've emphasized throughout this book, is powerful stuff. A knowledge network can be effective without fancy software, but it can't be effective without trust. People must feel safe to pour out what they know and believe to be true. Stories not only provide an easily interpreted explanation of knowledge, but they also reveal the storytellers as fellow humans, making them more real and trustworthy to the virtual audience.

SHARING KNOWLEDGE THROUGH STORIES

The story format is a teaching tool. A good story for imparting knowledge drawn from personal experience includes the following:

1. **Background: How you learned what you know**
2. **Context: Why it was important**
3. **Beginning: What you did or tried first**
4. **Middle: The failure or breakthrough that was the lesson**
5. **End: How you confirmed your success or failure**
6. **Reflection: What you've learned about it since**

Stories told online work best when kept brief and concise. As they say, "Brevity is the soul of wit." Most busy readers would agree.

The storytelling style should be modeled and encouraged in all online conversations aimed at sharing knowledge. Elements of effective storytelling should be part of the organization's training for knowledge community leaders and facilitators.

Describing how one learned something not only imparts the knowledge, it wraps that knowledge in an applicable lesson. True knowledge sharing is not the simplistic activity of asking and answering questions; it's a process of raising the collective intelligence and problem-solving capacity of the group or organization and providing the group with better handles for putting knowledge to work and implementing new ideas.

Stories also are more interesting to read and write than dry facts and information; they make participation in an online conversation more enjoyable and engaging, retaining more participants. In the pursuit of practical knowledge, stories provide context. They serve as a framework for delivering one's experience to others in ways that teach and inspire as well as inform and entertain.

Springboard Stories Go Online

Stephen Denning has a special view and purpose for telling stories. In *The Springboard*,[1] he describes the story as "a launching device aimed at enabling a whole group of people to leap—mentally—higher than they otherwise might, to get beyond mere common sense." This is more than a teaching function or simple knowledge exchange. It is more akin to intellectual stimulation or a call to action. Denning's stories are short and tend to describe possibilities based on actual events. They are carefully assembled and delivered. The springboard story is meant to catalyze organizational change.

Springboard stories share some common elements. They generally begin with a protagonist and what he calls "the predicament" that describes a problem the audience can relate to. They then move on to "the resolution of the predicament, embodying the change idea." This is meant to stimulate audience thinking, where they apply the change idea to their organization. The story wraps up either with "extrapolating the story to complete the picture" or with "drawing out the implications." Sometimes both elements are included. They help the audience connect the change idea with practical implications for their specific situations.

HOW A STORY CHANGED THE WORLD BANK

It takes one page in Stephen Denning's *The Springboard* to tell the story that he claims led to "an explosion of new energy and momentum" at the huge international organization. The story was a simple one, relating how email contacts brought the right expertise and appropriate solutions to fix rapidly deteriorating roads in Pakistan.

What made the story so powerful was its relevance to what was then a growing concern in the World Bank: that the global financial crisis was looking more and more unmanageable.

The rapid response and marshaling of road repair experience from around the world—as related in the short springboard story—*changed perceptions and raised hopes* that new solutions were at hand and that some of its people knew how to use them. Maybe there was light at the end of the tunnel after all.

The story inspired Denning's World Bank colleagues to recognize a solution that it could adapt to many of its international situations.

The potential power of a springboard story is proportional to the need for knowledge that must be satisfied. The right story, delivered at the right time, can mobilize people to adopt new practices and to effect change in the organization.

Denning's book assumes its readers will use his lessons in face-to-face situations. Drawing from his recommendations, we've adapted them to the virtual meeting place and present those adapted recommendations as follows:

1. Study and understand your audience. As Denning says, "You implicitly reflect the inner cravings of your audience." Your understanding will come across in your story.

2. In preparing a story for online presentation, emphasize qualities such as conviction, readiness, and a sense of ownership of the content of the

story. Unlike stories told face-to-face, online stories are not usually presented repeatedly to different audiences. But once an online story is posted, it may be distributed to many different groups and individuals.

3. Unlike Denning's in-person situation, posting a story online allows the author to continue interacting with his or her audience, expanding on the story's theme, or using it as a starting point for developing innovative ideas. Remaining available for follow-up discussion is appropriate in conversational communities.

4. Take care in composing stories to be presented as text. Be economical in the use of words. Tell the story as briefly and concisely as possible. Break up the story into small paragraphs for easier reading. Use proper punctuation and check your spelling. Select a readable typeface such as Times New Roman and double space the lines. Your presentation is important.

5. Do not complement your story with visual aids (such as Web graphics, Power Point slides, attached documents with charts) unless it's necessary. Don't distract the audience from the essence of the message, whether it's a lesson, relevant experience, or a moral meant to mobilize the audience to action.

6. Emphasize key points in the story through whatever conventions are available in the medium being used. **Embolden** or *italicize* words, or in plain-text email, use punctuation marks to *emphasize* specific words or phrases. Isolate key sentences or paragraphs to ensure that they stand out for readers.

7. Denning advises springboard storytellers, "As a presenter, you must above all believe in your presentation." In the impersonal environment of the Net, where each participant in a conversation sits alone in front of a keyboard, it's tempting to treat what one posts to the screen lightly. Yet, when the discussion environment is defined by a collective hunger for useful knowledge, a story told with deep belief is likely to be read with correspondingly deep attention and respect.

Stories fit well within all three of the community types we are about to describe. One story may be the seed that launches a conversational community, or storytelling may be the preferred style for a knowledge exchange community.

Change is a dire need in many organizations and an aspired-to value in others. The springboard story—brief, illustrative, relevant, sometimes inspiring, sometimes unsettling—is a valuable instrument for catalyzing and directing change. It can be used by managers and team leaders but can just as easily be applied by frontline workers. As an igniter of innovative conversation or as an initiator of a new knowledge-sharing community, a springboard story can be quite effective.

The Practice of Online Conversation

We described what we did on the WELL as "talking through typing." Although the physical act of pressing keys and constructing words and sentences was identical to that used in composing a letter or writing a book, the sense we had as we typed those words was one of responding to something that someone had just said to us. And in the course of an hour, we would find ourselves feeling as if we'd been in 10 or 20 different discussions covering that many topics and involving perhaps dozens of people.

Talking through typing takes some getting used to. It takes some suspension of disbelief that the participants in the virtual conversation are actually as remote from each other as they physically are. The fact that the other participants might be down the hall, on another floor, in another building, or in another country is not so important in the exchange of ideas. But that remoteness—along with the lack of visual and auditory clues that transmit mood, meaning, and style—must be compensated for in the online relationship. The style and quality of writing and reading can make a virtual conversation feel more sincere, detailed, trustworthy, and human.

As an aid to those engaging in continuing online conversation for the first time, we have compiled a list of basic competencies in effective online conversation (see Table 8.4). They begin with the practice of leading and initiating conversations, move into recommendations for composing messages and responses in a conversation, and gradually pull back in focus to describe ways of envisioning the conversational landscape.

Table 8.4 Basic Competencies in Continuing Online Conversation

KEY PRACTICES FOR EFFECTIVE ONLINE CONVERSATION	WHY THEY ARE IMPORTANT
Create a tone of invitation and openness	Leaders are recognized by the attention they pay to motivating people to participate. Welcome newcomers and thank contributors.
State the purpose and goals of the conversation	Make it clear what the discussion is about and what it is supposed to achieve. Be attentive to titles of discussions and subject lines of messages.
Manage time constraints	Lead conversations to reasonable resolution, especially if there are time limits and deadlines. Open-ended discussions can become time wasters.
Avoid unproductive argument	Argument is good, up to a point. When an argument cannot be resolved in the conversational forum, redirect it to email or "offline resolution" to avoid distracting the community.

Table 8.4 *(Continued)*

KEY PRACTICES FOR EFFECTIVE ONLINE CONVERSATION	WHY THEY ARE IMPORTANT
Facilitate disagreement	When two members are at odds, attempt to mediate their disagreement within the community's value in civility. Use *backchannels* to help resolve spats outside the conversation space.
Partition formal and informal conversation	Provide conversation areas for informal interaction that serve to build trust and strengthen relationships. Keep these areas distinct from those used for work, knowledge sharing, and problem solving.
Avoid opening excess conversations	Given the number of participants, only a certain number of active conversations can be supported. Open new conversations only when there is demand.
Identify people in official roles	Make it plain which members are in leadership positions or who have control over conversation management tools. Use special user names or symbols to designate them in the space.
Remember: It's a *postocracy*	Those who post the most words command the most attention, but they don't necessarily contribute the most useful knowledge. Make sure prolific posters leave room for others.
Follow up on your controversial posts	Don't post messages guaranteed to elicit strong reactions and then fail to show up to respond. It's a conversation, and it's rude to stir things up and leave.
Be accountable for your contributions	Be ready to back up information that is challenged. Again, in a conversation focused on knowledge, all parties should be fully engaged as information providers and experts.
Communicate clearly	Take pains to compose messages carefully. Use uppercase and lowercase appropriately. Check spelling and grammar. Break up messages into small paragraphs and be concise.
Be honest	Don't play a role different from who you really are unless the conversation manager has declared it to be virtual Halloween.

Leading Online Conversation

The tone and wording of the first content in a new online discussion are very influential on the subsequent interaction. When the words and tone are inviting and communicate openness and enthusiasm, they are more likely to elicit response than dry, businesslike remarks. It's okay to overdo the emotional content somewhat to offset the impersonal nature of the medium.

A conversation space for knowledge exchange has a purpose. The question is: How specific is the purpose? This should be clarified at the outset of every new conversation or collection of conversations. A reminder on the entry screen to the discussion space is a good idea, and attention to the labeling of topics helps remind participants of their focus of interaction. If there is a deadline or time limit on the conversation, a facilitator should be minding the clock (or calendar) and leading discussion toward resolution in advance of the deadline.

Facilitation may also entail regularly summarizing lessons learned, points made, and issues still left unresolved. A facilitator, if there is one, has specific responsibilities that also should be made clear to participants. In some cases, a facilitator will serve in the role of debate moderator or even referee, charged with helping to resolve or settle arguments. The classic role of a facilitator is to help meetings and discussions stay on track toward a goal by getting people involved and clarifying their contributions to the conversation. If there are disagreements of substance, the facilitator points out the relevance of the disagreement to the group and attempts to lead it to consensus or resolution.

If some people hold special roles in the community, as moderators, facilitators, hosts, or leaders, their identities should be made clear to the rest of the community. New joiners won't necessarily recognize which members hold positions of authority, and for the sake of convenience and orderliness, they should have special user names or other obvious designations in the online environment.

As important to smooth knowledge flow as any other factor is the building of trust and relationship. These may happen offline already, but if there are no opportunities for community members to meet in person and spend time with each other informally, the opportunities must be provided in the online meeting space. The kind of interaction that builds trust and relationship is not the same as knowledge sharing, so it's wise to make a clear partition between knowledge exchange areas and social hangout areas as the site is designed and organized. In a simple email conversation list, participants should take the time to correspond with each other individually rather than overload list recipients with social chitchat.

Participating in Online Conversation

Some veterans of the activity believe that online communities are good for extending conversations but bad for resolving them. Because in most cases the conversations happen without moderation or facilitation, they are subject to an effect that could be called *the last word obsession*. Everyone wants to get in the last word, and if the conversation has been left open to additional posts, the issue being discussed may never be settled. The cure for this is to include a moderator or facilitator in any discussion that must be resolved or in any community that shows tendencies to argue rather than reach agreement. Responsible participants can control their urges to get in the last word by simply paying attention to the sense of the conversation. Every conversation has a natural ending, and learning what that means is part of learning to be a good online conversationalist.

In the same vein, a knowledge-sharing community should learn the value of avoiding unproductive arguments. These not only distract other members from pursuing the knowledge they need, but they can poison the social well, eroding trust and making participation unpleasant enough to overcome whatever incentives drew people to the community in the first place. As the old Western sheriffs used to say, "Check your guns at the door." The purpose of the community is to get smarter, not dumber.

Some people avoid argument by posting something controversial and then logging out, without returning to deal with the responses they have provoked. This, too, can be deadly to a culture based on goodwill and trust. Accountability is important in professional communities, unlike some consumer-based forums where anonymous participation is invited. If you post something, take responsibility for it and be around for follow-up discussion. Be yourself; don't assume roles that will confuse people about your true identity, what you really think, and how you really behave. If the purpose is to exchange knowledge, don't mix fact with fantasy.

All participants in an ongoing online knowledge-sharing community have equal responsibility to be clear in their communication. This means being a good reader (the text-based analog to being a good listener) and taking part in coherent discourse. Good writing skills should be developed for the sake of the reading audience, and attention should be paid to details of spelling, grammar, composition, and the organization of thoughts. It all makes a big difference, not only in the regard in which the person will be held but also in the overall quality of the knowledge exchange. You'll appreciate good writers when you've been subjected to enough bad ones.

Remember that an online discussion community is a *postocracy* where those who post their comments and responses get more attention than those who don't. As Woody Allen said, 80 percent of success is showing up, and in an online community, that's how recognition works. If you make your presence known, you're part of the conversation. If you don't, then you aren't. And where reciprocity is a big incentive for participation, it's important that every member contributes his or her share to the knowledge pool.

Organizing the Community

In the simplest online communities for knowledge exchange, there is likely to be one focus, one purpose, and one fairly stable group of participants. Aside from the occasional scheduling intervention by leaders or initiators in the group, there are few organizational concerns. The main questions about membership are how many should there be and who should be invited.

As the community grows and diversifies—attending to wider ranges of knowledge and serving different groups and needs—organizational issues arise. These have to do with leadership, responsibility, and access rights. How will the discussion space be partitioned and controlled? Who will have access to the tools for managing the interface and the database of conversations? Will policies for participation be the same across all communities, or will there be different ground rules in different forums?

Each group must consider, for example, how it will determine membership. Will a certain amount of participation be necessary to retain access rights? Will members be allowed to read without contributing their own posts? Will *lurking* (reading the contents of online conversations without even logging on to the discussion space) be allowed or encouraged? In some cases, this can be a good thing; it allows people who are considering joining an online community to look through a virtual window and decide if it's the kind of interaction they'd like to be part of.

An original knowledge-sharing community has to decide if it wants to divide into subcommunities, and if so, how to arrange it socially and technically. It may also have to decide, once the original focus begins to break down, if those *daughter* communities should be spun off into their own separate conversational forums.

We described some best practices for leading online communities, but in terms of leadership, there are other roles to consider beyond moderator and facilitator. When there are many conversations going on in parallel, a *coordinator* or *administrator* may be needed to take care of the content and to do *housekeeping* through the discussion interface. This involves archiving or deleting old conversations, retitling conversations whose original titles don't match their content, and scheduling intentional conversations when specific knowledge needs arise in the organization.

The ideal situation in an online community is to achieve a level of self-governance that minimizes the need for oversight, leadership, and external control. Self-governance must be learned collectively; early attempts are prone to power struggles between people with differing views of what self-governance entails. The presence of what we call a *benevolent dictator* can quell small civil wars before they threaten the community and maintain control of the tools for removing damaging content and restricting access. A determined disruptor can ruin a community before it has a chance to grow, and it's sometimes necessary to ban such people until they understand the necessity of civil discourse.

Community health is of interest not only to the members but should be of interest to other people in the organization who depend on the knowledge generated and shared in its conversations. Social breakdowns do occur, and although there are no objective measurements to indicate the health or sickness of a community, there are ways to assess it that have meaning. A community leader should, for example, keep a conversation open for discussion of *meta* issues—the social and behavioral aspects (as opposed to the knowledge-sharing aspects) of the community as a whole. Meta conversations occur when the community talks about itself and how it's doing. They provide clues pointing to potential threats to trust and openness that can short-circuit knowledge exchange. They bring up warnings about dissatisfaction of key participants or problems with the interface that need to be remedied. Meta discussions are also important in establishing the community's sense of itself as a distinct social entity, which is an important aspect of the identification of its members with the group.

Spontaneous Conversational Communities

"Let's get together and talk about it."

That's the spontaneous beginning of a dialogue in which two people exchange their unanswered questions, their viewpoints, and their stories. Or that's the beginning of a discussion in which a group of people with a shared interest does the same. The stimulus for these conversations may be a pending deadline, a potential project, a crisis in the organization, or mutual curiosity. The only requirements for making the conversations possible are agreed-upon time and place—a time when the participants can communicate and a place where they can gather. The Net simplifies those requirements. People can now get together without synchronizing their schedules and without meeting physically.

The Organization's Stake

Spontaneous communities that provide value to the organization are more likely to be approved, supported, and promoted. How do they provide value? Here are several ways:

1. They discover useful knowledge and solutions that more formal groups often miss

2. They learn on their own how to manage collaborative online conversation and group process

3. They incubate new ideas and develop prototypes that can then be put to use by others in the organization

4. They develop teachers and leaders for more widespread practice of online conversation and knowledge exchange

Spontaneous communities form (and dissolve) constantly within organizations whether the management is aware of them or not. Many of them make use of the internal resources such as paid time, office space, and bandwidth on the intranet. It's in the organization's interest to get some value out of them.

Some grass-roots groups come together spontaneously to form true communities of practice. We'll describe their special case later in this chapter. Other groups are less focused on pursuing common interests and more interested in having convenient access to an online forum where they can get reliable and expert answers to their questions. Such forums may form spontaneously, using whatever communications tools are available. Or they may be provided by an organization on its intranet as part of its knowledge management strategy. Often, though, spontaneous communities appear to fill a vacuum, becoming the organization's first experiments in online community.

ENCOURAGING AND INHIBITING SPONTANEITY

The organization can provide the following support and training aids to foster the emergence, survival, and effectiveness of spontaneous conversational groups:

1. Quick and easy access to an online meeting medium
2. A purpose recognized as important and interesting
3. Unwavering focus on that purpose
4. A founding core group of participants
5. Agreement about presence or absence of a leader
6. Regular input by the core group
7. Room for informal relationship building
8. Internal critique of the process and content
9. Consideration for the convenience of fellow participants
10. Attention to keeping messages as brief as possible
11. Agreement about whether or not to include copies of previous messages in all responses

Factors such as the following inhibit spontaneous groups from forming or surviving:

1. Red tape that slows initiation of the group
2. Lack of agreement on what the conversation is about
3. Rules too strict to attract participation
4. Too many participants
5. No sense of ownership by participants
6. Failure to affect the organization
7. Poor email management by participants
8. Disregard for the convenience or feelings of others

Spontaneous communities may be the explorers and pioneers in an organization's migration to new cultural practices and new customer relationships. Working behind the scenes, they take chances and occasionally suffer setbacks, but at minimal cost to the organization. They gain experience in managing the social processes of online conversation and relationship building. They learn to deal with the shifting dynamics of group interaction over time. They become the organization's local experts in virtual community. Their accumulated experience is an asset that the sponsoring organization should both realize it has and put to good use.

Knowledge-sharing networks initiated by workers are fertile incubators for new ideas and practices that can enhance the organization in many ways. Collaborative networks build intellectual and social capital for the company. The initiators and leaders of productive spontaneous communities may help the organization to expand knowledge-sharing practices as internal consultants. Experienced knowledge networkers can author training programs to disseminate new collaborative skills throughout the organization.

Who Is Responsible?

Where do grass-roots efforts fit within an organization's hierarchy and management processes? Who owns these bottom-up projects and who makes use of their output? Who harvests the knowledge they generate through their conversations and the social techniques they invent? Who decides whether they are a valid and productive use of resources? How involved should a company be in providing and maintaining the technical means for their formation and operation?

Peer-to-peer networks link individuals and offer perhaps the optimum in personalization through the network. They encourage and support each user's decisions about who is included in their personal network and how to interact with each member of that network. The individuality of the interface in a program such as Groove may work both for and against fluid collaboration. The exclusivity that each individual can enforce can eliminate extraneous communications, but it can also block what could be valuable input. In practice, a P2P knowledge-sharing network should be managed in much the same way as an email list. If used as the operational base for a spontaneous knowledge network, the members of the network must pay attention not only to the focus of their interest but to what they might be missing by using an interface separated from the intranet.

There's a romanticized idea that cabals of workers, meeting in secret and independently developing projects below the radar of the organization—so-called *skunk-works* teams—are good things for the organization. Because of a few notable successes, legend has it that skunk-works teams are made up of geniuses, and their inventions invariably revolutionize the company, which looks dumb for having forced its best employees into secrecy.

In fact, skunk-works teams are not commonly composed of geniuses and do not often invent successful products. We don't hear much about their failures, of course. And because of their invisibility, whatever good things they do discover in the way of new knowledge and process are not made available to the organization. So although spontaneous communities might warrant some protection from the effects of overexposure and overpopulation, they should remain visible and active contributors to the organization.

That said, here are five recommendations for realizing value from spontaneous knowledge-sharing communities:

1. Appoint or hire someone to serve in the role of *knowledge coordinator*, or KC. The KC, in this case, is the recipient and distributor of things learned in spontaneous groups.

2. Announce to all employees that the company will support any spontaneous group conversation on its intranet or email system that identifies a representative who will stay in regular contact with the KC.

3. Make it clear that the company management will not interfere with the natural formation and development of these groups and their interactions unless it is specifically invited to participate. If appropriate, such groups can operate with restricted access. Groups that wish to remain private should be respected as long as they communicate with the KC.

4. Create a means by which knowledge of use to other groups or to the organization as a whole can be extracted from the spontaneous communities. These may be discoveries about the company, its products or services, suggested interface improvements, or the process of managing group interaction toward goals. A periodic community made up of community representatives and the KC may convene to build more knowledge about knowledge-sharing practices.

5. Report to the organization as a whole valuable lessons learned in spontaneous communities. If appropriate, evangelize discovered practices that improve on current practices. As spontaneous groups build histories, have their leaders, representatives, and active participants report on their experiences and best practices in meetings and online Q&A sessions.

In objective and dollar terms, the returns from spontaneous networks are difficult to measure. Anecdotal evidence is useful, though, because it's also difficult to measure the time lost and frustration experienced in seeking vital knowledge through database searching and not finding relevant answers. Spontaneous networks don't cost the company much to support and administer, but to make them as productive and useful to the company as possible, there are things the company can do to bring out the best in them.

Fostering Spontaneity

Self-starting, self-governing, self-sustaining innovative teams that provide new knowledge to the organization are valuable assets. The same can be said about employees who communicate and collaborate productively without the need for micromanagement or IT handholding. A company can build these assets for the relatively cheap price of some meaningful cultural support. Creative people aren't as likely to initiate spontaneous networks if they suspect the company doesn't approve of such activities. They're much more likely to start networks if they know it's not only okay but appreciated by the company. So an unambiguous statement by the leadership of the organization, as we described a few paragraphs earlier, is important.

PROJECTS AS KNOWLEDGE TRAPS

Spontaneous online communities are often formed to implement projects, but these teams and their activities, like skunk works, may not enhance the organization's overall knowledge-sharing culture. As Davenport and Prusak write in the updated preface to *Working Knowledge*, "projects are by definition peripheral to the rest of the business. Projects 'bottle up' knowledge and treat it as something separate."[2] What the project team learns in the course of its work is not recorded or communicated to the rest of the organization in a helpful way.

This problem of "lost project knowledge" can be overcome if the project team communicates and records its activities through online conversation. Although slower than voice and in-person meetings, online collaboration provides a medium through which lessons learned can be referenced by others.

A knowledge strategy must tap into gold mines like project teams to learn from its most able and active teachers—the focused, time-pressed, coordinated, collaborative, and organized members of project teams. Online debriefings by team members, participating in Q&A sessions with other interested parties in the organization, are an alternative method for capturing project-generated tacit knowledge.

As we all know from our office lives, most people are satisfied to use whatever means are convenient and available to meet with and learn from each other. We meet in the company's cafeteria, in hallways and lobbies, or in temporarily vacant offices. It's not the environment that matters; it's the contact, the content, and the effectiveness of the communication.

In the online realm, people who simply want effective communication with a small group may be satisfied using email or the commercial messaging clients they download from Microsoft or AOL. They don't think in terms of asking the company to provide them with a new software platform. People intent on spontaneous group communication don't look for elegant solutions; they tend to adopt what is familiar to group members.

If the organization is aware that such groups are forming and recognizes potential benefits from their collaboration, it can provide support to help them succeed. It may be in the form of technical help in setting up email lists or custom configuring a private discussion space on the company intranet. It may be in providing authorization and entitlement for restricted access to the group's online home. It's important that the culture make people feel safe in proposing new knowledge-sharing groups and in selectively supporting them when they come forward with their ideas.

One characteristic of participants in spontaneous knowledge networks is their sense of independence and freewheeling exchange. As organic entities, they may invent or adopt styles of interaction unique to their groups and very different from the visible *artifact* level of the organization's overall culture. In an online environment, a very strong sense of unity is possible. That sense may be creative but also rebellious, confident but also vulnerable and wary of any management attempt to control or interfere with its self-governance. The relationship between an organization and the spontaneous knowledge networks it supports should resemble patron and artist: The sponsor supports the artist from a distance with faith that the creative spark will pay the patron back, and then some.

This is not to say that the organization must support every group that wants to use its network infrastructure as a regular meeting place; resources do have limits. But given limited resources, the organization should first support the aspiring communities that are most important to (and aligned with) its strategy. In Chapter 3, "Strategy and Planning for the Knowledge Network," we described "knowledge of maximum leverage," explaining how groups that seek, share, and generate such knowledge should get priority treatment and support.

Successful spontaneous communities advance strategy and cultural change most effectively if their work is transparent to the organization. They should serve as prototypes and learning models to bring maximum value to their sponsors. As Davenport and Prusak write: "it's not terribly difficult to envision ways of using knowledge more effectively in business strategy. The difficulty, of course, is in making changes to strategic programs and adopting the necessary behaviors throughout your organization." Spontaneous knowledge sharing helps push those changes along while modeling those necessary behaviors.

Life Cycles of Spontaneous Communities

Communities that form spontaneously are just as likely to dissolve spontaneously. Because they are powered by passions and interest, they are subject to the periodic fading of those power sources or to the loss of key participants and leaders. The sponsoring organization should stay aware of the various segments of its knowledge network, not only to learn from them but also to know which of them are vigorous, which are dying, and which are going through periods of activity and quiet.

Networks formed by special project teams fire up quickly at birth and burn brightly, fueled by high focus and motivation until the project is done or the problem is solved. The knowledge sharing required to meet the deadline is intense. After that, their members disband and the activity fades out. Their reason for being has disappeared, and their purpose has been fulfilled.

Other networks form for a purpose that remains vital; the problem doesn't ever get completely solved but changes shape and requires the group constantly to adapt. These groups may show cyclical ebbs and flows in their activity and creative spirit. The organization should be aware of these dynamics in its management of the communications platform and support of the groups that are using it. There should be regular communications between the leaders of spontaneous networks and a clearly identified administrator of the communications platform being used so that communities going through lulls in activity are not mistaken for communities that have ceased to be.

Though we recommend that they serve as prototypes for the company, the success of a spontaneous conversational community can be its worst enemy. When such a group is regarded as a best practice example, labeled by the company with a gold star, it may gain prestige but lose the anonymity that was part of its appeal. Suddenly, waves of people want to join the community or observe what makes it tick. Executives in the organization want to analyze it and break it down for replication. Tech magazines may even want to write an article about it. Its world is changed into a fishbowl, and the uninhibited spirit that was responsible for its initial success is threatened. Most people stop feeling so open and creative when thrust into the roles of cast members in a dramatized online *demo* community.

External forces can shut down free-flowing conversation, but equally damaging to the creative spirit can be the inflated sense of self-importance that cohesive communities often develop, especially after being recognized as exceptional and successful. Such communities may become isolated from the rest of the organization, too exclusive to accept input from nonmembers. The WELL became that way after it began getting mentioned in the national press in the late 1980s. As new members appeared, they were challenged. Members began to be preoccupied with the value of their words and of the WELL's conversations to the detriment of the quality of the discourse that had attracted the press attention in the first place.

So how can the organization make the best use of a successful community's example without "killing the goose that laid the golden egg"? First, don't allow the online meeting places of such groups to become tourist attractions; keep them closed to all but their natural community members. If the community has something to teach the organization, arrange an online forum, event, or in-person meeting where its members can answer questions and describe their techniques. In general, use discretion when heaping praise on grass-roots conversational groups or on any productive collaborative groups, regardless of their sources. Learn from their success and provide a repository for lessons learned about their techniques, mix of talents, and style of communication, but don't turn the glare of the spotlight on them and distract them from their good work.

Beyond the realm of organizational values, missions, and policies, though, there must be an online medium available to people in the workplace through which they can participate in such communities. One medium remains, after almost 40 years, the most ubiquitous and understood means of group communication over the Net: email.

Enabling Email Groups

The founding participants of the Kraken at Price Waterhouse saw themselves as a group of "self-selected creatives" looking for a way to collaborate more innovatively than they could within the established structure of the large consultancy. To that end, they made use of their Lotus Notes email, a tool that was accessible to all employees and could be configured appropriately without having to submit a formal proposal, wait for funding, or explain their needs to IT.

Their technique was simple: Make a list of email recipients that was shared by all of the original members. Every message reached everyone on the list. Every response to every message reached the same list. Any individual was free to read or ignore each message. Success relied only on regular participation and the perceived value of new knowledge (or of appreciation) that each member realized by participating.

They named their interactive email list after a mythological sea creature of great power (the Kraken) that lived largely out of sight. Word soon got around about this low-profile but exceptionally productive knowledge exchange, and others were allowed to join—to have their names added to the email list. Even after the merger of Price Waterhouse with Coopers & Lybrand (another large accounting and consultancy firm), the Kraken continued to exist and grow to about 500 members. Its success has since spawned new internal email lists for knowledge exchange within the firm, serving different purposes and including different categories of expertise.

The Kraken is notable as an example of spontaneous knowledge exchange for several reasons:

1. It formed around recognition of common needs

2. It used a familiar and readily available communications interface

3. It followed no company-dictated agenda or schedule of deliverables

4. It cost practically nothing to create and to maintain

5. Its members saw it as an effective means for innovative collaboration

This last reason is especially telling because following the merger, PriceWaterhouseCoopers put in place an elaborately designed interface called KnowledgeCurve to expand its knowledge management activities. KnowledgeCurve was not used as often or with as much enthusiasm as the email-mediated communities. It was not considered by employees to be as effective in disseminating usable knowledge.

The strength of email is that it is so basic and adaptable. Every employee with a networked computer on the desktop now has an email account and knows how to send and receive messages. No new software is required; the IT department doesn't need to install or integrate new software into its systems. People are free to adjust their participation according to their available time. The tool does not drive the worker, so there is less resentment of its use.

Nevertheless, some practices should be learned and adopted to make email productive for knowledge sharing. Because there is so little structure—for example, an email conversation does not live on a specific Web page and cannot be seen as a scrolling list of responses on a series of Web pages—motivation and incentive serve as the only bonding agents to initiate the conversation and keep it going. New messages to the group must be circulating almost constantly or people tend to pull their heads out of the conversation and forget it's even going on.

Because most ongoing email conversations happen without leadership or moderation, it's contingent on the participants to maintain the focus, to make the list readable and worthwhile, and to occasionally reflect on what has been discussed, decided, and accomplished through the interaction. The original sense of purpose must be reconfirmed regularly to keep incentives for active participation alive.

An email list should be set up by having IT provide the initiator with ownership of a *listserv* run through the organization's mail server. Listservs offer options for managing the correspondence that personal email clients don't have. They offer convenient means for registration and joining the list and allow the owner to control access through the member list. A company portal can even provide the means for individuals to start listservs without help from IT.

One of email's main assets is also one of its main liabilities: the lack of a distinct *home* on the computer screen. Except for when new messages arrive, there is no location where the conversation can be found and revisited. There is less to keep track of, but when one wants to review the messages that made up a recent conversation, the medium makes such a task clumsy and time-consuming. For many people, an identifiable location on the Net where conversations can happen and be stored for reference makes more sense.

Providing a Place for Discussion

If the organization's culture is friendly to it, spontaneous knowledge sharing will happen when virtual meeting rooms are easily available. Many, if not most, corporate portals feature links to "community" or "collaboration" where discussion boards can be found. These are often dedicated to the business line associated with the employee, but some companies provide discussion space for general use and access, permitting conversation across business lines. As we pointed out in Chapter 7, "Choosing and Using Technology," commercial portal products vary in their ability to integrate applications from different vendors. Many portals bundle the eRooms message board, whereas others allow standalone discussion interfaces such as Web Crossing to be integrated. For spontaneous communities, the feature set is not as important as the easy availability. The motivation of the spontaneous group can overcome many shortcomings in the interface.

Email, as a home for ongoing focused discussion, has many limitations for scaling, expanding, and diversifying the conversation. In Chapter 6, Taking Culture Online, we described the differences between linear and threading discussion interfaces and their effects on social interaction. Either one of these offer advantages over an email list in that they both provide a clear, graphic depiction of the conversational landscape. Coherent conversation in email relies on the conscientious use of the Subject line to distinguish one thread from another amidst the flow of messages, but discussion interfaces display conversations and related threads in stable formats that can be navigated easily by new members of the community. Discussion systems provide a history of the conversations and how they developed. They include member profiles that can be referenced to add context and credibility to the opinions and knowledge expressed. Some of them include the ability to search the content of their discussion databases.

Discussion interfaces offer more options and flexibility than email lists, so spontaneous interaction can take different forms. It may include separate topics for new member introductions or the identification of a core problem to tackle or interest to explore. The initiator may want to conduct one conversation as an interview of an expert while creating a related conversation for open discussion of the expert's specialty.

Thus, open access to a discussion board located on the company intranet may be an improvement over the email approach. The board could provide an area for innovation where any member of the organization could start a collection of conversations, or a site administrator could answer requests by opening new private discussion areas for specific communities of knowledge exchange. Leaders of these areas could be granted the power to invite and provide access to members of a group, or the areas could require new joiners to go through a registration process. Either way, a discrete meeting place would be provided that would hold a record of all conversations and would be available for participation at any time of day.

Within certain populations, moderation or facilitation of the conversation is appropriate. This entails selection of which submitted messages will be passed on to the recipient group in the case of a moderator. Or it may entail regular guidance, clarification, summarization, and direction of the conversation in the case of the facilitator. The group as a whole must decide how much intervention is helpful or how much is distracting. More creative populations will opt to manage the conversation on their own, allowing the topic to drift in exploratory directions at times and then pulling it back on topic when required. Groups that are more interested in finding the missing knowledge held by its members and using it to solve ongoing problems may not care as much about having the freedom to widen the conversation.

Transitory Conversation for Immediate Solutions

Bringing people together online for the purposes of instruction, education, or inspiration certainly falls under the description of knowledge transfer. So does crisis management, and for many organizations not yet ready to support ongoing online conversation, the occasional *time-bound event* is a good way of getting the attention of many people at the same time and of persuading them to use online group communication tools that they don't normally use in their daily work lives.

Transitory networks aren't constantly active, but they benefit from the ready availability of a software platform that key participants can use without training or lengthy preparation. Unambiguous leadership, intense focus, clear goals, and hard deadlines usually define such task-based communities. They have little time to build trust and no guarantee of a future once they have achieved their purpose. They are convened for a limited time for learning activity, after which there may or may not be any follow-up interaction.

We refer to these as *transitory* networks because they are created temporarily to serve a special purpose as simply as possible. They may not be the ultimate solution to the organization's knowledge paralysis, but they don't require the planning and maintenance of continuous strategic online interaction or the motivated self-governance of spontaneous knowledge sharing.

What transitory solutions do require is a technical solution that can be prepared and put to use quickly and economically. If the production of each online event must start from scratch,-, with no technology in place or integrated into the local network and with no leaders and moderators trained in its use, the expense in terms of technology and labor will rival that required to build a permanent online community space.

In this section of the chapter, we describe some of the more useful applications of time-bound knowledge conversation and how to use them for different purposes, including the following:

1. To expose an audience to special expertise about a shared interest

2. To mobilize involvement in a special project or discipline

3. To gather input from a specific population

Jump-Starting Knowledge Transfer

When IBM produced its WorldJam event, inviting all of its 320,000 employees to log on to a site that it had spent multimillions of dollars to design and build, it had no guarantee that the results would pay for themselves. It was meant to be a wide-open brainstorming and knowledge transfer opportunity, but its greatest value to the company may have been in the publicity it attracted. The scale of an online event has a lot to do with its success, as does the focus. In IBM's case, both of these parameters were unbounded. It came up with a technical solution that could handle a larger real-time participating audience than had existed up to that point, and it committed itself to months of follow-up analysis of employees' suggestions, opinions, and reactions to the event. This is not the route we would recommend that any organization take to learn what its employees think. But it did illustrate some useful principles.

First of all, WorldJam got the attention of 320,000 people who shared an interest in their company's success. An invitation to submit feedback and ideas is difficult to ignore, even if one has nothing new to offer or believes that their contributions would be lost amidst such an avalanche of feedback. In fact, only 52,600 employees logged on (to the reported delight of event managers), and only 6,000 proposals and comments were posted during the 3-day duration of the site. So one of six IBM employees thought enough of the idea to check it out. If that caused most of them to feel better about their employer or gave them hope that IBM was interested in what its employees—from top to bottom of the hierarchy—had to say, then it may have paid for itself in worker loyalty and goodwill.

Second, WorldJam was probably the first experience in online conversation for thousands, if not tens of thousands, of IBM employees. For them, the idea of online conversation is now a new option, another potential solution, for collaboration in the workplace. It's difficult to get people to try new methods, and by putting on such a widely publicized event, the individual risks were reduced. More people were willing to give it a try because it was not targeted at an elite or advanced group within the company.

And finally, many of those 52,600 people who logged on to WorldJam certainly got their eyes opened by reading opinions from others that either matched their own, conflicted strongly with their own, or exposed them to ideas they'd never seen expressed within the company. To those people, the possibilities of knowledge exchange through online channels became much more significant.

Training and Education

On a more practical scale, Cisco Systems has, for several years, been escalating its use of Webcasts to leverage its expertise around the world. Claiming cost savings of 80 percent over its previous techniques of sending speakers and trainers to hundreds of geographic locations, the company now works with Yahoo! Broadcasts (http://business.broadcast.com) to produce seminars and individual training events to update global employees and business partners and to build a larger population of Cisco-certified technicians.

These events pair graphic presentations with streaming audio, video, and chat windows to broadcast information while allowing audience interaction. These are usually asymmetrical knowledge exchanges, with knowledge sources doing the broadcasting and the knowledge recipients attending and submitting their questions through chat, email, or even voice via conference calls. Yet they offer the possibility, like WorldJam, of stimulating audiences to be involved and contribute ideas and suggestions to the forum based on their own experiences or expertise.

Transitory broadband events are too expensive to produce to be used as a company's main format for conversation. They are appropriate for episodic communications, between which their audiences can study on their own or follow up with new practices learned from the latest event. They are also useful for kicking off the opening of new, more persistent online communities. Because they bring broadband communications to the desktop in the form of voices, they are more attractive to many people than having to read comments and interpret their emotional component.

But transitory networks don't have to use broadband media to be effective. Special purpose meetings and symposia can also be staged using asynchronous platforms. They are more attractive to people who want to get deeper into subjects and who don't have the flexibility of schedule to allow them to participate in real-time events. For the same reason, they may be able to attract experts and instructors whose schedules don't match up.

Group Jazz (www.groupjazz.com) is a small consulting company that, among its other services, produces asynchronous "time-bound" meetings for organizations. The viewpoint of its founder, Lisa Kimball, is that virtual meetings that have beginnings, middles, and ends can be more productive than open-ended online conversations that don't feel the need to resolve and wrap up their ideas by a certain time. A time-bound meeting can have many of the features of a face-to-face conference or seminar, with keynote addresses, slide shows, break-out sessions, papers to download, and even the all-important "hallway conversations" where most of the valuable knowledge transfer takes place. Sponsors can advertise their wares, and people can trade business cards.

By working with client companies on the design of online environments for virtual meetings and helping to train their employees in the skills of virtual facilitation, Group Jazz provides comprehensive support and enables the client to manage most, if not all, of its events. It may introduce technologies appropriate to specific events that the client will want to purchase or contract on its own once it has learned how to use them productively. And for organizations that would prefer to enable knowledge-sharing conversations on an as-needed basis rather than support them all of the time, it's cost effective to have these technical platforms and the people who know how to implement them on standby for whenever they are needed.

Maintaining Resources for Transitory Networks

Transitory networks are purposeful networks that lend themselves to success because of the focus their audiences bring. Once the production and user experience has been mastered (and the technologies themselves have also been learning steadily over the past few years), subsequent events are cheaper to produce and bring more predictable success. The technologies—whether broadband subcontracted services, such as Yahoo!, Broadcast, Placeware, and Webex, or asynchronous platforms, such as Web Crossing and Caucus—can be formatted for future use and modified cheaply for each new event. The skills gained in moderating and facilitating the initial events become assets that can be smoothly put back into action when required. Ideally, a production team— either contracted from consultants or trained in-house—should be kept intact and available for whenever needed. The real cost in convening transitory networks is in the original design, production, and staff training. Once a successful formula has been arrived at in terms of design, promotion, implementation, management, and follow-up, additional costs per event become minimal.

Transitory events can become such regular occurrences that they are no longer transitory but become part of the organization's strategy. Just as Cisco's use of real-time interactive broadcasts have become integral to the training programs that enhance the value of its technologies, a company may find that regular production of online meetings is an important aspect of its branding and product identification.

Planning to Reinforce Knowledge-Sharing Culture

Strategic knowledge networks are meant to help weave the fabric of an organization. They are the social embodiment of the value the company puts into constant learning and optimum use of its intellectual capital. Once an organization accepts the fact that it will never know enough, and that the Net can be a very efficient environment for learning collaboratively, it can effectively incorporate the process of online knowledge networking into its long-range strategy.

Spontaneous and transitory knowledge networks are both good learning bases for planning and designing more permanent environments and practices for companywide knowledge exchange. Strategic networks may be inspired by collaboration born in the company's divisions and lines of business, but they are initiated higher up in the management structure.

Compared to spontaneous and transitory networks, strategic ones take longer to design and launch and take longer still to reach their optimum conversation flow. But if they incrementally incorporate the feedback and input from their users to improve their design and operation, these long-range networks will ultimately reach more people and result in more widespread adoption of new practices. They can indeed bring about change in the organizational culture.

Spontaneous networks bring together expertise, focus, motivation, and initiative to begin online conversations that are likely to survive their early and inevitable technical problems, social problems, and difficulties in translating knowledge into getting things done. They make robust prototypes, with enough resilience to correct their errors and model successful practices.

Transitory networks attract novice audiences and expose them to the possibilities of online knowledge sharing. They don't ask for a long-term commitment from participants and are therefore viewed as "safe" personal experiments using new formats for conversation. They open the minds of people who might otherwise resist joining anything called a "community" on the company intranet.

The organization should use all that it learns from its experiences in online social networking in designing more permanent strategic knowledge networks both on the technical and social management sides. It may have its intranet already in place. It also may have portals designed specifically for its distinct lines of business or departments. And its portal software already may include group communications interfaces such as email, message boards, and instant messaging. But in designing for effective conversation for sharing knowledge, it must be prepared to introduce different software and, more important, structure its culture and human assets to serve the needs of people and their open interaction.

A strategic design for knowledge sharing is more likely to succeed if its authors have learned from the spontaneous exchange that goes on among the company's employees. When actual workers, rather than executives, initiate conversation to share the knowledge that helps them do their jobs, the prospects for their success are high. The greatest risk in starting strategic knowledge networks is that executives identify knowledge needs that the rank-and-file members of the network don't see as crucial to their job performance. Strategies must be translated into the practical language that working groups use in their job-focused conversations.

Fostering Roles and Culture

We've written an awful lot about culture in these pages, and we don't intend to repeat it all here. But in the context of actually implementing strategic knowledge conversation, it must be emphasized that unless the culture is aligned with the overall strategy, the benefits of a technical infrastructure will be severely limited. Design for knowledge networking that will serve an organization's strategic goals begins with an admission that, even at the top of the hierarchy, the organization is starving to learn more.

The motivation to learn and to recognize the value of each person's contribution to mutual learning must be strong throughout the company. The importance of skills such as online community leadership, online meeting facilitation, and online meeting production must be elevated. The idea that an individual's knowledge is more valuable when hoarded than when shared must be debunked through new incentive programs and attitudes. The positive results of a group's collaboration around shared knowledge must be publicized and praised. Training to help all employees understand how to represent their work skills and experiences should be easily available.

A strategic approach means that the entire company must be included in the new knowledge-sharing attitude. Communities may be broken down by project, department, or profession, but all aspects of the organization should be invited and encouraged to engage in the online conversations that will enhance their performance and productivity.

Summary

Online conversation can serve to effectively share and spread practical knowledge within the organization if and only if the conversation advances strategy. The participants must be sufficiently motivated to reveal what they know and sustain the interaction that keeps new knowledge flowing. There is much that an organization can do to promote online knowledge sharing among its employees. It should foster a culture that encourages knowledge exchange and provide appropriately designed online environments, training, and staffing that enable groups to make the best use of their skills, experience, and information resources.

Technology is less responsible for success than social factors such as agreement on common focus, motivation to accomplish goals, competent group leadership, group skills in effective online conversation, and procedures for constantly transferring lessons learned in conversations to other parts of the organization that can use them. People learn in the course of their work and interaction, and the use of online discussion provides a means for recording that interaction as part of the knowledge database.

Spontaneous conversation groups are formed out of commonly recognized needs. They make use of whatever communications opportunities or media are most readily available and accessible to all of their members. Their high motivation and cohesion may compensate for inadequacies in communications technologies chosen out of expediency. The organization that recognizes their potential for generating valuable knowledge will support them with improved technology but will avoid disrupting or attempting to steer their self-governed knowledge-sharing activities. Spontaneous groups form and grow organically around their acknowledged purpose and may need to be asked to share what they have learned with the rest of the organization.

Transitory conversations have intentionally limited life spans and serve immediate, short-lived purposes such as training, education, group alignment, or the attraction of target audiences for marketing. They usually feature expert presenters and an audience of people coming to learn something. They may last through an hour-long Webcast or through a week-long asynchronous discussion. Transitory conversations generate knowledge in the interactions of their members and in the behaviors and demographics of their attendees. They may serve as teasers to upcoming, more permanent online conversations.

Strategic conversations are started at the behest of upper management to further the goals of the company. They are usually provided with specialized interfaces, including message boards and content management. They tend to be built in the order of strategy-technology-community, whereas spontaneous conversations grow in the order of strategy-community-technology. For success, their conversational communities will require the same grass-roots motivation and focus that drive spontaneous communities. Therefore, management should tap into the experiential knowledge of existing communities that began their conversations spontaneously within the organization to learn and apply their best practices to the design of the communities it wishes to initiate.

CHAPTER 9

Conversing with External Stakeholders

To paraphrase the poet John Donne, no company is an island. Businesses rely on their customers, suppliers, shippers, and investors. Nonprofit organizations rely on funders, donors, constituents, and supporters. All of these groups are stakeholders in the organization's success. The easier it is to communicate with people in these external (but integral) parts of the organization, the more effective they can be in their relationships to it. To continue—just as in any online community—the communication must be perceived as mutually beneficial by both sides.

Donors want to know how their giving is being put to use. Supporters want to volunteer their advice or influence. Customers look to companies to support the products they sell. Some customers even want to be involved in the product design process. To win (and keep) their involvement, the company needs to understand how these stakeholders think, plan, and make their decisions. The company needs the insight that stakeholders can provide to help it make *its* decisions.

These vital communications can take place in several ways: The company can open channels and invite its customers to talk to it directly; the company can share what it knows with its stakeholders; and the company can help its stakeholders share what they know with each other. All of these actions can benefit the company by forging stronger relationships with customers and constituents. External conversations can take place in the context of business-to-customer (B2C) relationships and business-to-business (B2B) relationships.

In this chapter, we cover the why and how of conversing online with external groups. The technical means are now available for organizations to become better listeners to their constituents and to respond more promptly and informatively to them. For most organizations, there is ample room for improvement in both of these areas, and relevant to the subject of this book, there is great potential for using enriched external knowledge to drive twenty-first century organizations.

Just as internal conversations require a thirst for knowledge to initiate and sustain them, external conversations require a *need for engagement*, commonly recognized by the organization and the members of the external group. The relationship defined by that need is likely to be asymmetrical; the contact is more important to the organization than it is to its stakeholders. In a free and competitive market, the business will always need the customer more than the customer needs the business. For that reason, everything the company does in its online conversations with external stakeholders must be done to please the stakeholders. That begins with internal attitude and extends to the communication technology and design.

In this chapter, we provide a variety of best practice examples. We've included *screen shots* with many of them to illustrate the importance of clear presentation on the Web page as an incentive for external groups to engage. Organizations are looking for cost-effective ways to gain access to the vital tacit knowledge contained in the interests, experiences, and opinions of their Web-connected stakeholders. Online conversation is an effective route to that knowledge.

Building External Relationships

Through the Internet, organizations can open ongoing conversations with thousands of customers. They *can*, but why should they? The most compelling reason is that, if they don't and their competitors do, those crafty competitors will have some big advantages. They will be building closer relationships with a very communicative and influential segment of customers. They will be gaining loyalty and access to viral marketing channels. But more important, they will be learning from their customers, in a more engaged manner, about how to make their products and services even better. External conversations build more informative relationships with more customers.

There is still resistance in many organizations to opening "that can of worms," which is how some people describe public, uncontrolled conversation opportunities with customers. They see more potential for trouble than upside in a forum that puts powerful companies and their customers on equal footing. The examples in this chapter demonstrate how some companies conquered this fear and resistance and moved ahead to realize solid benefits.

The Importance of Innovation

Using the Internet to converse with customers is still a pretty innovative idea. It's new enough to still be questioned within companies, often because people fear the public criticism that could appear in those conversations. That mindset fails to appreciate the reality of today's networked world. That criticism is probably already happening somewhere on the Net, if not on the company's site. To not move forward and engage in those conversations is to remove the company from an increasingly important aisle of the marketplace.

Seth Godin is one of the pioneers of Web marketing. He is also author of *Permission Marketing* and *Unleashing the Idea Virus*, two of the more creative books about attracting customers through the Internet. In a column in *Fast Company*,[1] he takes the reader through an analysis of how criticism stifles innovation. It may apply to your company. We think it applies aptly to the innovation of online customer conversation.

Companies that are market leaders are often the most afraid of innovating. Godin cites the following examples:

- The fall of many retail giants to Wal-Mart

- The lag in producing organic, nonengineered food products by Kraft

- The lack of much content on cable or on the Net from CBS

Microsoft is an example of a company that forges ahead with innovation in spite of almost constant, scathing public criticism, he points out.

The stakes get higher, he explains, when companies have been successful because they feel that they have more to lose—that all they have built might come crashing down if they take a risk and change something. The fear often lies within the top-level executives who might have been the original innovators in the company but have become conservative behind the success of their original ideas.

Godin believes the main sources of criticism are the people who staff the company. Companies, he writes, "are far more likely to hire people to *do* jobs, as opposed to hiring people who figure out how to *change* their jobs for the better." Those *do job* people are more likely to support the status quo that brought them there. Why rock the boat with new ideas that may affect your job status?

The result of these combined tendencies to stand pat are that when a new idea comes along, such as creating a forum where customers can talk to each other about the company and its products, that idea and its *worst* possible outcomes are compared to the status quo and its *best* possible outcomes. It's an unfair comparison, of course. To get approval for such an innovation, it must promise to be vastly superior to the current methods for relating with customers.

Opening an online dialogue with customers does involve some risk. Your company may do a poor job of designing the interface. It may drop the ball on responding promptly and candidly to questions posed in public forums. The forums may be poorly managed. But these negative possibilities must be compared with the new reality—that your company, if it's known at all, *already* is being talked about somewhere on the Net.

If you're not involved in that conversation on the Net, you've already lost control over your public relations. You don't get to respond to your critics. You don't get a chance to win the loyalty of skeptical customers. You don't learn from their experience, opinions, and viewpoints. Do you have to be everywhere on the Net, responding to everyone? No, and you don't have to try to be everywhere. There are plenty of more practical options.

Lessons from the Dot Coms

The first wave of business presence on the Web was a very expensive and very visible experiment. Some people made a lot of money and more people lost a lot of money, but there was much to be learned in this first venture into such an interactive and public environment. One lesson was that the companies that took the best advantage of the Web's interactive properties to build relationships with customers stood the best chance of surviving the experimental stage. Two well-known survivors have included conversations among their customers as vital elements of their online presence and branding identities.

While most of the new *pure play* Internet companies were burning through their venture capital building name recognition, the established *brick-and-mortar* companies were learning and adapting. They were leveraging their brands and the loyalty of their customers as they tried to figure out their place in relationship to the Web and how to change their strategies to make the best use of it. Some sooner than others, they began to buy domain names, build home pages, and establish a presence on the Web. The smartest of them observed and learned from the waves of new companies as they spent gobs of money attempting to use the Web to provide better service to retail markets, selling everything from pet food to software to automobiles.

ESSENTIAL TEACHINGS OF THE DOT-COM EXPERIENCE

- Relationships established through online interaction are compelling
- It takes time to establish and prove the value of relationships
- Advertising alone does not bring loyal customers
- Customer input is inexpensive but valuable content
- Trust is important to the buying decision
- People trust the advice of their peers
- Companies need to use the Internet to get closer to their customers

The lesson these observers learned is that customers and their loyalty can't be bought through advertising; they must be earned through service. Relationships grow out of trust, and a customer's relationship with a business grows largely out of the perception that the business is sincere in its efforts to please. If customers see steady improvement in the way they are treated (and spoken to) by the business, they are likely to remain customers. The Web provides a convenient way for many companies to speak to *and listen to* many customers.

It's not a very complex formula, yet so many first-wave companies failed to connect with their user-customers that the exceptions stand out. Companies that relied on advertising, for both revenue and for branding purposes, did not attract large enough loyal followings to make a profit. Companies that emphasized customer relations as essential to their business models tended to build loyal markets that carried them through as they trimmed expenses.

If you ask consumers today which dot coms have survived the great downfall of 2000–2001, most—even those who have never shopped on the Web—will probably include eBay (www.ebay.com) and Amazon.com. Those two companies stand out not only for their name recognition but because they have provided two of the most successful models for businesses relating with customers through the Web. We'll describe how they each use conversational techniques later in this chapter, but both of these companies illustrate a third lesson of the dot-com experiment: Act on what customers tell you and make it easy for them to reach you with their input.

Unlike the B2C models of eBay and Amazon.com, the early B2B models for the Web looked to eliminate inefficiencies in how companies dealt with suppliers, buyers, and partners. The idea of online *business exchanges* grew out of the recognition that old processes had become more and more inefficient over time; they had failed to adapt. Customer tastes were changing faster than new products could be designed, assembled, and provided. By the time products came to market, tastes had changed and competitors had altered the market. Companies found themselves stuck with large inventories; they had too little time to get competitive bids on supplies; competition was fierce to innovate faster and cut costs.

The relationship between businesses is different in quality and purpose from that between businesses and their customers. However, there is still a need for communication and trust that the software interfaces of most online exchanges do not support. Lessons have been learned here, too, in the wreckage of many first-wave ventures.

The Online Business Exchange

Exchanges were envisioned as open marketplaces on the Web where multiple buyers and sellers could find one another through a common interface and where the bidding, ordering, procurement, and shipping processes could be made more efficient to fit *just-in-time* manufacturing models. Parts could be bought more cheaply and quickly, inventories could be kept low, and shipping could be tracked more accurately; business, legal, and transactional standards could be followed. Exchanges were meant to be online shortcuts in the normal flow of business.

Facilitating Business Transactions

Companies such as Ariba (www.ariba.com) and Commerce One (www.commerceone.com) were among the first to provide specially designed software to build exchange sites. Features to optimize routine procedures were incrementally added to what were primarily procurement-focused platforms; these included credit checking, financing, real-time order fulfillment, and invoicing. Yet although their platforms supported what they referred to as *collaboration* and *interaction*, they did not provide interfaces for buyers and sellers to meet online and converse. Those communications were still left to email, the telephone, and fax, which for most people meant switching from one medium to another to complete a transaction and service a relationship.

Many business exchanges were formed to attract and serve both horizontal and vertical industries, and many of them failed. A research article about B2B exchanges[2] blames most of the failures on there being too many of them, with too little quality control over the performance of vendors who sold on them and a reluctance of many companies to change their practices to fit the exchange model. Because vendors joined exchanges but didn't follow through on orders placed through them, buyers stopped relying on them. It doesn't take many negative experiences to extinguish a willingness to try something new.

The exchange model, says the article, needs to be refined, and many analysts agree that, in time, online exchanges will be successful. The main caution voiced by some analysts is that powerful exchanges, by bringing about the consolidation of vertical markets, might violate antitrust laws. But the article goes on to say, "One of the potentially most interesting effects of exchanges is their impact on supplier relations, customer loyalty, and customer retention." Furthermore, "customer/supplier intimacy is increasingly critical to a company's ability to differentiate itself from the competition." Intimacy comes through better communication, and a well-designed online exchange should provide the means for that communication.

VerticalNet and the Community Theme

VerticalNet (www.verticalnet.com) was founded and designed to provide a software platform to build portals to serve any vertical marketplace. Besides tools for all of the processes involved in procurement and selling, its interface included features to support conversation and relationship building among participants. An editor would be hired to manage content for each vertical marketplace, and a message board was provided for use as a knowledge-sharing forum. VerticalNet almost got it right by providing a framework that could be used by many different markets, but its timing and execution haven't yet brought the success its founders had hoped for. It has upgraded its process-oriented features to include what it calls "Strategic Sourcing, Collaborative Planning and Order Management," but most of its clients have yet to make optimum use of the site's message boards.

In VerticalNet's portal for aerospace buyers and sellers, shown in Figure 9.1, the community forum appears to be a quiet place in spite of the good selection of resources. Note the few discussions and old dates of last responses. A perusal of other VerticalNet exchanges shows this lack of participation to be pretty typical. One possible reason for the slow adoption of VerticalNet's message board could be gleaned from a study done by IDC, discussed in *Cahners-Interstat*,[3] of the acceptance of knowledge management practices across many vertical industries.

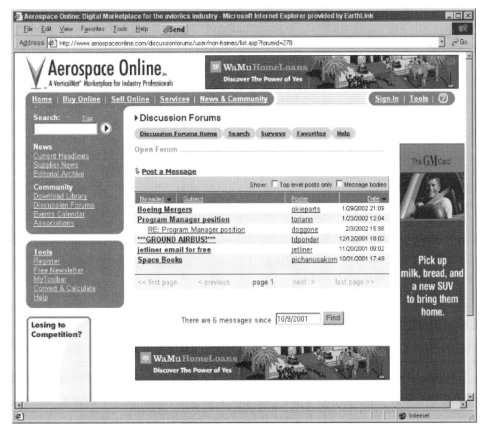

Figure 9.1   VerticalNet's exchange portal for aerospace buyers and sellers.

In an industry survey of companies serving 13 specific vertical market segments plus a category for "other," it was found that 10 of the 14 groups named "nonsupportive culture" as one of the two top challenges to implementing KM. Participation in the parts of the business exchange that involve person-to-person learning, as opposed to those that lead to closing deals and simplifying supply chain management, may not be deemed culturally important.

The study also concluded, "KM customers want to establish best practices to retain expertise, particularly related to customer support." So it may be that a platform such as VerticalNet can overcome cultural resistance to using its discussion boards by providing forums where users of the vertical portal discuss best practices discovered in putting the business tools to use.

Like many Web-based ventures from the 1990s, VerticalNet was early for its market, and in attempting to serve dozens of vertical marketplaces with one service, it may have overreached. But its founders understood the importance of social interaction in establishing a trusted trading environment. Vertical marketplaces define communities of interest. Those communities gather at conferences and trading conventions all the time. The challenge is not in proving to them that conversation is a valuable part of doing business; it's in convincing them that conversation in the online business exchange will work for them.

As the research paper cited earlier indicates, providers of business exchange sites need to be more selective in providing access to the exchange. Vendors and buyers must be committed to responding to transactions and interaction once they are members. And users—the buyers and sellers—need to learn how to maximize the potential benefits of their membership by understanding how the exchange can make a positive difference in their bottom lines.

Many people regard eBay as a consumer's business exchange. In our description of eBay later in this chapter, we point out the importance of building a culture of trust and open interaction among traders and between traders and site management. Marketplaces have their own cultures that define the rules of transaction and sustain their activity. Until business exchanges attract enough traffic and begin establishing social networks, most companies will continue to rely on traditional means of dealing with buyers and sellers, communicating through phone, fax, and email.

Learning about (and from) Your Customers

Organizations are still getting accustomed to the new and continually evolving capabilities provided by the Internet, the Web interface, and other new technologies for communication. The people outside organizations, whose only options for connecting with them used to be letters and telephones, now have many new formats for airing their views, providing their feedback, and issuing their complaints.

Markets are conversations that can lead to insight on both sides. The buyer and seller learn about each other and, if they so choose, work toward win-win situations. Conversations build the relationships that companies must nurture to excel. Conversations can help organizations and stakeholders work their way toward win-win solutions.

STAKEHOLDER TRANSACTIONS IN ONLINE CONVERSATION

Here are four widely recognized transactions that can happen in conversations between your organization and its external stakeholders:

1. Customers can tell you why they buy your products and why they stopped buying
2. Stakeholders can inform you how to fix your business and improve your service
3. They can help you design your next product and warn you if your competitor is making a better one
4. Customers can save you money by helping their fellow customers make the best use of your product

---

By conversing with your customers online, you can tap into all of this and give them another reason to stay in the relationship: You care enough about what they think to make it easy for them to talk to you. Indeed, they are likely to refer their friends. Any organization whose stakeholders establish lasting, mutually beneficial relationships with it has gained a powerful asset.

Customer Research Goes Online

Businesses (and increasingly nonprofit organizations) spend tons of money learning about their customers' preferences and habits. For years, they've spent it on marketing studies, surveys, and focus groups. They once believed that conducting such research through the Net would yield invalid results; the population would be skewed toward the demographic groups who were more likely to be online. But now the online population is far more representative of the population as a whole than it was then. Online market research has arrived and is here to stay.

Recipio (www.recipio.com) provides what it describes as "the only Web-based customer relationship intelligence solution that allows leading companies to aggregate customer dialogue and turn the voice of their customers, employees and partners into a strategic asset." It may not be the "only" such solution, but in an article about the impact of online research,[4] John Ellis described how Procter & Gamble—"the biggest buyer of market-research services in the world"—uses Recipio's software to support online surveys and customer participation in discussion, advisory boards, focus groups, and collaborative product design.

Procter & Gamble and Its Customer Advisors

Who knows how many people use Tide detergent or Ivory soap or who eat Pringles or brush their teeth with Crest or take Nyquil for a cold? P&G, it would be safe to say, has products in just about every American household and in tens of millions of households elsewhere in the world. With dozens of brand names to support, it's no wonder that it spends so much on market research. And it's no surprise that it figured out how to use the Web to reinforce and advance its market research.

Anyone can register at www.pg.com, where—in addition to tips and resources about family, household, and personal care—they invite visitors to "help us create." To that end, they provide a variety of formats for submitting feedback to, and for interacting with, Procter & Gamble. Once registered, a customer of P&G can, as Figure 9.2 shows, "talk to us about our products." Depending on the customer's preferences and available time, this can mean becoming an "advisor" or joining "Consumer Corner" where surveys are offered and one can be part of a customer panel. And beyond gathering advice and feedback from customers, P&G even offers to acquire new inventions or ideas for new products from visitors to its site. Given the high penetration of their products, as word gets around about such opportunities for customer involvement, odds are good that they'll attract a significant enough population to make the effort and the cost of Recipio's software and the staff to host the resulting communities of customers well worth the expense.

Hallmark's Community of Ideas

Hallmark, of greeting card fame, is another pioneer in using online conversation among customers as a strategic tool. To collect customer insights, Hallmark developed the Idea Exchange. In an interview provided for its software provider, Communispace,[5] Tom Brailsford, head of Hallmark's Knowledge Leadership Team, explains the genesis of Idea Exchange.

Brailsford had long been involved in consumer research and "the voice of the marketplace" and had observed how technology developed for doing surveys on the Internet. He wondered if there was a way to use technology to get closer to consumers and to change the interaction from the episodic process of repeatedly asking a question, then doing a study, and then getting an answer, to a more ongoing conversation with the marketplace.

Hallmark understood that consumers are a constituency that companies sell to but not a group that companies actively involve on an ongoing basis with product development or other internal knowledge-based processes. Hallmark decided to allow its customers to become involved, and it set up the consumer communities of Idea Exchange to use as an experimental research tool.

Figure 9.2   Procter & Gamble's variety of customer feedback formats.
© Procter & Gamble

At first, Brailsford wanted to recruit volunteers to participate in this experiment and call them Honorary Hallmark Employees, but the company finally settled on calling them Consumer Consultants. Tom's group recruited the first 100 volunteers by contacting some people who had made purchases on the Hallmark Web site and calling some on the telephone. The volunteers were asked if they would like to participate—to answer questions and share their thoughts, feelings, and opinions about Hallmark products and ideas.

It was originally assumed that Hallmark would have to provide incentives for people to participate, and an elaborate incentive system was devised. They were surprised to find that people would have participated with no incentives at all because they were so happy—in fact, they were "starved"—to get the chance to have an active voice in a company they liked. The Idea Exchange is managed as a facilitated community. The facilitator, who helps guide discussion, is known to members of the community, and the members have become familiar with one another. The Exchange, as of the interview, had 200 members and would not be allowed to grow beyond that size in order to maintain that familiar atmosphere, but other communities were being planned.

Tom Brailsford is a member of the Conference Board Council on Knowledge Management and Learning Organizations and is a member of the advisory board of the "Mind of the Market Lab" at Harvard Business School. As he explains it, online consumer communities are appropriate for all companies because consumers these days feel a disenfranchisement from companies. He points out that consumers say they have a lot of information and ideas to contribute, and they emphasize to companies, "we're not dummies."

Brailsford believes that companies tend to see themselves in a sort of parent-child relationship with their customers, which does not motivate the customer to share knowledge with the company. Hallmark sees the relationship as more of a triangular system, consisting of feedback from the consumers to the company, news updates and information from the company to the consumers, and an ongoing relationship among the consumers themselves. This latter component has proven to be a big selling point in convincing consumers to participate and has resulted in participants telling their friends and family about the consumer communities. Now there are waiting lists of customers who want to sign up to be Consumer Consultants in Hallmark's expansion of new communities in the Idea Exchange.

The Revenue Connection

The original impetus for setting up Hallmark's online consumer communities was a straightforward business goal: to increase revenue. The company had come to recognize ideas as the *new capital of growth*. Thus, the Idea Exchange was created to tap into a wealth of good ideas that Hallmark was convinced already existed in the marketplace, ideas for everything from new products to completely new businesses.

Originally, many of the Hallmark questions for the Consumer Consultants came from the editorial side of the company. The creative staff asked people what specific words they used to describe certain situations and also paid attention to the casual language used by the consumers in their informal conversations with one another. Today, Hallmark proactively explores themes with the community by asking them to brainstorm about certain questions: "What if we did this?" "What if we called it this?" "What idea or feeling would come up for you if we did this?"

In response to traditional marketing people objecting to this type of feedback as "statistically insignificantly valid," Brailsford responds that the Idea Exchange is not a substitute for quantitative tools but an adjunct to them. Unlike quantitative analyses, the Idea Exchange is not used for predictions but for insights and insight generation. Customer Consultants are asked for input on internal strategic business unit discussions and help with diagnoses. Tom considers their advice and input to be "way upstream" from quantitative research tools. In fact, the Idea Exchange members have even designed questionnaires, which Hallmark uses in more traditional consumer polling.

The results after the first 6 months of the project showed that the Consumer Consultants were more positive toward Hallmark. Those who had never bought Hallmark products bought some. Those who already had bought products bought more. They are grateful to Hallmark for giving them a voice and a way to contribute and are telling their friends about it. They are recruiting people for the next communities.

In sum, the Idea Exchange has proven to be not only a rich source for insight and idea generation but also an effective viral or social network-based marketing tool. Since Hallmark believes that communities need to be small to be actual communities, the plan is to open more communities of 200. The question then becomes: What if you want to have thousands of people involved in one large knowledge network? We begin with the basics of customer relations.

Customer Relationships in Cyberspace

The field (let's call it an industry) of customer relationship management (CRM) has focused company attention on using network capabilities to learn more about customers. As one of the first special applications to branch off from knowledge management, CRM seeks to use all available information about customer behaviors and interaction with the company to build better profiles of typical and (especially) high-value customers. Using those profiles, the company can better predict customer behaviors and, by improving its customer service, increase high-value customer loyalty.

The Rising Cost of Customer Service

The continued rise in the use of the Internet is forcing advances in the technology and practice of CRM, and the cost to companies of new CRM technologies for gathering and analyzing customer data has been increasing steadily. A report by *Cahners-Interstat* projected increases in total worldwide CRM software application revenues from $9.4 billion in 2001 to approximately $30.6 billion in 2005. Yet many executives and experts are challenging the perception that technology is the real answer to the question of attracting and keeping customers. In fact, if the goal of CRM is to deliver better customer service, technology may be part of the problem by making customer service more complex.

Charles Fishman, in an article in *Fast Company*,[6] describes how Sprint PCS, the phone service, trains its customer service representatives for 6 weeks to provide support to people who are able to buy a phone and get on the service in 15 minutes. The increasing complexity of products and services available to non-expert customers makes this support correspondingly more expensive to provide. Customer satisfaction numbers for services is declining across all industries. Whether support is delivered over the phone or through online interaction, companies often find themselves unable to please customers no matter how much they spend on call center technology, CRM applications, and training.

In 1993, Don Peppers and Martha Rogers published the first edition of *The One to One Future: Building Relationships One Customer at a Time.*[7] The title succinctly describes their approach, which was prescient because the Internet had not yet become the marketplace that would position the customer as a powerful and informed shopper. By surfing the Web, the customer now can study companies and decide, based on how the company represents itself online, which are most worthy of a relationship. This expanded capability to compare vendors has reinforced a consumer trend toward demanding more personalized service.

Personalized service means that the company, through its Web site, treats each customer differently based on past buying behaviors and expressed preferences. If you've bought products through Amazon.com, you know how it greets you on subsequent visits and presents you with products it thinks you might like based on your past purchases. Personalized service also can work through customer support call centers by allowing support representatives quickly to look up your transactions with the company and remedy problems efficiently.

Peppers and Rogers rode the wave of these marketplace realities and now manage a very influential consulting company (www.1to1.com) that emphasizes changes in strategy and process as well as in software. But although personalization of software interfaces is important in their approach, conversation is not emphasized as much as we believe it should be. Indeed, it's becoming more and more difficult to deliver custom service to one customer at a time. Leveraging technology to provide personalized service through company Web sites is one solution. Enabling online conversation that will distribute service-oriented knowledge is another.

Consumers in Conversation

The Internet empowers consumers to make choices and to converse with each other about products, services, politics, and the marketplace. Word gets around fast in its constantly connected environment. When companies first began to get feedback through the Net from people who might never have taken the time to call their 800 numbers or write them letters, they took notice. They began to hear that customers and potential customers "out there" on the Web were exchanging opinions about their products and businesses. Customers were getting some one-to-one service, but it was from fellow customers, often sharing gripes and complaints. It was a public relations front companies hadn't recognized, and they have scrambled—with widely varying success—to deal with it.

As we mentioned in Chapter 2, "Using the Net to Share What People Know," some pioneering technology-based companies early in the Web's history provided places on their corporate sites for customers to connect with each other. Leaders of these companies figured that if customers were willing to communicate with each other (and with the company) within the relatively neutral environment of the Web, maybe there was less need to fabricate more contrived and less personal opportunities for customers to submit their opinions and preferences.

Market research, focus groups, and scientifically sampled surveys are, after all, contrived and truncated conversations, limited in what they can deliver in the way of customer insight. They don't convey detail and subtlety, and focus groups are known for eliciting views more representative of the participants' desire to please each other than of their true feelings. Plus, an online survey isn't likely to raise levels of customer loyalty.

But though the early practice of engaging customers in conversation worked for some companies, most others had (and still have) many questions about how to do it effectively and economically. Most still see CRM as the practice of identifying and aggregating all of the right numbers and statistics rather than one of establishing channels for trusted communication.

CRM, as understood by most companies, is not the same as customer relationship *development*. The Web provides technology to support relationship development through *series communications* with customers—what, in essence, are online conversations. Relationships now can be established and maintained that bring the design and marketing of products and services much closer to the people who will purchase and use them. Those relationships build trust and loyalty with Web-enabled buyers and donors. Relatively few companies, such as Hallmark, have realized the potential of putting online customer conversations to work, and their experiences serve as valuable lessons for doing business in a networked world.

Listening First to Many Voices

Enterprise-level companies with huge populations of customers must be selective in opening their online conversations. That's why Hallmark limited its first Idea Exchange community to 200 members. But large businesses already have input streams of feedback, complaints, and queries from customers. Analysis of that input can help them decide which conversations, with which customers, will be most effective for them.

The same software provided on the Web site of Ask Jeeves (www.ask.com) is used internally by more than 65 companies, including Nike, Office Depot, and Dell. The companies pay an average of $250,000 per year to accept queries from customers and then generate daily, weekly, or monthly reports analyzing the questions and sorting them by content, date, time, and geography. The input received has been put to use by client companies to change and add new practices and products.

An article in *Forbes* magazine[8] describes how the online securities trading company Datek Online was motivated by input through its Ask Jeeves interface to add an options trading component to its site. And Daimler-Chrysler, responding to a stream of "how-to" queries about specific vehicle models, embraced the idea of "owner sites" that allowed owners of its vehicles to log on and get model-specific maintenance, warranty, and service information.

By providing a means through which customers can ask questions and make suggestions that can then be analyzed and sorted, a business can identify different categories of customers and needs, which in some cases can be addressed by appropriate online conversations. The closer the company can get to understanding the mentality of its customers, the better prepared it will be to opening online dialogue. If customers come to a company's site and find conversational opportunities that speak to their needs, they are much more likely to dive in and participate. The company will have shown that it has done its homework.

Customer-to-Customer Knowledge Exchange

Knowledge networks form spontaneously on the Internet, just as they do on company intranets. Where there's a need for shared knowledge, there are now tools to support the communication and exchange. Consumers don't need the initiation or even the participation of a company to build an online community around the company's product or service. If the company is too slow to respond to this need, customers somewhere will begin a conversation on a message board or through email to find what they're looking for.

It's important for organizations to understand that people may be talking about them online and that those conversations could hold value. The knowledge shared among customers is richer than that owned by a single customer. A kind of informal collaboration happens when people talk about a product they all use, and the resulting shared insights often contain an elusive understanding that the company's product development and market research people would pay dearly to have. A discussion that takes place on a neutral site—not under the sponsorship of the company—is likely to be more candid and creative than a focus group or a discussion initiated by the company. We say "likely" because the example of Hallmark demonstrates that a company doesn't have to sacrifice the candor of its customers for control over the discussion space.

The Net-Savvy Marketplace

The rise of e-commerce exposed organizations to the new phenomenon of a Net-savvy marketplace. Consumers, on their own, gathered on publicly accessible community sites to discuss topics of common interest. Many of those discussions contained veins of pure marketing gold in conversations, observations, and opinions that would have been of interest to almost every business, cause, and profession that cared to know what its customers, constituents, and colleagues valued. Yet for years, public online discussions went unnoticed by businesses preoccupied with figuring out how to effectively market themselves through the Web environment. Those were the years of blind faith in banner ads.

Citizen-consumers found each other online to converse about health and medical frustrations; they swapped opinions about cars, fashion, music, technology, current events, and celebrities. They emailed each other links to recommended Web sites. A microbudget movie, *The Blair Witch Project*, rode a tsunami of brilliant guerilla-marketed Internet buzz to a record profit margin. Viral marketing enlisted interpersonal relationships to spread the word about notable products such as Napster, the peer-to-peer software that enabled millions of music fans to download from one another's PCs. Relationships built entirely through online conversation formed the bases of networked, interrelated online communities. Through the Web, people were telling each other what they liked, what they didn't like, and why. The Web has become the world's biggest ever word-of-mouth network, where keyboards rather than mouths spread the word.

Before the Web came to prominence, companies accepted surveys, focus groups, and polls as "good enough" means for assessing consumer preferences. But those measuring tools missed not only the passion and analysis that many consumers devote to products; they missed the *reciprocal relationship* that more conversational formats could provide. The nature of an ongoing conversation is to lead what might be a single idea and a single response into a deeper, more detailed interaction. A few intrepid companies and entrepreneurs recognized this kind of conversation happening in public chat rooms and message boards and decided to help facilitate it.

Pioneering companies, including those we mentioned earlier, found it quite natural to engage with their customers online because many of them shared the same skills and professions as the engineers or programmers who designed the company's products. So, as we describe later in the chapter, Sun Microsystems was one of the first examples of a business supporting a *strategic* online customer community. But people by the thousands already had begun engaging with each other around products of common interest in *spontaneous* communities not related to any specific companies.

eBay's Secret Ingredient

If any pure play Web business model stands as an example of perfect adaptation to the networked environment, it is eBay. Employing the Web's speed and ability to organize information and to support a product display and bidding process, it provides a virtual *flea market* interface, where anyone can register and sell goods for the highest offer. The main technological features of eBay are its categorized auction interface and the tools it provides for personalization and reporting the trustworthiness of participants in its marketplace. One personalization feature, illustrated in Figure 9.3, is the eBay member's *My eBay* page. The one pictured is of the author's personal page, showing how it keeps track of auction items of interest, items being bid on, and items on which the member has made winning bids. The tracking tools encourage involvement by active traders. The power of the individual member is enhanced by such features, but as its CEO, Meg Whitman testifies, the not-so-secret secret of eBay's success is in its support of community.

Community drives eBay's word-of-mouth marketing and its rapid adaptation to customer needs and preferences. It has built its reputation and its base of regular members through grass-roots selling and buying, and it's in the interest of members to attract new members and expand the marketplace in which they trade.

Many other auction sites, including Yahoo!Auctions, have been launched on the Web, and software platforms for supporting the auction model have been produced and sold, but eBay distinguished itself early in its history by deciding to steer many of its decisions based on the input of its members. Mary Lou Song was

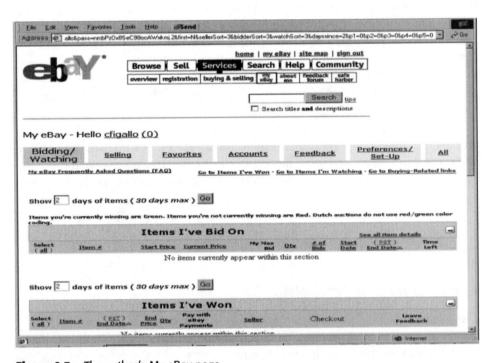

Figure 9.3 The author's My eBay page

the third employee at eBay, and when she joined the company in 1996, it had 15,000 members; it now claims over 16 million. Song helped develop its young community, building the cooperative relationship between the community and the company through combining traditional product marketing—to attract the right people, with online community marketing to win their loyalty once they had joined. Her goal was, and still is, to make membership a fun and safe experience.

For the designers of both the interface and the business process (a company spared of the obligations to handle merchandise or shipping), eBay was an ongoing learning experience based on conscientious *customer listening*. And for the community managers like Song, the community was a source of essential feedback and an audience that needed to be kept informed. Even policy questions—an area usually dealt with by companies in locations far beyond the reach of customers—have been brought into the public forum as shown in Figure 9.4.

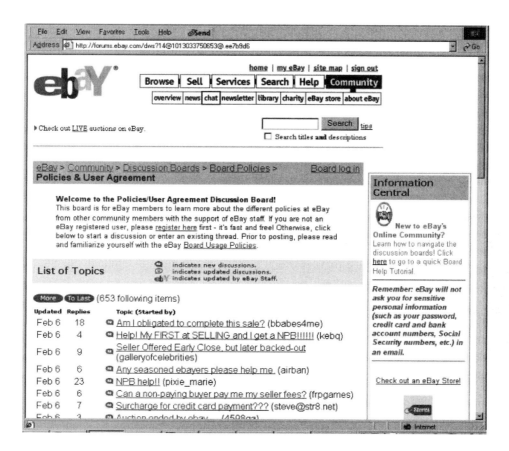

Figure 9.4   Members discuss policies and agreements on eBay.

Through experience and attention, eBay has learned the following important lessons about including their members in decisions that affect their buying and selling activities:

Lesson 1: Make your policies clear and bring discussion of policies out into the open. Where customers depend on policies to put their trust in a business or social process, and where the company depends on customers for its success, it's smart to invite the customers into the policymaking discussion.

Lesson 2: Be proactive. Note the security reassurance about not asking for sensitive personal information in email.

Because of the open nature of its auction activity, eBay is frequently in the news for the items that some people attempt to sell—from bogus famous paintings to human organs. At one point, the company instituted a policy of not permitting the sale of firearms. It did this for its own ethical reasons but failed to include its members in the deliberative process before making the announcement. It learned from indignant customer reactions that, even in cases where its corporate mind was made up, it needs at least to confer with its member population before implementing a policy change.

The auctions on eBay also have been subject to occasional fraudulent behavior over the years such as sellers taking the money and not delivering the goods and buyers receiving the goods and not sending the money. At times, goods sold were not delivered as described. The software, in combination with the participation of members, has attempted to address these betrayals of trust by providing a means for members to assign other members a *feedback rating* based on the total of positive, negative, and neutral reviews of their transactions.

A prospective buyer will want to see the *feedback profile* of the person selling an item. The rating page will show the number of positive, negative, and neutral ratings given to the seller over the past 6 months and will display any comments written about the seller by people who have bought from him. Still, there is the possibility of fraud, as *shills*—associates of the seller or phony members created by the seller—might be providing the positive ratings. So eBay has devised more comprehensive fraud protection: insurance that will reimburse members a portion of the money they lose in a bad transaction (see Figure 9.5). Fraud had been perpetrated on eBay members on several very publicly visible occasions, so the company chose to address it head-on in discussions with members and in this policy.

Though eBay began as what would be considered a trading site, where individuals sold items to each other as if it were a virtual yard sale, it has adapted its technology and its culture to include retail sales, where companies offer goods for sale beginning at set prices. The trust-enhancing qualities of its com-

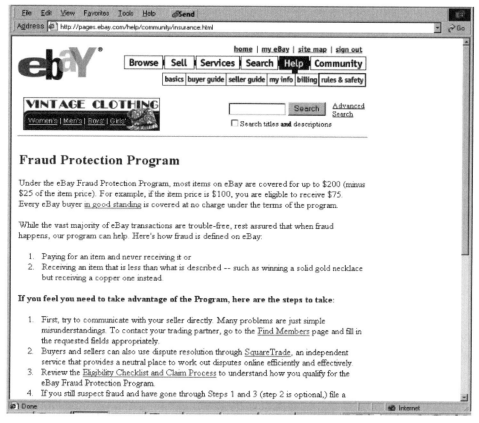

Figure 9.5 Fraud protection: another important trust reinforcement feature of eBay.

munity approach have been extended to cover small to large businesses, and many of the original individuals who once sold the occasional item now make their livings by selling through eBay. The culture has evolved, but the focus has continued to be on maintaining a trusted marketplace through encouraging conversation among members and between members and the eBay staff.

Cisco Attracts a Technical Community

We've used Cisco's NetPro community as a case study in previous chapters. Here we use it as an example of a company creating a place on its Web site to attract a specific group that already has an established, unaffiliated meeting place. In Cisco's case, the group consists of the networking professionals that install, configure, and maintain the kind of technology Cisco provides.

As we've noted previously, technical communities were the first ones to form on computer-mediated networks. Technicians just happened to be the people designing and building the networks, so it's natural that they were the first ones to inhabit them. To this day, technical people naturally form online communities to share knowledge, mostly using email or the conventions of Usenet. One newsgroup, comp.dcom.vpn, is all about *virtual private networking* (VPN), the technology that allows employees to connect to the corporate intranet through a secure remote modem connection. In this newsgroup, networking professionals exchange knowledge about VPN, and it doesn't matter what company they work for.

Cisco produces and sells VPN technology and equipment for many other aspects of Internet and intranet functionality. The company wanted to attract the same professionals who were using comp.dcom.vpn and other online communities to discuss networking hardware. They had to offer incentives to get them to change their behavior; most workers don't have the time or social bandwidth to be members of more than one community addressing a single interest. Cisco's main appeal was its status as the largest producer of networking equipment in the world. Since some of that equipment was regarded as the global standard for Internet connectivity, the promise of learning more about Cisco equipment and having a closer relationship to Cisco was important, career-wise, to many of the targeted professionals.

Similar situations can be found today among companies and professionals whose products and interest lie outside the technical realm. Users of products—cars, bikes, gardening equipment, stereo equipment—gather spontaneously on the Web, and the makers of the products they're talking about invite them to gather on their product support sites. If the conversation switches venue from the nonaffiliated message board to the company-sponsored message board, the context changes. The meeting place is no longer spontaneous and independent but is created, owned, managed, and maintained by the company.

A professional community, once it convenes on the company site, stands to lose some of its autonomy and ability to self-govern. The company, meanwhile, takes on a new obligation: to provide the meeting space while keeping the professionals happy with the trade-off they have made. Both the company and the professional community are seeking an arrangement of mutual benefit.

Cisco was cautious in its approach to the networking professionals. It first attempted to attract attention and stir interest by staging online events: slide presentations with live audio featuring product managers and engineers representing its VPN team. These experts answered questions from a moderator and from the online audience. Out of those events, Cisco identified professionals who registered and posed questions and then contacted them about becoming founding members of its planned discussion community.

As the initial online interface was designed and the back end of the system was assembled, the decision was made to begin the community with a narrow focus, VPN, but to be ready to expand into other technical topics likely to be of interest. IP telephony was one alternative and security was another. The system was launched with a small population that helped Cisco's community team iron out the bugs in the interface. As the design was tuned, more participants arrived and the community began to grow, driven by word of mouth. Cisco learned to manage the community to the satisfaction of its members.

Now the Networking Professionals Connection is a lively knowledge exchange where the professionals learn from one another and Cisco learns from their conversations. Members can choose from a variety of activities and information resources (see Figure 9.6) and are invited to submit input to Cisco about the community, its design, and its administration. The NetPro community, as it's called, began with one main topic: virtual private networking. As the community expresses its interest in other topics, the focus of the community is expanded. As Figure 9.6 shows, there are now topics on emerging technologies.

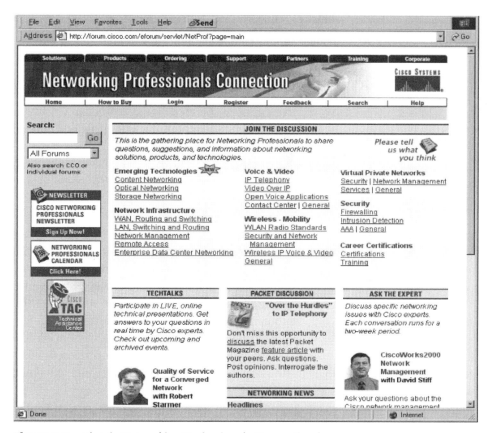

Figure 9.6 Cisco's Networking Professionals Connection home page
© Cisco Systems

How to Learn from Customers

Michael Ruettgers, president and CEO of EMC Corporation, a $4-billion provider of intelligent enterprise storage systems, software, and services, claims to be "relentless" in keeping up to date with what his customers want and value. The challenge, as he describes it in an article on the *Chief Executive* Web site,[9] is in implementing practices to learn from customers "consistently and methodically." In answer to that challenge, his company follows four principles, which he claims "not only look outward to our customers, but also bring customers into the heart of our product development process."

FOUR PRINCIPLES FOR LEARNING FROM CUSTOMERS

EMC Corporation recognizes these as the keys to delivering what its customers want:

1. **Customer closeness should start in the boardroom**
2. **Create a customer trust loop**
3. **Strike a balance between leading the customer and following their lead**
4. **Invest for customer activism**

The first principle is that customer closeness should start in the boardroom. At EMC, the chairman and founder, even though retired from management activities, spends considerable time meeting with customers one-on-one and in "chairman's dinners." By getting customers—from the easy-to-please variety to the most demanding—to confide in him, he learns about what they really need and care about. His obsession with knowing the customer has rubbed off on upper management and the entire organization. The need to get closer with all of the company's customers has led to the development of IT systems and online means for finding out what they want.

The second principle is to create a customer trust loop, which involves "listening, responding, validating, refining, revalidating, delivering, fine-tuning" and then repeating the process. Only through constantly going through this loop will the organization know that its perspective of what the customer wants is, indeed, the customer's perspective. In our experiences managing online communities, we have kept this trust loop going continually, listening and then validating, acting on suggestions and then asking customers, "Is this what you meant?" Just as you would with your employees, you keep the communications channels open and respond promptly to input. Only by staying responsive and delivering on the suggestions you are hearing from customers can you win and maintain their trust and valuable feedback.

As eBay does, EMC invites customers that it identifies as highly motivated to come to its headquarters and meet intensively with EMC executives and managers, who listen to what they have to say and then go through the response-validation-refinement loop to make sure the customers' needs are truly understood. This is face-to-face stuff, where relationships are built that will remain strong when the communication reverts to virtual channels. A core of loyal customers who understand the sincerity and motivations of the company can be a strong influence on the majority of online customers, who may only know the company through conversation on the Net.

The third principle followed at EMC is to strike a balance between leading the customers and following their leads. As Ruettgers points out, it was not customer leadership that brought the invention of the electric light, the laser, intermittent wipers, and the minivan. The same could be said for the World Wide Web. Customers tend to ask for refinement and improvement in what they already have. They want things to be faster, cheaper, easier to use. But innovators within companies need the input of customers to know if the products they are developing are on the right track for usability, convenience, and design. Likewise, companies need to be able to collaborate with their suppliers in designing parts and components as new products are created.

Investing for customer activism is EMC's fourth principle. The investment is in terms of executive involvement, primarily, for the CEO can create a tone in the organization that is welcoming to customer input and fosters strong relationships between the company and its customers. The investment also includes making it as easy as possible for customers to provide input into the product design process. The company invests in quick turnaround of product improvements that are suggested by customers. And it invests in providing products that have been well thought-out concerning the customer's life cycle with their products, simplifying their purchase, use, and upgrading. EMC believes in reinforcing the innovative intelligence of its customers and investing to tap into that resource.

Self-Organized Communities of Consumers

Observant pundits and analysts recognized the rise of spontaneous *consumer communities* as soon as they began forming on the Web. One of the first attempts to aggregate communities and content according to special interest was called The Mining Company. It provided a template for building focused Web sites and invited people with experience and expertise in a subject area to become a combination online community leader and editor, organizing the sites, linking to relevant information, providing original content, and managing online conversation. These so-called *guides* were paid a percentage of the company's advertising revenue, and the best sites became known as expert knowledge-sharing communities where users exchanged techniques and opinions about various products. The company later changed its name to About.com (www.about.com) and still stands as a good example of what user-driven portals can be.

Topic-focused communities on About.com cover hundreds of hobbies, interests, skills, and fields of knowledge. Included in the site's contents and discussions are thousands of products and services that serve these subject areas and attract people with varying amounts of expertise. A visit to the Fresh Water Aquarium community reveals product reviews and online discussions about different types of fish, tanks, water conditioning, and diseases. The experience represented by participants is much broader than could be found on any one product provider's site. But product review is not the main mission of About.com. Other Web sites have been created to specialize in that area.

In 1998, *Consumer Review* magazine brought its professional product testing and evaluation services online as ConsumerREVIEW.com. Through the Web, it began accepting input from paying subscribers to complement its own objective studies and ratings. In 1999, Epinions.com (see Figure 9.7) was launched to provide a specially designed gathering place for people to submit their own reviews and ratings of products and to research what others thought about those and other products or services. The Epinions interface allows every registered member to build a personal Web of Trust made up of credible reviewers and the people who also find them credible. Trust is important to offset any mis-

Figure 9.7   Epinions lets consumers comparison shop and advise each other
© epinions

leading ratings and reviews that might be posted by corporate *shills*—unidentified company reps posting good reviews of their own products.

Consumers began using these review sites as important shopping guides, reporting the results to each other. Eventually, companies whose products were critiqued positively or negatively began to get wind of the feedback. Some began regularly monitoring Web sites where their products were being discussed. In the case of strictly ad-supported review sites, there is no guarantee of survival, but Epinions now earns revenue by generating leads for retailers to whom it provides links from its product review pages. ConsumerREVIEW.com, on the other hand, has two steady revenue sources: subscription fees for both their print magazine and their Web site. Together, this income supports its publishing activities and its product evaluation work.

In the difficulty encountered by companies searching for feedback about their products and services in the vastness of the Web, another business opportunity was recognized. New ventures were created to perform the searching and monitoring of the Web for companies hungry for knowledge of consumer thinking and journalistic mentions. Going by names such as Cyveillance, E-Watch, CyberAlert, WebClipping, or NetCurrent, they provided a kind of digital clipping service, sending their clients daily electronic reports of quoted conversations and mentions in the online press.

An online service called PlanetFeedback (see Figure 9.8) makes most of its revenue by providing these services. Its Web site also provides a single point of access for consumers to send complaints and suggestions to businesses. As the company's CEO, Pete Blackshaw, explained as financial justification for companies making use of its services, "If you totaled the money the Krafts, Unilevers, P&Gs and [Johnson & Johnsons] spend listening to consumers tell them how to improve a product, you're going to be in the hundreds of millions of dollars."[10] Subscribing businesses get to see the feedback but don't necessarily respond to any of it. And as we described earlier in the chapter, P&G has its own online methods for soliciting customer input.

PlanetFeedback recently merged with another technology firm called Intelliseek, which originally provided a service for dealing with two problems facing companies: the overabundance of information and the variable reliability, importance, and impact of that information on the company. Intelliseek not only found relevant information, but it filtered out the "noise" from the truly useful stuff. Now the merged service can deliver relevant and meaningful reports from online conversations and publications to its clients.

Services like PlanetFeedback are useful when there are active conversations happening on the Web about your company. But they don't provide you with a convenient opportunity to respond—to make amends for a customer's dissatisfaction, to assure customers that a problem has been corrected, or to invite the customer to describe how your company could improve itself. And with the collapse of the business models that have supported many of the public discussion

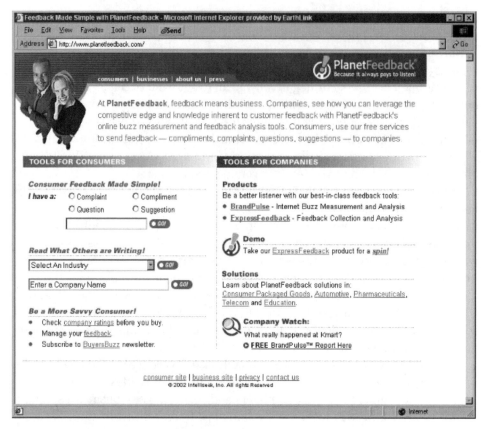

Figure 9.8 PlanetFeedback, where consumers talk and companies listen
© PlanetFeedback Division of Intelliseek, Inc.

sites, there's no guarantee that those useful conversations will continue to be available for harvesting by these special purpose search engines. Yet the value of that feedback is such that forward-looking companies must provide their own channels for it.

Hosting the Customer Conversation

The online conversations among customers and those between customers and representatives of the company have many similarities to the online conversations among employees we described in Chapter 8, "Initiating and Supporting Internal Conversation." Trust among participants is necessary for most people to reveal what they know and think. Leadership is important in building that trust and in setting the focus for knowledge sharing. Facilitation is often useful to help people express themselves and to stimulate the social interaction. Site design and organization must be appropriate to the needs of the community not only to reduce barriers to participation but also to allow participants to find what they need with minimal hassle. But there are some significant differences, too, between communities composed of employees of an organization and those composed of external stakeholders.

An organization is limited to exerting less control over the content and direction of online conversations among customers or constituents. It can set no goals or deadlines or deliverables as it can for an internal project team. The policies it imposes cannot be too restrictive or people will refuse to participate. It must spend more of its time listening and helping participants explain what they are trying to tell the organization rather than keeping the conversation aligned with its strategy. The incentives it offers for participation must be stronger because there is no compensation structure or prestige attached to a customer's input to a business. The position of the company with respect to its customers is a supplicant asking humbly for contributions. Yet, if invited in the right way, many stakeholders will be excited by the opportunity to help make a company's products or services better.

Inviting Customer Input and Collaboration

The social aspects of initiating and supporting conversation across the firewall—between representatives of the organization and external groups—are trickier than they are on the intranet. There is less room for error in relationships between a business and its customers or between an organization and its constituents. In effect, *they* are the guests and the organization is the host to the interaction. The host is obliged to extend courtesy and to be tolerant of transgressions. With internal conversation, there is room for conflict, multilateral disagreement, debate, and even the occasional insult. Vigorous debate may, in fact, be encouraged. Try any of that with a customer and the ripples of bad PR will spread far and wide, with the speed of email.

Interface design is more important in supporting external relationships for the same reason: There is less room for mistakes like downtime and clumsy navigation. The company can't be constantly tweaking the interface when the users are guests; that would be considered inconsiderate at best and incompetent at worst. The interface must be designed with the convenience and needs of the customer or constituent in mind rather than the needs of the internal groups doing the listening and outreach. Staff members don't quit their jobs because the discussion board is tricky to use, but customers will abandon a Web site that forces them to go through a tricky learning process.

You can invite people to give you feedback and help you to satisfy them, but there are costs and preparations associated with acquiring their deep input and ongoing collaboration:

- People who provide your company with valuable input will expect some valuable takeaways in return. You must know what those expectations are.

- People expect you to provide an intuitive and comfortable interface for their participation and input.

- Appropriate and timely content combined with a prompt, courteous response from staff will keep people coming back.

With a wise investment of time, research, and training, combined with good execution, a company can turn the initial trickle of curious and hopeful participants into a population of loyal and regular collaborators. Building the relationships that anchor that loyalty takes commitment and purpose.

A Business School and Its MBA Candidates

The Wharton School not only studies businesses; as a prestigious academic institution, it is itself a business. In an article on its Web site[11] (knowledge.wharton.upenn.edu), it describes how companies learn from online customer dialogue and how it uses message boards as a recruiting tool.

One of the school's marketing professors says, "even if negative comments come up in the online discussions, companies seem willing to live with that for what they feel is a positive overall experience of talking about products and services." (That occurs if they overcome the initial internal resistance to the idea.) Another marketing professor is not so optimistic, venturing the opinion that online word-of-mouth is nothing special. Of course, that's not to say that online interaction doesn't work; it just may not be *more* effective than offline talk. We'll grant that, except that companies can talk to far fewer people offline.

The Wharton School itself provides message boards for students and prospective students. Alex Brown, associate director of MBA admissions, says these have proven to be a great way to help market the school and its programs. MBA candidates are no longer captive of dialogue controlled by the business schools and their admissions departments. Candidates, he says, "are talking to each other about what we offer and how it compares to other schools."

After setting up their discussion boards, Wharton wondered if it should "take the next step and host those discussions or ignore them." They decided to participate in them and embrace them "rather than let the rumor mill take over." Students and prospective students interact and answer questions for one another. Those who are looking for a place to continue their studies get a taste of the culture of the student body and staff. They get beyond the surface promotion of brochures and the superficial physical impressions of buildings and classrooms.

The debate between the professor who favors organizations hosting online dialogue with stakeholders and the professor who is skeptical of the value of such dialogue revolves around the trustworthiness of the input. As the skeptic expressed his doubts, "I would hesitate to draw any conclusions about chat on a company-based Web site. Those are squeaky wheels seeking grease on those sites. And who knows if the company is monitoring the discussion or steering it in a direction that the company desires?" Of course, when done right, the company fosters candid relationships and is monitoring discussions and responding truthfully when appropriate. The squeaky wheels may not represent all customers, but they do represent a motivated portion of them. And motivated customers provide especially valuable input.

A Gathering Place for Creative Users

In Chapter 2, we described the early users groups of Apple computers and how they exchanged rare information first in face-to-face meetings and then through computer BBSs. Technical populations, enthusiastic about using technology to communicate, led the way in giving advice to each other and to product vendors about innovation and improvement.

Sun Microsystems (www.sun.com) has long relied on the ability of programmers and computer engineers to communicate through the Net. It was one of the first companies to provide space on a Web site for users of its products to converse with one another. Today, it continues to host a variety of what it calls "developers forums" for discussion of different products and their applications. These range from communities for system administrators of Sun-powered installations to software developers using Sun technologies like Java and Jini. Figure 9.9 shows the Java Developer Connection, a kind of peer-to-peer knowledge exchange similar in purpose to Cisco's Networking Professionals community.

As Sun describes another of their forums, "Dot-Com Builder Discussion Forums are an interactive area where Sun's Web developer community can share knowledge by posting messages to a message board. Messages on the message board are organized by topic, cover all aspects of server-side architecture and Web development, and include community member comments, opinions, questions, answers, and technical tips." Of course, Sun also benefits greatly by having access to the creative conversations that go on among experts in using its products.

For one of its software technologies, Sun has provided a community site away from its home site. Jini allows dissimilar processes and devices to communicate and work together. Its potential uses are so numerous that Sun initiated a special development community, complete with a constitution, for sharing new solutions. The community (at www.jini.org) was begun with several high-level Sun engineers serving as facilitators. The goal was to make the community self-governing, and to that end, a community constitution was composed by its members to state the agreed-upon procedures for sharing solutions and setting standards. The participants in the Jini community preferred to stick

Figure 9.9 Sun Microsystems' Java software language has relied on collaborative innovation by its users.
©Sun Microsystems

with email as their platform for interaction. They were comfortable with it, and combined with the ability to create Web pages that could be shared with other members, it was the most appropriate technology for their collaborative needs.

Only a cohesive group with a goal of mutual benefit can reach this level of agreement. However, there are many products that would lend themselves to such an arrangement if only the companies that produce them would recognize the potential. Clearly, the more solutions that are devised by the Jini community for applying the technology, the more Sun has to gain.

Providing the Basic Support Community

At one time, online community was envisioned as an ad-supported revenue center. When this failed to pan out, the focus shifted to view online community as part of customer relations—a cost of doing business like marketing and PR. But some companies see it as a *cost-cutting* activity, replacing some of the expense of customer support. If done well, customers not only provide each other with advice that the company was once liable for, but customers provide *better* advice because it is experientially based and the customers are professionals.

Click on the Technical Support link on Hewlett-Packard's home page (www.hp.com) and then on the link to Forums for IT Professionals and Businesses. You reach the IT Resource Center (ITRC), a Web page that leads you to what HP identifies as its four main categories of customers: IT professionals, business professionals, developers and solutions partners, and home and home office customers. And as HP states on this page, "Different forums may have different rules and guidelines."

It's significant that home and home office customers aren't provided with actual discussion forums in ITRC, whereas the other groups are. Managing a discussion community composed of tens of thousands of owners of hundreds of models of HP PCs and printers would be a daunting and expensive task. All of the customer communities get indexed troubleshooting menus, search tools for solutions, and company support provided through email. The forums aimed at professionals in the other three support areas *do* encourage interaction and knowledge exchange.

HP recognizes the potential bottom line benefits of users helping other users to the extent that it set up a points system to recognize users who answer a lot of questions. The leaders in accumulating points are recognized on the forum's home page and by symbols displayed by their posts in the discussion space. By accumulating points as valued knowledge resources, they can rise in rank from Pro (symbolized by a baseball cap icon) to Graduate (a mortarboard icon) to Wizard (magician's hat) to ITRC Royalty (a crown). HP claims that it may (but is not obligated to) award gifts to such participants.

In its terms of use, HP describes, in part, its relationship to the Communications—the content of user discussion in its forums. The terms say, "HP may, but is not obligated to, monitor or review any areas on the Site where users transmit or post Communications or communicate solely with each other." This relieves it of responsibility for inaccurate or offensive posts written by users, but it's very likely that Communications containing information of value to HP will be noticed and made use of. Indeed, as on most corporate sites, the company claims the right to make use of whatever information its users post. "HP and its designees will be free to copy, disclose, distribute, incorporate and otherwise use the Communications and all data, images, sounds, text, and other things . . ." in any way it chooses.

Designing to Support Health Needs

One of the Web's most effective uses is as a reference resource for people with questions about health and medicine. With the rising cost of health care, people are using the Web to research their own conditions and treatments. The more serious the health problem, the more vital the information. The motivation to collaborate with others around different conditions is very high compared to almost any other topic, whether business-related or personal. The trick is in providing reliable information and managing helpful online conversation.

The American Cancer Society (ACS) recognized the importance of fostering a sense of community among cancer patients, survivors, their families, and ACS's donors and volunteers. Coping and survival are at the core of these groups' overlapping missions. So, in redesigning their Web site at cancer.org, they studied their users, especially cancer patients, to find out how best to provide them with connections to their most relevant support communities. They wanted to know how visitors to their site moved through it and where they would need links to community-enhancing features.

Most Web sites that include message boards segregate them under a "community" link that, if followed, leads the visitor to an environment quite different from that found elsewhere on the site. There is likely to be no information other than the topics and responses of the participants—a discussion ghetto. ACS wanted to weave the idea and the access to community throughout its site so that visitors, no matter where they were on the site, would have easy access to chat rooms or message boards. As Figure 9.10 shows, the site also links to compelling stories and an invitation to donate. ACS hopes to convert eager volunteers into eager donors.

In redesigning its site, ACS provided a good example of how to go about identifying the needs and tendencies of the user community. It hired a consulting company, Sapient, to help it with the analysis. As an article in *CIO* magazine[12] described, Sapient "had clinical psychologists and cultural anthropologists spend time with cancer patients at various stages to develop an 'experiential model'." Based on that model, they imagined scenarios that would describe how different hypothetical individuals would move through the Web site.

Someone recently diagnosed with breast cancer would, for example, come to cancer.org looking for information about the disease, its prognosis, and its treatment. So links directing that person to that information should be prominent on the home page. Once informed, the patient would be interested in finding local support groups (see Figure 9.11) of breast cancer patients and survivors. A place for the patient to enter her zip code also would be located on the home page, as would links to general information about breast cancer. The patient, at this point, would be looking for an opportunity to ask questions, so links to chat rooms and message boards also would be posted on the home page. The invitation to join a network also offers the option of connecting by telephone for those who prefer that medium to online conversation.

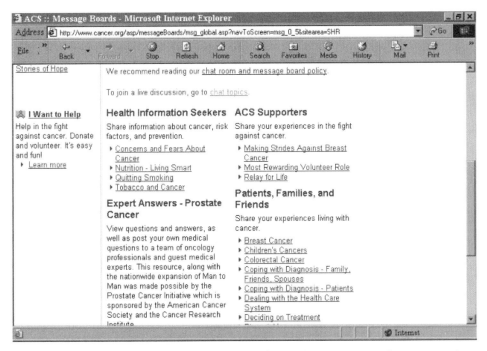

Figure 9.10 The American Cancer Society's site directs visitors to appropriate conversations in its message boards.

Reprinted with the permission of The American Cancer Society, Inc.

ACS is devoted to supporting patients and families in their dealings with the disease and its aftermath, so its design keeps evolving to better support that purpose. The organization also expects to reap some bottom-line benefits from helping people share knowledge and caring. They hope to grow relationships with people that will lead them to donate to the organization, if not in money then in volunteer time. If the Web site and its communities can build a sense of loyalty among members, ACS can expect some of them to be regular supporters of the organization. And as James Miller, ACS's director of Internet strategy, put it, "that means you're always going to be at the top of a person's mind when they start thinking about donations."

Where Customers Gather on Their Own

The days may be past of the *Cybercities*—vast so-called online community sites like Geocities and The Globe that provided ad-supported, easy-to-build personal home pages and online discussion spaces. But it's relatively cheap to set up a site to support the content and discussion needs of a focused community.

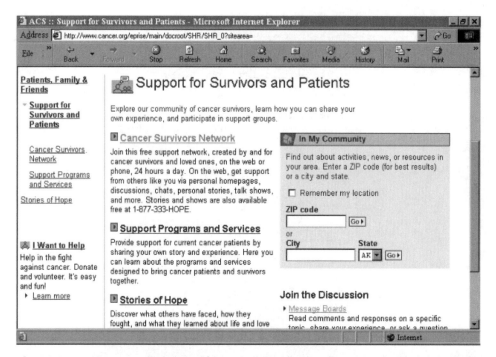

Figure 9.11 A community page within cancer.org shows where members can search for local support groups by zip code.
Reprinted with the permission of The American Cancer Society, Inc.

There still are countless gathering places on the Web where consumers converse about their hobbies, their professions, and their opinions of what companies should be doing with their products.

Today, when a company fails to address its customers' needs through the Web, there's a good chance that its customers will take things into their own hands. This can make the company look all the worse for its negligence; customers are almost sure to refer to the company in negative or derisive terms. But such neutral sites offer a chance for redemption; the company can listen in and learn how to satisfy customers who have gone to the trouble of getting together on their own to deal with an important company and its products or services.

Here are two examples of motivated customers creating communities of interest and support that the companies themselves should be providing. In one case, the initial cause was to amplify complaints that the company seemed to be ignoring. In the other case, the cause was to share enthusiasm for a product and, in the process, share knowledge that the company was reluctant to provide.

A Customer-Run Complaint Department

The following story may not address the post-9/11 state of affairs in air travel, but it does illustrate what can happen through the Web to companies that don't do a good enough job of communicating with their customers.

In June 1996, Jeremy Cooperstock had some terrible traveling experiences on United Airlines. Over the next 2 months, his unsuccessful attempts to get a response from the airline through two polite letters of complaint led him to create what he called a "poor show" Web site that soon began attracting support from other disappointed United customers. In April 1997, after almost a year of trying to get the airline to improve its customer service policies, Cooperstock launched the Untied Airlines site (www.untied.com), unabashedly mocking the logo and style of the airline's own site and providing a forum for people sharing his frustrations.

Months after the new site went online and after some legal threats, Cooperstock received an apology from United. Then, with donations received from other dissatisfied customers, he built a complaints page (see Figure 9.12) that forwards messages to the director of United's customer relations department. An insider at United later admitted that the company was circulating complaints received from Untied's site. As "evidence," Untied.com keeps a database of both customer complaints and United Airline's responses to them.

Today, a visit to the United Airlines site at www.aul.com reveals a heightened attention to customer service including a Statement of Customer Commitment and services ranging from baggage liability to ticket refunds to information about dealing with delayed flights. Maybe these improvements in service would have happened without the nagging of Cooperstock's community, but the probability that disgruntled customers on the Web will find a way to raise their voices in unison should be a sobering reality to all businesses.

The lesson: Customers can and will demonstrate creatively what they need from businesses. If not supported in demonstrating this on the company's own site, they are likely to build or make use of another venue on the Web to "get things off their chests."

Customer-Provided Order Tracking

In the spring of 2000, Daimler-Chrysler released a new car model called the PT Cruiser. We were among the people who loved the design as much as many others hated it. There was such great advance demand for the car that dealers were told to take orders with thousand-dollar deposits. On an impulse, we put down our money in May and were told not to expect delivery for about 6 months. We were so enthusiastic that when we got home we went to the Daimler-Chrysler site and looked for some current information on supply, demand, and projected delivery dates. We found nothing but a glorified advertisement.

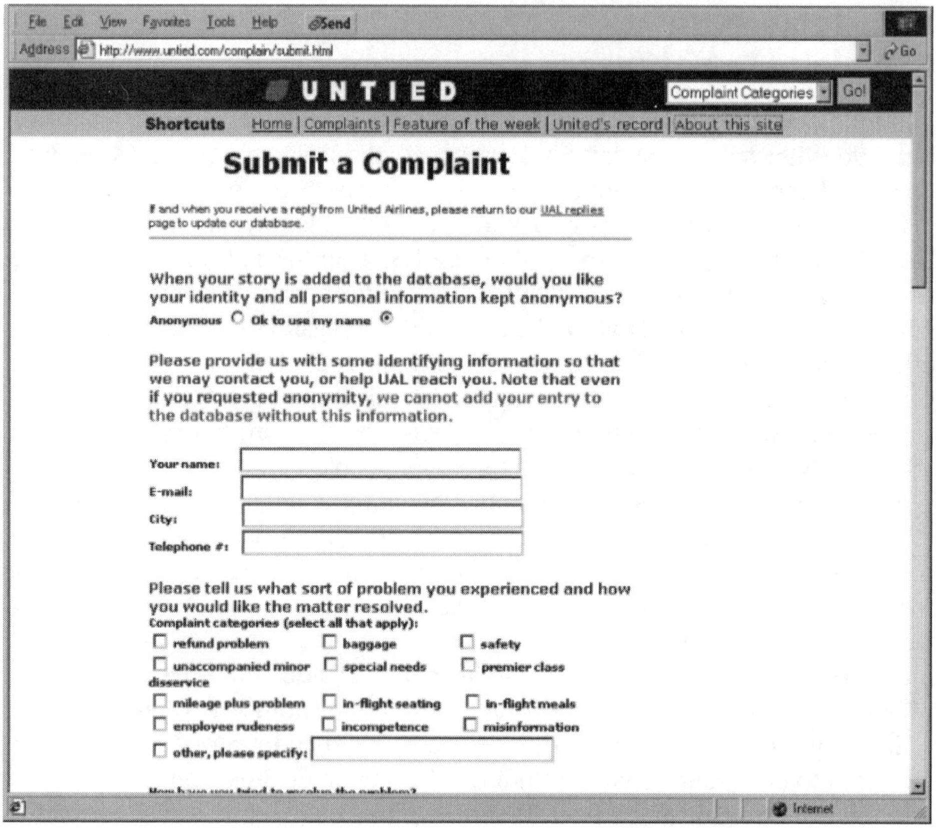

Figure 9.12 You won't find a form like this on the United Airline's site, but on the Untied site, your complaints will be forwarded to the airline with its agreement.
©Untied.com

So we did a search on "PT Cruiser," found the PT Cruiser Club (www .ptcruiserclub.org), and began monitoring its public discussion boards. We found a spontaneous gathering of PT Cruiser owners and people like us who had made deposits on vehicles. There we learned about the confusing practice of "dealer allocation," which could result in people who ordered their cars after us getting delivery before us. We learned how to track orders using a special sheet that dealers might or might not share with us. We learned from people who had gotten their new Cruisers that the automatics were sluggish accelerators and the five-speed versions weren't much better, but that the attention people on the street paid to your car made up for the poor performance. They *looked* faster than they actually were. We found people sharing tips on boosting the performance of their Cruisers (see Figure 9.13). We also learned that some dealers had raised the guaranteed MSRP sticker price once the car arrived on their lot.

As it turned out, the company ran out of the 2000 model year cars before they built ours, and we canceled our order, angry at the dealer, angry at the car company for not being more open and honest with people who were—as Daimler-Chrysler had hoped—*passionate* about the vehicle. The company did hold several public chat events, responding to customers and prospective customers, but did not provide a clear way—displayed on their Web site—for people with cars on order to check on the status of their orders. The PT Cruiser Club invited representatives of the company to visit their forums or to listen to their comments, but without success. Daimler-Chrysler so far has missed this chance to learn from the customers who truly care about their products and make efforts on their own to customize and improve them.

The lesson: Especially if your new product is expected to attract a passionate community of buyers, provide a place and invite them to get together on your

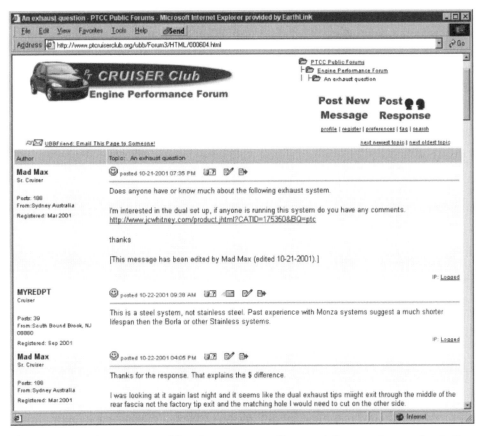

Figure 9.13 Where to get advice the company will never tell you: a forum about after-market exhaust systems for the PT Cruiser.

©PTCruiserClub.org. Used with permission.

Web site. Daimler-Chrysler could have won a lot of customer loyalty by doing so with the PT Cruiser, but instead, it failed to leverage the enthusiasm for its new vehicle and thus earned a lot of new enemies.

Summary

The essential social elements for productive conversation outside the company firewall are much the same as those for conversation on the company intranet: trust, leadership, and ease of use. Each company must decide on the most appropriate venue and format for these conversations, and every company must realize that it may be the topic of conversation somewhere on the Internet. Understanding the needs and habits of stakeholders is necessary to designing an interface that they will use. This may involve initiating or inviting conversation with a representative group of stakeholders.

The most successful examples of the use of online conversation with external stakeholders demonstrate the importance of incremental design and growth—building an initial interface for contact and activity, listening closely to what users say about it, and then adapting to their expressed needs. The bond between company and stakeholder is strengthened through mutually beneficial collaboration. The Web with its many tools lends itself to such cooperative work.

The Path Ahead

Changes came fast enough in the eighties and nineties, but the year 2001 really lit the afterburners. The collapse of the dot-com bubble was followed in turn by the ripple effects from September 11 and the extremely upsetting collapse of Enron. As businesses scramble to respond, these three very different but powerful events have created challenges for organizations on three fronts:

1. They must reposition the Internet in their business plans

2. They must plan for wildly unforeseen world events

3. And they must conduct complete reviews, if not complete restructuring, of their financial reporting

This is all for the good, of course. These seemingly unrelated but cascading events have forced issues that needed to be reformed. They are issues that call for change and increased communication within the organization and beyond it.

In this chapter, we explore trends that already are taking hold in large companies and will trickle down to smaller companies as reports of their success, best practices, and value circulate. We've alluded to some of these trends already. We point out the need for changes in accounting practices for businesses to quantify the value of their knowledge *networking* assets. Return on investments made to foster productive online conversation must be demonstrated to justify further investment in building both social capital and knowledge flow.

We can see much of the future forming in the present. To help put these trends into words, we call on some of our favorite technical observers and social philosophers, including Thomas Davenport, David Weinberger, and Etienne Wenger.

Davenport, coauthor of *Working Knowledge*, is a systematic investigator of organizational behavior who combines the knowledge of an insider with the analysis of an academic. Weinberger, coauthor of *The Cluetrain Manifesto*, is a "big picture" guy who views the human adoption of the Net in terms of the cultural climate of our era. To him, the Net is underhyped; is radically changing society, and businesses are still very much in denial about the depth of change that the Net is making in the marketplace. Wenger, visionary leader of what could be called the *communities of practice movement*, understands how focused groups work and is helping organizations learn to lead by following the natural human tendencies of their most creative workers. His work is less conceptual and more "just do it": Knowledge-sharing conversations want to happen, so put them to work. Whatever organizations do right now to make knowledge sharing more effective through the Net is the necessary preparation for future sustainability.

Interdependence and Infoglut

The rapid expansion of the global Internet and the explosive growth in the number of people and organizations using it have radically transformed communications and the ways by which we relate to one another. This transformation presents us with a double-edged sword. The vast improvement in our ability to interconnect has invited many more people to send messages and allowed many more people and organizations to produce, provide, and send information. The challenge and reason for forming effective knowledge networks are to balance the advantages of connectivity with the overwhelming amount of information there is to sort through.

Global Connectivity

Humanity is now almost totally interconnected, not in terms of people with access to the Internet—where with 6 billion still lacking access we're just getting started—but in terms of news being able to reach most locations around the globe in a matter of minutes. When 19 terrorists crashed four airliners on 9/11, the immediate effects of destruction, death, and horror proved to be only pebbles dropping into the pond. As the ripples radiated outward around the world, the travel industry lurched to a halt, jobs associated with travel disappeared, and then whole regional economies reliant on tourism went into a swoon. Many companies not directly related to the events of 9/11 were affected severely by its repercussions. With the ever-increasing amount of interdependence in the world today, all organizations going into the future will stand a higher chance of being affected by events in the world. Surprises are likely to come at any time, so the rising challenge is to be ready and adaptable.

As the effects of the 9/11 attack spread around the world, lower Manhattan, still covered in the dust of the World Trade Center, saw the stock market return to activity amazingly quickly. The interconnectedness and redundancy of its networked systems and the survival of key personnel brought the system back online while other parts of the New York City infrastructure were just beginning to dig themselves out. Networks—of computers and of people—are good insurance against sudden disaster and instability. Networks help organizations adapt to changing circumstances.

Conversational knowledge sharing is a natural way for people to distribute relevant information and experience as they deal with rapid change. Using the Net as the conversation environment allows a broader population of participants, bringing in viewpoints and expertise from more locations. Through the Net, organizations can get closer to their customers, and workers from different parts of the organization can connect and form closer working relationships with one another.

Ongoing conversation is an adaptive group behavior in which participants share observations, ideas, and their diversity of information sources. When it goes on within an organization, it can expand the thinking and problem solving of senior executives whose perspectives may be limited in scope due to their isolation from the workplace and the consumer. Wide-ranging conversation is the organization's equivalent of ants waving their antennae about, reading the environment for scents indicating potential threats and opportunities. Those antennae will become required equipment for organizations in the future, but to develop them, they have to align their cultures with the values that make knowledge sharing happen.

More Voices, Faster and Louder

Tom Davenport's latest book, written with John C. Beck, is titled *The Attention Economy*[1] and describes the workplace and the marketplace that have been transformed by the Internet and the accelerating flow of information. In the book, Davenport describes the world most of us have gotten to know only too well. It's a world where the competition for our attention has become so great that organizations must now figure out how to (1) focus their workers on the information and tasks that matter most to the company and (2) distinguish themselves, in the minds of consumers, from the blizzard of ideas, products, and other organizations that compete for their attention.

The Internet continues to grow in importance as the number of people using it increases and as it sees improvements in speed, interface design, and software. Access to the Net has brought changes in business process, communication, and the distribution of knowledge. But as its rapid growth continues, we are all challenged in our attempts to adapt and deal with the unprecedented volume of information the Net brings to us.

As technology advances and broadband connections increase the speed of information, how will we pull the important and timely information we depend on out of the nonstop avalanche of data, polling results, queries, opinions, ideas, suggestions, invitations, and junk mail that floods our monitors and inboxes? There's a crying need for the foolproof, personal searching-filtering-archiving system, but *systems* don't think like people do.

As individuals, our most insightful and understanding filters are other people. A community of trusted sources, each networked with other trusted sources, can not only understand what you want to know, but it can also respond to *the reason* you want to know it. Information filtered through an active knowledge-sharing community will have a much higher hit rate than an advanced Google search.

Selective engagement in online conversation is a very effective (and elementally human) method for directing one's limited time and focus. As the practice of online communication becomes more prevalent and normal, people will have more choices in where they spend their time looking for vital information and with whom they converse in their searches. In a future filled with bigger pipes and faster delivery, information overload will continue to balloon to absurd levels, and people will seek the most meaningful and productive ways to spend their limited attention on the Net.

Conversation Proliferation

With too much information to process already, why would organizations want to foster more conversation among their workers? Why would they expect workers to participate if it might overload them? The answers are that organizations have some critical problems to solve, and the wise use of group interaction may be the best and most economical way to find solutions. Workers will participate if they know it will help them do their jobs. But improvements must be made in technology, in the way technology is applied, and in the methods organizations use to calculate the value of their online conversations.

In a recent interview with *Agilebrain.com*, Tom Davenport was asked, in light of the dot-com meltdown, where he thought we were along the path to making optimum use of the Internet. He answered: "The Internet is still there, and companies are still quite interested in how to take advantage of it more effectively. We're just at the beginning of thinking about how we change our processes and our cultures and our governance structures to do anything differently with it."[2] In other words, the impact of the Net has yet to reach the parts of business that most need to change to keep up with the very changes the Net is bringing to other parts of the business universe.

The processes, cultures, and governance that Davenport refers to are social rather than technical in nature and more internal to the company than external. Yet the ultimate aim of changing them is to deal better with the external online marketplace, which continues to grow in significance, although it still receives a small portion of most companies' attention.

The previous decade has shown that as more people join the Net, there is more information to choose from and there are more conversations taking place. Organizations that change their processes, cultures, and governance to better use the Internet to know and understand their external stakeholders will gain a competitive advantage.

Incentives to Engage

Adaptation within organizations to the increasing speed and information flow of the Net must happen on both the technical and social levels if they expect their workers to engage in the practice of online conversation. In previous chapters, we've described what we've found to be state-of-the-art approaches for supporting that practice both technically and socially. In our search for pioneering role models, only a select few organizations are blazing new trails. But as more organizations (and communities of interest and practice) discover incentives to adopt online conversation as a business tool, interface refinement will follow and the online conversation process will "learn itself" into being a more productive form of knowledge generation.

As more organizations implement knowledge-sharing technologies and practices, there will be more need, interest in, and accumulated track records of positive returns. When enough studies and analyses have been done to make a convincing case for the return on investment from the wide variety of internal and external online conversations, the incentives will be there for more widespread adoption.

More Efficiency through Technology

People already loaded with responsibilities, swamped by information, and working in companies that have reduced their staffs don't have the time or mental bandwidth to learn new skills and engage in new knowledge-sharing activities. To persuade such overloaded workers to change their habits, incentives are required, one of which is greater convenience through improved design of technologies. If the interface and the tools made available can help workers solve problems and do their jobs more efficiently (without falling behind while learning a new, untried process), they will be adopted and used.

Technology must be a big part of the solution to the info-glut problem it has made possible. Social reorganization alone won't make knowledge sharing as effective as it needs to be. Aside from lack of understanding and compelling need, *usability* is the main barrier to the adoption of new technologies. As new handheld devices with wireless Web access multiply, designs for customizing our interface with the Net—to bring us only the information we want, just when we need it—will have to improve.

Peer-to-peer models allow the more ambitious and technically adept to move ahead of the pack (and the intranet), unfettered by centralized systems that can only be improved at the pace of an often overburdened IT department. By using basic email, instant messaging, or more sophisticated software like Groove, spontaneous knowledge networks, virtual teams, and CoPs may be supported, but P2P is not an ideal solution for the majority of workers as we explained in Chapter 7, "Choosing and Using Technology." Most workers don't want to go it alone without the handholding of IT. They simply need more useful interfaces provided through the company intranet.

Portal design is developing rapidly in a competitive market. Eventually, as application integration meets personalization, workers will be able to create and easily configure their own personal *dashboards* to increase their efficiency and effectiveness. A dashboard may contain links to prioritized and custom-sorted information and contacts, with gateways to (and automatic updates from) conversations in which the worker is engaged. In effect, the worker will choose to engage in numerous simultaneous conversations—some with people, some with database servers—and will be able to filter the input from all of them to fit time and attention constraints and to get just the right knowledge at the right time.

Recognizing the Value of Knowledge Flow

If intellectual capital is like cash in the bank, then *knowledge flow* must be like cash flow. Intellectual capital (IC) is gradually being recognized as a true asset to organizations, though there are many theories on how to measure it. Like IC, knowledge flow will become recognized in the future as a strong indicator of the organization's capacity to adapt, to innovate, and to survive.

Many businesses are now learning from knowledge already contained in their databases and in the minds of their workers and customers. To that end, they have spent considerable money on advanced software and systems integration to move data around and turn it into information that can be learned from. That doesn't necessarily mean that they actively promote knowledge exchange among their employees or with their customers. Some, as we've described, are beginning to do that, and many enterprise-level companies now recognize the value of communities of practice. There are now enough success stories to at least provide best practice examples that can be adapted to current business models.

But business models will have to adapt continuously as the rules and growth of the Internet press harder on large organizations still held back by tradition and older technology. Though some of these large companies are beginning to leverage the potential of online CoPs, most of them still have a long way to go before they can tap into the full value of the Net. When a valid and widely accepted means for measuring the knowledge flow in an organization is available, the results may persuade large companies to make the changes necessary to be competitive with companies that already are putting online conversation to work.

As businesses get wired, both technically and socially, the overall business environment evolves, and online communication skills become more important in job descriptions. Computers will continue to take over more of the tasks they do best, and humans will be spending more time in what they do best: collaborating, conversing creatively, and innovating for the benefit of the organization. Innovation is even more important to the survival of organizations today because world events may preclude long stretches of stability in the economy. Organizations today must become more communicative and lighter on their feet.

Mapping Social Networks

A school of study has been developing over the past decade that will become increasingly relevant as organizations make use of knowledge-sharing networks. *Social networks*, as we've mentioned in previous chapters, are made up of connections between people and connections between people and content. These connections range from the close and important *ties* of cohesive communities to the loose and episodic ties that characterize most relationships within organizations and between businesses and their customers. But as more people are given the opportunity to join online knowledge networks, the mapping methods of social networking analysis (SNA) will be put to greater use.

In his book *The Tipping Point*,[3] Malcolm Gladwell wrote of Connectors (people who know everyone) and Mavens (experts who love to teach) as catalysts of social *epidemics*. In social networks, these are the kinds of visible and influential people who attract and nurture communities. Identifying and empowering such people in an organization can jump-start knowledge networks. It's likely that the natural teachers and facilitators in organizations have spontaneously begun to do that already. Social networking analysis is a valuable technique for understanding how knowledge flows within communicating groups.

The principles of SNA are described well in a paper titled "Researching Organizational Systems Using Social Network Analysis,"[4] by Michael Zack. We've included many of these principles in our descriptions of the various roles in knowledge-sharing networks. Emergent leaders, who have the skills, experience, and confidence to step forward in new online meeting places, are key actors in SNA. The degrees of reluctance and enthusiasm that surround the introduction of new social technologies are measured by SNA techniques based on the ties that people have with other people. The influence of those ties can be affected by how close the people are located physically in the workplace, how close they are in their working relationships, and how dependent they are on each other.

As your company pays more attention to the social techniques of fostering productive communities of practice, you'll want to learn more about SNA. It may help you choose and configure technologies to support your online social interaction. One of the leaders in the development of SNA is Valdis Krebs, whose paper, "An Introduction to Social Network Analysis,"[5] can be found at www.orgnet.com/sna.html. It's a starting point for further study and is worth reading to gain a different perspective of the workings of your organization and its various overlapping and interwoven internal communities.

The Sustainable Organization

The challenge for organizations in the future is to adapt and sustain their meaningfulness in a fast-changing world. To meet that challenge, they will need to accept and embrace some different ways of operating and relating with people inside and outside the organization. Rigid structures and hierarchies will have to give way to more distributed ways of managing that provide less control but more flexibility. Human knowledge will need to be identified and used more effectively as the limitations of software are reached. Companies that are slow to adapt will be pushed to speed up the change process as smaller, quicker, less encumbered competitors seize opportunities. Companies will need to get closer to their customers to understand where the market is heading as early as possible. Faster learning, increased collaboration, and greater emphasis on building trust within the organization and with its stakeholders will be the drivers of organizational success in the future.

More than ever before, organizations are recognizing knowledge as an asset—not only the knowledge held by their company officers and well-educated professionals, but also the knowledge of every worker who understands his or her job. For strictly bottom-line reasons, companies need to preserve the knowledge of all workers because it costs more to replace them and retrain their replacements than it does to keep them and help them share what they know. This is especially true as organizations seek to "go lean" and cut staff numbers to the minimum.

Every bit of experience, know-how, competence, and individual learning counts now. Good workers need to share what they know and be rewarded for both knowing and sharing. It's in the self-interest of the organization to help workers collaborate and understand the value to the company of what they know about their jobs. This is true today, but the future will see the most successful organizations changing their cultures and values radically to become adaptable and sustainable entities.

Messiness Is In

The knowledge held by workers is not just valuable to their workmates; it is also increasingly of value to customers. Workers in positions that historically have been out of sight and out of reach of customers now find that they represent key links to customer loyalty and involvement. Product designers, systems engineers, and sales and shipping clerks all hold keys to the positive customer experience. When they do their jobs well, the company prospers because customers are pleased. Some companies have chosen to expose these previously anonymous servers of customer needs. The designer of the Daimler-Chrysler PT Cruiser, for example, became a star and a celebrity to owners and fans of the vehicle.

In the future, there will be more direct links from customers to the desktops of "back room" workers and innovators. They will be invited to respond directly to customers because the knowledge that can be shared between a customer and the designer of his tool, or the person who sends that tool to him, will become a competitive advantage. In the eyes of the consumer, the hierarchy of the business looks increasingly flat. People can track the packages they send through UPS on their home PCs. The shipping clerk who gets the product to the customer promptly is becoming a more meaningful contact to the consumer than the CEO ever was. To most company leaders, accustomed to keeping customer communications compartmentalized, this view of the future looks threateningly chaotic and filled with risk, but some see it as an inevitable reality.

Dave Weinberger, in an interview with *CIO* magazine said, "Businesses are taking on the structure of the web—decentralized, messy, self-organizing."[6] In the same interview, he also gave this warning to companies determined not to loosen their hierarchical ways: "Many businesses are devoted to maintaining the org chart through everything from disciplinary action to body language, so hyperlinked teams route around org charts." People are able to contact whom they want and need to contact, and they will do so if it means they can get their jobs done more easily or if it can bring them better service. The Net has changed the playing field to one with its own built-in rules that are not necessarily compatible with those of old-style organizations. Resistance to the messy ad hoc efficiency of hyperlinking is futile. Organizations must change proactively rather than adapt reactively to the changing marketplace and to the changing character and growing independence of their workers and customers. But a reactive change is still better than no change at all.

Speaking the Customer's Language

Weinberger also strongly promotes the need for companies to communicate with their customers in normal conversational language. The voice of the consumer is all over the Web, interpreting the marketing and sales messages of business that don't seem to be emanating from fellow human beings. Conversations among consumers are becoming more sophisticated at sorting the wheat from the chaff and the truth from the BS.

Weinberger, in his *CIO* interview, notes this ongoing translation of obscure business-speak into the natural language of the Web-enabled marketplace: "Business information now is wrapped in human voices, and that's an essential part of our ability to make sense of this information." More consumers are demanding an open dialogue with companies, but companies insist on obscuring their message, talking *at* their customers instead of *with* them. Consumers confront a smokescreen of marketing jargon and are finding ways to penetrate it. They are also choosing which companies to do business with based on the companies' willingness to address them as peers rather than as submissive customers.

Along with the adoption of the Net as a conversational environment, businesses need to realize that consumers are more willing to converse with them if they speak back in voices not scripted through the marketing or PR departments. Customers are tired of being spoken to like children. They just want to connect as fellow consumers (since even those who sell products must also buy products) and get the respect they deserve.

Learning about Learning

The idea of the learning organization has caught on, but how much of what has been learned has turned into increased productivity and profit? As the economy struggles to rise out of recession, early attempts to implement knowledge management solutions are being evaluated, and some truths about online knowledge sharing are becoming clear as indications for the future. Organizations in the future will do a better job of finding relevant knowledge, distributing it, and putting it to use because some pioneering companies and analysts are discovering today what works and does not work.

Smart People Trump Smart Software

In an interview after publication of *The Attention Economy*, Tom Davenport was asked, "What's going on in knowledge management these days?" He responded that the greatest treasure to be found in KM is the *insight* that it brings to companies, but that *business intelligence*, rather than the sharing of best practices, was the area currently seeing the greatest advances. He also said, "The smart companies realize it takes a lot of very bright human beings around in addition to the software, and that's sort of a knowledge management-oriented insight."[7] Software meant to mine data for information can only take a company so far. Unless it has smart people around who can convert data and information into usable knowledge, the output of software brings limited improvement.

Those "very bright human beings" are often the ones starting and participating in spontaneous knowledge-sharing communities. These communities use a variety of technologies, often simple and often in applications different from the purposes for which the company provided them. When communities of practice build email lists to collaborate and share, they are adapting social intellect rather than trying to invent or design new technologies. When workers independently download and install popular IM clients like ICQ so that they can stay in more immediate contact on project development, they are choosing simple technological solutions instead of elaborate and expensive software structures.

As Deloitte Research reported in a paper describing collaborative communities, "virtual communities defy many hierarchical practices."[8] Members of these communities are smart people seeking the most efficient ways to get their jobs done using whatever technologies are available, from their Web-enabled desktops to Blackberry mobile devices. The companies within which these communities operate must first of all know that they are present and identify them. Company leaders must get to understand them and what they are about and then carefully go about connecting them with each other so that knowledge can be shared among them appropriately. The Deloitte paper concludes, "Companies that learn to manage and leverage these networks effectively will be more agile, more efficient, and more innovative than those that do not."

MONITORING AND FACILITATING NETWORKS OF SMART PEOPLE

Deloitte Research concluded that company leaders "must understand that one of their jobs is to monitor and facilitate the linkage of communities of practice to form collaborative knowledge networks."

To accomplish this without ruining the creative spark that makes these communities so valuable, company leadership "must also understand that effective communities are about trust—trust by employees that their participation will be valued, and trust by companies that workers will make responsible decisions."[9]

Empowering Creative Thinking

Company leaders also must understand that their smartest employees may bring more value than expensive technologies, but *appropriate* technologies can raise the effectiveness of those employees and of their spontaneous communities of practice. Though many productive CoPs use email as their meeting environments, that original choice of platform is often made based on the lack of available Web-based discussion environments that allow multithreaded conversations and more accessible records of those conversations. The Web, with its ability to hyperlink between resources and its capacity to weave content with conversation and personal profiles, offers significant improvements over email in terms of the effectiveness of its support for knowledge sharing.

A study by *Forrester Research*,[10] surveying 50 Fortune 1000 companies, showed that although the great majority use email in collaborative product development, only a small percentage use Web-based tools. Executives responding to the survey projected that without a Web-based approach to collaboration, in-house best practices would take an average of *27 months* to be conveyed from one part of the organization to another, even in the best of firms. That time represents money lost. If the easy linking capabilities of a Web-based environment can cut the time of best practice dissemination in half or even better, the conversion from email is almost certain to have a positive impact on the company's bottom line.

It's not just the creative people inside the company who need to be empowered and leveraged; the helpful customers outside the company need to be hooked into the network, too. The Deloitte paper recommended that companies wishing to get full value out of their spending on CRM projects begin treating customers "as partners in anticipating, designing and delivering on their current and future needs." To build that partnership around customer-centric strategies, companies must create "an environment that allows for ongoing, consistent dialogue."[11] Again, this calls for simultaneous change in organizational culture and in improved access between knowledge-sharing groups both inside and outside the organization.

Adjusting to the Changing Marketplace

As markets are conversations, the marketplace is changing fast in part because the number of conversations is rapidly increasing. Companies that relate to their customers understand that the question no longer is simply "what do they want?" but "how do they want it?" The first generation dot coms may have been unrealistic in their visions of how fast their new business models could be established, but they were very practical when it came to serving consumers through a commonly available interface. In that respect, at least, they set the new direction of the changing marketplace.

The Net Waits for No Company

Change has occurred much faster and on a wider scale than has the adaptation of many enterprise-level businesses. Large companies, even those that take action to modernize their technology, change slowly. In Tom Davenport's interview, he says, "We've had ERP [enterprise resource planning] for 20 years, and only a small fraction of companies have started to change the way they manage using the systems. I think that will be true of the Internet."[12] If it takes 20 years for some companies to adapt their management to the changes in the Internet-powered marketplace, there's enough time for a second generation of dot-com frenzy to take place between now and then that could still grab business opportunities from slow-to-change competitors.

There is evidence, though, that large companies are continuing to try to keep up, at least on the technological end. In a paper titled "Communities: Sociology Meets Technology,"[13] the Gartner Group made some high-probability (Gartner-rated at 70 percent chance or higher) predictions for the year 2002. We list them in Table 10.1.

Table 10.1   High-Probability Predictions by the Gartner Group for 2002

GARTNER PREDICTION FOR 2002	IMPLICATIONS
The market for Web conferencing will exceed $500 million, doubling by year's end.	A lot of that expense will go for expensive virtual meetings through interfaces like Placeware and Webex. The more budget-minded companies will be installing discussion boards and instant messaging applications.
A wide range of "smart mobile devices" will begin to proliferate through the year.	These include wireless technologies for virtual team collaboration. Some other examples of their use: media content management, voice portals, geospatial information management, and personal knowledge management.
Six or more companies will offer packaged "smart enterprise portfolios."	These will integrate the functions of the portal with content and document management, KM, and collaboration products. Gartner believes many of these will include e-learning features. Such platforms can support self-managing knowledge communities in the same way that the software platform (described in Chapter 7, "Choosing and Using Technology") is designed to do.
Technology for locating experts in the workplace and for managing the searching and profiling functions will grow the fastest in terms of expanding its user base.	More than half a million workers will have access to such tools by year's end. People look for other human resources—as mentors, as sources of experience, for fact checking, and for inviting into collaborative relationships. Once these resources are found, conversations can begin.

Proving the Return on Investment

Purchasing new technologies that promise to solve knowledge-related problems is slowed, for the most part, by lack of proof that they will be worth their expense. An article in *Infoworld*[14] highlighted the continuing concern over new communication technology's ability to pay for itself. ROI continues to be relied on as the main justification for adopting collaborative practices and technologies, and if the ROI case cannot be proven using traditional metrics, the adoption of new practices and technologies doesn't happen.

In the *Infoworld* article, George Paolini, the chief marketing officer of the email-on-steroids application Zaplet (see Chapter 7), claimed that businesses still see collaboration as a "nice-to-have, not a must-have" system. The must-have status will only be recognized, he said, when current practices prove to be costing the company instead of saving it money. It's still easy to picture thousands of workers, perfectly happy with their simple email and scheduling application and the routine exchange of attached documents. Why pay for an upgrade if they are satisfied with what they have now? As Paolini explains, the ROI from software-mediated collaboration can only be demonstrated *after* a company has adopted and developed the new practice. Thus, companies relying on proof of ROI to trigger change are likely to adopt the new practice only when the current system's costs in inefficiency prove to be intolerable.

The article also acknowledges that the benefits of collaborative software, although not easily quantifiable, contribute indirectly to ROI through increased efficiencies such as "opening up communication bottlenecks, improving information redundancies, and combining disparate knowledge." As investments in collaborative technologies grow, it will be interesting to see how traditional measures of ROI evolve to include their contributions to the business.

Most cases of failed ROI from collaborative technologies reflect two basic management errors: an overinfatuation with cutting-edge software as the solution and the inappropriate application of software solutions to socially based networking situations. In fact, only a small part of the genre referred to by industry and the press as "collaborative technologies" is software to support online conversation; much of the attributed costs for that genre go for very expensive system-level technologies, systems integration, and middleware rather than for tools meant for interpersonal interaction.

Return on investment is more easily achieved if initial investments are kept small and increased incrementally only as paths for successful use are discovered. For conversational technologies, companies that follow a path that includes leveraging spontaneous communities, keeping the technology as simple as possible, starting small, learning and following a phased growth plan—with the users of the system leading the expansion—will prove effective in keeping initial costs low and seeing direct benefits more clearly.

Changes in organizational culture that make collaborative tools effective are happening, but slowly. Likewise, the proof of ROI is gradually emerging from the use of those tools. Soon, we believe, companies that have invented and implemented collaborative solutions over the past few years will have abundant proof to justify those investments. In the future, we believe that the period for proving the ROI of technologies that enable knowledge sharing will be extended beyond the traditional single-year timeframe. Investments that require social as well as technical integration and are meant to build the sustainability of the company must be given more time to become ingrained in organizational culture and practice.

Truly Knowing the Customer

Organizations whose products and purposes relate to lifestyle communities will gain both loyalty and knowledge by providing opportunities for customers and constituents to converse on the Net. As attractions to these natural communities, organizations like REI—the outdoor equipment store that began as a cooperative and now manages one of the more effective online shopping sites—become hubs of customer interaction and sources of valuable market intelligence.

The key functions of these community opportunities are described clearly by REI in its "Learn & Share" area, pictured in Figure 10.1. Customers, who originally come to the site to shop for outdoor gear and clothing, can learn from fellow backpackers, skiers, and canoeists how to select the right equipment for their conditions or fitness. They can offer their advice to those coming to the online forums to learn. They can find partners for their adventures and suggest favorite hiking routes. By facilitating the contact between people with interest in outdoor activities, REI helps to build a loyal and informative market for its products.

Because of experience gained in its brick-and-mortar stores, REI understood its customers before it built its Web site. Many companies, though, have fallen behind their customers in learning how to communicate. They have to catch up. Dave Weinberger says, "The web is enabling markets to become much smarter, much faster than businesses can hope to—at least businesses along the old model."[15] The market becomes as smart as its smartest person because "the web enables global conversations in which people speak the truth to one another in their own distinctive voices." Again, the issues of trust and genuine voice arise. This is not about the technology as much as it is about the company providing the interface and the words that customers understand as they look for solutions. REI is a good example for the future because its employees and the editors of its Web site are outdoors enthusiasts just like its customers. It speaks the language of its customers.

Consumers as Consultants

In Chapter 9, "Conversing with External Stakeholders," we described Hallmark's Idea Exchange, an online community composed of Hallmark customers and

Figure 10.1 Learning and sharing opportunities help REI win customers and sell products.

consumers invited to participate through phone calls and email. We believe that more companies will adopt the Hallmark model of close consumer involvement with product design and service feedback in the future, so in February 2002, we conducted an interview with the initiator of the Idea Exchange, Tom Brailsford.

Since the report that informed our initial description of the consumer-as-consultants project, Hallmark has started two more online communities: one for grandparents and one for Hispanics. As with the original community, made up of mothers with young children, the company plans to limit the populations to about 200 members at a time. Additional communities—specifically, their composition—are under discussion within the company. Brailsford says that one way consumer communities save his company money is by enabling faster research. "There's a financial value associated with time too."

Brailsford set up the original Idea Exchange so the company could have an ongoing dialogue with its customers rather than just "point in time" focus groups or surveys. Part of customer loyalty, he maintains, involves the customer thinking of the company as a partner. He recognizes that for these communities to work the participants must also have a compelling reason to want to talk with one another, such as exchanging child-raising tips or having a voice about issues that are deeply important to them.

The communities, Brailsford says, are always "morphing"; that is, they are living, organic, works in progress. Members regularly leave and new ones are recruited (or join voluntarily) to replace them. At first, the company's goal for the Idea Exchange was to come up with one good new product idea a year from the insights generated there. Last year he believes they came up with at least two ideas for entirely new businesses.

Hallmark's employees don't participate as regular members of the Idea Exchange communities but can visit and observe by using guest passes. The availability of these passes is made known within the company by word of mouth; they have not been advertised or promoted. So far, more than 400 people have used the guest passes, and although the members of the consumer communities are aware when a guest is present, the guests themselves are asked not to interfere or disturb the normal interactions of the consumer members. Hallmark tries to be very careful to preserve its trusted relationship with the consumer community participants. It is aware that if the communities are overly influenced by Hallmark, the Idea Exchange(s) may no longer be a valid market research tool.

Members of the communities are empowered to start their own discussion topics and to launch their own surveys. Hallmark's creative writers take special note of the language that consumers use to describe day-to-day life events and feelings. Brailsford projects that in the future they may allow the consumers to do their own recruiting for their communities and become even more self-governing than they are today. He considers what Hallmark is doing with consumer communities to be a kind of online anthropology where the company can observe consumers interacting in a relatively controlled but uninfluenced environment.

The New Shape of Organizations

"Many companies are moving toward decentralized and team-based work environments to improve their responsiveness." So says the Deloitte Research paper on knowledge networks.[16] Such companies have realized how far the marketplace has pulled ahead of them. Their old, rigid, hierarchical structures could not respond fast enough. Now they need to go faster and grow leaner to save money and learn from where they've been. This defines a clear need for the efficiencies and adaptability of conversational knowledge sharing.

Speeding Up the Learning Process

Tom Peters wrote *In Search of Excellence*, a book that years ago helped bring attention to exemplary companies that had recognized and were adapting to the changing marketplace. In an article in *Fast Company*, he says that companies "need to achieve liberation. Today, it's all about the freedom to try new things."[17] He compares this to the days when he wrote his groundbreaking book, way back in 1982, when he concentrated on "people, customers, and action." Today, he says, "it's about ideas, liberation, speed … the power of good ideas that passionate, motivated, fully engaged people can generate." The speed that Peters is talking about today is "speed to learning," and it's a kind of speed that doesn't waste time worrying about what just happened. It's a forward-looking speed, eager to anticipate and adjust to the future.

Similarly, Tom Davenport sees companies today not worrying about what just happened, but trying to gather their wits and move ahead as smartly as possible. Speaking at the end of year 2001, he said, "Right now, we're sort of in a period where there's no really big new ideas, and a lot of managers, employees and organizations just want to take all the ideas that have come along for the past several years and put them together, integrate them, simplify them and get some value out of them. They're all looking to extract some value from their existing infrastructures and, at this moment, cut costs from their existing infrastructures."[18]

How much time they have to do such analysis will depend on the patience of their markets. What Davenport describes is a characteristic of the new *lean* company model, where only the essentials to success are retained and where no extraneous infrastructure or staff is carried that will slow the company down and cut into its profitability. The companies he describes are gearing down for their anticipated acceleration into the fast-learning lane described by Peters.

The Rising Emphasis on Collaboration

A study done by consulting giant Accenture indicated that more than 70 percent of surveyed executives from Fortune 1000 companies see the Internet as one of the most important factors in fostering greater collaboration with key business partners because of the visibility it provides in the supply chain.[19] Collaboration, in this context, is a necessary result of executives outsourcing more of their business functions like transportation, logistics, and procurement and working harder to eliminate supply chain inefficiencies. Although this doesn't mean that they are fostering more online conversation, the results of partner collaboration—sharing or integrating software so that data are compatible with partnering organizations—are certainly a form of collaboration that is likely to require more direct online communication.

Other clues point to increased emphasis on conversational collaboration in the workplace. The previously cited study by the Gartner Group also included interesting projections about online communities and interaction. Companies will implement more online *business* communities from now through 2004, and Gartner predicts that *employee-focused* communities (B2E) will appear in the greatest numbers. This makes sense because employees have established reasons to communicate and share common communication technologies. Interest, though, will be highest in building *customer* communities (B2C) because companies are being asked increasingly by their customers to provide better channels for support. Leading the way in measured ROI will be partner communities (B2B), probably because they are closer to actual business transactions than the others. We believe that by 2004 more valid and accepted ROI measurement techniques for the B2E and B2C communities will drive their adoption by more companies.

Gartner believes, based on its research, that by 2007, "the time spent interacting with others in the virtual world will exceed the physical connections by a factor of 10-to-1." And by the same year, "more than 60 percent of the European Union and U.S. population will carry or wear a wireless computing and communications device at least six hours a day." These numbers, if they prove even close to accurate, will certainly have an impact within business practice and culture.

These projections describe a very communicative and collaborative workplace—one that organizations should be preparing for today in their strategic planning and in their changing operations. As communication among workers increases, the productive value of specific technologies, online leadership, and online conversation skills will stand out. Innovation spurred by interaction between customers and companies will become more important, and the amount of tolerance and flexibility ingrained in an organization's culture will prove to be either a lubricant or a source of friction on its path to sustainability. Yet the increase in interpersonal interaction in the virtual world must be metered carefully so as not to become another form of information glut.

Making Collaboration More Effective

Not surprisingly, as one senior executive says, "Nobody in reality wants to collaborate for the sake of collaboration." Darren Lee, senior VP of NextPage, admits, "We're finding [collaboration] only has significant value when it's combined ... with mission-critical information, attached to a business-processing context."[20] That's a fancy way of saying that working people need to get things done and that online collaboration needs to be made as efficient as possible.

We agree that "collaboration for the sake of collaboration" can be wasteful of valuable time, but we also warn against holding too high a standard for what "mission-critical" means, at least when the collaboration involves online conversation. Informal practice of online communication skills is important; it leads to learning and allows people to develop the new skills, habits, and trust required for productive interaction.

But besides practice, productive online collaboration also requires appropriate software environments and interfaces for the specific community and task. Often, the community finds an available environment for online meetings—for example, email combined with content on Web pages—and settles in with it rather than seeking more powerful software that might actually be more useful for its purposes. The end users can't be relied on to be the ones pushing for change in the collaborative interface. End users are often the most conservative forces in terms of pushing for change and new things to learn.

As Andrew Mahon, senior director of product marketing at Groove Networks, notes, "Collaboration usually is aimed at the long-term efficiency and effectiveness of a group, but that's not how people behave—they behave in their short-term best interest."[21] Mr. Mahon is referring to the lack of demand in the workplace for tools like Groove. He can't be blamed for wanting businesses to buy Groove, just as Mr. Paolini wants them to convert to Zaplet Appmail. But workers aren't yet demanding change on the level that would drive institutional demand for their products.

Email and instant messaging may be the platforms of choice and may indeed work well in the short term. But when collaboration is adopted as a long-term solution in the company, software that can make every collaboration more efficient—providing document sharing, calendars, and project management time-lines—will be more appropriate and effective for the company as a whole.

A Return to Community Values

As innovative thinking and action become more important to organizations, so will inspirational leadership and stimulating culture. Businesses must learn to be less mechanical and more social because people communicating can create and adapt for situations better than computers and machines. And as the Net brings people outside organizations closer to people inside them, the human side of the organization must be nurtured. Tom Davenport was asked in an interview about the importance in workplace culture of "how you manage people's spirits." He responded, "If you want employees to think creatively and share their ideas and so on, you have to work on that kind of stuff."[22]

Managing people's spirits is not the stuff of traditional business, but increased internal communication is changing the way organizations see themselves. Referring to his latest book about the scarcity of attention, the interviewer asked Davenport about online communities, pointing out that they get attention, sustain attention with user participation, and encourage knowledge sharing where novices learn from experts. Did Davenport see companies embracing the idea of internal and external online communities?

"I think online communities are great and they have a number of positive attributes," he said, "but I think a lot of companies try to do them on the cheap, and they don't really take experts and put them in roles to facilitate communi-

FOSTERING INNOVATION

Margaret Wheatley is president of The Berkana Institute, a charitable global foundation. She has been an organizational consultant and a professor of management in two graduate programs. These ideas for managers, which call for a lot of communication between people, are from her writing in the book *Leading for Innovation:*[23]

- "Meaning engages our creativity." Find out what is meaningful to people by paying attention to them, being around them, communicating with them. Things don't become meaningful to people just because you tell them they should be. Stay open and listen actively.

- "Depend on diversity." Just as it is with crops, monoculture can be dangerous in organizations. Diversity and deviance raise the possibility that new solutions will be devised quickly when new problems arise. Invite unique personal perspectives because that reflects the complexity of the real world.

- "Involve everybody who cares." Participation is necessary, so leaders must invite everyone who will be affected by a change into the creation process. Organizations are complex, so "engage the whole system so we can harvest the invisible intelligence that exists throughout the organization."

- "Diversity is the path to unity." By airing and discussing their differing viewpoints, perspectives, and predispositions, groups can build trust and discover common interests and goals and shared meaning for the work they do together.

- "People will always surprise us." We have to take the time to hear each other's stories and get to know people. Applying stereotypes and labels to people only serves to reduce the number of people who are invited to help create new solutions.

- "Rely on human goodness." People need each other to make work worthwhile and to figure out the solutions that will make their organizations sustainable. There is cynicism among workers, but inviting them to be part of the meaningful conversation and listening to them can win back their trust.

ties." Because they can be so difficult and expensive to facilitate, he sees online communities evolving into what he described as "kind of another unit of organizational structure." Employees will work within a specific department of the organization, such as accounting, but they may actually be active in communities that cross the boundaries of departments. Community structures will define a constantly changing organizational network within the organization.

Tearing Down the Walls

We see online communities in the future spanning not only internal boundaries but boundaries between the company and its customers. The people who design and market products share a common interest with the customers who buy and use those products, and together they comprise a community of focus and purpose: to end up with the highest quality product. The Internet now provides the potential meeting place for these potential collaborators. To open the conversation between them, companies must change themselves from within.

Michael Hammer wrote *Reengineering the Corporation*, a book that helped set off waves of reorganization and change in the way businesses were managed. That was 1993, and today his viewpoint has evolved with the marketplace. He now believes that the equation has changed "from scarce goods to scarce customers." Customers are more educated today and have become more particular, so companies must reengineer in this age to "face the customer, to serve the customer, and to make life easier for the customer."[24]

The Net makes this obvious to those of us who have been online steadily for years, but as more people log on and become more comfortable doing business through the Web, the pressure for companies to open up to the market through the Net will become irresistible. The customer will be more and more defined by what happens through the Net, where the marketplace expects there to be a conversation.

Deviance as the Source of Solutions

The innovative company of the future will need to find sparks of creativity in places it has never looked before. Organizations can learn from customers, consultants, and other external sources, but when looking for solutions to internal problems, ideas drawn from outside the company often hit cultural roadblocks. Solutions developed within the framework of a culture, rather than introduced from outside it, are more likely to be adopted and sustained. This is human nature. But an organization looking inward for solutions may wonder where to begin its search.

Recognizing internal *deviants* in the culture as innovators (rather than crackpots, eccentrics, or rebels) is one approach to finding fresh new solutions. People deviate from the norm for different reasons, but one is that the norm is not effective enough for them; they feel it is holding them back. So they try different ways of doing things. Sometimes they break rules or ignore protocol. Sometimes they download and install software not provided or approved by IT. Sometimes they create their own discussion groups just to learn something new about their job or profession. Their behavior may go against corporate norms of playing it safe and submitting to the organization, but deviation can be recognized as leadership rather than rebellion.

Resisting Solutions from Outside

Jerry Sternin's job with Save the Children was to help save starving children in a specific region in Vietnam. Faced with an impossible timeframe for figuring out and implementing lasting solutions, he decided to look for the rare examples of children that were not starving in the region. Compared to the vast majority of families whose children were suffering, these deviant cases might provide workable solutions for everyone. But that was only part of the challenge. The most important challenge was in getting these solutions adopted by many families and in changing entrenched cultural behaviors.

Sternin knew from experience with businesses that when outside consultants come into an organizational culture and introduce new practices, they may be adopted for a while, but once the consultants leave, the tendency is to revert to old practices. Cultural trust is a powerful thing. Foreign intervention, no matter how helpful, is still foreign. As Sternin said: "The traditional model for social and organizational change doesn't work. It never has. You can't bring permanent solutions in from outside."

Sternin knew that the most effective way of introducing new ideas was to find successful but unusual practices that were working for some people, in some circumstances, in the organization and "amplify them." People sometimes unwittingly discover paths to success that can benefit the entire organization. They need to be discovered and to have their ideas disseminated. But acceptance by others in the organization can be tricky. People like to think that they have discovered the ideas they adopt. They tend to resist having new ideas imposed on them, even if they are improvements over their current practices. When people feel that they have a part in discovering a solution, they "own" it, trust it, and are more likely to continue using it.

Adopting Solutions from Inside

In Viet Nam, Sternin found families whose children were not malnourished and studied the differences in their diets from the norm. He and his wife introduced other families to the foods in these deviant diets, but they did so casually, without proselytizing. This let the families feel that they were discovering the new foods on their own rather than having them introduced as part of a "nutritional program."

Applying the deviant solution approach to organizations, the incremental successes of deviant groups (like spontaneous communities of practice) can be publicized in a low-key manner through the intranet, where other groups can appreciate the new ideas and adopt them as they choose to fit their situations. To overhype the specific deviant group ("Everybody go look at what the widget team is doing!") could endanger its effectiveness. To force all groups to form communities of practice is sure to breed resentment and awkwardness. But spreading exceptional practices by *seeding* them as ideas through the organizational culture introduces the elements of choice and creative collaboration— elements that contribute to group trust, creativity, and loyalty.

EIGHT STEPS TO USING POSITIVE DEVIANCE

Jerry Sternin has some dos and don'ts drawn from his experiences in organizations and in other cultures:[26]

1. **Discover solutions within the existing culture.** Don't bring solutions from outside of it. Identify deviants who have found solutions on their own.

2. **Solve for a distinct group culture.** Don't try to solve across cultures. Everyone in the group must identify with the others, must face the same challenges and rely on the same set of resources to come up with answers.

3. **Let them do it themselves.** Set up a situation in which people—including those who need to change the way that they operate—can discover, on their own, a better way to do things.

4. **Identify and clarify the conventional wisdom of the average and of the majority.** What is accepted behavior? What do most group members do?

5. **Identify and analyze the deviants.** As you track how all people in the group go about their tasks, and as you begin to list the behaviors that they all have in common, the positive deviants will naturally emerge.

6. **Let the deviants adopt deviations on their own.** Once you find deviant behaviors, don't tell people about them. It's not a transfer of knowledge. It's not about importing best practices from somewhere else. It's about changing behavior. Let the people who have discovered the deviations spread the word in their group. Don't require adherence to the new practices, but do offer incentives for it.

7. **Track results and publicize them.** Post the results, show how they were achieved, and let other groups develop their own curiosity about them. Celebrate success when you achieve it. Go back on a periodic basis and observe how different groups have changed, and track the results quantitatively to show how positive deviance works. Chip away at conventional wisdom, and gradually alter low expectations by showing, in indisputable terms, the results that come with doing things differently.

8. **Repeat steps one through seven.** Make the whole process cyclical. Once people discover effective ways to deviate from the norm, and once those methods have become common practice, it's time to do another study to find out how the best performers in the group are operating now. Chances are that they've discovered new deviations from the new norm. The bell curve of performance keeps moving up, as long as you disseminate the best deviations across the curve and continue to discover new examples of positive deviance among the next group of best performers.

Redefining Success

The dot coms pioneered some novel ways of measuring success. Page views were as good as money for several years. In 1999, click-throughs were going to be the standard for setting ad rates. Eyeballs—the number of unique visits or unique visitors—drove share prices. Being first to market was an automatic symbol of success, and winning dominant market share was seen by the stock market as worthy of huge investment. Revenue and profit would come in their natural course, eventually.

But page views didn't sell product. Click-throughs stopped happening, and eye-balls did not reliably translate into revenue for anyone. Profit and ROI were reclaimed as the bedrock measures of business success. But the Net, in speeding up the flow of information and introducing many new ways of relating people and information, did create some new benchmarks for performance measurement. These will be refined, adopted, and used in the future, led by the most innovative companies who understand the importance of monitoring their real-time performance as they constantly try new ideas and react to shifting markets.

Performance Measurement

Michael Hammer is one of those who believes conventional business measures have fallen behind the marketplace and must be changed. In a September 2001 interview,[27] he calls most conventional measures "worthless" and charitably labels the others as only "dangerous." What measures is he referring to and what's his complaint? "Financial measures—profitability, return on investment, discounted cash flow, or any of the technically complex measures used by financial engineers—tell you little, if anything, of what you need to know about your business." He calls the basic profit-and-loss statement "an autopsy." Hammer does accept, though, the importance of a strong balance sheet and healthy P&L but only as *outcomes*, not as the most useful measurements of business health.

Hammer believes businesses should be tracking more measurements of their actual performance: how much they are getting done and how well they are doing it. "The fundamental language of business is about things like customer satisfaction, speed, and error rates," Hammer says. He wants "[real] operating measures, metrics that matter not to the accounting department, but to the all-powerful customer." Customers don't care and can't tell if your company made a profit last month, but they do care and can tell if your delivery came on time and if the invoice you sent them was correct. Customers can be lost if service is bad, even though the company's balance sheet looks healthy. In a fast-changing marketplace, service and performance must be monitored constantly.

Knowledge Generation as Performance

Performance measures as described by Hammer help describe a company's effectiveness as tied to its customer satisfaction. We believe that knowledge exchange also must be measured as a kind of intellectual performance that can be tied to cost savings and to revenue-generating ideas and relationships. Conventional measures of business success must be expanded in the future to recognize the effects of communication through the Net on efficiency, innovation, knowledge generation, and the overall health and prospects of companies. In a more communicative wired marketplace, companies will be valued in part by how well adapted they are to that environment.

Thus, in addition to ideas like those suggested by Michael Hammer, we would add other measuring criteria such as:

- How many new product or business ideas have been stimulated by direct interaction with customers?

- How many employees are involved on a daily basis in knowledge-sharing communities?

- How many customers are participating in company-sponsored online conversation?

- How fast do best practices disseminate through the company?

Conventional accounting doesn't include any means for recognizing the value of a company using the Net to engage in conversation with its customers and partners. As Tom Brailsford of Hallmark's Idea Exchange asked in our phone interview with him, "What is the value of thinking?" Conversations in which knowledge is shared amount to collective thinking. The fact that it is happening within an organization identifies the potential for generating useful as well as mission-critical knowledge and ideas. Correlating conversations with the value of their creative results—new products, more efficient processes, faster time to market, improved customer and employee satisfaction—should be considered the new frontier of accounting in the knowledge-focused marketplace.

Business has been paying attention to the brainpower within organizations for many years. Measuring intellectual capital is not a new idea by any means, but the Internet continues to spawn new examples of group intelligence that don't yet fit into recognized categories for measuring intangible assets. Dynamic knowledge generation and its positive by-products need to be integrated with parameters like *competency models, balanced scorecard, benchmarking,* and *business process auditing.*[16] If a company invests in using the Net to harness the power of consumer input and feedback, if it grows communities of reliable consumer consultants, then those assets should be represented somewhere on the balance sheet.

The New Skill Set

Online knowledge sharing is a new way of doing business and will require the learning and adoption of a new set of skills. Depending on a person's role and the nature of the conversation, these skills can be as natural as starting and maintaining an interesting conversation or as challenging as herding cats. The personal assets that make a productive online conversationalist can be as mundane as good typing skills and as elusive as inspirational leadership.

Every organization and every culture will need its own special skills to manage this virtual social activity. We describe only general categories here because skills such as effective message writing, operating in a flattened hierarchy, applying online etiquette, and conversational leadership are important to any wired organization, but to different degrees. Every cultural unit, whether a distinct company or a line of business within a company, needs to discover on its own how these skills should be tailored to its particular needs.

For his book on the scarce resource of human attention in the information-flooded workplace, Tom Davenport studied what business leaders pay attention to. This is important to know because wherever executives spend their limited attention is more likely to influence the strategies they implement. In his interviews at Agilebrain.com,[28] Davenport described what executives chose to zoom in on. It turns out that, at least in the case of online communication, executives behave a lot like the rest of us.

Getting Attention

Davenport and his coauthor asked executives which medium they paid the most attention to. They responded: email. The executives were then asked which attributes of an email message were most important to them in deciding whether it was worth further attention. Their responses ranked the attributes in the following order, beginning with most important:

Personalization of the message. Executives looked first at messages written specifically to them rather than to a group.

Brevity. Keeping the message "short and concise" was likely to convince them to spend time reading it.

Emotion. If the message evoked either a positive or negative emotion, it was more likely to draw their interest than if it did not.

A trustworthy source. Even long, dry, impersonal messages from someone known and trusted would get a look.

Over the years, we've found the same attributes of online interpersonal communication to be important for most people. When the number of messages—whether email, message board, or IM—becomes too great, people apply their own sorting and prioritization systems. First to get ignored always seem to be the least personal messages, followed by the long time-consuming ones. Boring messages are a labor to read, and those coming from unknown sources probably don't have as much relevance as those coming from friends, associates, and workmates.

People (and businesses) have to work hard to become known as trustworthy sources and thereby to attract attention. Businesses and business leaders who need to contact many people at once also must work hard to make their messages seem personal. These factors apply to messages posted in message boards or anywhere in the online environment. The new skill set of the knowledge-sharing future includes an understanding of how to attract attention when the audience, not just executives, is learning to filter its input and aim its attention based on factors such as personalization, brevity, emotional impact, and trust.

Future Leadership Skills

In the flattened hierarchy of the Net, leaders are recognized more by their communication skills than by the number of people who report to them. In companies where executives spend most of their attention on email, they may not spend any time in group conversation environments such as discussion boards or as member/participants in ongoing email lists. But as online conversations become more popular as meeting places and collaborative environments, executives will find it more difficult to keep a finger on the pulse of the organization without spending time involved in some of those conversations. Leadership must become accustomed to proving its mettle in Cyberspace.

Peer-to-Peer Management

Dave Weinberger, who campaigns constantly for businesses to express themselves like normal people, also thinks that business leaders need to learn the importance of addressing the marketplace with substance rather than spin. "An important new skill is being required of our best communicators," Weinberger says. "They need to stand for something, to care about what they're talking about, to be able to talk from the heart in their own words."[29] Michael Hammer strikes a similar theme when he says, "You're not going to get passion in your organization by talking about shareholder value. You have to give people a sense of transcendent purpose."[30]

Millions of people have now used the Net as a medium for serious, heartfelt, passionate communication. They understand that it is not a toy and is not a broadcast medium like television where they can simply mute the commercials if they offend. The Net is a two-way medium among virtual peers. People expect to get back in truth and sincerity what they put out. They expect leaders to be able to use the medium to communicate from the heart and to inspire people behind common causes.

Weinberger recognizes that in a communications-rich marketplace, leaders must be more than managers of people in offices. They must, as he says, "earn respect by being out in the fray, by being able to laugh ... especially at their own mistakes." Respect is earned, he says, "by being a participant just like everybody else. That's pure democracy."[31] That's also consistent with the very real flattening of the hierarchy in the modern organization. The Net makes it so. Networks need competent and trusted coordinators more than they need commanders.

Hammer says, "The old leader was a guy who sat on the 59th floor and made financial decisions. The new leader must be a charismatic persuader, someone to whom others can relate, a person who can set sights higher than the next quarter's earnings report."[32] The next era of reengineering, he says, will depend on "on qualities that emanate from the right side of the brain: devotion, trust, empathy, and all of their touchy-feely cousins." We may be 30+ years beyond the end of the sixties, but Hammer sees management entering an age of "empathic identification." The Net makes us all more exposed to each other, businesses and consumers alike. It's time to accept that fact and learn how to take best advantage of it.

Effective Facilitation

Facilitation means to make something easier. The leaders of sustainable organizations will be responsible for making it easier for workers and knowledge-oriented communities to communicate and learn. Those leaders will have to understand how online conversation works. And to do that, they will have to use the tools their workers use so that they can experience and join online conversations. Leaders of sustainable communities will be active members of knowledge networks and will therefore understand their needs.

Facilitation also means making productive conversation easier for participants. There are specialists who do this for a living or who fill this role in online discussions, but we believe online facilitation skills will become common to knowledge workers in the future. Good facilitators maintain focus, help people understand one another, and bring the group to resolution within set time limits. They pay attention to every individual and to the conversation as a whole. Good facilitators understand the practical attention limits and capabilities of people conversing online. They manage meetings according to the time and attention people are most able to give. They perform helpful tasks like clarifying points people attempt to make. They provide summaries of past meetings and agendas for future meetings.

The more people in any online meeting who are participating with a facilitator's level of attention, the more productive the meeting can be. Not every online conversation needs a facilitator, but where efficiency and time are involved, every online knowledge-sharing conversation should be managed as a facilitated meeting. In a knowledge-sharing environment, we expect group communications skills will become more important as a requisite skill. We foresee companies providing training and practice to get all of their workers up to a much higher level of sophistication than exists today.

Future Technical Paths

In Chapter 7, we described a range of technical genres, platforms, interfaces, and approaches that can serve the needs for knowledge exchange within and across the firewall. We included some products and ideas that we believe represent the future, or at least the next step of technology for the virtual knowledge-sharing organization. In this last part of the final chapter, we'll touch again on some of the technical themes we believe will support the expansion of online conversation in the workplace and marketplace.

Decentralization is one theme. Application integration is another. But as we've emphasized many times in this book, self-motivated knowledge-sharing communities are not limited by the shortcomings of centralized systems or the slow pace of integration. They find tools that work in the present because they need to converse and learn now, not later.

The recognition of businesses as communities and of communities within businesses also will affect the direction of technical development for and within organizations. Communities of practice are catching on in corporations, and some of the best practices for tapping into customer knowledge are now known to involve online conversation. The future of knowledge networking will feature more personalization and more ongoing collaboration between IT, Web designers, and portal builders. Workers dependent on their knowledge-sharing communities will need the technical means to stay engaged remotely through different devices. But beyond these few assumptions, the technical future of knowledge sharing will depend on where the actual practice of knowledge sharing leads it.

Next-Generation Portals

Portal design today is a very competitive business, with many companies trying to serve widely varying corporate needs by including just the right mix of information searching, application integration, employee profiling, and collaboration tools. The portal market is being driven by increasing dissatisfaction with existing intranet deployments and the recognized need to move toward Web-based interfaces as the standard for information delivery and knowledge sharing. All of the major business infrastructure providers such as SAP, Oracle, and PeopleSoft have rewritten their programs for operation as Web applications.

We expect knowledge sharing to be one of the more sought after functionalities in future designs because portals will be where more employees spend their time and get their information. Portals will become the means through which more enterprises tap into what their employees know and provide the means for employees to share with each other what they know.

The ability to provide mobile, remote, and distributed workers with organized access to the applications, knowledge, and information they need for sound decision making has become vitally important for businesses striving to be productive, agile, and profitable. The attractiveness of Web-based computing combined with the need to expedite information access and skills training has led to the design of what are called *e-learning* portals.

Centra (www.centra.com) is, like Placeware, a provider of real-time Web-based communications. Through integrating its services into the local portal, companies can bring virtual classrooms into the organization. The importance of bringing an entire staff up to speed on new skills is crucial to organizations needing to keep pace with the fast-changing marketplace, and portals will be the primary channel through which the necessary training will be delivered. E-learning portals will connect directly and seamlessly with enterprise resource planning (ERP), business intelligence, customer relationship management (CRM), and other mission-critical enterprise systems so that workers can learn within the actual information environments that define their jobs.

Open source technologies allow programmers to build new platform-independent applications for virtually any device, including wireless and handheld communication devices and information appliances. Mobile users will be able to move seamlessly from one device to another and receive consistent, personalized learning and knowledge. These applications will be integrated into portals where all information and personalization options will be located—where individual workers will configure and maintain their personal dashboards.

Integration Technologies

Three main approaches to integrating technologies are developing today that will open the doors to wider collaboration in the B2B, B2E, and B2C arenas: Web services, application service providers (ASPs), and virtual network organizations. Many businesses are unable to collaborate with each other because of incompatibilities among the applications they use. Two different ERP systems may not be able to exchange information, for example, preventing the time-saving efficiencies that could be realized if data could be smoothly exchanged. Because such relationships are blocked by incompatibilities, the need and opportunity for conversations among potential collaborators do not exist. Integration solutions will allow different applications to be shared by different organizations under different technical arrangements, thus allowing many more collaborative relationships to form in the future.

Web Services

We've mentioned Web services previously in the book, noting that they still face some problems in standardization and cross-company implementation. They represent the next natural evolutionary step in the development of tools for the distributed network of the Internet. Using current industry standards like XML to build them, they are software tools that can be used by other software applications.

Web services rapidly can interconnect existing applications and information. Their use can wean end users from the complexity of incompatible legacy systems. And in the words of Dirk Spiers, describing the consensus expressed at *Infoworld's* Next-Generation Web Services Conference in January 2002,[33] they will "cause the Internet to become a big, programmable software soup, with virtually unlimited components that can mix and match themselves."

At the conference, the cofounder of one Web services provider admitted, "We tend to underestimate the speed at which we do simple things and overestimate the speed at which we do hard things." For even as Web services are being developed and deployed at a rapid rate, the perception of many speakers at the conference was, as Spiers described, that the industry "remains some distance from a solid set of services upon which real businesses can be built." What "some distance" means is anybody's guess, but the need is indeed there for what Web services can do. Locally—integrating the applications used within a single organization—the implementation of Web services is less problematic than it is between different companies with different software and cultures. So in the short term, we will see Web services used internally, in combination with portals to provide consistent interfaces for workers to what would otherwise be incompatible applications.

This internal integration will aid knowledge-sharing communities by providing them with more flexible access to the information coming from different processes in the organization. Cross-company knowledge communities— involving both CRM and marketing, for example—will be able to learn better from each other when the information provided by their distinct software applications is delivered through more standardized interfaces. The CRM staff will be able to access and interpret marketing data and marketing will be able to do the same with CRM data, providing context for more productive conversation.

Application Service Providers

When a company runs part of its technology through an ASP, it spares the IT department of certain responsibilities and expenses. It allows the company to concentrate on its core competencies rather than manage peripheral applications, and it reduces pressures to hire the professionals it would need to run the applications internally. For an ASP solution to work, there must be sufficient *secure* bandwidth connecting the company with the ASP. So far, this has been one of the bottlenecks in adoption of these solutions, and it is where ASPs intersect with the virtual network organizations to be described.

System integration is not necessarily smooth in the use of ASPs. The application may be run and managed remotely, but it still must fit smoothly into the overall business system so that it can be used most effectively. This applies in arrangements like B2B exchanges where different companies using the exchange will come with their own different applications. Integration might mean building interoperability for many vendors and buyers with a single ERP system. This is where Web services intersect with ASPs. And there are still problems in matching the design assumptions of the ASP with the organizational realities of the ASP client. As Tom Davenport opined, "I think it's fair to say that few companies or industries have solved [ASP integration] yet. What you're getting into is inter-organizational reengineering, and it's very time-consuming and very expensive."[34]

Virtual Network Organizations

One expected voice of optimism is John Chambers, CEO of Cisco Systems. He was asked in an interview if the Internet had lived up to his expectations. His response was interesting, especially in light of the tremendous slide his company had taken over the prior 18 months as demand fell for the boxes that his company supplies for Internet expansion.

"The Internet has overachieved my expectations," he said. There is too much pessimism about the role of the Internet and its capability, he argued. "We'll see wave after wave of applications of the Internet. One will be a *virtual network organization*,"[35] which happened to be his company's message at the 2002 Comdex. He's probably right, though, in spite of his marketing spin, for the model of the virtual organization is one in which the company uses a network to tie together all of its functions—outsourcing to ASPs the functions that other companies are better at, continuing to do the functions that the company excels at, and creating what Chambers calls, "the ultimate killer application." But there still seems to be the hanging problem of Web services at the software integration level.

The Collaborative Future

All organizations recognize the need to solve integration problems to move forward with collaboration, both internally and with other companies. The current challenges will eventually be solved, led by companies that are most willing to change established practices and legacy systems. The efficiencies of collaboration are too great to ignore or to delay, and as leading companies solve the technical and social puzzles that block their ability to exchange information and share knowledge efficiently, the competitive map will be altered to their favor.

But this still seems all too mechanical as a description of the future of conversational knowledge sharing. Where are the people and the personal relationships, the trust and the familiarity, in all of this system integration? What if organizations chose to concentrate on building environments where the emphasis was on creative interaction in virtual meeting places rather than on information and data exchange?

We thought a good ending for this book would be to envision a future that went beyond the limitations of text on a screen and relationships built entirely around words. What if the future of online knowledge sharing looked more like a game?

Collaborating in Simulated Communities

Some years ago, we had a computer game called SimCity, produced by Maxis Software. Players could design and build a city from scratch, including factories, power stations, water systems, roads, businesses, and homes. The trick was not to run out of money and not to allow the city to burn down or wash away because there was insufficient investment made in public safety or environmental safeguards. It was a fascinating game, and millions of people got hooked on it. SimCity had hired some very good urban planners to advise them on the structure and content of the game.

Now years later, the concept of the player building a virtual environment is offered on the Web as The Sims.[36] The scale has changed from SimCity's god-like (or at least, mogul-like) viewpoint—operating from an aerial view of the town—to a more human viewpoint, from which the player lives on screen as a character in a household. The Sims' characters come with options for predefined personality traits (neat, outgoing, active, playful, nice) and straightforward needs (hunger, comfort, hygiene, bladder, energy, fun, social, and room).

As described by J.C. Hertz, founder of Joystick Nation, "The Sims is a remarkable example of how a company and its customers can help a product evolve to the point where customers not only do a large portion of the innovation and marketing but also produce as much intellectual capital as they consume."[37] Player/participants in The Sims can build houses, rooms, and gardens. They can buy hot tubs, swimming pools, and big-screen TVs. They can exchange houses, families, and music albums using a *teleportation device.*

Sims' players interact. They use the Sims' home page as their portal and home base where players can chat, converse in message boards, link to each other's sites, and *teleport* their families and albums for everyone to see. The Sims' site also is like the general store, where objects and other utilities can be downloaded. It looks and acts so much like a portal, but includes so many ways to exchange and collaborate, we wonder if the Sims, at least in function, might be a hint at the next generation of collaborative software.

The Sims supports a huge virtual economy, with many fan sites, many artists creating custom content, and tens of thousands of collectors of custom-created objects. Players don't need any programming skills to create and modify their standard-issue Sims' characters and to create custom objects of just about any description in their Sims' environment: chairs, automobiles, lamps, ladders, and so forth. Hundreds of fan sites in over 14 languages furnish 90 percent of the game's content.

J.C. Hertz, an online gaming expert who has studied the Sims as both a gaming and social phenomenon, believes it provides two lessons for the business community:

- "The first is that interactive design trumps graphics." The experience of the Sims derives its richness and complexity from the people who create and manipulate the characters, and from their engagement with each other and with the place. The knowledge-sharing conversation needs richness and complexity. It needs to feel the humanity of its participants to become an attraction rather than a duty.

- "The second lesson is that online businesses don't just exist, like buildings, in space. They exist, like cities, in human context over time." We have always said the same thing about communities: A great part of their value is in their learning and history. Yes, they are messy and never finished. They evolve and their members become more and more interconnected, not just bigger. The collective experience is part of the ride. And as J.C. Hertz says, "When you open your window, there's a *there* there."[38]

It very well could be that 10 years in the future, workers will log on to assume graphic online personas in a virtual marketplace of things and ideas, meeting in rooms of their own design with customers and coworkers to learn and share not only what they know but also what they have created. The rich knowledge-sharing environment of the ancient bazaars will be realized again as the virtual conversational marketplace of ideas, opinions, and experience.

Summary

As always has been true, those who communicate more learn more and learn faster. Groups who use the Net to collaborate and share knowledge will excel over those who don't. Such groups are not limited to who is local and can show up at a meeting. They are not limited by widely separated time zones and conflicting schedules. They are not limited by the need to print and mail documents.

There will always be groups within an organization who spontaneously organize and use the Net as a key meeting place. But there are still too many valuable resources going wasted, not being tapped because they have not been invited to sit at the table and share what they know. There are still too many organizations that, wittingly or unwittingly, inhibit their workers from collaborating for the common good. There are still too many people who, for many reasons, haven't learned to use the Net as a regular communications tool. And there are too many people who don't trust the Net because they haven't learned how to use it.

The future of online knowledge sharing will feature many more conversations as companies encourage and enable them. The study of social networks will become more widespread as organizations look for better ways to analyze the group power of their human resources. And as more people in and outside their workplaces become more accustomed to using the Net as both a social channel and a business environment, the potential for sharing knowledge and experiences will open new and unanticipated doors. The organizations that make the best use of that undeniable trend will best be able to deal with a future that is sure to include instability, unpredictability, and a need for trusted conversation.

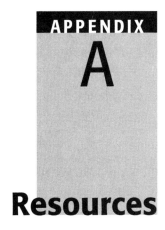

APPENDIX A

Resources

Suggested Reading

1. Bloor, Robin. *The Electronic B@zaar: From the Silk Road to the eRoad.* London: Nicholas Brealey Publishing, 2000.

   Bloor describes the brave new world in which an economy based on paper-based information is rapidly transforming into one in which the market, money, and its supporting information are all electronic.

2. Boyett, Joseph H., and Boyett, Jimmie T. *The Guru Guide to the Knowledge Economy: The Best Ideas for Operating Profitably in a Hyper-Competitive World.* New York: John Wiley & Sons, 2001.

   This is a valuable distillation of the wisdom of 115 successful business titans who describe what it takes to survive and succeed in this new global, knowledge-intensive, increasingly high-tech world. Peter Drucker, Seth Godin, Bill Gates, Alan Greenspan are among those featured.

3. Bressler, Stacey E., and Grantham, Charles E., Sr. *Communities of Commerce: Building Internet Business Communities to Accelerate Growth, Minimize Risk, and Increase Customer Loyalty.* New York: McGraw-Hill, 2000.

Bressler and Grantham provide a detailed look at e-commerce and online communities such as Cisco, Yahoo!, Amazon, Lands End, MarthaStewart.com, and others, describing how well-run communities of commerce can help your company achieve record profits.

4. Davenport, Thomas H., and Prusak, Laurence. *Working Knowledge: How Organizations Manage What They Know.* Boston: Harvard Business School Press, 2000.

   Two of the leading thinkers in the knowledge management field explain the how-tos of how organizations can and do put knowledge to work as a source of competitive advantage in today's marketplace.

5. Denning, Stephen. *The Springboard: How Story-Telling Ignites Action in Knowledge-Era Organizations.* Boston: Butterworth-Heinemann, 2001.

   Denning teaches the science and art of using storytelling as a powerful tool for organizational change and knowledge management.

6. Levin, Rick, Locke, Christopher, Searles, Doc, and Weinberger, David. *The Cluetrain Manifesto: The End of Business as Usual.* Cambridge: Perseus, 2000.

   The book that reminded us that "markets are conversations." Read this book to shake up your perception of how businesses will communicate internally and with customers in the networked future.

7. Pfeffer, Jeffrey, and Sutton, Robert I. *The Knowing-Doing Gap: How Smart Companies Turn Knowledge into Action.* Boston: Harvard Business School Press, 2000.

   Businesses can waste millions of dollars by pouring it into fancy knowledge management systems and what the authors call the "smart talk trap." Pfeffer and Sutton outline how to turn knowledge into action and use examples that show how some companies overcome the knowing-doing gap, why others try but fail, and how your company can avoid the gap.

8. Tiwana, Amrit. *The Knowledge Management Toolkit: Practical Techniques for Building a Knowledge Management System.* Upper Saddle River, N.J.: Prentice Hall PTR, 2000.

   A nuts-and-bolts guide that includes sections on infrastructure, knowledge audits and analyses, systems deployment, measuring ROI, the role of the CKO, and reward structures. Includes a CD-ROM with tools for mapping, data mining, modeling, and workflow.

9. Van Doren, Charles. *A History of Knowledge Past, Present, and Future: The Pivotal Events, People, and Achievements of World History.* New York: Ballantine Books, 1991.

An insightful historical perspective of human knowledge sharing and the definition of knowledge. Good for reminding you that knowledge networks are far from a new idea.

10. Von Krogh, Georg, Ichijo, Kazuo, and Nonaka, Ikujiro. *Enabling Knowledge Creation: How to Unlock the Mystery of Tacit Knowledge and Release the Power of Innovation.* Oxford, England: Oxford University Press, 2000.

    The authors provide clear insights into building workplace cultures that are conducive to knowledge creation and sharing. They also describe practical instructions for how to instill a knowledge vision, inspire knowledge activists, encourage and manage knowledge conversations, and more.

Suggested Web Sites

Here is a useful selection of sites worth bookmarking for the latest writings and articles on knowledge networking, social use of the Net, and related online technologies.

1. *Brint Institute's Online Book on Knowledge Management*: www .kmbook.com.

2. *Brint Institute's WWW Virtual Library on Knowledge Management*: http://kmbrint.com.

3. *CIO Magazine*: www.cio.com.

4. *Darwin: Business Evolving in the Information Age*: www.darwinmag .com.

5. Destination CRM's knowledge management site: www.destinationcrm .com/km.

6. *Intelligent KM*: www.intelligentkm.com.

7. *IT Toolbox for Knowledge Management*: http://km.ittoolbox.com.

8. *IT-Director.com*: www.it-director.com.

9. *KM World* magazine's site: www.kmworld.com.

10. Knowledge at the Wharton School: http://knowledge.wharton.upenn.edu.

11. *The McKinsey Quarterly*: www.mckinseyquarterly.com.

12. *New Architect: Internet Strategies for Technology Leaders*: www .newarchitectmag.com.

13. *Open P2P.com* by O'Reilly: http://openp2p.com.

14. Pew Internet & American Life site: www.pewinternet.org.

15. *Technology Review* by M.I.T.: www.techreview.com.

Notes

1. John B. Horrigan, "Online Communities: Networks That Nurture Long-Distance Relationships and Local Ties," Pew Internet & American Life Project, at www.pewinternet.org/reports/pdfs/PIP_Communities_Report.pdf.

2. Steven Johnson, *Emergence: The Connected Lives of Ants, Brains, Cities, and Software*, Scribner's, New York, 2001.

3. David Sims and Rael Dornfest, "Steven Johnson 'Emergence,'" O'Reilly Network at www.oreillynet.com/pub/a/network/2002/02/22/johnson.html.

Chapter 1

1. *Time*, February 13, 1995, vol. 145, no. 7.

2. Christopher Locke, Rick Levine, Doc Searls, and David Weinberger, *The Cluetrain Manifesto: The End of Business as Usual*, Perseus Press, Boston, 2000.

3. Charles Van Doren, *A History of Knowledge*, Ballantine Books, New York, 1991, p. 151.

4. F. W. Taylor, *The Principles of Scientific Management*, Harper, New York, 1911.

5. Stephen B. Adam and Orville R. Butler, *Manufacturing the Future: A History of Western Electric*, Cambridge University Press, New York, 1999.

6. Edgar Schein Web site at http://web.mit.edu/scheine/www/home.htm.

Chapter 2

1. "Knowledge Management: Making Sense of an Oxymoron," David Skyrme Associates Web site, www.skyrme.com/insights/22km.htm.

2. "As We May Think," *Atlantic Monthly*, July 1945, at www.theatlantic.com /unbound/flashbks/computer/bushf.htm.

3. "The History of Notes and Domino," from the Notes site at www.notes.net /whatisnotes.

4. "Groupware: Introduction," *Usability First*, from www.usabilityfirst.com /groupware/intro.txl.

5. Marketing Terms.com, dictionary at www.marketingterms.com/dictionary /network_effect/.

6. Howard Rheingold, *The Virtual Community: Homesteading on the Electronic Frontier*, Addison-Wesley, Reading, Mass., 1993. Full text available online at www.rheingold.com/vc/book/.

7. Michael Hauben, "The Social Forces Behind the Development of Usenet," in *Netizens: An Anthology* at www.columbia.edu/~hauben/netbook/.

8. Arie de Geus, "Planning as Learning" *Harvard Business Review* (1988). http://www.hbsp.harvard.edu/hbsp/prod_detail.asp

9. Etienne Wenger, "Themes and Ideas: Communities of Practice," from his Web site at www.ewenger.com/ewthemes.html.

10. Applefritter: the Apple I Owners' Club at http://applefritter.com/apple1/.

11. The Stanford University Library Macintosh history site at http://library .stanford.edu/mac/userg.html.

12. Chris Woodyard, "Firms Use Web Lurkers for Customer Service," by *USA Today*, June 21, 2001, at www.usatoday.com/life/cyber/tech/2001-02-06-lurker.htm.

13. "Online Extra: Q&A with Hallmark's Tom Brailsford," *Business Week*, July 9, 2001, at www.businessweek.com/magazine/content/01_28/b3740626.htm.

Chapter 3

1. Steven Johnson, *Emergence: The Connected Lives of Ants, Brains, Cities, and Software*, Scribner's, New York, 2001.

2. Andrew Leonard, "The Emergent New Order," *Salon.com*, at www.salon.com/tech/feature/2001/11/28/emergence/index.html.

3. Yogesh Malhotra, "Knowledge Management for E-Business Performance: Advancing Information Strategy to 'Internet Time,'" Brint Institute's *Online Book on Knowledge Management* at www.kmbook.com/.

4. "Crawling from the Dot-Com Wreckage," *Business Week Online*, December 19, 2000, at www.businessweek.com/bwdaily/dnflash/dec2000/nf20001219_800,htm.

5. "A Nation Online: How Americans Are Expanding Their Use of the Internet," report published by the National Telecommunications and Information Administration and the Economics and Statistics Administration at www.ntia.doc.gov/ntiahome/dn/index.html.

6. "Essential E-Business Numbers for Marketers," *eMarketer* at www.emarketer.com/statistics/essential_numbers.

7. "Hot Off the Net," *Nielsen/NetRatings* at www.nielsen-netratings.com/hot_off_the_net.jsp.

8. "Internet Demographics and eCommerce Statistics," *Commerce Net* at www.commerce.net/research/stats/stats.html.

9. "Online Communities: Networks That Nurture Long-Distance Relationships and Local Ties," The Pew Internet & American Life Project at www.pewinternet.org/reports/toc.asp?Report=47.>.

10. Press release: "Total Time Spent Using Instant Messaging Jumps 110 Percent at Work and 48 Percent at Home versus Last Year, Reports Jupiter Media Metrix," www.jmm.com/xp/jmm/press/2001/pr_111401.xml.

11. Stephen Denning, *The Springboard: How Storytelling Ignites Action in Knowledge-Era Organizations*, Butterworth-Heinemann, Boston, 2000, p. 27.

12. Thomas H. Davenport and Laurence Prusak, *Working Knowledge: How Organizations Manage What They Know*, Harvard Business School Press, Boston, 1997, p. 58.

13. Mark Monmonier, *How to Lie with Maps*, 2d ed., University of Chicago Press, 1996.

14. "Empowering Social Change at the World Bank Institute" found on Tomoye Web site at www.tomoye.com.

15. Davenport and Prusak, *Working Knowledge*, p. 36.

16. Jakob Nielsen, "The 10 Best Intranet Designs of 2001," *Use It.com Alertbox*, November 2001, at www.useit.com/alertbox/20011125.html.

17. "Interview: Jakob Nielsen on Usability and Intranets," *IT-Director.com*, December 3, 2001, at www.it-director.com/article.php?id=2383.

18. Chuleenan Svetvilas, "The Human Factor: Intellectual Capital Guru Nick Bontis Discusses KM's Missing Link," *Intelligent KM* at www.intelligentkm .com/feature/010723/feat1.shtml.

19. "Solutions That Drive Bottom-Line Business Benefits," *AskMe.com* at www.askmecorp.com/solutions/default.asp.

20. Nielsen, "The 10 Best Intranet Designs."

Chapter 4

1. "Executives Unaware of Internal Security Risks," KMPG survey report at Nua.com, November 20, 2001, at www.nua.ie/surveys/index/cgi?f=VS&art _id=905357423&rel=true.

2. Michael Vizard, "CommerceFlow CTO Explains Why Application Integration Remains Overly Complicated," interview with Erik Swan in *InfoWorld*, October 24, 2001, at www.infoworld.com/articles/hn/xml/01 /10/26/01 1026hnswan.xml.

3. "Interview: Jakob Nielsen on Usability and Intranets," *IT-Director.com*, December 3, 2001, at www.it-director.com/article.php?id=2383.

4. "Measuring Returns on IT Investments: Some Tools and Techniques," *Managing Technology*, on the Wharton School site at http://knowledge .wharton.upenn.edu/articles.cfm?catid=14&articleid=396.

5. Ibid.

6. Thomas H. Davenport and Laurence Prusak, *Working Knowledge: How Organizations Manage What They Know*, Harvard Business School Press, Boston, 2000, p. 26.

7. Michael Koenig, "User Education for KM: The Problem We Won't Recognize," *KMWorld*, November–December 2001.

8. Ibid.

9. WhatIs.com at http://whatis.techtarget.com.

10. Katherine C. Adams, "Mapping the Enterprise Software Market," *KMWorld*, September 2001.

11. Robin Hourican, "Tools to Maximize Performance," *Knowledge Management*, September 2001.

12. David Smith, "Tackle Instant Messaging's Security Risks—Now," report by the Gartner Group, October 12, 2001.

13. Eric Woods, "P2P," *KMWorld*, October 2001.

14. Koenig, "User Education for KM."

15. "Intranet Design Annual: 10 Best Intranets of 2001," by the Nielsen Norman Group, available for downloading at www.nngroup.com/reports /intranet/2001/.

16. Woods, "P2P."

17. Fara Warner, "He Drills for Knowledge," *Fast Company*, September 2001.

Chapter 5

1. James C. Collins and Jerry I. Porras, *Built to Last*, Harperbusiness, New York, 1997.

2. Brad Bollinger, "Civility and Grace Not Just the H-P Way," *Santa Rosa Press Democrat*, May 6, 2001.

3. Carl Frappaolo, "Ushering in the Knowledge-Based Economy," by The Delphi Group Symposium, available at www.delphigroup.com/research.

4. Rebecca O. Barclay, "Leading the Knowledge Enterprise: CIOs, CLOs, CKOs, and Beyond," *KM Briefs* and *KM Metazine* at www.lamarheller.pair .com/technology/knowledgemgmt/leadingtheknowledgeenterprise.htm.

5. Emelie Rutherford, "End Game: A Conversation with David Weinberger," *CIO*, April 2000.

6. Barclay, "Knowledge Enterprise."

7. Rutherford, "End Game."

8. Barclay, "Knowledge Enterprise."

9. Nathaniel W. Foote, Eric Matson, and Nicholas Rudd, "Managing the Knowledge Manager," *The McKinsey Quarterly*, 2001, no. 3.

10. Andrew S. Grove, *Only the Paranoid Survive: How to Exploit the Crisis Points That Challenge Every Company and Career*, Currency/Doubleday, New York, 1996.

11. Etienne Wenger, "Themes and Ideas: Communities of Practice" at www.ewenger.com/ewthemes.html.

12. John Harney, "Intellectual Stimulation," *Intelligent KM*, January 1, 2002, at www.intelligentkm.com/020101/501feat1_1.

13. Rutherford, "End Game."

14. Barclay, "Knowledge Enterprise."

15. Rutherford, "End Game."

16. Barclay, "Knowledge Enterprise."

Chapter 6

1. John Suler, Ph.D., "The Geezer Brigade: Steps in Studying an Online Group" at www.rider.edu/uses/suler/psycyber/geezerb.html.

2. Michael Schrage, "Don't Go There," *Fortune*, October 29, 2001.

3. Thomas A. Stewart, "The Case Against Knowledge Management," *Business 2.0*, February 2002.

Chapter 7

1. Fara Warner, "He Drills for Knowledge," *Fast Company*, September 2001, p. 189.

2. Etienne Wenger, "Supporting Communities of Practice: A Survey of Community-Oriented Technologies," a "shareware" report available at www.ewenger.com/tech/.

3. Shar VanBoskirk with Charlene Li and Jennifer Parr, "Effective Email Marketing," *Forrester Research*, August 2001.

4. Home page of the Learning.org mail list at www.learning-org.com/LOinfo.html.

5. Chris Lindquist, "Zap to It: Zaplet Suite Makes E-mail Work," *CIO.com*, January 7, 2002, at www.cio.com/online/techtact_010702.html.

6. Overview page at Jabber.com Web site at www.jabber.com/about /index.shtml.

7. John Udell, "Can IM Graduate to Business?" *OpenP2P.com* at www .openp2p.com/pub/a/p2p/2001/12/20/udell.html.

Chapter 8

1. Stephen Denning, *The Springboard*, Butterworth-Heinemann, Boston, 2001. p. 82.

2. Thomas H. Davenport and Laurence Prusak, *Working Knowledge*, Harvard Business School Press, Boston, 2000. p. x.

3. Clerity, Inc. Web site at www.knowtoday.com/solutions/eks.asp.

Chapter 9

1. Seth Grodin, "Change Agent," *Fast Company*, May 2001.

2. Mary Tumolo, "Business-to-Business Exchanges," *Information Systems Management*, Spring 2001.

3. "The 3 Faces of CRM: Analysis of the Worldwide Customer Relationship Management Market, Part 1: Operational CRM," *Cahners-Interstat*, July 2001.

4. John Ellis, "In My Humble Opinion," *Fast Company*, September 2001.

5. Interview with Tom Brailsford of Hallmark, provided by Communispace. Available through Fishman, "But Wait, You Promised … ," *Fast Company*, July 2001.

6. Don Peppers and Martha Rogers, *The One to One Future: Building Relationships One Customer at a Time*, Currency/Doubleday, New York, 1997.

7. Ian Zack, "The Question Is the Answer," *Forbes*, August 6, 2001.

8. Michael C. Ruettgers, "I Pledge Allegiance to This Company: From Customer Satisfaction to Allegiance," *Chief Executive* at www.chiefexecutive .net/mag/.

9. Jack Neff, "PlanetFeedback Happy to Hear Consumer Gripes," *AdAge.com*, October 2, 2000.

10. "How Companies Sponsor, Listen in and Learn from Chat Rooms," Wharton School, at http://knowledge.wharton.upenn.edu.

11. Stephanie Overby, "Healing Channels," *CIO*, December 1, 2001.

Chapter 10

1. Thomas H. Davenport and John C. Beck, *The Attention Economy: Understanding the New Currency of Business*, Harvard Business School, Boston, 2001.

2. Christian Sarkar, "Attention, Management! An Interview with Thomas Davenport," *Agilebrain.com*, at www.agilebrain.com/davenport.html.

3. Malcolm Gladwell, *The Tipping Point: How Little Things Can Make a Big Difference*, Little Brown & Company, Boston, 2000.

4. Michael Zack, "Researching Organizational Systems Using Social Network Analysis," paper on the Northeastern University College of Business Administration Web site at http://web.cba.neu.edu/~mzack/articles/socnet /socnet.htm.

5. Valdis Krebs, "An Introduction to Social Network Analysis," paper at www.orgnet.com/sna.html.

6. Emelie Rutherford, "End Game: David Weinberger Talks about the Impending Death of Corporate Life as We Know It," *CIO*, April 1, 2000, at www.cio.com/archive/040100/end.html

7. Sarkar, "Attention, Management!"

8. Deloitte Research, "Collaborative Knowledge Networks" at www.dc.com.

9. Ibid.

10. Navi Radjou, with Ted Schadler, Amanda J. Ciardelli, and Stephanie Smith, "Collaboration beyond Email," *Forrester Research* 1999.

11. Deloitte Research, "Collaborative Knowledge Networks."

12. Sarkar, "Attention, Management!"

13. Kathy Harris and Waldir Arevolo De Azevedo Filho, "Communities: Sociology Meets Technology," Gartner, Inc. Web site, July 9, 2001, at www.gartner.com.

14. Stephanie Sanborn and Cathleen Moore, "Collaboration Comes Together," *Infoworld*, December 7, 2001, at www.infoworld.com/articles/fe/xml/01/12 /10/011210fecollab.xml.

15. Rutherford, "End Game."

16. Jean Graef, "Measuring Intellectual Assets," *Montague Institute Review*, 1997, at www.montague.com/le/le1096.html.

17. Tom Peters, 'Tom Peters's True Confessions," *Fast Company*, December 2001, pp. 78–92.

18. Sarkar, "Attention, Management!"

19. Eric Chabrow, "Survey: Internet Key to Collaboration," *Information-Week.com*, February 6, 2002, at www.informationweek.com/story /IWK20020202602060007.

20. Radjou et al., "Collaboration beyond E-mail."

21. Ibid.

22. Sarkar, "Attention, Management!"

23. Frances Hesselbein, Marshall Goldsmith, and Iain Somerville, eds., *Leading for Innovation and Organizing for Results*, Jossey-Bass, San Francisco, 2001.

24. Daniel H. Pink, "Who Has the Next Big Idea? An Interview with Michael Hammer," Fast Company, September 2001, pp. 108–116.

25. David Dorsey, "Positive Deviant," *Fast Company*, issue 41, December 2000, p. 284.

26. Dorsey, "Positive Deviant."

27. Pink, "Who Has the Next Big Idea?"

28. Sarkar, "Attention, Management!"

29. Rutherford, "End Game."

30. Pink, "Who Has the Next Big Idea?"

31. Rutherford, "End Game."

32. Sanborn and Moore, "Collaboration Comes Together."

33. Dirk Spiers, "Waiting for the Web Services Wave," *Business 2.0*, January 24, 2002, at www.business2.com/articles/web/0,1653,37356,FF.html.

34. Sarkar, "Attention, Management!"

35. "Cisco Chief: Future May Lie in Virtual Networks, Interview with Matt Krantz," *USA Today online*, November 12, 2001, at www.usatoday.com /life/cyber/tech/2001/11/12/comdex-cisco.htm.

36. The Sims' home page at http://thesims.ea.com/us/.

37. J.C. Hertz, "Learning from The Sims: A Sleeper Software Hit Shows How Customers Help Build Better Businesses," *Industry Standard*, March 26, 2001, pp. 90–91.

30. Ibid.

Index

!Kung tribe of the Kalahari, 9–10

A
About.com, 271–72
Accenture, 304
adaptable platforms, 113–15, 149, 174–176, 202, 237–38
Adobe, 50
Advanced Research Project Agency, 32–33
A History of Knowledge (Van Doren), 13, 16–18, 19
Amazon.com, 251, 260
American Cancer Society, 280–281, 282
Anadarko Petroleum, 110
AOL, 53–54, 192, 201
Apple computer users' group, 48–49
application integration
    enterprise application integration (EAI), 89–90, 317–19
    Extensible Markup Language (XML), 52, 89, 317–18
    personalization capabilities, 292
    platform independent applications, 317
    problems with, 88–89, 99–100

    Web services, 51, 88, 100–101, 298, 317–318
Application Service Providers (ASPs), 101, 174–175, 317, 318–319
Appmail, 181, 300
archivists, 102–3
Ariba, 252
ARPANet, 32–33, 38–39
Ask Jeeves, 261
AskMe, 79–80
ASPs (Application Service Providers), 101, 174–175, 317, 318–19
assembly lines, 20–21
assessments
    cultural, 120–121, 141–142, 209–210
    ROI, 81, 300–301, 312
assets, organizational, 30–32
associates. *See* stakeholders
"As We May Think" (Bush), 32, 33
asynchronous
    events on the Web, 242. *See also* email; message boards
asynchronous interfaces. *See* discussions
AT&T Bell Labs, 38
The Attention Economy (Davenport & Beck), 289

auctions, 263–267
audio/video conferencing, 142–143, 148, 172, 241
auditoriums. *See* forums

B
B2C (business-to-customer), 274–76. *See also* stakeholders
Baillargeon, Victor, 128, 129, 134–35
bandwidth
    for audio/video conferencing, 142–43, 148, 172, 241
    as depth of social contact, 40–41, 67
banner ads, 36–37
B2B (business-to-business). *See* stakeholders
BBSs (bulletin board systems). *See* message boards
B2E (business-to-employee), 317
Beck, John C., 289
The Berkana Institute, 307
best-of-breed integration solutions, 99–100
BITNET, 33
Blackshaw, Pete, 273
Boccaccio, Giovanni, 16
Bontis, Nick, 79
bozo filter, 45, 145–146